Providence **Community** Library
OUR NEIGHBORHOOD LIBRARIES

This book has been purchased in honor of

LINDA J. KUSHNER

one of the four founders of
Providence Community Library
to acknowledge her tireless efforts in ensuring
that all Providence residents have access
to libraries in their neighborhoods.

ALSO BY KIM MacQUARRIE

The Last Days of the Incas

Where the Andes Meet the Amazon

Peru's Amazonian Eden:
Manu National Park and Biosphere Reserve

Gold of the Andes:
The Llamas, Alpacas, Vicuñas and Guanacos of South America

LIFE AND DEATH

IN THE

ANDES

On the Trail of Bandits, Heroes, and Revolutionaries

KIM MacQUARRIE

SIMON & SCHUSTER

New York London Toronto Sydney New Delhi

¹⁰/₁₉/₁₆ KMA

Simon & Schuster
1230 Avenue of the Americas
New York, NY 10020

Copyright © 2015 by Kim MacQuarrie

First Simon & Schuster hardcover edition December 2015

SIMON & SCHUSTER and colophon are registered trademarks of Simon & Schuster, Inc.

For information about special discounts for bulk purchases,
please contact Simon & Schuster Special Sales at
1-866-506-1949 or business@simonandschuster.com.

The Simon & Schuster Speakers Bureau can bring authors to your
live event. For more information or to book an event, contact the
Simon & Schuster Speakers Bureau at 1-866-248-3049 or
visit our website at www.simonspeakers.com.

Interior design by Ruth Lee-Mui
Maps by Paul J. Pugliese

Manufactured in the United States of America

10 9 8 7 6 5 4 3 2 1

Library of Congress Cataloging-in-Publication Data

MacQuarrie, Kim.
   Life and death in the Andes : on the trail of bandits, heroes, and revolutionaries / by
Kim MacQuarrie. — First Simon & Schuster hardcover edition.
      pages   cm
   Includes bibliographical references and index
   1. Andes Region—History.   2. Andes Region—Biography.   3. Andes Region—
Description and travel.   4. Andes Region—Social conditions.   5. Outlaws—Andes
Region—Biography.   6. Heroes—Andes Region—Biography.   7. Revolutionaries—
Andes Region—Biography.   8. Death—Andes Region—History.   I. Title.
   F2212.M25   2015
   980—dc23   2015017288

ISBN 978-1-4391-6889-9
ISBN 978-1-4391-6892-9 (ebook)

To Ciara

All men dream, but not equally. Those who dream by night in the dusty recesses of their minds, wake in the day to find that it was vanity: but the dreamers of the day are dangerous men, for they may act on their dreams with open eyes, to make them possible.

—T. E. Lawrence, *Seven Pillars of Wisdom*

CONTENTS

*Atlantic
Ocean*

*Pacific
Ocean*

Medellín•

VENEZUELA

GUYANA

SURINAME

FR.
GUIANA

Cali•
•Bogotá

COLOMBIA

ECUADOR

EQUATOR

*The
Galápagos
Islands*

*Route to
Galápagos
Islands*

PERU

SOUTH

AMERICAN

PLATE

THE ANDES

Machu
Picchu

Lima•

Ayacucho•

•Cusco

BRAZIL

NAZCA

PLATE

•La Paz

BOLIVIA

Arequipa•

•La Higuera

San Vicente•
•Tupiza

PARAGUAY

Pacific Ocean

CHILE

THE ANDES

URUGUAY

The Galápagos Islands

Genovesa

*Darwin
Bay*

*Tortuga
Point*

Santiago

Baltra

*Santa
Cruz*

Fernandina

•*Puerto Ayora*

Rabida

*San
Cristóbal*

Isabela

*Tortuga
Bay*

Floreana

ARGENTINA

*Atlantic
Ocean*

PATAGONIA

N
W   E
S

South America
Showing the Author's Route

*Tierra
del
Fuego*

•Ushuaia
— *Cape Horn*

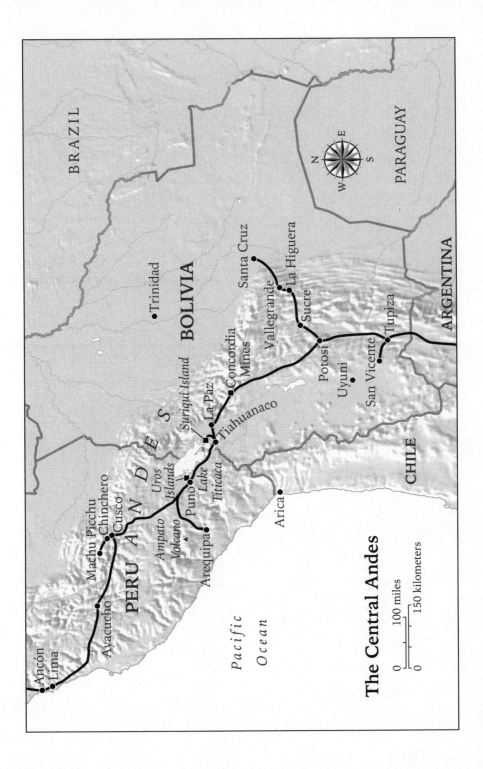

The Central Andes

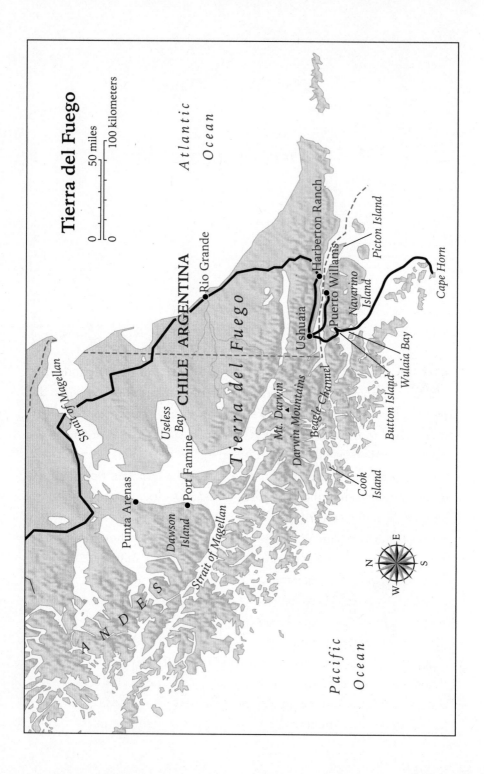

Tierra del Fuego

50 miles
100 kilometers

Atlantic Ocean

Pacific Ocean

ARGENTINA

CHILE

Tierra del Fuego

Strait of Magellan

Punta Arenas
Dawson Island
Port Famine
Strait of Magellan

Useless Bay

Rio Grande

Mt. Darwin
Darwin Mountains

Ushuaia

Beagle Channel

Harberton Ranch
Puerto Williams
Navarino Island

Picton Island

Button Island
Wulaia Bay

Cape Horn

Cook Island

A N D E S

N E S W

PREFACE

When I was a boy, growing up in Nevada, during the long, hot summers I used to read a lot. On bright, burning days when the temperature outside hovered well over a hundred degrees and when if you tried to cross an asphalt street you'd singe your bare feet like a couple of grilled vegetables, I'd remain inside, would lie on my back on our floral-patterned couch, would open a book—and then would immediately find myself plunging across icy seas or tunneling deep into other worlds. One of my favorite authors growing up was a German-American sailor named William Willis, who wrote true-life accounts of his various adventures. Willis had sailed on square-rigged ships as a teenager and, later in life, eventually made his way to Peru, on the western coast of South America. There, he lashed together some balsa logs and sailed across the Pacific Ocean—for no other reason than adventure. Willis's descriptions of being alone on his raft at night, peering down into the translucent blackness where he witnessed great luminescent creatures rising from the deep, still haunts my imagination. At around the same time, when I was about eight or nine years old, I stumbled across Edgar Rice Burroughs's "hollow earth" series, which tells the tale of how a man burrowed down through the Earth's crust with a machine, only to discover an exotic, interior world called Pellucidar. Within the Earth's interior, it turned out, existed a world full of half-naked tribes and powerful beasts (mostly dinosaurs), rich, luxuriant vegetation, beautiful women, and so much adventure that I remember spending an entire summer there, immersed in a world as far removed from the deserts of Nevada as the Earth is from Mars.

Many years later, after eventually becoming a writer and documentary filmmaker, I was touring with a film I'd recently made on a certain Amazonian tribe when a magazine writer asked me what had motivated me to spend so much time in South America. Without even thinking, I blurted out "Edgar Rice Burroughs." The journalist, it turned out, had gone to public school with Burroughs's grandson and, about a month later, a package arrived at my door. Inside was an original edition of Burroughs's *At the Earth's Core*, published in 1914, the first in the "hollow earth" series. Burroughs's grandson had signed the book, saying that his grandfather would have been pleased to know that his work had propelled me to the far reaches of the Amazon. It was while fingering through its pages, however, that I suddenly realized a certain truth: that some of the worlds we visit in books when we're children become so buried within our minds that, even though they may remain deeply submerged, they may still prompt us to later subconsciously search for them—much as adoptees might search for their biological parents, or as adults might search for long-lost childhood friends.

While motivations remain mysterious, I do credit Burroughs with having created a vision that eventually took me to South America, a continent that, in many ways, contains everything that the best of Burroughs's writing ever did: a massive mountain chain, epic in its proportions; colossal continental plates that continually collide, thrusting up volcanoes and even lifting entire lakes twelve thousand feet into the air; and a cloud-wreathed rain forest that stretches more than halfway across a continent—a jungle so replete with sloths, giant snakes, bizarre animals, and uncontacted tribes that you'd think you had somehow left the modern world and stumbled instead into a world as primeval as Pellucidar.

My own journey to South America began in the late 1980s, to Peru, at the height of the Shining Path guerrilla war. Within a few months, amid Lima's curfew-ridden city, I began entering high-security prisons as a journalist and interviewing members of the Shining Path. I then began traveling in the Andes through some of the Shining Path's "liberated" zones, where red flags with hammers and sickles fluttered alongside dirt roads—roads whose bridges had recently been blasted into ruined hulks and where guerrillas routinely pulled anyone who worked for the government off buses and shot them in the head. One day, while busy doing graduate work in anthropology at the Universidad Católica, I read a small notice in the paper about a reed raft, called the *Uru*, which was about to depart on a voyage across the Pacific. With memories of William Willis in my mind, I quickly went down to the port, learned that the crew was exactly one member short, and promptly volunteered my services. It was a Spanish expedition, however, and the captain wanted an all-Spanish crew. The day the *Uru* departed from the port of Callao, I met there the Norwegian explorer Thor Heyerdahl, of *Kon-Tiki* fame, who later invited me to spend some time with him while he excavated ancient Moche pyramids in northern Peru.

Ultimately, I visited Heyerdahl, which I describe later in this book, and then later lived for half a year with a recently contacted tribe called the Yora, in Peru's Upper Amazon. While with the Yora I participated in their ayahuasca ceremonies and also listened to their rather spellbinding stories of how they had previously perceived the outside world, which some believed to be the land of the dead. The Yora told me about their skirmishes with outsiders, how they'd shot six-foot arrows at invading oil workers, and how, at one point, they'd shot so many arrows into some hapless intruder that afterward he'd resembled a Huicungo tree—a type of palm whose spines resemble those of a porcupine. Later, fascinated by the discovery that the Incas had built a jungle capital not far from where the Yora lived and had fought on against the Spaniards for four decades *after* their conquest, I wrote a book about the collision of those two worlds called *The Last Days of the Incas*.

Throughout the four years I lived in Peru, however, there always lurked in the back of my mind the idea of one day traveling the full length of the Andes, all 4,300 miles, from one end to the other. What could be a greater adventure? On the day I finally set out, my idea was not so much to travel from point A to point B, but rather to investigate some of the most interesting stories that South America had to offer. To travel down the Andes collecting stories the way others might fill a basket with ripe, exotic fruits. I wanted to explore stories and characters I'd always been fascinated with, but I was also looking for historical events that might help illuminate certain aspects of South America's present and past. Where did the first inhabitants of South America come from—from across the isthmus to the north or from across the seas? And where had the continent's first civilizations come from? Did they arise independently, or had they been imported by white, godlike emissaries from other continents, as Thor Heyerdahl had believed? How and why did the Andes float like icebergs on the Earth's crust—and why did the Incas sacrifice their children on top of its peaks? And what relationship was there between the Spanish conquistadors's desperate search for El Dorado—the mythical native king who possessed unlimited quantities of gold—and ruthless drug lords like Pablo Escobar, the leader of the Medellín cartel? These were some of the questions—questions that probed into the very heart of South America—that I set out to explore. Each of the stories, I soon discovered, was interwoven with the others, like some vast, intricate tapestry spread over a continent.

In Colombia, for example, I investigated the cocaine trade by searching for a certain police colonel who'd once turned down a $6 million bribe from Pablo Escobar. The colonel had not only refused the bribe, but afterward had actually tracked down Escobar. What kind of person, I wanted to find out—offered the choice between almost certain death or of becoming a multimillionaire—would choose the former? I traveled through Colombia, to Bogotá, Lake Guatavita, and Medellín to find out.

Off the coast of Ecuador, amid the Galapágos Islands, I went in pursuit of where and when, exactly, Charles Darwin had come up with his theory of evolution. Was it in the Galapágos? Or earlier, in Patagonia?

Or not until he'd returned to England? And was it true that Darwin had so bungled his famous bird collections on the Galapágos that he was never able to use them to support his theory of evolution?

Farther south along the Andes, in Peru, I went in pursuit of a story I'd heard that the leader of the Shining Path guerrilla movement had eventually been captured not by the army but instead by a certain police colonel whose identity and methodology had remained a state secret for more than a decade. But was the story true? And who was the upper-class ballerina who had reportedly hidden the Shining Path leader—protecting a revolutionary dedicated to overturning the very class system from which she benefited?

On the border of Peru and Bolivia, fascinated by a series of high-altitude archaeological discoveries in the central Andes, I went in search of a young Inca girl who'd been sacrificed on top of a 20,700-foot volcano and who was recently discovered, still frozen after more than five hundred years. Who was this girl, why was she sacrificed—and how did she and other children end up on top of some of the highest mountains in the Andes, almost perfectly preserved?

Traveling farther southward, I next went in search of the extraordinary floating islands on Lake Titicaca, some 12,500 feet up in the Andes. I was curious to know why Thor Heyerdahl, who'd once crossed the Pacific on the raft *Kon-Tiki*, had later flown a trio of Aymara boat-builders all the way from Lake Titicaca to Egypt, to the base of the ancient pyramids. What secret did Heyerdahl believe these three men possessed that he would later entrust his *life* to their creation? On the shores of Lake Titicaca, not far from the legendary ruined city of Tiahuanaco, I tracked down one of the men, who told me his surprising story.

Meanwhile, in eastern Bolivia, curious to know how worldviews can sometimes collide with reality, I went in search of where the Argentine revolutionary Che Guevara had been captured—and how his dream of founding a communist utopia had foundered in an isolated area of the Andes. In the town of Vallegrande, I tracked down the schoolteacher who'd given the wounded revolutionary his final meal and had chatted with him on numerous occasions. The schoolteacher, now sixty-three years old, told me the remarkable story of what had actually happened on the last day of Che Guevara's life—and how those events had changed her life.

In a similar fashion, in the far south of Bolivia, I sought out how the legendary characters Butch Cassidy and the Sundance Kid had met their ends. Did the duo really depart this world in a hail of bullets—as depicted in the Hollywood film—or were rumors of a murder-suicide pact closer to the truth? It wasn't until I traveled to the dusty mining town of San Vicente, nine thousand feet up in the Andes, and met the grandson of a man who had lived there during the shootout, that I learned the answer.

Finally, at the southernmost tip of South America, I tracked down a woman who is the last speaker of the Yámana language and who now lives on a windswept island off Patagonia. Three of the woman's ancestors had once shared a ship with Charles Darwin, had toured London, and had met the English king and queen. They'd then been transported back to Patagonia as part of a grand social experiment. But what had become of them? And what had become of the experiment? And who on Earth had ever come up with such a crazy idea in the first place?

The stories included in this book, then, investigations really, are all the result of my meandering voyage down the Andean spine of South America, stories that I have strung together geographically from north to south, much as the white peaks of the Andes lie along that vast mountain chain, like a glimmering set of pearls.

What ultimately links all of these stories together is that the characters within them lived at least a portion of their lives in South America and all of them struggled to control, adapt to, or explore the rugged landscape that exists along the westernmost rim of the continent. Most of them, in addition, were the kind of characters that T. E. Lawrence ("Lawrence of Arabia") would have called "dreamers of the day"—the most dangerous kind, he felt, because these types of people always put their dreams into action. Che Guevara, Thor Heyerdahl, Abimael Guzmán, Hiram Bingham, Nilda Callañaupa, Chris and Ed Franquemont, Butch Cassidy and the Sundance Kid, Charles Darwin, Thomas

Bridges—even Pablo Escobar—all were dreamers who actively tried to convert their dreams into reality. And, whether they realized it or not, they also viewed South America through the lenses of their culture and time. In some cases, this proved fatal, for as the writer J. Solomon noted, "Worldviews act somewhat like eye glasses or contact lenses . . . in either example, an incorrect prescription can be dangerous."

The revolutionaries Che Guevara and Abimael Guzmán, for example, intensely dissatisfied with social conditions in their native countries and convinced of the wisdom of Marx's prescription for building a political utopia, tried to transform society at the points of guns. In doing so, however, they unleashed forces that ultimately overwhelmed them.

Charles Darwin also arrived in South America with his own set of cultural perceptions, which in certain cases prevented him from perceiving facts that now seem obvious. Somewhere during Darwin's long journey, however, his ideas about the world shifted and he began peering at it freshly, from a different point of view. That shift ultimately led him to conceive of the theory of evolution.

The Incas, by contrast, saw not the Andes of modern science but a sacred landscape controlled by their gods. Confronted by an environment of erupting volcanoes, deadly earthquakes, and unpredictable droughts, the Incas offered up sacrifices, sometimes in the form of children. By doing so, they hoped to restore balance to their world.

Nearly five hundred years ago, a Spanish chronicler and soldier of fortune named Pedro Cieza de León spent eleven years traveling in South America, journeying southward through the recently conquered Inca Empire, which stretched from what is now Colombia into central Chile. In the preface to a book dedicated to the Spanish king, he wrote,

O most serene and gracious Lord . . . to describe the wonderful things of this great kingdom . . . would require one who could write like [the Roman] Titus Livius, or Valerius, or some other of the great writers that have appeared in the world, and that even they would find some difficulty in the task. For who can enumerate the mighty things . . . the lofty mountains and profound valleys over which we went conquering and discovering? The numerous rivers of such size and depth? The variety of provinces, with so many different things in each? The tribes, with all their strange customs, rites and ceremonies? So many birds, animals, trees, fishes, all unknown[?] . . . Much that I have written I saw with my own eyes, and I travelled over many countries in order to learn more concerning them. Those things that I did not see, I took great pains to inform myself of, from persons of repute, both Christians and Indians. I pray to Almighty God that . . . He will leave you to live and reign for many happy years, with the increase of many other kingdoms.

Cieza de León died having never visited all of South America. I can attest, however, having traveled the length and breadth of the continent and having visited much of the same territory that he did, that many of the miracles and marvels he described still exist, and that the wonders of South America—a world I once half imagined as a child and was later fortunate enough to experience—still remain.

1

THE HUNT FOR PABLO
ESCOBAR AND THE SEARCH
FOR EL DORADO (COLOMBIA)

He stated that [Colombia] was a land rich in emeralds and gold . . .
he told of a certain king, unclothed, who went on rafts on a pool to
make oblations . . . anointing all [his body] with . . . a quantity of
ground gold . . . gleaming like a ray of the sun . . . [and] the [Span-
ish] soldiers . . . then gave [that king] the name El Dorado [the
Golden One].

—Juan de Castellanos, 1589

Sometimes I am God; if I say a man dies, he dies that same day . . .
There can only be one king [and that king is me].

—Pablo Escobar, leader of the Medellín cartel, who spent seven
years on *Forbes* magazine's billionaire list (1987–1993)

Someday, and that day may never come, I'll call upon you to do a
service for me. But until that day, accept this [retribution] . . . as a
gift on my daughter's wedding day.

—Don Corleone, *The Godfather*, 1972

nock, knock, knock!

The knock on Colonel Hugo Martínez's door that signaled his possible death came at 11:30 a.m. on a Wednesday morning in the La Castellana neighborhood of Bogotá. The knock came during the height of the Medellín drug wars and, Martínez knew, the only way to access Martínez's home on the fifth floor of this particular upscale apartment tower was after being screened by the watchman downstairs. It was the latter's job to confirm whether the apartment dweller was there, to ask for the visitor's name, and then to announce the visitor's arrival via the intercom. Only if an occupant granted permission was a visitor allowed to enter the building, which was mostly inhabited by the families of high-ranking Colombian police officers. On this particular morning, however, the intercom had been silent. It must be a neighbor, Colonel Martínez thought—but how had anyone known that he was *here*? The colonel, whose job was to hunt down the leaders of the Medellín cartel, moved carefully to the door. All about him, on the floor, lay shards of glass from the bomb explosion outside that had shattered the windows and his television set a week before.

Knock knock knock!

The colonel was a lean man, six foot tall and forty-nine years old, with short-cropped brown hair and closely set, coffee-colored eyes. He'd been in the midst of packing up his family's belongings when the knock caused him to momentarily freeze. The apartment had lain empty for a week, the clock still ticking silently on the wall, clothes strewn about, his children's toys in their rooms, just as they had left them before his wife and two children fled. No one was supposed to know that he was here, alone in this particular apartment and in Bogotá at this particular time. So who was knocking at the door?

A week earlier, the cartel had exploded a powerful bomb in the street below, spewing jagged shrapnel and creating a cloud of smoke that had risen into the air. A number of people had been wounded, although none had been killed. Martínez had been two hundred miles away in Medellín at the time and had called his wife frantically when he'd heard. He'd then flown back to Bogotá and had arranged for her and their children to go into hiding. The cartel, Martínez realized, could have killed his entire family. Instead, they'd chosen to send the bomb as the sort of message they knew the colonel would understand:

We, the Medellín Cartel, know your family lives here. We can kill them anytime we wish. If you continue to pursue us, your family will cease to exist. This is a warning.

For much of the last three years, Colonel Martínez had been living an almost monastic life in Medellín. There, he was quartered on a police base with the rest of the handpicked members of the special police force that he'd helped to create and currently led—*el Bloque de Búsqueda* (the Search Bloc). In 1989 the Colombian government had selected Martínez to command what both he and his fellow officers believed to be a suicidal mission: hunting down Colombia's most powerful and feared drug lord, Pablo Escobar, and dismantling Escobar's Medellín cartel.

Martínez hadn't wanted the job. In fact, most of his colleagues felt that he'd be dead within a few months, if not weeks. But an appointment was an appointment, Martínez believed. After all, he'd spent his entire life in the police, ever since becoming a cadet.

Duty was duty. If *he* didn't do it, then someone else would be ordered to instead. After years of giving and receiving orders, Martínez wasn't about to disobey one now. At the same time, the colonel realized, perhaps that's why he'd been given the mission in the first place. While others might resign or try to pass the assignment on, Martínez's superiors knew that he was one of the few who never would. He was well known, in fact, as the kind of officer who got things done. His record was clean. He'd not only obtained the rank of colonel but also had graduated from law school at the top of his class. Martínez was now middle-aged, was married with three kids, and was on track to become a general. But only if he could survive his present mission.

Martínez and his family had been living in Bogotá when he'd received his new command. The assignment called for Martínez to move immediately to Medellín. There, he was to conduct operations in a city where the cartel had already paid off most of the local police. Law enforcement in Colombia was a poorly paid profession, after all, while drugs were bringing in billions of dollars. Corruption was at an all-time high. So many Medellín judges, police, and politicians were on the cartel's payroll, in fact, that Pablo Escobar was considered "untouchable" in his hometown.

The cartel, of course, made the payments to protect its major business—the exportation of cocaine. Bribes were thus one of the cartel's unavoidable operating expenses. If certain individuals proved troublesome and could not be bought—or if other individuals cheated or betrayed them—then Escobar and the cartel employed a veritable army of thousands of specialized hit men, called *sicarios*,* who enabled the cartel to enforce its will. By the late 1980s, some two thousand *sicarios*—mostly young teenagers—swarmed Medellín's crowded streets, often riding tandem on the backs of small motorcycles. The one in front was the designated driver; the one behind, the shooter. Escobar, who, according to some, had worked as a *sicario* himself in his teens, had sent out word to his young killers regarding the kind of assassinations he preferred: two bullets in the forehead, placed just above the eyes. A person might survive *one* of those bullets, Escobar advised, but never *two*.

In Medellín, assassination for the cartel was such a lucrative business that an entire cottage industry had sprung up. With an ever-increasing number of targets, delivering death smoothly, rapidly, and anonymously had become a highly sought-after skill. By 1989, the year that the colonel and four hundred members of the Search Bloc arrived in Medellín to take on Escobar, Medellín was already considered the most dangerous city in the world. No other metropolis came close to the rate at which living human beings were so abundantly converted each day into the dead.

That the members of the Search Bloc would be exposed to extreme danger was a given: for that reason, neither the colonel nor his men had brought their families along. To have done so would have

---

*The word *sicario* comes from the Latin *sicarius*, or "dagger men," originally referring to a small group of Jewish guerrillas, in the first century BC, who attempted to expel Roman occupiers by using concealed daggers for assassination.

immediately transformed their loved ones into targets for the cartel. Instead, the Search Bloc families lived in various homes in other cities and frequently moved for security reasons. Recently, as the Colombian government had turned up the pressure on the cartel and violence had correspondingly increased, Colonel Martínez and his wife had abruptly withdrawn their children from school. Even a police escort could no longer guarantee their safety. No, after the recent bomb explosion outside, the colonel realized, even Bogotá had become too dangerous. For that matter, so had practically every corner of Colombia. To Martínez, the cartel increasingly seemed like an enormous octopus with innumerable tentacles, some thick, some small, with more tentacles constantly sprouting. The cartel could reach whomever it wanted, even outside of Colombia. Anyone who, for any reason, tried to stop or hinder the cartel's growth automatically became a target for assassination.

Knock, knock, knock!

The knocks were harder, louder, more insistent.

"Who's there?" Martínez called out.

There was silence. Then a muffled voice.

"Who *is* it?" he called again.

This time, he heard a name. A name he recognized. But it was a name he hadn't heard in years.

Martínez opened the door. Before him stood a man about forty-five years old, dressed in a suit and tie, with brown skin and a pained expression on his face. It was a man Martínez recognized—a former police officer whom he hadn't seen in more than four years. The officer had once lived in a house alongside his own in another city, and Martínez had once asked him, because of certain irregularities, to resign.

The man stood there, a look of shame mingling with fear on his face. He had difficulty meeting the colonel's eyes.

"I come to you with a message, *mi colonel*," he finally said. "I come to you *obligated*."

Martínez looked at him, frowning. The man then looked up.

"The message is from Pablo Escobar," he said.

"If I didn't come—they'd kill me. Or my family. That's the threat I'm under."

Martínez stared at his former colleague, still wondering how he'd appeared so easily at his doorway.

"What's the message?" he finally asked.

"Escobar's sent me to offer you six million dollars."

The man looked at Martínez carefully, judging his reaction, before continuing.

"The only thing he asks is that you keep on working, that you continue your job, that you keep carrying out operations. But," he added, staring hard at the colonel, "if you're sending an operation to capture him—then you must first make a phone call. To let us know. If you agree, then the money will be delivered to any account you want.

"Six million dollars," the man repeated.

Colonel Martínez stared at the former officer, who was clearly uncomfortable and sweating, despite the cool air. Two thoughts now entered the colonel's mind. The first was the realization that Escobar was making him the standard cartel offer of *plata o plomo*, "silver or lead." Literally, "money or death." The bomb explosion a week earlier had been the first part of that offer—the threat of *plomo*, or death—unless Martínez changed his behavior. Now his former colleague was here with the second part: the *plata* or, in this case, the $6 million. It was up to Martínez which to accept.

The second thought that entered Martínez's mind, as he watched the cartel's messenger shift uneasily before him, was that Escobar wouldn't be making this offer if he wasn't feeling pressure. Already, the colonel and his men had captured or killed some of Escobar's top lieutenants, including Escobar's cousin Henao, his right-hand man. Escobar, the colonel now realized, must be worried. His offer was thus a sign of weakness, not strength.

"Tell them you couldn't find me," Martínez said quietly.

"But, *mi colonel*, I can't do that," the man pleaded.

"We never spoke," the colonel said firmly.

And then, despite the man's pleading, the colonel closed the door.

When Pablo Escobar was seven years old and his eldest brother, Roberto, was ten, armed mobs, or *Chusmeros*, arrived in the village of

Titiribu where the Escobar family lived, with the intent of slaughtering the inhabitants. The year was 1959 and, as Escobar's older brother Roberto later recounted,

> They came to our town in the middle of the night, dragging people out of their houses and killing them. When they reached our house they started banging on the doors with their machetes and screaming that they were going to kill us.

Most of the inhabitants in Escobar's village belonged to Colombia's Liberal Party. The armed mob, by contrast, was made up of Conservatives. Eleven years earlier, in 1948, the internal tensions in Colombia had come to a head with the assassination of a Liberal political candidate, Jorge Gaitán, who was predicted to win the presidency. Gaitán's death became a trigger point that set off in Colombia a kind of collective nervous breakdown, unleashing a home-brewed explosion of violence that was as brutal as that in Rwanda some forty years later. If, as the Prussian general Carl von Clausewitz said, "War is simply a continuation of policy by other means," Gaitán's death motivated Colombians to take their political opinions out of the realm of the ballot box and into the countryside, where ideology was now enforced with machetes, knives, and guns. In a country with only eleven million inhabitants, *three hundred thousand* Colombians soon lost their lives in the violent mayhem that ensued. Another six hundred thousand to eight hundred thousand were injured. To make matters worse, in Colombia the transformation from political discourse to open civil war had a particularly barbarous edge: the goal became not simply to kill one's opponents but to do so in the most horrific manner possible.

During the mass hysteria that would later become known as *La Violencia*, methods of murder became so ghastly that a new lexicon emerged; new forms of language had to be invented for acts that had never before been seen, or at least not to such extremes or on such a scale. Colloquialisms soon sprang up, for example, such as *picar para tamal*, "to cut like a tamale," which in this case meant to slowly chop a person's body apart until he or she died. Death through *bocachiquiar* derived from the manner in which Colombian fishermen cleaned *bo-cachico*, a fish so scaly that numerous slits had to be cut into its flesh in order to remove the scales. In the human version, a person was sliced repeatedly until he or she bled to death. Village-wide rampages broke out that included cutting off people's ears, scalping inhabitants alive, bayoneting children and babies, and, for men, inflicting the signature *corte de corbata*, or "tie cut"—which meant cutting someone's throat open and then pulling out his or her tongue through the open wound.

Thus, eleven years after Gaitán's assassination, when shouts, lights, and torches arrived at the Escobars' home in the middle of the night, the entire family knew what probably lay in store for them. According to Pablo's brother, Roberto, as fists and machetes began to bang on their door, and as the screams of neighbors punctuated the night,

> My mother was crying and praying to the Baby Jesus of Atocha. She took one of our mattresses and put it under the bed, then told us to lie there silently and covered us with blankets. I heard my father saying "They're going to kill us, but we can save the kids." I held on to Pablo and our sister, Gloria, telling them not to cry, that we would be all right . . . The door was very strong and the attackers failed to break through it, so they sprayed it with gasoline and set it on fire.

At the last minute, just before the Escobars were roasted alive, the Colombian army arrived and put the crazed marauders to flight. When shortly afterward soldiers banged on the Escobars' door, telling them it was safe to come out, at first the family didn't believe them. Eventually, forced out by the intense heat, the family stumbled into what was now a ravaged village, the soldiers leading the Escobars and other survivors to the local schoolhouse. Recalled Roberto,

> Our road was illuminated by our burning house. In that strange light I saw bodies lying in the gutters and hanging from the lampposts. The *Chusmeros* had poured gasoline on the bodies and set them on fire, and I will remember forever the smell of burning flesh. I carried

[seven-year-old] Pablo. Pablo held on to me so tightly, as if he would never let go.

The sudden and savage outbreak of violence made it obvious to the rest of the world that Colombia, for whatever reason, had been a country coiled like a spring, a spring to which had been fastened hand grenades. The assassination of Gaitán had in fact cracked the country's normally polite exterior and had allowed its inner tensions to explode, much as lava occasionally bursts forth through sudden cracks in the Andes. It wasn't the first time, however, that Colombia had suffered such a fiery eruption. Fifty years earlier, between 1899 and 1902, another civil war had broken out, one equally as savage and during which *eight hundred thousand* people had been slaughtered, or about 20 percent of Colombia's population.

"The immeasurable violence and pain of our history are the result of age-old inequities and untold bitterness," wrote the Colombian novelist Gabriel García Márquez in his 1982 Nobel Prize acceptance speech, "and not a conspiracy plotted [by Communists] three thousand leagues from our home."

Historians would agree. Most state that the roots of modern violence in Colombia stretch all of the way back to the original Spanish conquest. That is when a band of fewer than two hundred Spanish conquistadors, led by thirty-one-year-old Gonzalo Jiménez de Quesada, arrived in 1537 upon a high plain dotted with Indian villages. The Spaniards were searching for an Indian chief named Bogotá who was rumored to possess great quantities of gold. They soon stumbled upon the Muisca culture, a loose confederation of Native American states whose inhabitants lived in conical huts, practiced agriculture on abundant, fertile fields, wore cotton tunics, and mined or traded for emeralds, copper, and gold. Each Muisca state had a chief, or *cacique*, and the confederations—some of the most complex to have ever existed in the Andes—covered a mountainous area the size of Switzerland.

The Muisca spoke Chibcha, part of a language family that extended up into lower Central America. Like many other native South

Americans, individuals did not own property. Instead, the land, water, and game animals were commonly owned. The Spaniards, by contrast, who had arrived from a Europe that had only recently invented capitalism, saw not a commons but a land ready for the taking—a country that was ripe for the institution of private property to be introduced. Here, fields, plains, and forests could be seized and demarcated; resources could then be quickly scooped up and exported for profit. Wrote one sixteenth-century chronicler,

> When the Spaniards set their eyes on that land [of Colombia], it appeared to them that they had reached their desired destination. Therefore, they set out to conquer it.

Wrote another,

> Marching along on the campaign, Jiménez [de Quesada] . . . initiated the conquest of this New Kingdom . . . [they] entered the territory of the most important lord in all the land; they call him Bogotá . . . it is rumored that he is extremely rich because the natives of this land claim that he has a house of gold and a great number of very precious emeralds.

Gold, emeralds, and the idea of quickly obtained wealth excited the conquistadors to a man for, as the historian John Hemming noted,

> The men who went on these ventures were not mercenaries: they received no pay from the expedition's leader. They were adventurers who took passage to the Americas in the hope of making their fortunes. In the early days of the conquests, any reward for these desperadoes had to come from the Indians themselves. They were predators hoping for easy plunder. Their food and personal service came from the Indians they hoped to rob . . . The Spanish adventurers were like packs of hounds, roaming the interior to pick up a scent of gold. They sailed across the Atlantic full of bravado and ambition

and then filled the tiny coastal settlements, hoping to grow rich as parasites on the native population.

On the high, fertile plains where later the Colombian capital of Bogotá would be founded, Jiménez de Quesada and one hundred and sixty-six men—the only survivors from the nine hundred men who had begun the expedition two years earlier—continued searching for the Indian lord, Bogotá. Recounted one chronicler,

> The next day they continued ahead two leagues where they came across a brand-new settlement, recently built by a great lord . . . Bogotá. The town was quite splendid; the few houses were very large, and made of finely worked thatch. The houses were well fenced, with walls made from cane stalks, elegantly crafted . . . two walls enclosed the entire town and between them was a great plaza . . . A message was sent . . . to tell their *cacique* [chief] to come forward and make friends with the Christians. If he did not, the Christians would raze the town to the ground, and wage war against those who chose not to come in peace.

Chief Bogotá, for reasons that seem obvious today but for some reason were not so obvious to the Spaniards, refused to come out as desired. The Spaniards then, true to form, immediately began killing and enslaving the local population, seizing their emerald mines, capturing the native chiefs, killing or ransoming some of them for gold, and gathering up as many portable resources, or spoils, as they could. After eventually murdering chief Bogotá, the Spaniards then hunted down one of the Muisca federation's last remaining leaders, demanding that the latter turn over the supposed fortune in gold they suspected chief Bogotá had hidden from them. Wrote a chronicler:

> [The captured chief] Sagipa responded that he would, with great pleasure, give them the gold. He asked them to extend him a reasonable deadline in order to do so, promising that he would fill a small

house with Bogotá's gold; but he needed a few days in order to gather [it] . . . but when the deadline expired Sagipa had not complied. He handed over three or four thousand pesos of fine and low-grade gold, and nothing more. Seeing this, the Christians began to plead with Lieutenant Jiménez [de Quesada] to place Sagipa in irons and have him tortured . . . after which point the Christians proceeded to torture Sagipa in order to compel him to hand over Bogotá's gold and confess where he had hidden it; in the end, Sagipa died.

Chief Sagipa didn't just "die," of course; rather, he was tortured to death. A few days later, the Spaniards founded *Santa Fé de Bogotá*, which ironically means "The Sacred Faith of Bogotá," named after the very native chief whom they had just murdered. Thus, amid the despoiled Muisca highlands, smeared with blood, gold, emeralds, and death, began Colombia's written history, a first bloody chapter that set the stage for many more to come.

One day at the Hacienda Nápoles, the luxurious country estate and hideaway that Pablo Escobar owned about a three-hour drive from Medellín, he was entertaining guests beside his kidney-shaped swimming pool when an employee was led out before him. In the distance, on the hacienda's grounds, imported giraffes, ostriches, and gazelles gamboled about. A bit farther away, in a nearby river, feral African hippopotami snorted water and wiggled their ears. Escobar had imported four of these massive animals—some of the most dangerous in Africa—and their numbers were increasing. On this particular day, Escobar was dressed in his trademark blue jeans, white Nike tennis shoes, and a T-shirt. The employee who now stood before him with bound hands had been caught stealing from one of the estate's many rooms, Escobar was told. He was a thief.

"You're lucky you confessed," Escobar told his captive calmly and in his usual quiet voice. "Because that way you protected your family." As the

guests lounged in their chairs and sipped from their drinks, Escobar rose and methodically began kicking and beating the man until he fell to the ground. The world's wealthiest and most powerful drug baron, who by this time owned more than four hundred properties in Colombia and nineteen mansions in Miami, each with its own heliport, now proceeded to savagely kick the man until the latter fell into the pool. As the man's thrashing body sank slowly toward the bottom, Escobar returned to his guests.

"Now, where were we?" he asked them with a smile.

I meet retired general Hugo Martínez—the man who once turned down $6 million rather than sell his soul to Pablo Escobar—in an upscale apartment tower in the *Chico Norte* neighborhood of Bogotá, in the condominium of one of his friends.

"The general doesn't like to have visitors at his home," I am told by his friend Maria, a journalist who spent time covering Martínez and the Search Bloc during the height of their war against the Medellín cartel.

"He prefers to meet people he doesn't know outside of his home."

No doubt from his years of being pursued by the cartel, I reflect.

The general is now sixty-nine years old, yet remains tall and lean, his dark hair shot through with gray. He has thin lips, a soft handshake, close-set eyes, and looks Spanish or European in complexion. When in 1989 Hugo Martínez was assigned the job of going after Escobar and the cartel, he had been a colonel. Today the retired general is wearing slacks, a gray sweater, a pressed shirt with thin blue stripes, and is amiable and relaxed. Twenty years after his epic battle with Escobar and the cartel, the memories of that period still remain fresh in his mind. They also remain seared into the collective mind of many Colombians. Even more so, perhaps, as only recently a lengthy television series called *Pablo Escobar: El Patrón del Mal* (*Pablo Escobar: The Boss of Evil*), was broadcast throughout the country. It was the most expensive and successful television series in Colombian history, with millions tuning in every evening. The series was only the latest offering, however, in a plethora of Colombian crime dramas dealing with narco-trafficking, many of which tend to paint the lives of various drug lords as "colorful" while at the same time portraying the police officers and politicians who pursue them as corrupt.

"Colombians are fascinated by all of this," Maria tells me. "But they don't know the reality; the younger generation doesn't know how *brutal* it all was."

The man selected to hunt down Escobar, meanwhile, was born in a small town called Moniquira about eighty miles northwest of Bogotá. Moniquira was the kind of town where people rode about on horseback and wore *ruanas*, Colombia's traditional woolen ponchos. Both Martínez and Escobar, in fact, were born into the lower middle class and grew up in large families. Escobar had six brothers and sisters; Martínez had eight. Escobar's father was a small farmer; Martínez's was a small shop owner selling suitcases and leather goods.

Escobar's maternal grandfather, however, was a well-known bootlegger who used to smuggle locally brewed liquor in bottles hidden inside coffins. Martínez's family, by contrast, had a long military thread running through it. Martínez had an uncle who had been an admiral in the navy. Another relative had been an army general. Not surprisingly, as a young boy Martínez joined the Boy Scouts.

"I have some photos of myself with other scouts," Martínez tells me, breaking into a laugh as he remembers it. "We're standing around, and all the kids are relaxed. And there I am, stiff and straight as a board in my uniform and very serious. I was about eight years old," he says, shaking his head.

When Martínez began secondary school, his family sent him to a nearby town as a boarding student, as his home town had only a primary school. Martínez boarded with a local family. One day during Easter vacation, when most of the students had returned to their home towns, Martínez was still living as a boarder when two older friends arrived with a friend for a visit. All three were cadets living in a different town. The newcomer was about Martínez's size so Martínez asked him if he could try on his uniform. The cadet agreed and changed into regular clothes. "I took off my clothes and put on his uniform," Martínez says, straightening himself up and throwing his shoulders back. "Then I stood before the mirror, put on my cap, and went out into the street. I spent the entire afternoon walking around, showing off. I even played billiards for a while. Finally, the cadet was searching everywhere until he found me. "Hey! What got *into* you?" he said. "You almost got me kicked out of cadet school!"

As a boarder, Martínez was somewhat isolated, so he spent a lot of time reading, mostly dime novels about gunfighters in the Old West and especially crime novels. "I liked to read stories about solving crimes, about bandits," he tells me. "But the funny thing is, when I finally joined the police—it wasn't anything like the novels!" Nor was wearing a uniform or handling a gun like he had imagined it. By the time he, too, became a cadet, he'd had to polish and press his uniform so many times that he no longer enjoyed wearing one. Martínez soon experienced the same disenchantment with guns.

> When you first become a cadet, you see that everyone else is carrying a rifle and a sword. But you are given nothing, only a stick, which you simulate a rifle with. That lasts for eight months, eight months during which you can't carry a gun—instead you learn to clean it and polish it and assemble it. By the time the eight months are over—you no longer want a gun! Or a uniform!

A maid brings us a plate of cookies, cakes, and espressos, setting them down before us on a knee-high table. Martínez doesn't touch the sweets but does take an espresso. He's straightforward and a good communicator, occasionally touching one's arm for emphasis, as many Colombians like to do. He's relaxed and has no airs about having been a general. Martínez sips the bittersweet coffee and continues.

Despite his aversion to guns and uniforms, he says, he did like his classes in criminology. He liked studying sociology. When he finally graduated and was a young sub-lieutenant, his superiors sent him to

Bogotá for the first time, to complete a year of *práctica*. At the end of that year, the station where he was assigned threw a party for him, as he was about to be transferred to another locale. At the party he met a girl named Magdalena, "the most beautiful girl I had ever seen." Martínez was twenty-three, and she was seventeen; he asked her for her phone number and she complied. Their first date was a movie. A year later, when his superiors told him that he was about to be transferred to another city, he knew he had to make a decision. "She was very pretty, so I knew if I didn't marry her, she would no longer be mine," he tells me, draining his espresso and setting the cup back on the table. Martínez asked his father for advice: "If you love this girl—*marry her!*" his father counseled. "If you don't love her, *leave her!*"

So Martínez married Magdalena, started a family, and gradually began moving up through the ranks: first sublieutenant, then lieutenant, then major. For a safety net, however, Martínez decided to study at night for a law degree, which he felt would complement his day job. Five years later, he graduated at the top of his class. As an award, he received a scholarship to study criminology for a year in Spain.

By the time he was in his forties, Hugo Martínez was a colonel in the national police, had a law degree, and had studied advanced criminology abroad. Working as the commander of a police school in Bogotá, he also supervised the work of intelligence officers who analyzed crime data from every region of Colombia. By now, Martínez and his wife had three children, the eldest of which, Hugo Martínez Jr., had just become a police cadet and seemed destined to follow in his father's footsteps.

All was running smoothly until, on August 18, 1989, the news broke that a presidential candidate named Luis Galán had just been assassinated, most likely by the Medellín cartel. Galán was a front-runner in the presidential elections and had sworn to uphold the current extradition law, which allowed Colombian criminals to be extradited to other countries such as the United States. A few days after Galán's assassination, Martínez learned that the government had decided to assemble a task force of four hundred officers from different departments—all from elite forces—and move them en masse to Medellín. The new group would be called the *Bloque de Búsqueda,* or "Search Bloc." Their assignment was to go after the Medellín cartel—to capture or kill Pablo Escobar and the rest of the cartel's leaders.

Galán's assassination, it turned out, thoroughly angered Colombia's elite: the government's reaction was to declare war on the cartel. The very same day that Martínez learned about the new task force, he received a phone call from the director of the police. Martínez had been selected to lead the *Bloque de Búsqueda,* the director informed him. He was to pack a bag and leave immediately for Medellín.

In 1551 a thirty-one-year-old conquistador named Pedro Cieza de León published the first of three chronicles about his travels through South America, which included years spent in Colombia and Peru. Curious about everything he saw, the Spaniard described plants, animals, and people that no European had ever seen. He also wrote about the widespread use of small leaves by natives in the Andes, harvested from plants they called "coca":

> In all parts of the Indies through which I traveled I noticed the Indians delighted to carry herbs or roots in their mouths . . . to which they apply a mixture which they carry in a calabash [gourd], made from a certain earth-like lime . . . When I asked some of these Indians why they carried these leaves in their mouths, which they do not eat . . . they replied that it prevents them from feeling hungry, and gives them great vigor and strength . . . They . . . use Coca in the forests of the Andes . . . The trees are small, and they cultivate them with great care, that they may yield the leaf called Coca. They put the leaves in the sun, and afterwards pack them in little narrow bags . . . This Coca is so highly valued . . . [that] there are some persons in Spain who are rich from the produce of this Coca, having traded with it, sold and resold it in the Indian markets.

For centuries after Cieza de León's description, however, the precise reason the coca plants had such powerful grip upon Andean natives remained a mystery—only to be unraveled nearly half a millennium later.

"Do you know what Colombia's greatest 'sport' is?" asks Alexander, a twenty-eight-year-old Colombian teacher from Bogotá. Alexander is giving me and two of his friends a ride out to Lake Guatavita, the sacred lake where the story of El Dorado was born.

"Soccer?" I suggest, staring through the windshield from the front seat.

"No," he says, shaking his head.

He looks over at me, and I shake my head, too.

"Murder," he says matter-of-factly, shrugging his shoulders. Alexander swerves to give a wide berth to a tight cluster of bicyclists on the right-hand side of the highway, their helmeted heads down, their black and yellow outfits gleaming in the early morning sun. Bicycling and bicycle racing is a popular sport in Colombia, and on Sundays it seems like half of Bogotá puts on tight shorts, shirts, and helmets and takes to the streets. The cyclists remind me of the fact that Pablo Escobar's older brother, Roberto, was once a champion bicycle racer before he joined Pablo's growing drug business.

"So why *is* there so much violence in Colombia?" I ask.

"Genes," Alexander says, without missing a beat.

He looks at me, and I shake my head again, not understanding.

"We were conquered by murderers," he says. "Our ancestors were thieves and barbarians. Violence is in our genes."

In the backseat of Alexander's car sits Herman Van Diepen, a lanky, fifty-eight-year-old American expatriate who teaches English in Bogotá and who has been living here for the last five years. Herman is of Dutch extraction, hails from Modesto, California, and has blue eyes and what seems to be permanently sunburned skin. A year after he arrived in Bogotá, Herman married a Colombian flower vendor. (Colombia, it turns out, not only cornered the market on cocaine but is also the world's second largest exporter of cut flowers.) Her name was Maria and, like Herman, Maria was divorced. She had two sons and had put both of them through the best universities in Colombia. Maria was a hard worker and eventually bought two small brick apartments she had paid off by running the small flower business. Today both Herman and Maria are riding with us, in the backseat of Alexander's Toyota.

I turn to Maria, who's wearing jeans and a sweater, and ask her the same question I had asked Alexander:

"Why has there been so much violence in Colombia over the years?"

"*Desigualdad*," she says without hesitation. "Inequality."

"A few people have everything, a lot of people have nothing. That's the root," she says, nodding her head, her long black hair lightly streaked with gray.

"Yet," says Herman, "despite the violence, Colombians are some of the happiest people in the world. Some of the friendliest people I've ever met."

"But we have an inferiority complex," Alexander says, as we drive through countryside that looks a bit like Switzerland or southern Germany, with rolling hills and patches of dark green forest, intermixed with cultivated land. To the left, rows of strawberry plants stretch up and over a low hill.

Recently, Alexander says, Colombia played a soccer match against Ecuador. For almost the entire match, Colombia completely dominated the team from the smaller nation to the south. But, he says, in the last few minutes Ecuador scored not once but *twice*. The match ended 2–0.

"That's why we have an expression here," Alexander says: " 'We *played* as never before—but we *lost* as usual.' "

Maria laughs.

Alexander teaches English in the same college that Herman does. He lives in a small apartment and graduated from the university in linguistics. He's married, has two small boys, and shakes his head.

"I love Colombia," he says. "But this country is still pretty fucked up."

We turn off the highway, the sky overcast with ragged gray clouds, and pull into Sesquilé, a small town with a colonial church set at the base of forested green mountains. In a small café with a wooden balcony, we look out onto the square below and order a breakfast of rib soup, croissants, and small cups of piping hot chocolate.

"Beautiful mountains," I say, admiring the jagged hills that rise behind the church. The church is made of orange brick, and its two towers are layered in green shingles.

"Yes, 'beautiful mountains,' " Alex says sourly, wiping croissant crumbs from his neatly pressed sweater and slacks. "Beautiful mountains that are full of guerrillas."

Just outside of town, Alex pulls to a stop and asks an old man wearing a straw hat and a *ruana*, or woolen poncho, if this is the right way to Lake Guatavita.

"You're pretty much lost," the old man says. He has dark brown eyes set in leathery skin. "But you'll find it," he says, gesticulating vaguely toward the hills.

A half hour later, we find the entrance to the *Reserva del Cacique Guatavita* and are soon following a Muisca guide through damp, bromeliad-infested hills, home to spectacled bears and small night monkeys called *martejas*. Moss and lichen cling to the trunks of small trees while an iridescent green hummingbird flits about, dazzling us when struck by the sun.

Our guide is from one of the five local indigenous groups in the area. His name is Oscar Chauta, he's twenty-eight and has straight black hair, a soft voice, and pleasant, musical laughter. Oscar's ancestors used to speak Chibcha, he says, the same language the conquistadors encountered here. But no one speaks Chibcha anymore, he explains, not even his grandparents—they only spoke a few words. Oscar's last name, Chauta, means "man, being, to sow the seed," he says. King Carlos III of Spain outlawed the speaking of Chibcha in 1770, Oscar says, in an attempt to rid Colombia of its indigenous heritage.

The law remained in place for more than two centuries, until 1991, the same year Colombia's congress outlawed extradition, thus protecting drug traffickers from being prosecuted abroad. By then, however, the Chibcha language had long since gone extinct.

Alexander, Maria, Herman, six other Colombian tourists, and I huff and puff up the trail to nearly ten thousand feet, sometimes walking through natural tunnels of vegetation. Ferns protrude out toward the stone-flagged trail. We pass groves of pine trees, the clustered needles of which hang like shrunken heads, low to the ground.

At one point we pause, looking out over rolling hills and patches of dark green forest. I ask our guide if in the past Muisca villages weren't scattered over the hills, if this land in fact hadn't once been a quilt-work of villages and fields.

"No," he says, "this whole area was sacred. It was *un ecosistema sagrado,*" he says, a "sacred ecosystem." "There were no villages here— only the sacred forests and lakes."

We finally emerge onto a crest and discover that we are standing on the rim of a giant crater where, some hundreds of feet below, stretches an emerald-colored lake. This is Lake Guatavita, one of a series of lakes sacred to the Muisca. A breeze alternately ruffles and stills its surface, so that sometimes it's corrugated and at other times is as smooth as glass.

Our guide gathers us on the crater's rim and begins to tell the story of how, back in the days of the Muisca, certain boys were chosen to be *caciques,* or chiefs. As part of their training, Oscar says, the boys were kept isolated in a cave for twelve years, without being permitted to leave. The first six years, he says, they were taken care of by their mothers. For the next six, they were raised by their fathers. When they finally reached puberty and after lengthy instruction from their elders, each boy was "tested" to see how "pure" his heart was, by surreptitiously offering him a tempting array of virgin girls. If the teenager failed the test, Oscar tells us, his black hair framed by the green mountains behind, then he was killed. If the teenager passed, then on a certain resplendent day attendants covered him in resin and blew gold dust onto his body with tubular reeds. Afterward, the teenager was fitted with golden breastplates, diadems, and sparkling nose and ear ornaments. Early in the morning, Oscar says, gesturing toward the lake below, attendants rowed the prospective chief out onto the water on a reed raft. Up on the crater's crest, where we are standing now, a thousand or more onlookers gathered, awaiting the emergence of the sun. Finally, at the appropriate time, certain natives blew conch shells as the anointed prince—whom the Spaniards later called El Dorado, or "the golden one"—raised his arms toward the newly arrived sun. The prince then threw golden ornaments into the lake as offerings to the lake goddess and to the sun.

"Do you believe he threw gold into the lake?" Oscar concludes dramatically, looking carefully at our small group. We nod solemnly. We can hear the sound of wind in the trees, and I can see it begin to carve the lake surface far below.

"The Spaniards did," Oscar says, now pointing at a large gash on the northern edge of the crater, a kind of wedge cut into the rim that cleaves all of the way down to the lake's surface. "They tried to drain it over and over again," Oscar says, "but they never could. They never found the bottom."

Oscar is only partially right, it turns out. A long line of Spaniards and Colombians *did* try to drain the lake in the sixteenth century, beginning with bucket brigades and culminating in the 1580 excavation of a huge wedge in the crater's side, which lowered the lake by sixty feet. The gash later collapsed, killing the native workers, and the effort of cutting farther into the crater's rim was abandoned. The Spaniards found enough jade and golden ornaments along the newly exposed lakeshore, however, to encourage further efforts. In 1801 the German scientist Alexander von Humboldt visited Lake Guatavita in the midst of his South American explorations. Humboldt carefully measured the circumference and later estimated that possibly the equivalent of $100 million in gold might lie at the lake's bottom.

A century later, an English engineer named Hartley Knowles took over a Colombian extraction company and went to work applying modern technology in the form of steam engines to bore holes into one of the crater's sides. Hartley spent a dozen years at the task, gradually draining the lake lower and lower, all the while hiring local workers to scour the newly exposed lake beds for gold. By 1912 Knowles had discovered enough ancient Muisca offerings that he auctioned off sixty-two lots of golden ornaments and jewels in London, which netted him $20,000. That same year, a reporter from the *New York Times* interviewed Knowles in New York City, where the Englishman had gone to show some of his smaller treasures to specialists. According to the reporter, Knowles poured some of the golden ornaments into the reporter's outstretched hand.

"El Dorado," the Englishman said quietly. "El Dorado after centuries. The gifts of the golden man. The treasure of the sacred lake."

A photo that later accompanied the reporter's article showed the result of Knowles's handiwork: instead of a lake now stretched a massive crater, almost completely drained, with two men standing on its bottom amid pools of water, mud, and slime.

"The lake is drained as dry as I [currently] want it," Knowles told the reporter. "If it is completely drained the mud at the bottom may solidify, and we do not want that. What we are after now is to dig down to what was the bottom of the lake 456 years ago. The present bottom is, of course, a sediment of years . . . It took four years to drain the lake. Now we are excavating."

Unfortunately for Knowles, his workers ultimately *did* drain the last pools of water, the lake bottom *did* solidify, and excavation efforts had to be abandoned. Eventually his company went bankrupt, the rains came as they always did, and the crater filled up once again.

In 1965 the Colombian government purchased Lake Guatavita and the surrounding area and turned it into a reserve, thus putting an end to four centuries' worth of efforts to dredge the lake for gold.

"To the Europeans, gold was money," Oscar tells us, as the late afternoon sun illuminates his face. "To the Muisca, it was different. The gold was sacred. It had meaning. It was an element that never tarnished, an element that never became corrupted."

Oscar looks around at us, and we nod. I turn to the great gash that still scars the lake's edge and think of all the reed rafts and of centuries of golden men and of the worshippers who once stood on the crater's rim, like we are standing now, waiting for the glorious emergence of the sun. And then I think of the endless parade of treasure hunters who later arrived, hoping to find a substance that could make them wealthy, hoping to find an element that could make them powerful, hoping to find a treasure that could completely transform their lives. One of the latest and most infamous of this line was the drug lord Pablo Escobar. The only difference was that Escobar chased after neither myths nor buried treasure. Instead, he focused his full attention on a plant-derived substance now literally worth its weight in gold.

Pablo Escobar Gaviria was born the third of seven children and grew up in Envigado, a suburb of Medellín. The Escobar family had moved to Envigado from the countryside after the ravages of *La Violencia*. Although his father was a farmer and his mother a schoolteacher, Escobar in his early teens soon fell in with the "wrong crowd," dropped out of high school, and embarked on a life of crime. At first, he stole cars, then he robbed banks, before he eventually moved into contraband goods, kidnappings, extortion, and murder.

By 1975, when Escobar was twenty-four, he had already spent a decade honing his criminal skills. Five foot six and with wavy brown hair, he was by now a master at stealing cars and also at smuggling contraband. By a strange quirk of fate, Escobar's mastery of the local contraband trade just so happened to coincide with changes occurring thousands of miles north. By the early 1970s, US citizens who had been regularly smoking illegal marijuana for decades were just beginning to experiment with cocaine. Small amounts of the white powder had been wending their way northward from South America since the late 1960s. By the early 1970s, the flow of cocaine had started to increase exponentially. Colombia was a natural transshipment point for illegal drugs from the Andean countries as it straddled both the Pacific Ocean and the Caribbean as well as the land isthmus that led north. And the economics made sense. In 1975 a kilo of unrefined cocaine paste, called *pasta básica*, could be bought in Peru or Bolivia for roughly $60. Once refined into pure cocaine and smuggled into Miami or New York, a kilo could be sold for $40,000. Among the small-time criminals who lived in the provincial city of Medellín, none took a more intense interest in those profits than Pablo Escobar.

Escobar began his move into the cocaine business as a bottom-rung drug smuggler at the age of twenty-four. In 1975 the young criminal outfitted three French Renaults with a secret compartment under their chasses, bought a kilo of cocaine paste in Peru, then drove the first car with Peruvian license plates to the border. There he switched to the second car with Ecuadorian plates, then switched again to a third Renault at the Colombian border. Once across the border, Escobar drove without any problems to Medellín, where he personally refined the paste into purified cocaine in his own bathtub. He then sold the drug to local traffickers who knew how to smuggle cocaine into the United States. Dissatisfied with selling his hard-won product for local Colombian prices, however, Escobar soon began searching for a way to gain access to the distribution system that connected Colombia to the rest of the world. It was only by selling abroad, after all, that the really huge profits could be made. Eventually, Escobar learned of a local smuggler in Medellín named Fabio Restrepo, a medium-level drug dealer who had begun shipping forty to sixty kilos of cocaine several times a year to Miami. Escobar quickly did the math: forty to sixty kilos—purchased in Peru as *pasta básica* for roughly $2,400 to $3,600—could be converted into cocaine and sold in the United States for 1.6 to 2.4 million dollars, a markup of nearly 1,000 percent. Local US distributors, meanwhile, would add various worthless substances, such as cornstarch, to the cocaine, thus "cutting" it, or expanding the volume and weight, up to three times. The original kilo would thus become three kilos—resulting in a final markup value of nearly 3,000 percent.

Eager to gain access to the distribution system linked to those profits, Escobar soon contacted some of Restrepo's men and arranged to sell them some cocaine. At the time, Escobar was living in a grungy, ill-kept apartment and had been storing the cocaine he had refined in a dresser drawer. The two men who showed up were unimpressed by the small, soft-spoken young man who ultimately sold them fourteen kilos of cocaine. A few months later, however, those same men were surprised to learn that their boss, Restrepo, had been killed and that Restrepo's organization—themselves included—was now being run by the same small-time supplier they had previously met and had obviously underestimated: Pablo Escobar.

"Escobar was a criminal, through and through," says General Hugo Martínez, the former Search Bloc leader who had been sent to capture Escobar and dismantle the Medellín cartel.

"He was very cunning, very smart, very ruthless. He wasn't a businessman; he was a gangster."

A year after Restrepo was killed, two agents from Colombia's security police (DAS) arrested Escobar, having caught him smuggling more cocaine. According to Colombian law, Escobar now faced a possible sentence of multiple years in prison. The mug shot taken of him the day of his arrest, however, showed not a young man who was worried about his predicament, but instead a smiling, confident man who clearly seemed to view his arrest as an adventure or a lark. Sure enough, after paying off the proper authorities, Escobar walked free a few weeks later. According to his brother Roberto, who was soon to join his younger brother's organization, Escobar later had the two DAS agents who had arrested him killed:

> Pablo promised "I'm going to kill those motherfuckers myself" . . .
> I have heard from others that Pablo had them brought to a house,
> made them get down on their knees, then put a gun to their head
> and killed them . . . [In any case,] the newspapers reported finding
> the bodies of these two DAS agents who had been shot many times.

The murder of Restrepo and the two agents offered an early glimpse into what soon became Escobar's standard operating procedure: kill or muscle your way into a lucrative illegal activity; eliminate competition and obstacles via hired killers; pay off police, judges, and politicians so that your illegal activities are protected or ignored; then expand your markets and control by repeating all of the above.

Immediately after taking over Restrepo's drug network, Escobar began working to increase the size of his operation. The man who had once processed a single kilo of *pasta básica* in his own bathtub was soon sending forty to sixty kilos of refined cocaine to Miami by small plane *per week* and earning roughly $8 million of profits per month. By reinvesting those profits, Escobar continued to expand, increasing his drug flights to two or three times per week. Within two short years, Pablo Escobar possessed a fleet of fifteen large aircraft. Each was capable of carrying 1,200 kilos of cocaine—worth more than $80 million—to the United States at a time. Those on the other end of the supply chain—at first trendy young Americans with disposable incomes and later the poorer inhabitants of the inner cities—had no inkling of the death, bribes, and sheer criminality that followed the journey of the fine white powder from the Andes all the way up into their noses. In 1977 a *Newsweek* reporter chronicled the explosive impact the powerful new South American drug was having in the United States:

> Cocaine's popularity has spread so vastly within the last few years that it has become the recreational drug of choice for countless Americans . . . At certain restaurants in Aspen, Colo.—which one DEA official called "the cocaine capital of the US"—devotees can ask for "Booth D" to be assured of a table where they can safely take the drug . . . Among hostesses in the smart sets of Los Angeles and New York, a little cocaine, like Dom Pérignon and beluga caviar, is now de rigueur at dinners. Some party-givers pass it around along with the canapés on silver trays; some fill ashtrays with cocaine and set them on the table . . . Some coke buffs wear neck chains with a razor blade and a tiny spoon dangling like amulets. Maxferd's, a San Francisco jewelry store, provides diamond-encrusted razor blades for $500 and custom-designed spoons that sell for as much as $5,000. The store, which sold $40,000 worth of cocaine spoons last year, also offers a double spoon. "We have to use calipers to measure the distance

from one nostril to the other," says Maxferd's owner, Howard Cohn. "It can get quite funny."

With his own nose glued to money, not powder (Escobar famously never imbibed cocaine—instead he smoked marijuana daily, getting high each morning before buckling down to business), Pablo Escobar quickly transformed himself from a car thief and extortionist operating in a provincial Colombian capital into an international cocaine baron. By 1982, at the age of thirty-two, Escobar was married, had two children, was a multibillionaire, and had helped create the Medellín cartel, a loose confederation of cocaine suppliers, refiners, and distributors. Amazingly, he had also just been elected to national office as an "alternate" congressman from Medellín. The latter position automatically gave Escobar both judicial immunity from prosecution and a diplomatic visa for travel to the United States. For the first time, Escobar could now legally travel to Miami and enjoy his mansions. Escobar did so on his Learjet, taking his family to see Disney World, the White House, and the FBI museum. Even while Escobar was vacationing in the United States, however, fleets of his planes, speed boats, and remote-controlled submarines were constantly heading north, returning to Colombia with so many bales of $100 bills that Escobar found it more efficient to *weigh* the money rather than count it.

Running for and winning political office, however, turned out to be a watershed moment in Pablo Escobar's career. It soon became apparent, in fact, that Escobar possessed a fatal flaw in his suite of criminal characteristics that, until now, had lifted him from complete obscurity up into the very stratosphere of the criminal elite. A man whose very profession required anonymity and whose business by necessity had to be carried out in the shadows, gradually revealed that he lusted after not only great wealth and power but also fame and renown. In a country where even four hundred years after the Spanish conquest 97 percent of the country's wealth was controlled by 3 percent of its elite, Escobar now wanted entrée and acceptance *into* that elite. Escobar's real goal, he informed his inner circle, was eventually to become Colombia's president. Yet running for and gaining political office couldn't be accomplished without simultaneously running the risk of Escobar exposing his vast, subterranean criminal enterprises. In the end, it was a miscalculation that would prove to be his undoing.

Escobar's enjoyment of his congressional seat, in fact, along with its twin perks of diplomatic immunity and a US travel visa, lasted for less than a year. Although Escobar had paid various henchmen to destroy his criminal records and had thus tried to whitewash his past, his sudden emergence onto the public stage invited both close public scrutiny and intense press coverage. Who was this thirty-two-year-old self-described billionaire who was now a Colombian congressman—and how had he made his money? Escobar claimed publicly that he had made his fortune through real estate. Rumors soon began circulating, however, that Escobar's story was invented, that it was in reality a mere façade.

"Escobar wanted it both ways," Hugo Martínez tells me, sitting in his friend's apartment. "He wanted the criminal world to fear him and not dare cross him in any way, yet he wanted the public not to know anything about his criminal enterprises! He tried to pass himself off as a 'businessman.' Here was the biggest criminal in the world—and he was telling everyone that he had made his fortune in real estate! And many people *believed* him!"

In August 1983, a year after Escobar's election, Colombia's justice minister, Rodrigo Lara Bonilla, revealed that Escobar was no real estate tycoon but rather a drug trafficker. The fact that Escobar was a congressman, Lara added, made a mockery of Colombia's justice system. Within days of the announcement, the newspaper *El Espectador* began publishing stories about Escobar's 1976 arrest for drug trafficking and the still unsolved deaths of the two DAS agents who had arrested him. The newspaper also published Escobar's 1976 mug shot, smiling and looking completely satisfied with himself, as if he were on a holiday, not in jail.

Like a building slated to be demolished and that has just had its support pinions blown out, Escobar's political career quickly began to implode. The head of the Liberal Party, to which Escobar belonged, soon denounced the cocaine baron, ejecting him from the party. Not long afterward, the US embassy revoked Escobar's diplomatic visa, Escobar's parliamentary immunity was then lifted, and Escobar was forced to resign from Congress. By January 1984, Pablo Escobar's short-lived political career was over. With his dream of one day becoming president of Colombia in ruins, however, one thing was predictable, at least to those who knew Escobar well: there was going to be all hell to pay for this humiliating disaster.

With his cover blown and his political career destroyed, Escobar no longer needed to pretend that he was anything other than the ruthless criminal he had always been, one who resorted to murder, violence, and terror as a normal part of his day-to-day operations. In retaliation for the loss of his political career, Escobar soon ordered a series of assassinations, first killing the Justice Minister, Rodrigo Lara, who had exposed him, then carrying out a prolonged campaign of violence against the Colombian state. Escobar's ultimate goal was to force Colombia to rescind its extradition treaty with the United States. To do so, however, meant altering Colombia's Constitution. And that meant forcing Colombia's elite, who wielded the political power, to bend to Escobar's will.

Bombings, kidnappings, assassinations, threats, and payoffs now became the norm, as Escobar launched a no-holds-barred war against the Colombian government. In August 1989, cartel *sicarios* assassinated the leading presidential candidate, Luis Galán, a man who had sworn to uphold the extradition treaty. Three months later, a bomb exploded in an Avianca jetliner that had just taken off from Bogotá, killing all 107 passengers. The bomb had been intended for César Gaviria Trujillo, who had become the leading presidential candidate after Galán's death and who had also sworn to uphold extradition. Gaviria, however, had changed his flight plans at the last moment and was not aboard.

Escobar's involvement in the killings of the justice minister and Galán, not to mention the downing of an international jetliner, had finally forced Colombia's government to take action. One thing had become painfully clear: for the Colombian state to survive in any form that resembled a democracy, Escobar and the cartel had to be eliminated. Either the government—or Escobar—was going to fall.

It was during this period of escalating violence, as he was sitting in his office in Bogotá, that Colonel Hugo Martínez received the phone call from his superior. It was not a long conversation, but when the colonel hung up, he knew that the call would ultimately change not only his life—but possibly the future of Colombia as well.

The city of Medellín, Colombia, is only a twenty-five-minute flight from Bogotá's El Dorado Airport, although culturally it's almost like flying to another country. "Keep your eye out for the women," my taxi driver on the way to the airport had urged me. He was a married man of fifty-nine, had put three kids through college, was retiring on a pension in a year, and assured me that the women of Medellín were the most beautiful in Colombia. *"Yo, como Colombiano, puedo asegurartelo,"* he said. ("I, as a Colombian, can assure you of this.") He also assured me that, like practically everyone else in Colombia, he had watched the recent series on television about the life of Pablo Escobar: *El Patrón de Mall, The Boss of Evil.*

"Escobar was and still is very popular in Medellín among his *paisas* [compatriots]," my driver said. "But it was all very calculated. He'd give a poor person a house, if the person asked him for it. But then he'd say, 'I may need your help one day.' Or he'd give a man some money, and then that man would be indebted to him. It was all very calculated," he assured me. "Basically, he was a *bandido*."

If you ask a Colombian what common characteristics all Colombians have, they'll generally shrug their shoulders. Colombians have no national character, one Colombian told me. They have only *regional* characters. People from Bogotá, for example, are called *rolos* and are supposedly very reserved, unemotional, conservative, and not very friendly. Those from the south are said to be slow and a bit thick. The people from the department of Antioquia in the west, of which Medellín is the capital, are called *paisas* and have always possessed the reputation of being good entrepreneurs, of being driven to succeed, and of being politically liberal. Escobar, it was obvious, was certainly a classic Antioquian, although an especially immoral one.

Medellín sprawls along the floor of a long valley with lush green hills on both sides. Various slums climb the hills, yet from a distance (and especially at night, when their lights come on) the slums look more like Italian villages, lit with twinkling stars, the lights camouflaging the poverty around them. I take a room in a hotel in the city's center, near Botero Plaza, then go out for a walk in the afternoon right after a rain. The eaves of the buildings still drip with water as I pass by a line of men selling plums, pears, and avocados from wooden carts. Each man has a microphone and a portable speaker system, trying to attract the notice of the pedestrians milling about: "Plums at fifteen pesos a kilo! Avocados at twenty pesos a kilo!" The noise makes it sound like I'm walking in a large stadium. I make my way across a wide street median where more vendors squat beside piles of shoes, bags, and watches, lines of cars spewing exhaust on either side, the street pungent with the smell of car fumes, urine, and the occasional strong smell of marijuana. I pass a man with short, vestigial arms wearing a blue T-shirt, past the bodies of homeless people sleeping on the wet, dirty cement using plastic bags as mattresses, past people picking their way slowly around stalled traffic, the car horns blaring, until I emerge onto the plaza that is lined with a series of colossal bronze sculptures, the bronze patinas streaked now with pigeon shit and rain. The sculptures depict corpulent men and women, a horse, a dog, a reclining nude, all with heavy haunches and fashioned by Medellín's best-known artist, Fernando Botero, now in his eighties.

It was here, to Medellín, that Colonel Hugo Martínez arrived to take command of the Search Bloc in September of 1989, amid the local *paisas* who speak with thick regional accents, amid the crowded streets where *sicarios* roamed on motorcycles, and amid a city of two million where resided the central nervous system of the Medellín cartel.

Within days of the group's arrival, Escobar and the cartel went grimly to work, quickly placing bounties of a thousand US dollars each for Search Bloc policemen, two thousand dollars for their lieutenants, five thousand dollars for their police majors, and so on. Within the first month, one hundred of Martínez's men had been gunned down, a number so alarming that the director of police in Bogotá was considering disbanding the group and ending operations. "I was constantly attending funerals," Martínez told me, shaking his head. "It was a war."

Martínez nevertheless went about his work, taking residence with the rest of his men on the grounds of a police academy in the northern part of the city. They soon ringed the school with cordons of security outside so that only those with passes were allowed inside. Martínez normally dressed as a civilian and, for security reasons, rarely left headquarters. Knowing full well that many of the local police had been paid off, Martínez early on had insisted on a simple rule: no one from Medellín or who had relatives in Medellín could join the Search Bloc. Everyone had to be from elsewhere in Colombia, lest friendships and family connections compromise their allegiance. Not surprisingly, Martínez's men were the crème de la crème of the various Colombian police forces, handpicked, well trained, and completely dedicated.

On one wall of his office Martínez soon constructed an organigram, or visual diagram of the cartel's organization, such as police intelligence then knew it. Gradually, he added to the sketch as his men captured criminals, tapped suspects' phone lines, and conducted surveillance operations.

After the assassination of the presidential candidate Galán, the Colombian government had quickly seized Escobar's sprawling Hacienda Nápoles ranch and many of his other properties. In addition, top secret US surveillance planes now flew over the city, invited by the Colombian government. The planes were tasked with recording Escobar's radio phone conversations and trying to fix his location by means of triangulation. A month and a half after arriving, Martínez and his men mounted their first raid, after receiving a tip that Escobar was visiting a particular ranch in the Colombian jungle. According to Escobar's brother Roberto, who was there at the time,

One of the radios Pablo had given to all our neighbors made a noise about 6:00 a.m. It was from one of the people who lived on a nearby farm . . . "Leave [the voice said]. The police are here. We've seen trucks and heard helicopters. Go now!"

Within a few seconds we heard the [Search Bloc] helicopters coming at us. . . . As they approached, they started shooting from the air. We ran, firing back as much as possible . . . Pablo was in his sleeping clothes without even a shirt or shoes . . . Bullets hit the ground and the trees and whizzed by my ear . . . It was later I found out that those damn mosquitoes [helicopters] had killed . . . Henao [Pablo's brother-in-law] . . . as he tried to get to the river. Pablo saw him get shot . . . that was the only time I ever saw Pablo cry.

Back in Medellín, after hearing radio reports of the operation and about those who had been killed or captured, Martínez walked over to his office wall and drew a line through Henao's picture. Henao had been not only Escobar's brother-in-law, he had also been his right-hand man; the two of them had pioneered new drug routes and had been arrested together in 1976. There was now one less leader of the Medellín cartel—and the Search Bloc's activities were just beginning.

Pablo Escobar fought back, continuing his campaign of bombings and assassinations across the country, selectively exterminating judges, police, prosecutors, and politicians, and assuming that by ratcheting up his campaign of terror, the government would eventually crack. Meanwhile, deep within the cartel's home territory, as lights twinkled on Medellín's hillsides and *sicarios* polished their guns, Martínez would sit each night in his office wearing a pair of headphones, listening to the intercepted conversations of Escobar speaking with his underlings. When Escobar finally realized that his conversations were being monitored, he eerily said into his radio phone one evening:

"Colonel, I'm going to kill you. I'm going to kill all of your family up to the third generation, and then I will dig up your grandparents and shoot them and bury them again. Do you *hear* me?"

Martínez's tactics nevertheless remained the same—he stayed on the offensive. For Escobar and the cartel, the colonel had now become Enemy #1. It was thus imperative that they somehow infiltrate the police compound and eliminate him before Martínez eliminated *them*.

One evening, as the colonel listened to phone calls the surveillance planes had recorded, a puzzling thing happened. In one conversation, Martínez heard a woman's voice speaking to a cartel member who was insistently demanding something from her.

"I'm here, but I don't *see* it," the woman kept saying.

"Then *look* for it!" the man insisted.

The woman's voice, the colonel realized, was familiar. But who was it and what was the man after? And where had he heard her voice before?

"I don't *see* it," she said over and over again.

Finally, the colonel realized who it was.

"There was a woman," Martínez told me, "who used to clean my office. Often I would stay there as she cleaned." The voice was that of the maid who cleaned up headquarters. The man, a cartel member, wanted her to remove his photo from the organizational diagram the colonel had made of the cartel on his office wall.

Shortly afterward, Martínez had the woman transferred so that she no longer had access to any of their offices. Members of the Search Bloc, meanwhile, soon discovered where she lived and also learned that the cartel had threatened her and her family. If she did not cooperate, the cartel had told her, she would be killed.

"They killed her anyway," Martínez told me. "She didn't give them what they wanted. So they shot her after we transferred her. She was a mother, and they shot her in her home."

Even after the discovery of the maid, Martínez gradually realized that the cartel must have another informer within his organization. Someone, somehow, had to be tipping off Escobar. As a routine precaution to throw off possible informers, Search Bloc operations would commonly leave headquarters in four convoys, each one roaring off through Medellín in a different direction. Only one of the convoys would be carrying out an actual operation, however—the rest were decoys to confuse the cartel. Yet despite their precautions, Escobar always seemed to know when they were coming. Martínez's men would raid a house they had received a tip on—one of many "hideouts" Escobar had in the city—yet inevitably they would discover that Escobar had recently departed, often just before they arrived. There was no question about it, Martínez realized: a rat had somehow infiltrated his organization. But *who*? And *how*?

On the floor where Martínez and a number of the Search Bloc officials worked, a young cadet was stationed. The cadet was often given guard duties and sometimes shined the shoes of the Search Bloc officers. At other times, the cadet spent his time carving small wooden figurines—of policemen or of helicopters—while standing near their offices.

Unbeknownst to Martínez, the cartel controlled the cadet—either through threats or money or both. Most likely, they had made him their typical offer: *plata o plomo*, silver or lead.

"The question," Pablo Escobar had once said, "is not *whether* someone will take a bribe or not—but how much they *want*."

Recently, the cartel had ordered the cadet to murder Martínez by putting poison in the soup that the Search Bloc's officers ate at lunch. Not only would the colonel die, but so too would the officers who ingested it. On the appointed day, however, instead of keeping the Search Bloc officer's food separate from the rest as he normally did, the cook used a larger kettle to cook with—twice as large in fact—for the non-officers to use, too. As he had been instructed, the cadet gained access to the kitchen, emptied his vial of poison into the kettle, then left. Although some of the men who ate it later developed diarrhea and cramps, they assumed that it had been because of contaminated food, not poison.

Exasperated, the cartel this time decided to take no chances, ordering the cadet to kill the colonel outright as he sat at his desk each night, listening to captured recordings. The cartel furnished the cadet with a pistol and silencer that the cadet successfully smuggled past security. On the appointed night, the young assassin crept up outside the colonel's office, watched him through the window listening with his headphones on, took out his pistol, held it out—then realized that the silencer had no aiming mechanism.

"If I fail," the cadet said to himself, "they will kill me."

Frustrated and undoubtedly promised a fat reward, the cadet decided that the wisest course of action would be first to practice with the pistol, then to kill the colonel the following night. The next day, however, tipped off that the Search Bloc definitely had an informer within, the colonel flew to Bogotá, realizing that his life was in danger. A week later, after an investigation discovered the source, the cadet was arrested, confessed, and eventually went to prison. The cartel had come up short again.

"Are you here for the Pablo Escobar tour?" the man asks me gruffly. The man is about fifty, wears blue jeans and a white T-shirt, has hairy arms, close-cropped black hair and eyebrows that meet above his nose. He looks at me suspiciously and frowns.

"Yes, I am," I say.

I'd arranged to meet the man, Jaime, who runs a private tour called the Pablo Escobar Tour, over the phone from my hotel. We meet at a Medellín café, near the Parque Bolivar. The café's open to the street and has round silver tables. Waitresses wearing white dresses like nurses serve hot *buñuelo* pastries and blended drinks of *maracujá*, *chirimoya*, and other tropical fruits. Colombia is one of the most biodiverse countries in the world, and its cornucopia of indigenous fruits is nothing short of astounding.

A short while later, I climb into the man's white van. As we pull out into traffic, he begins peppering me with questions.

"Are you a reporter?" he asks.

I shake my head.

"Work for TV?"

I shake my head again.

"Good, because Roberto Escobar doesn't give interviews," he says, referring to Pablo's brother, who spent ten years in prison before being released. He's now the highlight of the tour.

"He's almost blind, you know."

While he was imprisoned, Jaime says, and only weeks before his brother Pablo was killed, Roberto received a package. It turned out to be a pipe bomb.

I ask who had sent it.

"It was a 'gift,' " Jaime says, "from the Cali cartel."

The Cali cartel—named for a rival city and center of the cocaine trade in Colombia—was apparently trying to wipe out both Escobar brothers and the rest of the Medellín cartel, thus eliminating its main competitor.

"My cousin—I mean, my *friend*"—Jaime continues, making a verbal slip then looking at me sideways with a frown, "used to work for Pablo Escobar. We used to go out to the Hacienda Nápoles together," he says, steering the car with a hairy left hand and tapping my arm with the other for emphasis. Colombians like to occasionally tap another's arms while speaking, especially when making a point.

"When Roberto got out of prison," Jaime continues, "I asked him if he wanted to become part of the tour. There are other tours, you know," he says, tapping me again, this time on the chest, "but this is the only tour that includes Roberto Escobar."

The end game for Pablo Escobar and the Medellín cartel began in late 1993, in an upscale suburb of Medellín called Los Olivos. After two years of bombing and assassinations, Escobar finally made a deal with the Colombian government. Not surprisingly, the deal was almost completely on Escobar's terms. In exchange for ending his war against the state and halting his bombing and assassination campaign, Escobar agreed to plead guilty to a minor charge of drug trafficking and to turn himself in for a short stint in prison. After his release, he would be absolved of any previous crimes. Amazingly, the government also allowed Escobar to select the site and to build the prison himself. In addition, only Escobar and his men would be housed there, the prison guards would be hired by and would work for him, and the Colombian police would not be allowed within twelve miles of the prison.

Colonel Martínez, not surprisingly, was disgusted. After having lost hundreds of men, he felt betrayed.

"We felt we had lost the war," Martínez told me. "Just when he was at his weakest, he makes this deal with the government. But what could we do? Our job was to obey orders."

With the agreement signed, Roberto Escobar soon joined his brother in prison, as did other members of the Medellín cartel. The Search Bloc, meanwhile, was disbanded. Not surprisingly, Escobar soon gained complete control over the situation: he quickly outfitted the prison with luxury waterbeds, deluxe stereos, televisions, and radio communication equipment; in addition, he received any visitors he wanted and sometimes even attended soccer matches in Medellín. Escobar also continued to run his worldwide cocaine operation, the prison now a kind of legal sanctuary where he could no longer be bothered. A year later, however, when an embarrassed and exasperated government finally decided to transfer Escobar to a real prison, Escobar received a tip and escaped into the nearby hills, just as he was about to be transferred. The hunt for Pablo Escobar, once again, was on.

"It was a relief when he escaped," Martínez told me. "I was happy— because now that he was out, I knew we had a good chance of catching him."

Within a week of Escobar's escape, Martínez received a phone call ordering him to rapidly reassemble the Search Bloc team. A few weeks later, the Medellín cartel exploded a bomb in front of the apartment tower where Martínez's wife and two children were living. Martínez immediately flew to Bogotá and began packing up the apartment, placing his family in hiding. It was then that he received the knock on the door and a bribe from his former colleague of $6 million.

"I knew at that moment that Escobar must be weak," Martínez told me. "He was on the run. That's why he made the offer."

Due to the danger of refusing the bribe, the colonel decided to move his wife and children to the police academy in Medellín where the rest of the Search Bloc was housed. Anywhere else in Colombia, Martínez realized, was simply too dangerous. From now on, his two youngest children would be isolated from their peers and homeschooled.

The colonel's eldest son, however, twenty-three-year-old Hugo Martínez Jr., had already graduated from the police academy, had been on the police force in Bogotá for two years, and wanted to come to Medellín and help out. He urged his father to transfer him.

"It's just too dangerous," Martínez told him firmly.

"But I want to help you," his son repeated. Hugo Jr. had recently received training in electronics and was the best student in his class. His specialty was operating mobile radio tracking equipment from vehicles on the ground—a job that was conducted undercover with no police escort. To zero in on a radio signal, just two men—the driver and the radio tracker—drove about in an unmarked van, searching for the source of transmissions. The reason the tracking units had been created was simple: it had become clear that the American reconnaissance planes were unable to pinpoint a radio transmission precisely enough for the Search Bloc to mount a raid. The planes could locate the *neighborhood* the transmission was coming from, but not a specific location. With training in the latest radio tracking equipment, however, Hugo assured his father that Escobar's location could finally be pinpointed—but that ultimately it would come from the ground. "Let me help you catch him," his son urged. Finally, after weeks of going back and forth, Martínez relented. Father and son were now united together for the hunt.

According to the latest aerial surveillance, Escobar had remained in Medellín. Yet he was continually moving from safe house to safe house, knowing that if he remained anywhere for too long, he'd be located. Police searching for criminals, however, know that a criminal's family connections are often a liability. If the police are searching for a fugitive and Christmas is approaching, or the birthday of a criminal's mother, then the best chance of capturing the fugitive is to stake out the family and to tap their phone. Escobar—although a remorseless killer whose behavior often appeared to be that of a sociopath—nevertheless had a family that he was extremely attached to: his wife and their two children, Manuela, nine, and Juan Pablo, sixteen. By necessity, the three of them now lived in a high-rise tower in Medellín. Escobar was often desperately worried about his family's safety, especially since he knew that the Cali cartel wanted to kill them. In November 1993, the same month that his brother was blinded by a pipe bomb, Escobar finally succeeded in arranging for his family to fly to Germany, only to have the German government refuse to allow their entry. Instead, the government returned his wife and children to Colombia. The Colombian police opted to place the family in a police-owned hotel in Bogotá, under their protection. In a sense, Escobar's family was now a hostage of the Colombian government, and Escobar could do nothing about it.

Only ten years earlier, Escobar had been a Colombian congressman with diplomatic immunity. He'd possessed hundreds of properties and had bank accounts around the world. Although he was still a multi-billionaire, Escobar was now reduced to living in safe houses that only one or two people knew about, accompanied at most by one or two bodyguards, while police and narcotics forces from the United States and Colombia—and a horde of *sicarios* from the Cali cartel—searched for him. Escobar was also well aware that when he used one of his radio phones for more than three minutes, he ran the risk of being located. For this reason he owned a fleet of twelve taxis. Often, Escobar would sit in the backseat of one of these tinted-window cars, bearded and wearing sunglasses while making phone calls. While the taxi wove through Medellín's traffic, it was practically impossible to get a precise fix on his signal. As Roberto Escobar later recalled:

> Pablo made phone calls . . . [threatening] people what would happen if his family was harmed, but besides that there wasn't much he could do . . . now the Search Bloc, [the US] Centra Spike, [the US] Delta Force, the police . . . and [the] Cali [cartel] were getting closer to him. They had set up the family, and they knew that Pablo would do anything, even give his own life, for them. So the planes continued to fly overhead listening for his conversations, the experts with phone-tapping equipment drove through the city, soldiers roamed through the streets, all of them searching day and night.

Toward the end of November 1993, a few days before Escobar's forty-fourth birthday and a week after his family had been barred from entering Germany, Escobar placed a call from somewhere in Medellín that was picked up by a US aircraft circling the city. The plane's crew narrowed the location of the call to a neighborhood called Los Olivos, but before Colonel Martínez could scramble one of his three mobile tracking units, Escobar had hung up.

When Martínez informed his superior about the situation, the general told him to encircle the entire zone and begin a door-to-door search. The colonel, having attempted this in the past, stood his ground. "We've done this before," the colonel said, "and Escobar has always escaped. Let him make another call—and we'll have him." Finally, the general relented. Martínez knew that if Escobar didn't make another call, however, his relationship with the general might come to a head. Bombs, meanwhile, set by the Medellín cartel, continued to pound the country, as they had ever since Escobar's escape, accompanied by a constant flurry of assassinations. The pressure to capture or kill Pablo Escobar had reached a breaking point. The public wanted the war to end.

Martínez had quickly stationed mobile units in the Los Olivos neighborhood and waited. Twenty-four hours passed. And nothing. The general called the colonel repeatedly, asking for news. There was none. Another twenty-four hours went by, with the radio trackers sleeping in their vans, ready to spring into action. Still nothing. Not a word from Escobar. The pressure on the colonel continued to mount.

Finally, on December 2, a day after his birthday, Escobar made a call to his family in the police-guarded hotel in Bogotá. The colonel listened in as Escobar's wife wished her husband a happy birthday. Then Escobar asked his sixteen-year-old son to copy down answers Escobar had composed to questions previously submitted by a German magazine. The clock, however, was ticking.

Martínez's son, Hugo Jr., meanwhile, just happened to be in the tracking van closest to the radio transmission when Escobar made his call. He and his driver immediately scrambled to locate it. Hugo wore headphones and had a foot-long, gray metal box on his lap. On the side closest to him was a palm-sized screen displaying a single, wavering green line—Escobar's radio signal.

Alongside a small canal, on a quiet, upscale street, stood a line of two-story row homes. As Hugo and his driver drove toward the end of the block, the radio signal gradually became louder and the green line grew in intensity. Escobar's call seemed to be coming directly from a house at the end. To be certain, and amid growing excitement, the two drove around the block and approached the house from the other side. The luminescent green line indicated that the signal was coming from the same home. They had located him.

In his office at the Search Bloc, after three years of a desperate high-stakes game of cat and mouse, Colonel Martínez received a call from his son.

"I've got him located!" his son said. "He's in a house."

"Are you *sure?*" asked the colonel, who was at that very moment still listening to Escobar speaking on the phone.

"I can *see* him!" his son said.

Hugo and the driver, meanwhile, had returned to the front of the house, driving slowly, and had parked across the street. Hugo had then peered up at the second story, where there was a small window. Visible through its pane was a short, pudgy man with a dark beard talking distractedly on a phone, unaware of the unmarked police van and the excited young officer below. By this time, Escobar was accompanied by only a single bodyguard, a man nicknamed Limón, "Lemon."

"Cover the house," the colonel told his son. "You take one side, have the driver take the other. If he tries to get away, take him out."

I asked the colonel how he felt at this moment, with his son suddenly on the front line, an unknown number of criminals in the house and only two Search Bloc members—his son and the driver—outside. The nearest Search Bloc support group was about ten minutes away.

"Hugo was a great shot," the colonel answered. "Much better than me. He was several times a champion in combat tactical shooting."

In the end, Hugo covered the front of the house, where he had briefly seen Escobar, while the driver covered the rear. Meanwhile, his father ordered the nearest support team—a group of twelve men—to rush to the area. The colonel's order was to capture Escobar and whoever else was in the house and to shoot them if they put the team in danger—standard Search Bloc operating procedure.

As soon as the team arrived, they immediately took up positions around the house. Then, on a prearranged signal, two of them began breaking down the front door.

"Momento, momento. Está pasando algo" ("Hold on, hold on, something's happening") were Escobar's final words to his son, as he abruptly hung up the phone.

Inside the home, a window at the rear of the second floor gave access to a tiled roof and possible safety. It was the only way out. Escobar's bodyguard, Limón, was the first to try to escape, jumping onto the roof and firing at the police in civilian dress, who returned fire from below. Limón soon crumpled and fell from the roof onto a small patch of grass below, dead. Next came Escobar, holding a nine-millimeter pistol in his right hand, another pistol wedged inside his belt. The Search Bloc had obviously caught Escobar by surprise: the drug lord was barefoot and wore only a dark blue sport shirt and jeans. Escobar by now was also overweight from lack of exercise and from constant confinement, but he was not about to surrender. As Escobar fired, three bullets quickly took him down: one struck the back of his leg, another hit him in the back, just beneath the shoulder, and a third entered his right ear and exited the other side. Either of these last two shots would have been fatal. Less than ten minutes after arriving, a Search Bloc officer crouched over a motionless Pablo Escobar, checked to see if he had a pulse, and then called Colonel Martínez on the radio:

"Viva Colombia!" he shouted.

Pablo Escobar, the most wanted man in Colombia and one of the most sought-after criminals in the world, was dead.

On top of a green hillside, about five miles from where he was killed and overlooking the city of Medellín, Pablo Escobar now lies quietly in a grave at the *Cementerio Montesacro*, or Sacred Mountain Cemetery. On the day he was to be interred, crowds of people gathered, prying open Escobar's coffin and trying desperately to touch the lifeless body of a man who had once possessed powers so much more enormous than their own: the power to bestow great riches, the power to challenge armies of police, the power to challenge an entire nation, and the power to bestow, ultimately, life or death. Alongside Escobar is buried Limón, at the request of the latter's family.

Once Escobar was finally six feet beneath the ground, however, his power to influence events ceased. Within months of his death, the Medellín cartel was no more, all thirty-six of its leaders either dead or incarcerated. The Colombian government, with US help, soon dismantled the neighboring Cali cartel as well. The net effect of the two cartels' disappearance, however, left cocaine production unaffected: more cocaine was produced the year *after* Escobar's death, and in subsequent years, than in any year during Escobar's heyday.

The efforts thus far to stamp out cocaine production in the Andean republics, meanwhile, is known as la cucaracha, or "the cockroach," effect: just as you can kill a cockroach in one part of a room only to have another pop up somewhere else, the efforts of local and/or foreign governments to stamp out cocaine production in one Andean country have resulted only in cocaine production rising an equivalent amount in another. In the end, with the destruction of the Colombian cartels, the near monopoly over cocaine trafficking simply moved northward, where Mexican cartels quickly filled the void. Mexican cities along the US border soon became killing zones, as Mexican cartels began to fight with one another over the control of drug routes once controlled by Colombians. Between 2006 and 2015, more than one hundred thousand Mexicans died in the transplanted drug wars, with the US government continually pressing the Mexican government for more aggressive efforts to interdict cocaine. Nevertheless, roughly 150 tons of illegal cocaine are still smuggled into the United States each year.

Meanwhile, as we drive along a winding road up a tree-covered hill in the upscale Medellín district of Poblado, Jaime pokes my arm some more, emphasizing his latest point: "I tell you honestly, with all confidence," he says, lowering my confidence in him even further, "make sure you don't ask Don Roberto too many questions. He doesn't like questions."

The area we are driving through reminds me of the Hollywood Hills where my father grew up: small estates appear behind iron gates as we glide beneath large eucalyptus trees drooping overhead. The sky is overcast, and the paved road is washed out in parts. We finally arrive at a locked gate, and Jaime pulls to a stop. A gray-haired man arrives and opens the gate slowly, staring at us with no expression as we drive past. Shortly afterward, we arrive at a squat, one-story brick house painted white and with a tiled roof. Wrought-iron grates cover the windows to keep out burglars. Within an attached, open carport is parked a blue Wartburg sedan, an old East German model that Pablo used to like to drive around Medellín. One apocryphal tale describes how Pablo Escobar, the onetime car thief, was the only person in Medellín who never locked his own car. Instead, he left a small note in his glove box:

"This car belongs to Pablo Escobar."

No one ever touched it.

Before us stands the home of Roberto Escobar, now sixty-five years old (Pablo would have been sixty-two), who lives quietly in the forested hills overlooking Medellín. Jaime tells me that Pablo used this as a safe house prior to the one in which he was killed.

I follow Jaime inside the home, which is set up both as a living residence and as a kind of shrine to Pablo Escobar. The private tour of the house, apparently, is the prelude. Afterward is the main course: a meeting with Roberto, the onetime accountant for the Medellín cartel.

Framed photos hang on a wall, as well as yellowing newspaper articles of the many bicycle races Roberto won in his youth. On another wall hang thirteen carefully arranged photos of Pablo at various ages, from his first communion to his time as a Colombian congressman, wearing a flamboyant yellow suit. In a hallway on a small table stands a three-foot statue of the Virgin of Candelaria, an Escobar family saint. The home is as neat and immaculate as a funeral parlor.

Jaime leads me to a wall with a bookcase set into it, the bookcase edged with molding. He pushes on one side of the case, staring hard at me. The entire bookcase moves. I realize this is actually a revolving door, revealing a hidden compartment behind. Inside is a small space where one or two people could crouch. Pablo Escobar, after all, routinely kidnapped people throughout his life; it was in just such tiny cavities, hidden from the rest of the world, that his victims spent their time before they were either ransomed or murdered. In a desperate moment, Pablo could also hide there himself.

We walk outside, through sliding glass doors, onto a covered patio behind the house that has a red-tiled floor and views over a garden. From here I can see across the valley and in the distance the brick skyscrapers of El Poblado. Escobar once had his drug operation housed in a tower there, which was later attacked with a car bomb by the Cali cartel. In the middle of the patio squats a long green wooden table. Spread out on it is the raison d'etre of the tour: books, CDs, and photos are for sale.

"Bueñas tardes," says a soft voice behind me.

I turn and see a slight, bald man with thick glasses and a mouth whose edges seem permanently turned down, like a horseshoe. I recognize Roberto Escobar, onetime bicycle racing champion, cartel accountant, and a former inmate for ten years in Colombia's Itagüí prison. Roberto is about five foot six, the same height as Pablo, and has Pablo's long and sloping aquiline nose.

We shake hands. Roberto has gray-blue eyes, although his right eye appears cloudy behind his glasses. Comparing him to the photos on the wall back in the 1960s in his biking outfit, full of youth and energy, he appears more to me like a gnome—expressionless, opaque, as if his eyes and soul have seen too much.

"Did you like Washington, DC?" I ask him, referring to photos inside the house, which showed him in front of the White House.

"Yes," he says, in *paisa*-inflected Spanish, "very much. A beautiful city." While he and Pablo were in the US capital, he says, they took time to visit the FBI museum, out of curiosity. There on one of its walls they spotted a large WANTED poster with photos of his brother and himself that offered a $10 million reward. The poster, he said, had made him nervous, but not Pablo, who was always level-headed, even in the most desperate situations. After they went outside, Pablo tried to calm his brother. Pablo looked around for a few minutes, then turned to Roberto and said, "Watch." Roberto did, as Pablo went up to a policeman and asked for a light, using his heavily Spanish-inflected English. The policeman complied, unknowingly lighting the cigarette of the most powerful drug trafficker in the world. Pablo then calmly returned to Roberto and his son, took a drag from the cigarette, and exhaled. "You see," he said, "they don't know us over here."

I chat with Roberto, who seems to warm to the conversation. He becomes friendly and relaxed. Occasionally he pulls a small green bottle out of his pocket, withdraws an eye dropper, tilts his head back, and puts three drops into each eye. Although his eyes were damaged in the bomb explosion, Roberto's face is smooth and has no visible scars.

"Did you know about Colonel Martínez and that the Search Bloc were after you?" I ask.

"Yes, of course, we had our sources," he says.

"Do you think that if the *Bloque* had not been created that your brother would not have been killed?"

"No. It was Pablo going into politics. I was against it," he says, peering at me through his glasses. He explains that he was opposed to Pablo's ill-fated attempt to become a national politician. "Everyone began going after him then—along with the Cali cartel."

While he puts more drops into his eyes, I ask about the letter bomb in prison.

When the bomb blew up in his face, Roberto says, at first he saw angels. Then he saw the Lord. The explosion drew him closer to God, he says. It made him believe in an afterlife.

"Would you like to buy anything?" Jaime asks, impatient to leave and glaring at me for having asked so many questions. I realize that it's not Roberto who doesn't like questions—it's *Jaime*. This is all business to him. He wants to get paid and leave. I look around and agree to buy some photos.

Roberto sits down at one end of the table, then prepares a pen and a large inkpad. I begin handing him photos: one of Pablo dressed in a pinstriped suit, posing as the 1920–30s American gangster Al Capone, and holding a double-barreled shotgun; another of Pablo dressed as Pancho Villa, a personal hero of his, wearing a wide sombrero and a cartridge belt across his chest. Roberto signs each of them, presses his thumb into the ink pad, then carefully affixes his thumbprint beneath his signature, something that Pablo used to do when writing public letters. I hand him another photo, this one a copy of the wanted poster for $10 million, with photos of Pablo and Roberto at the top and the rest of the Medellín cartel leaders displayed in smaller photos below. Afterward, the former accountant carefully rolls up each poster and fits them into a small cardboard tube, which is also for sale. I would have thought that with so many billions of dollars, Pablo and Roberto would have had secret stores of cash and bank accounts all over the world. But if that were the case, then why would Roberto agree to receive tours and be selling photos of his brother and other knickknacks for a handful of dollars? Where did the billions go?

In the end, we shake hands. Roberto touches my arm as Colombians are wont to do. *"Mucho gusto,"* he says, and nods his head. I exit the door and head down the driveway. Roberto Escobar stares after me, a forlorn, gnomelike man who now seems utterly and completely alone.

Later that afternoon, I visit the Museum of Antioquia, the art museum on the Plaza Botero. Before leaving Medellín, I want to see two paintings by Botero. In a long, immaculate room with a shiny floor and a guard standing at one end, I find the first painting, a large canvas appropriately called *The Death of Escobar*. The somber-colored canvas depicts Medellín on a gloomy, overcast day. There, in the middle, Pablo Escobar stands on a tiled rooftop, his white button-down shirt open. Escobar is barefoot, wears dark pants, and clutches a pistol in his right hand, pointing it up in the air. A flurry of oversized bullets flow through him, left to right across the canvas, as if caught in a stop-animation sequence; some of the bullets have already punctured his stomach, neck, and chest, leaving small red wounds in Escobar's pale white flesh. Escobar's eyes are closed—he is still standing but dead, caught in the moment of impact, just as he is slain.

In another room, and as if from another scene clipped from the same film, I find the second painting. Escobar now lies on his side on the same rooftop, a gun still in his hand. His open shirt reveals a body riddled by bullets. Below in the street a police officer in a green uniform and cap points up at the fallen gangster. Alongside him a short woman in a red dress looks up, pressing her hands together, and prays.

As I exit the museum, I can't help but reflect that, two decades after his death, Pablo Escobar has long since been buried and now belongs to the realm of painters and writers and filmmakers and other mythmakers—and that his exploits are still being reshaped in the present. In a way, Escobar was Colombia's latest version of El Dorado, the Golden Man, a onetime king who daily anointed himself with gold dust so plentiful that he could easily wash it off and replenish it the next. Like the woman praying in Botero's painting, a sizeable sector of Colombians emulated, worked for, and/or admired Escobar, as if following the sun, blinded by the reflected gold of Escobar's enormous wealth and power, blinded by his fable-like, rags-to-riches story, blinded by the very myths that had risen up around him. As I head across the plaza it suddenly strikes me that the *real* golden man of Colombia, one who remained untarnished and incorruptible, was the former police colonel, Hugo Martínez. He is now retired and lives quietly with his wife in Bogotá. Tragically, his son Hugo Jr. died in a car accident in 2003. Nevertheless, when Martínez's own life and his family's lives were on the line—indeed, when the very life of the Colombian *nation* was at stake—here was a man who could be neither bought nor sold, who was motivated by neither *plata* nor *plomo*, but by principle. It was Martínez, not Escobar, who proved to be Colombia's El Dorado—the mythical, incorruptible, nearly unimaginable king.

2

EVOLUTION AND DENIAL IN THE GALÁPAGOS (ECUADOR)

And God made the beasts of the earth after his kind . . . and every thing that creepeth upon the earth after his kind . . . and God said, let us make man in our image . . . so God created man in his own image, in the image of God he created him; male and female he created them.

—Genesis 1:25–27

The main conclusion arrived at in this work, namely, that man is descended from some lowly organized form, will, I regret to think, be highly distasteful to many. But there can hardly be a doubt that . . . man is descended from a hairy, tailed quadruped, probably arboreal in its habits.

—Charles Darwin, *The Descent of Man*, 1871

I was fascinated with the evolutionary story, which is really the creation myth of the modern age. The first thing I noticed about it is that it contradicts the book of Genesis. It actually contradicts a whole lot more than that because, as the scientists define evolution, it is inherently a purposeless, mindless process that produced human beings as an accident . . . So did God create us? Or did we create God?

—Dr. Phillip Johnson, author of *Darwin On Trial*
and founder of the intelligent design movement

What you see depends on what you thought before you looked.

—Eugene Taurman

Charles Darwin had blown it. Deep in his bones, as he worriedly searched through his collection of birds from the Galápagos Islands, he knew that his work on the islands had been inexcusable. The year was 1837, and although he was already twenty-seven years old and presently living in London, he was just beginning his land-bound career after a nearly five-year voyage around the world. The voyage on the English surveying ship HMS *Beagle* had ended just three months earlier. The mockingbirds on the Galápagos, yes, Darwin realized, he'd gotten those right; he'd shot them on four of the islands, had eviscerated them and stuffed their bodies with cotton, then had labeled them according to which island he had found them on. Now an ornithologist in London had carefully examined the corpses and pronounced them three different species, when Darwin had thought they all belonged to one! How could he have *known*? As to the finches, however—a complete disaster! Darwin realized that while he'd been on the islands, he hadn't even known that many of the small birds he collected *were* finches. Instead, he thought more than half of them were wrens, warblers, and blackbirds, some of which belonged to entirely different *families* of birds, let alone genera. Worse yet, he hadn't even bothered to label which islands many of these birds had come from and had mixed the tiny corpses from two of the islands together after collecting them. And now the same ornithologist at the Zoological Society had asked him an inevitable and terrible question: "Can you tell me *which* islands each of these birds has come from?" Sweating, Darwin knew he could not. What a *stupid* mistake!

Shortly afterward, Darwin realized that he'd made an even worse one: although he'd enjoyed observing the Galápagos's giant tortoises and had even ridden one of the enormous beasts, at the time he thought this species also lived on islands in the Indian Ocean and that they must have been brought to the Galápagos by pirates. It was only recently that he'd been informed that the tortoises he'd observed existed only in the Galápagos Islands! Worse yet, he hadn't bothered to collect a single adult specimen—let alone specimens from each island! Ironically, Darwin realized, he'd *eaten* these giant animals—as they'd become a favorite food among the crew—but he hadn't *collected* them. What if each of the islands contained a different species of tortoise, like the mockingbirds? Such an answer would be potentially useful to science and could also help him with some of the biological problems he was currently working on. But now it was too late to do anything about it. Obviously, Darwin knew, it was impossible to retrace his steps and travel six thousand miles back to the Galápagos. Back to that obscure little chain of volcanic islands poking up out of the Pacific where the tortoises and birds in question lived. (In fact, although he would live another sixty years, Darwin would never travel outside of England again.)

"It is the fate of every voyager," Darwin wrote later in his autobiography, "[that] when he has just discovered what object in any place is more particularly worthy of his attention, to be hurried from it." Right now, however, Darwin was so upset he could hardly eat. Then suddenly, in the midst of his panic, he hit upon a possible way of correcting his string of errors. The captain of the *Beagle*, Robert FitzRoy, had also made collections of various animals during their journey and so had several members of the crew. None of his former shipmates, however, were trained naturalists, so who knew whether their collections were properly labeled or whether they contained the birds he was looking for? Nevertheless, Darwin hurriedly dashed off a number of letters that, paraphrased, went like this: "Can you tell me if you collected any small birds on the Galápagos Islands—and, if so, whether you labeled the birds by *island*?"

Horse carriages clopped by outside, carrying gentry wearing suits and top hats as Darwin addressed the envelopes. As Darwin hurried to the post office, there was no way he could have known that perhaps the entire concept of evolution now depended upon the answers that FitzRoy and the other crew members might provide. Did each of the Galápagos Islands have similar yet different species, like the mockingbirds? And, if so, *why*? Or were the mockingbirds merely a strange anomaly? As the tall, lean, chestnut-haired, smooth-shaven young man with the bushy eyebrows and projecting forehead walked immersed in thought, he puzzled over why this small, unimportant chain of islands seemed to hold so many different yet related species. Why did the Galápagos have a greater number of species than an equally sized area on the mainland? What was the cause of that? Could these islands possibly hold a key to that "mystery of mysteries"—the origin of new species, or, more simply, how species as distinct as mockingbirds, earthworms, and men first appeared on Earth? Were species divinely created—as Darwin had believed all his life—or was there possibly some other, more "natural" explanation? An explanation rooted in the world that he could see, touch, and feel—rather than in the supernatural realm of religion? Deeply worried about the likelihood that his sloppiness in collecting might have forever ruined some of the most important data from his voyage, Darwin posted the letters. Now all he could do was wait.

"I don't believe in evolution," the elderly Chinese American gentleman seated across from me says. It's day two of an eight-day cruise in the Galápagos Islands, on our ship called the *Eden*. The elderly gentleman is a retired engineer, a grandfather, and has short gray hair and thin-rimmed metal glasses. He's originally from Taiwan. Long ago, his ancestors met Christian missionaries there and converted. The gentleman's forty-year-old son, his son's wife, and their three children—Jason, Sarah, and Sam—are seated at the lengthy wooden dining table in the boat's cabin, on both sides of him. The children are well mannered, have been homeschooled, live in California, and wear glasses. They have with them maps of the Galápagos and a book on Galápagos birds. The entire family—three generations' worth—are dyed-in-the-wool creationists.

"The theory of evolution's full of holes," the elderly gentleman says emphatically, pointing a fork at me. "It's like cheese—*Swiss* cheese," he says. The three kids laugh at the joke as their grandfather spears a piece of overboiled broccoli. The twelve-year-old daughter, Sarah, has braces and wears a jaunty white straw hat, set at an angle. She has long black hair and is dressed in brand-new khaki shorts and a button-down khaki shirt, as is the whole family.

There are a dozen of us on the seventy-five-foot ship, not including the crew, and we are midway through a lunch of fish, rice, beans, and canned vegetables. All of the food has been flown in from Ecuador, some 620 miles to the east and to which these islands belong. Our boat presently lies anchored alongside Española Island, one of thirteen main islands in the Galápagos archipelago.

"Take five and twenty heaps of cinders dumped here and there in an outside city lot," wrote Herman Melville, the author of *Moby Dick*, "imagine some of them magnified into mountains, and the vacant lot the sea, and you will have a fit idea of the general aspect of the . . . [Galápagos Islands]. A group rather of extinct volcanoes than of isles, looking much as the world at large might after a . . . conflagration."

Melville was only a twenty-two-year-old sailor on a whaling ship when he first visited the Galápagos in 1841, yet he was correct about their origins. The island of Española, for example, is actually the upper tip of an enormous underwater volcano, rising from a bulge in the Earth's crust thousands of feet below. This particular volcano stopped erupting about three million years ago, its molten rock cooled, and slowly, over thousands of years, various forms of life began to appear, tossed onto its flanks by the wind or sea, or piggybacking on the wings of birds or on floating debris. It's now May, the air is warm, the swells are moderate, and the *Eden* gently rocks to and fro so that the liquid in our water glasses tilts slightly to one side, then to the other.

"How's that book?" I ask the elderly gentleman, having noticed that he has a book called *Darwin On Trial* on the table. We had been discussing earlier how computer chips keep getting faster and faster, with circuits now being designed on the molecular level. The chips are evolving so quickly, he says, that it's difficult to predict how far they'll go. "Nanotechnology is the future of electronics," his son said. Both he and his father are electronics engineers.

"Chips are *designed*, by the way," the elderly gentleman had told me, "just like humans."

He turns the book around so I can see it. On its cover is a depiction of a marble statue of an aged, bearded Charles Darwin seated in a chair and wearing a large Victorian overcoat. Brooding glumly below the incriminating title and with a frown on his face, Darwin gives the appearance of being a reluctant participant—a biologist on trial for undermining the biblical account of creation.

"This book is exceptional," the elderly gentleman says. "Really shows how the world's been fooled by a cockamamie theory."

Sarah and her two brothers giggle at the word *cockamamie*.

The elderly man cuts a piece of fish and then looks across the table at me.

"It's written by a lawyer. The father of intelligent design. Phillip Johnson. Have you read any of his books?"

I shake my head while digging into a pile of beans.

"Do you believe we came from animals?"

The entire family pauses and looks at me. I also pause, suspending my forkful of beans in midair.

Since everyone except me is on vacation, I decide that the best course of action is to deflect the question.

"Does the book tell the story about Darwin's finches?" I ask, knowing how the kids, especially, are interested in birds. The elderly man frowns and shakes his head.

"How a single species got blown out here millions of years ago and eventually turned into thirteen different species?

"I don't believe it," he says. "I tell you, I don't believe in evolution."

"We saw finches during our walk this morning!" says Sarah brightly. "Little brown ones!"

"And blue boobies!" says eight-year-old Sam. The word *boobies* makes all three of the kids laugh.

This morning we *had* seen blue-footed boobies, which are currently nesting all over the Galápagos Islands, laying their eggs directly on the ground. The boobies are about three feet high, have large, webbed, cobalt-blue feet and small yellow eyes that are set forward toward their beaks. The placement of the eyes affords the birds stereoscopic vision; they thus have the unusual habit of looking directly at you, very intently, each eye peering around the beak and making the birds look like querulous, pint-sized librarians. "Booby" comes from the Spanish word *bobo*, which means "clown" or "fool." Waddling about on the rocks and appearing almost cross-eyed, the ungainly birds seem more like characters from some animated film than the fierce, fish-eating predators they actually are.

As we walked over the burnt landscape this morning, we could also see that the lava had once clearly flowed over the area like some thick, overflowing molasses, then had puddled and cooled. Gas pockets had ripped open the lava's surface, leaving jagged holes the size of your fist or head as the lava froze. Although we'd seen some small brown finches with short, stubby beaks, we were more impressed by the black frigate birds soaring overhead, looking like dinosaur-age pterodactyls with their sharply angled wings. Farther ahead, Sarah had pointed at a crowded thicket of giant lizards, black and about three feet long, with spiny crests and tough, beaded skins. Most had their heads up, gazing intently at the sea.

"*Look!*" Sarah had shouted. Her two brothers had run up beside her, elbows and knees protruding from their khaki outfits, pointing and shouting for their parents and grandfather to hurry and catch up. Slithering over the rocks and into the translucent blue ocean, the marine iguanas looked about as prehistoric as anything any of us had ever seen.

Nearly five hundred years before our visit, in 1535, a Spanish bishop, Tomás de Berlanga, had set off from Panama on a ship filled with men and horses, bound for the newly conquered Inca Empire on the western coast of South America. While the ship was off the shores of Ecuador, the wind suddenly died and, for the next six days, the bishop and his men drifted helplessly westward, carried by a strange cold current that swept up the coast of South America and then curled out into the Pacific.* On the seventh day, the crew finally sighted land—an island rising out of the middle of the sea. With his ship running low on water, Berlanga sent some of the crew ashore to search for a spring or stream. He was sorely disappointed by the result:

> On land they were not able to find even a drop of water . . . [and] found nothing but seals, and turtles, and such big tortoises that each could carry a man on top of itself, and many iguanas that are like serpents. . . . [on another island they found] many seals, turtles, iguanas, tortoises [and] many birds like those of Spain, but so silly that they do not know how to flee, and many were caught in the hand.

The "silly" birds were no doubt the boobies and other island birds on the Galápagos, which for some inexplicable reason had no fear of man.

On the first Sunday after his arrival, Berlanga went ashore and conducted a Catholic mass. Although Berlanga made no mention of it, the bishop was no doubt certain that all of the species of animals here, including the giant tortoises, had been created by God, that they'd remained here in their present forms since the time of creation, and that during the great Flood, these same animals had been taken in mated pairs into Noah's ark, later to be rereleased into the wild. Noah, the bishop knew, was nine hundred years old at the time of the Flood, which for five long months had completely covered the Earth, including the highest

---

*The massive ocean current—one of the largest and biologically richest upwellings in the world—was later named the Humboldt Current, after its scientific "discovery" by the German scientist and explorer Alexander von Humboldt.

mountain peaks such as the Himalayas. Somehow after their release, the tortoises and other animals had eventually found their way back to these islands, a minor miracle as the Galápagos are roughly seven thousand miles distant from Mount Ararat in Turkey, where Noah's ark is thought to have come to rest. As the bishop later wrote the Spanish king,

> On Passion Sunday, I had them bring on land the things necessary for saying Mass, and after it was said I again sent the people in twos and threes over different paths. The Lord deigned that they should find in a ravine among the rocks as much as a . . . [large cask] of [spring] water, and after they had drawn that, they found more and more.

The bishop was relieved to find water but nevertheless was puzzled to find so much volcanic rock in the middle of the ocean, writing that "it seems as though sometime God had showered [the island with] stones." Eventually, Berlanga and his crew made it back to the mainland and to Peru, but only after having lost ten horses, all of which died of thirst.

In his later report to King Charles V, the bishop wrote about the discovery of the previously unknown islands and also about the giant tortoises found on them, which he referred to as *galápagos*, a word current in sixteenth-century Spanish that meant "tortoises" but has since been abandoned.* The islands consequently began showing up on European maps as *Las Islas de los Galápagos*—or the "Islands of the Tortoises"—named after the eight-hundred-pound, six-foot-long reptiles so powerful they could carry a grown man.

The islands' inhabitants, subsequent European visitors agreed, *were* decidedly different from those any of them had seen elsewhere. Their uniqueness, however, did not endear the archipelago to early sailors

---

*The current Spanish word for "tortoise" is *tortuga*, such as in the Dry Tortugas Islands in the Florida Keys.

and explorers. Most, in fact, tended to view these volcanic outposts as bleak, nearly waterless crags whose twisted landscapes were reflected in their strange animal inhabitants, most of which either slithered, hopped, or crawled. Or, as Herman Melville later put it: "Little but reptile life is here found: tortoises, lizards, immense spiders, snakes, and that strangest anomaly of outlandish nature, the iguana. No voice . . . no howl is heard—the chief sound of life here is a hiss."

Reptile hisses were in fact the lingua franca of this primordial world, in addition to the booming sound of the sea pummeling the volcanic rocks and sending up great plumes of salty spray. Occasionally, volcanoes erupted, releasing huge clouds of billowing smoke, spewing fresh lava into the sea, and incinerating whatever animals and plants had managed to gain purchase on their flanks. For at least some visitors, the Galápagos' bizarre, freakishly sized tortoises and the hordes of writhing black iguanas seemed to hearken back to an earlier, antediluvian time. For others, the inhabitants seemed to resemble nothing less than some medieval European artists' depictions of the tormented creatures of Hell.

"Early in my school-days a boy had a copy of the *Wonders of the World*," wrote Charles Darwin in his autobiography, "which I often read and disputed with other boys about the veracity of some of the statements. . . . I believe this book first gave me a wish to travel in remote countries, which was ultimately fulfilled by the voyage of the *Beagle*."

By the time Charles Darwin arrived in the Galápagos Islands in September 1835, he had indeed already had as much adventure as he ever could have wished for, having experienced everything from rounding the Cape Horn while beset by enormous, bone-crushing seas—seas so powerful that they had rolled the *Beagle* over onto its side and nearly destroyed it—to visiting little-contacted Patagonian Indians, who ran about naked and smeared their bodies with the grease from seals. Darwin had crossed the rugged southern Andes both on foot and on horseback, had explored Patagonia, had discovered the fossils of gigantic and now extinct ancient mammals and reptiles, including an extinct rodent the size of a hippopotamus, and had collected countless living species completely new to science. Prone to seasickness, the six-foot-tall En-glishman had also somehow managed to survive the previous four years living in a cramped, five-foot-tall cabin, ten by eleven feet in size, while sleeping in a hammock that swung wildly in the often wilder seas. All the while he'd been diligently making a collection of South America's plant, animal, and mineral specimens. Now they were headed across the Pacific and, ultimately, home.

Before he'd left England at the age of twenty-two, however, on what was supposed to be a two-year voyage, Darwin couldn't have seemed a less likely candidate to make a name for himself in the sciences. Few people would have seemed as little inclined as Darwin, in fact, to write one of the most famous books of all time, *On the Origin of Species*, a book that would offer both a theory and a mechanism to explain how life had evolved from simple, single-celled organisms into such complex creatures as apes, antelopes, and humans. Darwin had been raised a Unitarian, a Christian sect that, like other Christians, believed that God had created the heavens and Earth in a day, had created Adam and Eve, and that Adam and Eve had eventually been expelled from the Garden of Eden.

Despite his religious training, Darwin had fallen in with a rather dis-sipate crowd as a teenager and had spent much of his time hunting with them for sport. "You care for nothing but shooting, dogs, and rat-catch-ing," his exasperated father, a physician, had once told his son, "and you will be a disgrace to yourself and all your family." Since Darwin's father and grandfather were both physicians, at the age of seventeen Darwin attempted to follow the family tradition by enrolling in medical school. He soon dropped out, however. Darwin had quickly discovered that he could neither stand the sight of blood nor the pain patients com-monly suffered during surgery before the discovery of anesthetics. In-stead, Darwin enrolled at Cambridge University, where he studied for a "general degree" before graduating at the age of twenty-two. During his final exams, Darwin scored his highest marks in theology, while barely scraping by in his other subjects. Although he had a passion for collect-ing beetles ever since he'd been a boy and had become quite interested in geology, Darwin's ultimate intention was now to become a pastor, with the idea that eventually he would live quietly in some small rural community, tending to the religious concerns of the local inhabitants. Cambridge had been an excellent choice for such a profession, as all of its professors had taken religious orders. At least half the students there had likewise been studying to become clergymen.

Shortly after Darwin graduated, an obscure ship anchored in Plymouth, England, and named the HMS *Beagle*, was quietly being prepared for a projected voyage to South America. Its mission from the admiralty was to finish surveying Patagonia, the region that encompassed South America's complicated southern coastline. The *Beagle*'s crew had begun the first part of this arduous task on a voyage some five years earlier. The ship's present captain, twenty-six-year-old Robert FitzRoy, knew they'd be away for a good number of years, so he'd decided to search for a young "gentleman"—someone who could serve as both an educated companion to the captain and also as the ship's naturalist. On the *Beagle*'s previous voyage, FitzRoy was aware, no naturalist had been aboard. There was one catch, however: whoever was selected would be offered free transportation but would otherwise have to pay his own board.

FitzRoy first offered the job to thirty-one-year-old Leonard Jenyns, a clergyman who was also an amateur naturalist and a personal friend. Already employed, however, Jenyns weighed his paying parish job with the proposed nonpaying, multiyear voyage and turned FitzRoy down. Eventually, one of Darwin's former Cambridge professors learned about the position and sent Darwin a note. The twenty-two-year-old Darwin couldn't have realized it at the time, but the message was about to shift his future as abruptly as a railway switch shifts the direction of an oncoming train.

Cambridge
24 Aug 1831

My dear Darwin,

. . . I shall hope to see you shortly fully expecting that you will eagerly catch at the offer which is likely to be made you of a trip to Terra del Fuego & home by the East Indies—I have been asked by [Professor

George] Peacock [at Cambridge] who will read & forward this [letter]
to you from London to recommend him a naturalist as companion to Capt
FitzRoy employed by [the British] Government to survey the S. extremity
of America—I have stated that I consider you to be the best qualified
person I know of who is likely to undertake such a situation—I state this
not on the supposition of your being a finished Naturalist, but as amply
qualified for collecting, observing, & noting any thing worthy to be noted
in Natural History. Peacock has the appointment at his disposal & if he can
not find a man willing to take the office, the opportunity will probably be
lost—Capt. F.[itzroy] wants a man . . . more as a companion than a mere
collector & would not take any one however good a Naturalist who was
not recommended to him likewise as a gentleman. Particulars of salary &c
I know nothing. The Voyage is to last 2 yrs. & if you take plenty of Books
with you, any thing you please may be done . . . What I wish you to do
is instantly to come to Town & consult with Peacock . . . & learn further
particulars. . . .

[Professor] J. S. Henslow

[P.S.] The expedition is to sail on 25 Sept [1831]: (at earliest) so there is
no time to be lost.

Although Darwin was excited about this unexpected opportunity, his father was decidedly against it. The senior Darwin would have to provide the money for the voyage, after all, and preferred that his son begin looking for gainful employment instead. He was still disappointed that Darwin had failed at medical school. Eventually, however, his father relented, and finally, on December 27, 1831, the young man who'd nearly become a pastor instead set off on a voyage that would not only change his life but would change our understanding of our place in the natural world.

Thirty-two years before Darwin's departure, a young German scientist named Alexander von Humboldt had set out on his own five-year scientific exploration, eventually traveling through Latin America and discovering in the process the link between the Amazon and Orinoco

Rivers. Humboldt also discovered the massive ocean current that would later bear his name, climbed Ecuador's volcanoes, collected new species of plants and animals, explored the Amazon and the Andes, and eventually returned to Europe, to instant acclaim, at the age of thirty-five. Unlike Darwin, however, Humboldt had prepared his entire life for his expedition, having been trained as a geologist, an anatomist, a botanist, a surveyor, and an astronomer. A polyglot, Humboldt had also received training in the use of almost every modern scientific instrument known at the time. Darwin, by contrast, eight years younger than Humboldt was when the latter had set off, had just graduated with a general degree at what was basically a theology school. Although Darwin had some training in geology, a passion for beetle collecting, and knowledge about bird taxidermy, in a very real sense he was a rank amateur. Darwin's job description on the *Beagle*, in fact, was simply to make collections of any interesting animals and plants that he encountered, to take notes on the local geology, and to serve as a dining companion for the captain, who otherwise, due to his rank, would have to dine alone.* The idea was that once the *Beagle* had completed its voyage, scientific experts in England would be able to study the young naturalist's collections and could then decide whether anything he had discovered was important. These same experts would also be expected to draw conclusions from the information gathered, if any notable conclusions were to be drawn. Darwin, it was understood, was to be a *collector*. The experts in London, meanwhile, were the bona fide *scientists*.

During the summer after his graduation, however, and before he'd learned about the opportunity on the *Beagle*, Darwin had read Humboldt's *Personal Narrative of Travels to the Equinoctial Regions of America, During the Years 1799–1804*, which Humboldt had published in 1825.

---

*The *Beagle*'s previous captain, Pringle Stokes, had committed suicide during the ship's first voyage to South America, and Captain FitzRoy had taken command of the ship soon afterward. Some believed that Stokes's personal and physical isolation at the end of the world had contributed to his demise. This is one of the reasons Captain FitzRoy sought a "gentleman companion," someone who might help relieve some of a captain's isolation. Pringle Stokes was ultimately buried on a lonely beach on the southern shores of Tierra del Fuego Island, the location marked by a single tall wooden cross.

Darwin later recounted that the book had a profound impact upon him. The methodical way the great German scientist had applied modern concepts of scientific measurements to everything he saw while deducing laws from a seemingly chaotic assortment of facts had stirred in Darwin not only a sense of wanderlust but also, as he later wrote in his autobiography, "a burning zeal to add even the most humble contribution to the noble structure of Natural Science." Little did Darwin know that he would soon get his chance. Less than six months later, the newly designated "ship's naturalist" and "gentleman companion" was packing his trunk for a voyage to the very continent Humboldt had explored. And one book Darwin made sure he included was a well-thumbed copy of Humboldt's *Personal Narrative of Travels*.

"I have real problems with God," says Rachel, a thirty-two-year-old, unmarried Israeli American Jew who is about to have a child with a married Catholic Puerto Rican. We're sitting on the rear deck of the *Eden* after a skin dive off Santiago Island. Rachel is short, wears glasses, has thin, closely cropped brown hair and blue eyes. She's a psychiatrist who works in Miami. Her boyfriend, the Puerto Rican, is also a psychiatrist. The problem is, he's still married and has three kids.

"I think as the years have gone by, I've become more of an agnostic," she says. "I find it hard to believe that God could have created so much suffering."

Earlier in the afternoon, we had flippered through an underwater world filled with king angelfish, barberfish, butterfly fish, goldrim surgeonfish, sleek barracuda, Galápagos mullet, graybar grunts, Mexican hogfish, rainbow wrasse, giant hawkfish, stonefish, and parrot fish, among others. The Humboldt Current is one of the richest biological upwellings in the world, and we are at the tail end of it here, after it has swept up the coast of western South America and curled out six hundred miles to the Galápagos. Departing from the platform at the back of the boat, we had glided over papaya-colored seaweed that swirled in slow motion, performing ballet-like movements below us, pulsing in and out with the surge. We had then flippered through blue grottos streaked with bands of sunlight that occasionally lit up a stray fish scale or bounced off the sides of a shimmering school of mullet, the school parting before us like some kind of mobile curtain, with each segment bearing eyes.

Even underwater, the creatures here seemed less afraid than normal, the fish allowing us to approach so closely that we could almost touch them with our fingers. Only at the last second would one give a leisurely flap of its tail and move away. Farther along, near a volcanic formation (Santiago Island is the product of twin volcanoes), a young sea lion had swum in circles beside me, bubbles streaming from its nose, outlining arcs like tiny Ferris wheels. It had then approached so closely that at one point it had been only a foot away from my face mask, its dark, globular eyes peering inside at mine. An hour later, with goosebumps still on our arms and saltwater still dripping, we sat sprawled out in chairs on the back of the *Eden*'s deck, drying off.

"My brother, Haim," Rachel says, continuing with her religious theme, "now, *he's* a believer. I mean *devout*. He lives on a kibbutz and has nine children."

Rachel had gone to medical school in the United States and then began working in a hospital, helping patients deal with the psychological aspects of their physical ailments. For years she had been dating a smart young Jewish man who was financially stable, whom her parents loved, and who, she says, had "security" written all over him. He was perfect in every way except for one thing: Rachel wasn't in love with him. Then, at the hospital, she had met Pablo, a psychiatrist a dozen years her senior. Pablo was smart and an excellent salsa dancer. An affair soon began. Pablo said that he was going to get a divorce, that he didn't love his wife, that they had agreed to separate—all the usual things. Five months later, Rachel discovered she was pregnant, yet still there was no sign of a divorce. Now, four months later, none of her family knows she's pregnant, she says, not even her brothers or her closest friends. With vacation time looming, Rachel had booked a cruise to the Galápagos with the intention of sorting out her life. Today is day four of our voyage, and she's currently sitting in a lounge chair in a black swimsuit. She says flatly that she's agnostic.

"I don't know. I grew up speaking Hebrew, eating only kosher food. I mean, we didn't eat calamari in my house because Jews only eat seafood that has fins and scales. So forget about lobster! We didn't eat filet mignon—*ever*—because the sciatic nerve runs through it. Do you know what a sciatic nerve is?"

I shake my head.

"I *know*! I only found out in *medical school*! No hard cheeses, only certain kinds of wine. I mean, *crazy*. And what does all of that have to do with *God*?"

"So do Jews believe in evolution?" I ask. I'd actually never really pondered this question before. Or really much about what other faiths might think about evolution at all. What do Shintos think about evolution? I had no idea. I only knew that the more conservative Christians in the United States had a problem with the idea of man evolving from other animals. In fact, I'd just read a recent poll that fewer than 47 percent of North Americans believed that evolution actually occurred at all. For some, the idea of Adam and Eve having slowly evolved from some other animal in the Garden of Eden remains a deeply disquieting thought.

"Most Jews believe in evolution," Rachel says, nodding her head up and down and squinting at me. She's holding a frozen strawberry daiquiri, which is the pièce de résistance of the bar on the *Eden*. "Well, a *kind* of evolution. They believe that God created the world and life, but that He also created the laws that allow evolution to take place. So that's how the world ended up with humans. But not everyone believes that. My brother Haim doesn't. He believes the world is six thousand years old or something like that and that God created man and that no Jew should ever eat calamari or work on the Sabbath."

At precisely this moment, a black frigate bird decides to alight on one of our ship's metal spars, which stick outward from the railings like pikes. The bird shuffles its wings, its feathers glistening, its long beak curled downward at its tip like a claw. It then swivels its head left and right, looking out at the ocean and ignoring us. Interestingly enough, that is the only annoying thing I've discovered about the Galápagos: after a while you tend to get mildly annoyed that so many of the animals behave as if you aren't there, as if you don't exist. The reason is because the internal alarm wiring for "predator alert"—so important on the mainland, so unnecessary on islands where no natural predators lurk—has long since disappeared. Instead, the islands' inhabitants tend to look at other, more interesting things. Like members of the opposite sex.

"What about you?" I ask. "What do you believe?"

"I used to have faith," Rachel says. "But I really don't anymore. I gave up being kosher. I think the best description is that I'm agnostic. That maybe there's some power out there—but I have no idea what."

"And what about evolution?"

Rachel gazes at the frigate, which is intently watching what other frigate birds are doing off to sea.

"It's hard to go through medical school with all that biology and not accept that evolution exists. Did I believe in evolution *before* I studied biology? No," she says, shaking her head. "When I was a little girl I used to love all the stories in the Torah. I *loved* going to synagogue. But I don't go anymore. Maybe that's why I'm now in such a pickle."

The frigate bird has a red throat pouch under its neck, a pouch that males inflate to attract females, like gaudy party balloons. No doubt this one has a female partner somewhere, pregnant or already with eggs in a nest. Now is the season of mass reproduction on the Galápagos Islands. It's not just Rachel who is pregnant and about to reproduce.

"Wow," she says, looking out at the view. "This is so great."

On September 17, 1835, as twenty-six-year-old Charles Darwin and thirty-year-old Captain Robert FitzRoy first rowed ashore to the Galápagos's San Cristóbal Island, Darwin, too, was having doubts about his faith. Darwin had grown up believing in a literal interpretation of the book of Genesis, which describes how God created the Earth and all of the animals and plants on it. But in the late eighteenth century, a Scots physician and amateur geologist named James Hutton, fascinated by geology, had begun investigating the exposed layers of the Earth that he sometimes came across alongside country roads, rivers, and ocean shores. After descending into sweltering mines and drawing sketch maps of everything he had seen, Hutton gradually deduced that the Earth's interior must be molten, that its heat must create new kinds of rock such as lava, that the Earth's surface is naturally eroded by the forces of wind and water, and that the results of that erosion are eventually deposited in horizontal layers at the bottom of seas. These sediments, Hutton theorized, were eventually turned into stone and in some instances were lifted high up into the mountains again. Eventually Hutton established a number of basic premises and from these drew a few simple yet important conclusions:

- That the same forces of wind and water operating today must have operated in the past as well.
- That even great canyons must have been formed by these slowly acting erosional forces.
- That due to the great amount of time the forces of erosion must have taken to form the Earth's present geological formations, the Earth's age must be vastly older than the biblically based estimate of 4,000 B.C.

The Earth, Hutton deduced, must be *millions*, not thousands, of years old. And he did not stop there. Applying both his conclusions about geological time and his process of inductive reasoning to life on Earth, Hutton wrote in 1794 that

> If an organized body [i.e., a living creature] is not in the situation and circumstances [environment] best adapted to its sustenance and propagation, then, in conceiving an indefinite variety among the individuals of that species, we must be assured, that . . . those which depart most from the best adapted constitution, will be the most liable to perish, while . . . those organized bodies, which most approach to the best constitution for the present circumstances [that is, the environment], will be best adapted to continue, in preserving themselves and multiplying the individuals of their race.

Hutton had clearly stumbled upon the realization that not all life forms successfully reproduce or, if they do, do not reproduce equally. Some do so better than others. Those animals or plants better suited to their environments will reproduce more successfully than those less suited. As an example of Hutton's reasoning, suppose a species of hummingbird that feeds on nectar within a certain two-inch-long flower ideally has a beak two inches long, a size that allows it to most efficiently and easily obtain nectar. If certain hummingbird chicks within a brood are born with shorter beaks than the two-inch ideal, however, then those birds would have more difficulty obtaining food. Hutton's theory would predict that those shorter-beaked individuals would tend not to reproduce as successfully, leaving fewer descendants. Meanwhile, the "best adapted" hummingbirds—those hummingbirds with two-inch beaks—would reproduce more successfully, leaving larger numbers of two-inch-beaked hummingbirds. According to Hutton's theory, then, hummingbirds with the ideal, two-inch beak length are "naturally selected," while those with different sized beaks are "naturally rejected"—not by God but by nature. In such a manner, hummingbirds are "naturally" adapted to their environment, which in this case means gaining full access to the nectar within the two-inch-long flowers.

Following Hutton's logic, however, what if, for one reason or another, these hummingbirds dispersed to a new area where the flowers were *three* inches long, not two? In this new environment (that is, an environment with longer flowers), hummingbirds born with longer beaks than their siblings' would now more easily gather nectar than those with two-inch or shorter beaks. Hutton's theory would thus predict that the hummingbird population would gradually shift to more individuals with longer beaks, as longer beaks would now be favorably "selected," while shorter beaks would be "rejected." With enough time and enough generations, the inescapable logic of Hutton's theory would predict that eventually a longer-beaked population of hummingbirds would emerge, while shorter-beaked hummingbirds—at least in this new area—would disappear. Almost miraculously, with no "forces" acting upon the hummingbird population other than those already present in nature, the "creation" of a new species would have occurred.

Hutton, however, was a religious man. And although he had just stumbled upon the principle of "natural selection," he fully believed that God had created individual species. Hutton thus didn't allow himself to contemplate the possibility that the very mechanism he had discovered that could change the *form* of a species could also possibly explain the *origin* of a species. Mentally unable to move beyond a biblical paradigm that had existed virtually unchanged for thousands of years, Hutton was unable to carry his new theory to its logical conclusion: that forces inherent in nature could create new species—independent of supernatural intervention.

Hutton's thinking, however, *did* lead him to modify slightly his view of Genesis: that although God had created all the animal and plant species on Earth, perhaps God had also allowed his creations to "fine-tune" or "adapt" themselves to their environments—even though this ability was not mentioned in the Bible. Hutton therefore could explain how new *varieties* might develop within a species—such as poodles and great Danes, which nevertheless remain dogs—but he stopped short of going any further. If the Bible stated that God had created all of the creatures on Earth, then it was not his place to throw doubt upon the matter. Hutton's main interest, after all, was geology. His discovery of how new varieties of species might emerge came almost as an afterthought and remained buried amid his 2,138-page, three-volume 1794 tome, *An Investigation of the Principles of Knowledge and of the Progress of Reason, from Sense to Science and Philosophy*. And there it remained, a theory virtually unnoticed by the rest of the world.

Forty-one years after Hutton's publication and six thousand miles away, Charles Darwin and Captain Robert FitzRoy finally stepped ashore the Galápagos Islands. Like Hutton, Darwin was passionate about geology, and, also like Hutton, he believed that God had created all of the animals and plants on Earth. During his long trip around the southern cone of South America, however, Darwin *had* begun to doubt the Bible's usefulness as a literal guide to the Earth's geological history. Darwin, for example, had recently read two texts on geology by another Scottish geologist, Charles Lyell, who had followed in Hutton's footsteps and had adopted Hutton's idea that the same forces operating in the past were still operating in the present, a concept known as "uniformitarianism." Earlier geologists had assumed that the features of the Earth had been created by God with some final changes having occurred during the great Flood—the latter event having been developed into a geological theory known as "catastrophism," from the catastrophic flood that God had unleashed on Earth. Lyell—a less religious man than Hutton was—clearly saw how the principle of uniformitarianism might be seen as a challenge to the story of Genesis and thus to the church. In 1830, on the eve of publication of his soon-to-become-classic *Principles of Geology*, Lyell wrote a friend:

> I trust I shall make my . . . [book] of geology popular. Old [Reverend John] Fleming is frightened and thinks the age will not stand my anti-Mosaical [i.e., anti–Old Testament] conclusions and at least that the subject will for a time become unpopular and awkward for the clergy.

Although the church's subsequent reaction to the book was mixed, Lyell's *Principles* was a revelation for Darwin. The book almost immediately stripped him of his previous belief that canyons, river valleys, and sediments had most likely been laid down during the great Flood. Instead, as the HMS *Beagle* visited a succession of ever-changing landscapes, Darwin now began to "see" geological formations for the first time as he had never seen them before. While the *Beagle*'s crew busily mapped Patagonia, for example, Darwin frequently disembarked and roamed about, discovering layer after layer of exposed sediments filled with the fossils of strange and extinct animals.

At one point, ten thousand feet up in the Andes, Darwin discovered beds full of fossil seashells. It was obvious, he concluded, that these same layers must once have lain far beneath the oceans and that unknown geological forces had somehow lifted them up. After careful examination, Darwin also perceived that it would have been impossible for these formations to have been created by natural processes during the last six thousand years. Influenced by his own observations and now by Lyell, Darwin agreed that the history of the Earth must stretch back for *millions*, not thousands, of years. The Earth was also not static, Darwin realized; rather, it was constantly changing. So what effect, he couldn't help but wonder, did these often radical environmental changes have on plants and animals?

On many of his explorations in Patagonia, Darwin was accompanied by Captain FitzRoy. The captain had also read Lyell's book on geology but ultimately found himself unable to see the world as either Darwin or Lyell did. Where Darwin now saw the evidence of geological forces operating incrementally through millions of years, FitzRoy continued to see only the results of the great Flood. FitzRoy, in fact, later wrote an account of their voyage. In a chapter titled "On the Deluge," he even utilized some of the same evidence that Darwin would later use to support his theory of evolution. In FitzRoy's case, however, that evidence only served to reinforce his deeply held belief in the biblical account of the Flood:

> In crossing the Cordillera [mountain chain] of the Andes Mr. Darwin found petrified trees, embedded in sandstone, six or seven thousand feet above the level of the sea: and at twelve or thirteen thousand feet above the sea-level he found fossil sea-shells, limestone, sandstone, and a conglomerate in which were pebbles of the "rock with shells." Above the sandstone in which the petrified trees were found, is a great bed, apparently about one thousand feet thick, of black . . . lava; and over this there are at least five grand alternations of such rocks, and aqueous sedimentary deposits, amounting in thickness to several thousand feet. These wonderful alterations of the consequences of fire and flood, are, to me, indubitable proofs of that tremendous catastrophe which alone could have caused them;—of that awful combination of water and volcanic agency which is shadowed forth to our minds by the expression "the fountains of the great deep were broken up, and the windows of heaven were opened."*

*FitzRoy is quoting from Genesis 7:11, from the King James version of the Bible.

The very firmament of South America, then, had become for Darwin and FitzRoy a kind of enormous Rorschach test: FitzRoy peered carefully at the continent's twisted strata and saw physical proof of the ancient story of the Flood. "My own mind is convinced, (independent of the Scripture)," FitzRoy wrote after his return, "that this earth has undergone an universal deluge." Darwin, meanwhile, often peered at the very same strata, yet, because of the influence of Lyell, believed that he was now peering deeply into the Earth's history, using logic to gain a glimpse of a primordial past that he had never dreamt existed before.

And yet although Darwin's mental model of Earth history had only recently undergone a transformation, on the day he stepped ashore the Galápagos Islands, his view of biology was still very much the same as that of other Victorian scientists. As already stated, according to Darwin's contemporary biologists, God had created the individual species on Earth, although some amount of biological adaptation seemed to have occurred after creation. In his *Principles of Geology*, Charles Lyell had written of "centers of creation," that is, of places on Earth where God had created individual species that had since undergone minor changes. In Australia, for example, God had clearly seen fit to create kangaroos. In Borneo, orangutans. In Africa, gorillas. In the Garden of Eden, man. Man, in fact, was a good example of "changes" or "varieties" within a species: in some areas men were black; in other areas, white; in still others, men possessed Asiatic characteristics; in others, aboriginal ones. But no scientist doubted that all of these different *races* belonged to the same species of *Homo sapiens* to which modern mankind belonged—or that these variations had originated from man's first "center of creation," presumably in the Middle East. Both animals and plants, many scientists thought, had the ability somehow to "adapt" themselves to new environments. But none had the ability to transform themselves into entirely new species. Only God could do that.*

---

*There were, of course, exceptions, the most notable being the French biologist Jean-Baptiste Lamarck (1744–1829). In 1802, seven years before Darwin was born, Lamarck published *Recherches sur l'Organisation des Corps Vivants* (*Researches on the Organization of Living Beings*) in which he proposed the idea that species transformed themselves by means

Thus when Darwin stepped on shore in the Galápagos Islands, he naturally assumed that the islands had been populated by animals and plants that had somehow arrived there from the South American mainland, where God had originally created them. If a mockingbird had arrived on one of the islands, therefore, it may have undergone slight changes in its new environment, but it no doubt still belonged to the same *species* that continued to exist on the mainland. Biological species, Darwin assumed, were immutable.*

Darwin's creationist assumptions explain why he ultimately did such a poor job in collecting bird specimens on the Galápagos. Darwin was not an ornithologist nor a botanist nor a taxonomist. Without the help of experts and without access to the large museum collections experts often used to compare and contrast different species, he was in no position to understand or confirm the identity of much of what he saw. Years later, while recalling how he had collected plants on the Galápagos, for example, Darwin wrote with some chagrin that "From my ignorance in botany, I collected more blindly in this department of natural history than in any other." He was referring to his attempt to gather duplicate specimens of the plants he was collecting on the islands. Such specimens could later be shared by different museums, a practice that was and still is common today. Darwin later realized, however, that due to his ignorance at the time, "I probably collected second and third species as duplicate specimens of the first." In other words, instead of collecting three samples of a single species as he had

---

of acquired characteristics. If a giraffe, for example, stretched its neck constantly during its lifetime, then the giraffe's neck would lengthen and this newly acquired characteristic would be passed on to its offspring. Neither Lamarck nor any other scientist, however, were ever able to find any evidence supporting his theory. Nevertheless, Lamarck became convinced that species underwent transmutation. Lamarck never did, however, discover the principle of natural selection, which eventually provided Darwin with the key to how evolution might occur.

*Darwin was unaware, by the way, of Hutton's theory of "natural selection," as was almost every other naturalist. That was because Hutton's theory had been buried within the 2,138 pages of his massive geological text. Hutton's theory was not even mentioned by Charles Lyell in his *Principles of Geology*.

intended, Darwin unwittingly collected three separate *species*, yet labeled them as one.

With the scores of small birds on the Galápagos, Darwin ran into similar problems. Since he hadn't visited the adjacent mainland, did not have access to museum collections, nor did he possess any ornithological books that might help him sort out the birds, his difficulty was not surprising. After all, many of the birds on the Galápagos Islands had never been described scientifically before. Darwin's task of trying to identify them was therefore a challenge.

Captain FitzRoy, meanwhile, who also made occasional collections of animals during the voyage with the intention of turning them over to the crown, was little concerned about identifications. Instead, he marveled at how God had created species that were so well suited for these islands:

> All the small birds that live on these lava-covered islands have short beaks, very thick at the base, like that of a bull-finch. This appears to be one of those admirable provisions of Infinite Wisdom by which each created thing is adapted to the place for which it is intended.

Darwin's job, by contrast, was to make some sense of the islands' ornithology and, when possible, to collect both a male and a female of each bird species.* In the end, however, he was unable to sort many of them out. The birds' lack of fear of humans nevertheless astonished him. On September 17, 1835, his first day in the Galápagos, Darwin wrote in his diary that

> After dinner a party went on shore [San Cristóbal Island] to try to catch Tortoises, but were unsuccessful. . . . The birds are Strangers to Man & think him as innocent as their countrymen, the huge Tortoises. Little birds, within 3 or four feet, quietly hopped about

---

*The *Beagle* thus served as a kind of Noah's ark, although in this case each male and female pair of a species was placed aboard the ship dead, not alive.

the Bushes & were not frightened by stones being thrown at them. Mr King killed one with his hat & I pushed off a branch with the end of my gun a large Hawk.

Eventually, Darwin collected twenty-six species of birds on the islands. Thirteen of these were finches, although Darwin was able to identify correctly only six of those as such. The other seven finch species were so different in form that Darwin didn't recognize them as finches at all. Instead, he labeled them as belonging to three completely different bird families. In addition, because Darwin had assumed that the small species of birds on each island must belong to the same species that existed on adjacent islands, he'd made few attempts to label which island these birds had come from. Darwin never suspected that there might be similar yet different species of birds on each of the islands. After all, why would God create different species of birds on adjacent islands? If one species worked well on one island, why would He create a similar species on another? Why not stick with one? Darwin therefore often labeled birds with the date they had been collected but omitted the specific island. Instead, he included only the general locality, which he listed as "the Galápagos Islands."

It took FitzRoy and his crew, meanwhile, five busy weeks to finish mapping the archipelago. During that time, Darwin visited and collected on four of the Galápagos' thirteen main islands, spending a total of about nineteen days on land. Before he left, and still a firm believer that God had created each of the individual species that he had observed, Darwin noted in his journal that

> I industriously collected all the animals, plants, insects & reptiles . . .
> It will be very interesting to find from future comparison to what district or "center of creation" the organized beings of this archipelago must be attached.

In other words, since he had not visited the adjacent mainland of South America, and since he assumed that the wildlife on the Galápagos had originally arrived from there, Darwin naturally wondered where, exactly, the original inhabitants had hailed from. Had they arrived from Central America? From Gran Colombia? From northern Peru? Or from a mix of all three? Where, exactly, had God originally created the ancestors of the animals and plants presently inhabiting the Galápagos Islands? Darwin realized, however, that he would have to wait more than a year to find out. Not until the *Beagle* returned to England, where specialists could tell him exactly what species he had found, would he be able to answer this question. All Darwin could hope for, meanwhile, was that he *might* have collected something of value for science.

When the *Beagle* finally hoisted sail and departed, no one would have been more surprised than Charles Darwin to learn that what he'd often failed to see and what he'd often mislabeled on the Galápagos Islands would eventually shake both his faith and, more important, the faith of much of the rest of the world.

"There are holes very deep in the Earth," our guide José is telling us, "in the crust. They're called 'hot spots.' " José is thirty-two and lives on Santa Cruz Island, one of five inhabited islands in the Galápagos. He is Ecuadorian, has black hair and a ponytail and a small "Buddha belly," which pooches out the bottom of his T-shirt. Across the front of his shirt is a tie-dyed blue booby and above it are the words: "I love Boobies!" José was born on Santa Cruz, has a thick Spanish accent, and is explaining how the Galápagos Islands were formed.

"The hot spot is a hole where the hot rock, the—magma?" José stops and looks at us, not sure if he has correctly pronounced the word. We nod. "Where the *mag-ma* goes," he says. "That creates the islands, the volcanic islands. That is how the Galápagos, these islands, were born."

Our entire group is here, the elderly Chinese gentleman and his family; Rachel, the Israeli American; a group of Dutch, two Swiss, a short Italian man, and three French Canadians. English is the lingua franca. Bartolomé Island, where we are presently gathered beneath a brilliant sun, is one of the youngest of the Galápagos Islands, which range in age from thirty thousand to eight million or nine million years. This morning we're climbing up to its extinct volcano, a cinder cone that now overlooks Sulivan Bay. Both the island and bay were named after a friend of Darwin's who was a lieutenant aboard the HMS *Beagle*, Bartholomew James Sulivan.

The Earth's crust, José is telling us, is extremely thin. An average of four miles thick beneath the ocean floor. The Earth itself is about four thousand miles thick. So if our planet were represented by a ten-foot-diameter ball, José tells us, the crust would be thinner than an eggshell. José looks around at us, smiling and waiting for a reaction. I look over and see that Sarah is holding her grandfather's hand. Both are paying careful attention.

Beneath the crust is the hot plastic mantle, José continues, and beneath that is the liquid core. Inside the liquid core, like a nested Russian doll, is the superheated solid iron core that forms the Earth's interior. Our planet is the densest of the eight planets in our solar system, José says, and one of only four planets that are solid, not gas.

"Fourteen billion years ago, the universe was smaller than a pinhead," José says, squeezing his two fingers together to demonstrate how small. "This small. Then it exploded. Four and a half billion years ago, the Earth is formed from dust, gas, and fragments."

For the first billion years of its existence, José says, the Earth remained a red hot, lifeless orb spinning through space and slowly circling the sun. Gradually, as the solar system cooled, a thin crust on Earth developed, yet the crust was often punctured by the molten magma below. Three and a half billion years ago, life began, first in water and then eventually—a full three billion years later—it finally slithered onto land, about five hundred million years ago.

"And then, we appeared," José says, holding his arms out with a flourish.

"A very long process, no?"

José had told us earlier that he is Catholic but that he accepts the scientific explanation of the world.

The Earth, then, is a very hot ball with a very thin crust on its surface and an equally thin film of water covering much of that crust. That film, José says, gesticulating out to the blue expanse surrounding Bartolomé Island, we call "the ocean." The ocean floats on top of the crust, but the crust, too, floats on top of the hot magma. The crust, therefore, is not solid but instead is divided into huge thin plates—"like cracked eggs, yes?" José says, lifting his eyebrows and looking for more nods before continuing. The ground appears rigid when we walk on it, but the plates below us behave, geologically speaking, more like stiff clay. Eight major plates float slowly over the Earth's surface, José says, due to the hot molten currents below. When one plate collides with another, the first slides beneath the second, eventually returning to the magma, where it's melted again. The edge of the second plate, meanwhile, often crumples from the impact, forming a mountain chain. The Nazca plate, which is about three thousand miles wide and extends from west of the Galápagos all the way to the edge of South America, collided about twenty million years ago with the South American plate, crumpling that plate's western edge. The collision formed the Andes Mountains, some of whose peaks rise more than twenty thousand feet into the air.

José holds his two hands out horizontally, fingers together and pointing at each other, then he moves his hands together with one hand diving beneath the other. He then bends the second hand's knuckles up, forming the Andes.

"*Capito*?" he asks in Italian. "Understood?"

We nod.

"So how old *are* the Andes?" Rachel asks. She's wearing a wide-brimmed straw hat and large, oval sunglasses. Her willowy blue blouse shows no hint that she's pregnant.

"Twenty-five to thirty million years," José replies.

"And the Galápagos?"

"Very young," José says, looking around at the volcanic cone we are standing on. "This island, Bartolomé, it is only two hundred and fifty thousands of years. A baby," he says, cradling his arms and looking around for a laugh.

Sarah and her two brothers giggle.

José kneels down in the dark volcanic sand and draws a line. He then draws an arrow below the line and pointing toward it.

"The arrow is a hot spot," José says, explaining that a hot spot is a kind of hole in the mantle that allows the magma to move upward, toward the crust.

"When the Nazca plate moves to the east toward South America, it moves over this hot spot, no?"

José forms a *T* with his two hands, then slides the horizontal hand above in one direction while holding the vertical one below still.

"When the crust moves over the hot spot, a volcano is formed. If it is big enough, it lifts up out of the ocean and explodes."

The elderly Chinese American man nods his head, intently peering down at José's sketch. Sarah and her two brothers mimic their grandfather's stance, bent over, hands against their knees. All three are frowning.

"It is like fire hose," José says. "Shooting heat up at crust. No?"

As long as a volcano is positioned over the hot spot, José continues, eruptions continue. Once the Nazca plate moves the island away from the hot spot below it, however, the island is severed from its volcanic roots. It's then no longer volcanically active, but dead. As the Nazca plate continues moving toward South America, it drags fresh crust over the hot spot and new volcanic islands continue to form. Eventually, a chain of islands is created, with the youngest, volcano-spewing islands to the west, still over the hot spot, and the oldest, dormant islands to the east, having long since been severed from their source. The youngest islands in the Galápagos archipelago, José says, such as Fernandina, are still rising from the ocean and are hundreds of thousands of years old. The oldest islands to the east were formed nine or ten million years ago. The entire Galápagos archipelago, José says, is moving toward South America at a rate of about one and a half inches per year, or roughly twenty-four miles every million years.

With his explanation finished, José ends his lecture and then turns and resumes hiking up the volcano. We follow, looking out over smaller cones and lava tubes below. The landscape here resembles the surface of a boiling cauldron that suddenly froze, the bubbling surface turned into jagged stone.

In 1825, ten years before Darwin's visit, an American sealing captain named Benjamin Morrell visited the Galápagos and, on February 14, was anchored in a bay off Isabela Island. Early in the morning when most of the crew was asleep, a massive explosion occurred: the nearby island of Fernandina, located directly over the Galápagos' hot spot, had begun its latest eruption. Wrote Morrell:

> Monday the fourteenth, at two o'clock, AM, while the . . . night was yet spread over the . . . Pacific . . . our ears were suddenly assailed by a sound that could only be equaled by ten thousand thunders bursting upon the air at once; while, at the same instant, the whole hemisphere was lighted up with a horrid glare that might have appalled the stoutest heart! I soon ascertained that one of the volcanoes of . . . [Fernandina] Island, which had quietly slept for the last ten years, had suddenly broken forth with accumulated vengeance . . . The heavens appeared to be one blaze of fire, intermingled with millions of falling stars and meteors; while the flames shot upward from the peak of . . . [Fernandina] to the height of at least two thousand feet. . . .
>
> Our situation was every hour becoming more critical and alarming. Not a breath of air was stirring to fill a sail . . . so that we were compelled to remain idle and unwilling spectators of a pyrotechnic exhibition. All that day the fires continued to rage with unabating activity, while the mountain still continued to belch forth its melted entrails in an unceasing cataract.

At one point, Morrell's crew inspected the thermometer and discovered that at 4:00 p.m. it registered 123 degrees Fahrenheit. They then placed the thermometer in the water and found that its temperature had risen from its normal 70 to 105 degrees. Fortunately, a breeze sprang up, Morrell and his crew hoisted their sails, then sailed through the strait between the two islands, with Fernandina exploding off their leeward bow. Morrell continued:

On passing the currents of melted lava, I became apprehensive that I should lose some of my men, as the influence of the heat was so great that several of them were incapable of standing. . . . Had the wind deserted us here, the consequences must have been horrible. But the mercy of Providence was still extended toward us— the refreshing breeze urged us forward towards a more temperate atmosphere . . . We now steered for . . . [Floreana Island] . . . and came to anchor in its northwest harbor at eleven p.m. Fifty miles and more to the leeward, in the northwest, the crater of . . . [Fernandina Island] appeared like a colossal beacon-light, shooting its vengeful flames high into the gloomy atmosphere, with a rumbling noise like distant thunder.

Darwin, arriving ten years later, witnessed none of this. However, the *Beagle* did sail close by Fernandina Island and anchored in the same bay where Morrell had witnessed the explosion. In his journal, Darwin wrote:

The next day, a light breeze carried us over the calm sea, which lies between . . . [Isabela and Fernandina Islands]. In the latter, high up, we saw a small jet of steam issuing from a Crater. [Fernandina Island] . . . presents a more rough & horrid aspect than any other; the Lavas are generally naked as when first poured forth.

Elsewhere, Darwin wrote of the Galápagos Islands that "the fragments of Lava where most porous are reddish like cinders; the stunted trees show little signs of life. The black rocks/heated by the rays of the Vertical sun, like a stove, give to the air a close & sultry feeling . . . The country was compared to what we might imagine the cultivated parts of the Infernal regions [of Hell] to be."*

Darwin clearly realized that the Galápagos Islands were newly

---

*The most recent eruption of Fernandina, which continues to be located over the Galápagos hot spot, was in April 2009. It has erupted nineteen times since Darwin's visit in 1835. The island—and the rest of the archipelago—has moved roughly twenty-two feet toward South America since then.

formed and that these isolated, rough-hewn crags had somehow emerged as lava from beneath the sea. Darwin knew nothing, of course, about plate tectonics, "hot spots," or how and why the islands had been born. He also believed that God had created all of the species on Earth.

Sometime during the remaining eleven months of the *Beagle*'s journey, however, as Darwin began to study in his cramped, unsteady cabin the birds he had collected on the Galápagos Islands in more detail, doubts began to creep into his mind. The young naturalist had collected mockingbirds on four of the islands he'd visited, all of which at the time had appeared to him to be the same species. Now on closer examination, however, Darwin noticed that three of the four specimens he'd collected had features that were not shared by the others, almost as if they were different species. But *were* they? Hampered by his lack of knowledge, Darwin couldn't be sure. Perhaps they were only varieties, he mused. Yet what if they *were* separate species? If so, why would three similar yet different species of mockingbirds live on islands that were adjacent to one another and with similar habitats? Why on God's Earth would that be?

Soon, other doubts began to trouble him. While Darwin was in the Galápagos, the English vice governor there had told him that local inhabitants could easily tell which island a giant tortoise was from simply by glancing at its shell. Darwin hadn't thought much about the statement at the time, but now the conversation bothered him. Was it possible that the tortoises on each island were separate species? If so, he realized—and no doubt suddenly experienced a pang of worry—then he hadn't bothered to collect a single adult! Darwin *had* collected four tiny tortoises but no mature ones. In a notebook where he routinely compiled his ornithological observations, Darwin wrote:

> I have [mockingbird] specimens from four of the larger [Galápagos] Islands. . . . The specimens from . . . [San Cristóbal and Isabela Islands] appear to be the same; but the other two are different. In each Isld each kind is exclusively found: habits of all are indistinguishable . . . [I now remember] the fact that from the form

of the body, shape of scales & general size, the Spaniards can at once pronounce, from which Island any Tortoise may have been brought. When I see these Islands in sight of each other, & possessed of but a scanty stock of animals, tenanted by these birds, but slightly differing in structure & . . . [occupying] the same place in Nature, I must suspect they are only varieties. . . . If there is the slightest foundation for these remarks [about the tortoises possibly being distinct species on each island, then] the zoology of [island] Archipelagos—will be well worth examining; *for such facts* [*would*] *undermine the stability* [immutability] *of Species.*

Darwin couldn't know it yet, but what he was beginning to suspect was true. The mockingbirds he'd collected were not varieties, but separate *species*. Instead of the six finch species that he thought he'd identified, there were actually *thirteen*, with many of the islands having their own distinct species. Eventually, Darwin would discover that most of the Galápagos' inhabitants were species found nowhere else on Earth. They were similar to, but completely different from, species on the mainland. It was that information—which Darwin was just beginning to suspect but while on the *Beagle* was unable to prove—that would completely push him from the belief in the Biblical story of creation into a wholly new world where the main principle of biology—that species were created by God and thus were immutable—would soon be turned completely upside down.

"Grandpa—*look!*"

It's Sarah and she is absolutely giddy with delight.

"It's *Lonesome George!*"

Sarah is squatting beside an adult Galápagos tortoise, three and a half feet long and 200 pounds—or about 150 pounds heavier than she is. We are on Santa Cruz Island, just outside of the town of Puerto Ayora, at the Charles Darwin Research Station. Puerto Ayora is a former buccaneer hangout that now consists of a motley collection of small bars, open-air restaurants, and stores. The buildings lie clustered along a boardwalk where weather-beaten, solitary sailors—some of whom look like human forms of the albatross—walk the boardwalks, their clothes faded, wearing hats with neck flaps down the back to keep off the tropical sun. Offshore, in the protected harbor, an ever-changing community of small boats lies anchored, rolling quietly on the southern swells. The water beneath them is the color of turquoise.

Behind the research station, Lonesome George inhabits a large, private enclosure that is open to the elements. Although Darwin had begun to worry on his return voyage that each island here might have a different tortoise species, all of which he had failed to collect, it turned out that the islands had just one: a single species but with fifteen different subspecies. Biologists now believe that the ancestors of the Galápagos tortoise must have floated to the islands accidently from South America about six million years ago. Tortoises are buoyant, after all, and can survive lengthy periods of time without food or fresh water. Pushed here by the Humboldt Current like so many reptilian seeds, the tortoises eventually came to rest on eight of the islands, clambering out of the surf and finding enough vegetation to survive. Suddenly without predators, the newly arrived migrants flourished. Eventually, they developed into fifteen different subspecies, four of which are now extinct. In 1971, biologists visiting tiny Pinta Island in the northern part of the archipelago discovered the last living representative of the Pinta Island subspecies *Chelonoidis nigra*. They soon moved the tortoise to the research station we are now visiting and, because he was the last of his subspecies, nicknamed him Lonesome George.

Only a little over four hundred years earlier, when the Spanish bishop Berlanga visited the Galápagos, an estimated 250,000 Galápagos tortoises inhabited these islands. In some areas with more abundant vegetation, the tortoises were so thickly distributed that early visitors could practically use them as stepping stones. The largest were over six feet long and weighed more than eight hundred pounds. By 1971, however, when biologists stumbled upon Lonesome George, the population had plummeted to about 3,000 individuals—victims of centuries of hunting by crews of whaling and sealing ships. Flipped onto their backs, the tortoises could be stored alive for up to a year during voyages, providing a constant supply of fresh meat. Meanwhile, introduced animals from the mainland, such as rats, ate the tortoises' eggs and young, while introduced goats and other animals consumed the tortoises' plant foods, causing them to starve to death.

By the time Charles Darwin visited the Galápagos, a number of the tortoise subspecies were already rapidly disappearing from some of the islands. That didn't stop the crew of the *Beagle*, however, from collecting as many as they could find for food.

"These islands appear paradises for the whole family of Reptiles," Darwin wrote. "The Tortoise is so abundant that [a] single Ship's company here caught 500–800 in a short time."

A week later, while visiting Charles (Floreana) Island and an Ecuadorian settlement there, Darwin noted that three of the four main tortoise predators were already on the island: goats, pigs, and men (only the rat was not mentioned):

> The houses are very simple, built of poles & thatched with grass. Part of . . . [the settlers'] time is employed in hunting the wild pigs & goats with which the woods abound . . . The main article . . . of animal food is the . . . Tortoise: such numbers yet remain that it is calculated two days' hunting will find food for the other five in the week. Of course the numbers have been much reduced . . . Where the settlement now is, around the Springs . . . [the tortoises] formerly swarmed. [The English vice-governor] Mr. Lawson thinks there is yet left sufficient for 20 years . . . Mr. Lawson recollects having seen a . . . [tortoise] which 6 men could scarcely lift & two could not turn over on its back. These immense creatures must be very old; in the year 1830 one was caught (which required 6 men to lift it into the boat) which had various dates carved on its shells; one was 1786. The only reason why it was not at that time carried away must have been that it was too big for two men to manage. The Whalers always send away their men in pairs to hunt [for the tortoises].

The English vice governor's prediction, however, was incorrect: within fifteen—not twenty—years of Darwin's visit, the Floreana Island subspecies, *Chelonoidis nigra nigra,* had become extinct. Those on Fernandina, Rabida, and Santa Fe Islands soon followed. Roughly one hundred years later, in 1959, the Ecuadorian government declared 97.5 percent of the Galápagos Islands a national park (the other 2.5 percent was already inhabited). In 1964 an international nonprofit organization based in Belgium created the Charles Darwin Research Station, dedicated to carrying out biological research on the islands that could help Ecuador with the islands' conservation. By this time, however, the Galápagos tortoise population had plummeted 98.8 percent since the islands' discovery; four of the fifteen subspecies had gone extinct; and another one—the Pinta Island tortoise—was represented by only Lonesome George. Meanwhile, five of the thirteen main islands had been colonized by Ecuadorians (Baltra, Floreana, Isabela, San Cristóbal, and Santa Cruz). The human population of the Galápagos has steadily increased from roughly two thousand inhabitants in 1959 to more than twenty-five thousand people today.

Along with the first human visitors to the Galápagos came a veritable deluge of invasive species that accompanied them: goats, pigs, dogs, rats, cats, mice, sheep, horses, donkeys, cows, poultry, ants, and cockroaches, as well as a great number of invasive plants. The island chain originally had roughly five hundred species of native plants. Humans have since introduced an additional seven hundred species of invasive plants. Many of these have completely altered native habitats and, in some cases, have caused endemic plant species to become extinct.

Since many of the Galápagos' native animals had no predators, they had no fear of the newly introduced ones. Feral dogs and cats, for example, easily killed native birds and destroyed the nests of birds, tortoises, and sea turtles. Introduced pigs similarly destroyed the nests of tortoises, turtles, and land iguanas as well as ate the native foods of all three. In 1959, when Lonesome George was approximately sixty years old and living on Pinta Island, local fishermen introduced one male and two female goats to the island, with the idea that the goats would reproduce and provide meat that could be hunted. By 1973, fourteen years later, the National Park Service estimated that the original trio of goats had increased to *thirty thousand* individuals, completely destroying much of the local tortoise habitat. Not surprisingly, by that time only Lonesome George was left.

Here at the Darwin Research Station, Lonesome George's enclosure has low rock walls, a cement tank for water, and shrubs and trees within it, which George can graze upon.

Other giant tortoises from different islands and belonging to different subspecies live in adjacent enclosures, which have pathways through them that tourists can walk along. With his long neck and massive scarred shell, Lonesome George looks more like an old, battered World War II tank than a reptile. Instead of treads, he has four thick, elephant-like, leathery gray feet as well as wrinkled haunches that protrude from the back of his shell. George is now about one hundred years old and is presently standing up on all four legs, his neck extended out about a foot and a half, peering with dark, implacable, watery eyes at the small girl squatting before him. For the last two decades, researchers have tried to encourage George to mate with two females that genetic testing had discovered were closely related—but to no avail. It seems probable that with his death, the subspecies *Chelonoidis nigra abigdoni* will become extinct.*

In 1965 the Darwin Research Station began a captive breeding program for the various endangered subspecies of tortoises, along with attempts to remove invasive species from their original island habitats. That especially meant ridding the islands of dogs, pigs, cats, and goats. Because the tiny, two-inch tortoise hatchlings were vulnerable to rats and other predators, researchers found that if they could protect the hatchlings in captivity for the first four or five years of their lives, until they weighed about eight to ten pounds, then their chances of survival

---

*Lonesome George died in his pen on June 5, 2012, of an apparent heart attack, prompting the president of Ecuador, Rafael Correa, to pay tribute to the deceased tortoise in an address to the nation. Although Lonesome George never did successfully reproduce, scientists from the Frozen Zoo at San Diego Zoo's Institute for Conservation Research saved some of George's tissue cryogenically shortly after his death. It is therefore possible that a second Lonesome George might one day be cloned in the future.

in their original habitats would be greatly increased. By that time, the young tortoises' shells are harder, and the tortoises are more difficult to prey upon.

The program has thus far been largely successful. In 1977, for example, only fifteen tortoises remained on Española Island: three males and twelve females. Members of the subspecies *Chelonoidis nigra hoodensis*, these survivors were so few in number and were so dispersed on their island that breeding no longer occurred. Extinction appeared imminent. Scientists instead brought the tortoises to the research station on Santa Cruz Island where, during the next four decades, the three males and twelve females produced more than 1,200 baby tortoises. Most of these have been repatriated back to Española Island, where they are now reproducing on their own.

Further research has shown that the Galápagos tortoises are actually a "keystone" species on the islands, acting as major seed dispersers. Adult tortoises eat up to eighty pounds of vegetation a day, excreting much of it as they wander about. They also crop the thick undergrowth so that sunlight can help diverse plant seedlings sprout. Acting on this information, researchers in 2010 released thirty-nine tortoises on Pinta Island—the original home of Lonesome George—in order to begin "reengineering" the vegetation back to its original state. They also launched a major goat eradication project, using "Judas goats" as herd locators. The latter are radio-collared goats that have been released and that soon join local herds. All the goats are then shot, except for the Judas goats. A few weeks later, park employees return, locate the radio-collared goats that by this time have joined another herd, and destroy the goats again. Researchers believe that only by "reengineering" the Galápagos Islands can the original habitat be restored so that the native tortoises can thrive again.

Outside, we visit large concrete pens full of eight-inch tortoises, their dark, shiny, helmet-like carapaces marked with a set of small yellow or white numbers to indicate their date of birth and to which subspecies they belong. In 1835, when the *Beagle* set off from the Galápagos for home, Darwin's ship carried forty-eight adult tortoises aboard, turned upside down and stored in the hold for food. The *Beagle* also carried four baby tortoises—some only a few inches long—as "pets." Darwin named three of the tortoises "Tom, Dick, and Harry." The name of the fourth tortoise—if it ever had one—is unknown. Darwin had collected Tom on Santiago Island; Captain FitzRoy had collected Dick and another small tortoise on Española Island; and Darwin's servant, nineteen-year-old Syms Covington, had collected Harry on Floreana. The tortoises grew about two inches during the year it took the *Beagle* to return to England, living in a box in Darwin's cabin while their older relatives were one by one gutted and served to the crew.

Although the vice governor of Floreana Island had told Darwin that the tortoises on each island were so different they could be recognized at a glance, the information didn't register with Darwin until well after the last adult tortoise on board the *Beagle* had been eaten. It would take decades, meanwhile, before the four tiny captives would display their adult morphological forms so that they could be studied. Roughly three months after he arrived back in England, Darwin took his tiny visitors to the British Museum so that they could be examined by a reptile specialist. What happened to the tortoises after Darwin's visit, however, is not clear. A story still circulates in Australia that, after realizing the English climate was less than ideal for his captives, Darwin eventually gave three of the tortoises, Tom, Dick, and Harry, to John Clements Wickham, a former officer on the *Beagle*. Wickham was soon to retire to sunny Australia and had volunteered to take them there. Eventually, and well into the next century, Tom and Dick are said to have died in captivity. Harry, meanwhile—actually a female who was renamed Harriet—lived on, ultimately finding her way into the Australia Zoo in Queensland owned by the late television personality Steve Irwin. Harriet died there in 2006—a full 176 years after Darwin had presumably collected her. Darwin, meanwhile, had passed away more than 120 years earlier, but not before leaving his idea of evolution—and some of the tortoises that he had collected—behind.

By mid-January 1837, Darwin had been back in England for three months, had delivered his collection of mammals and birds to the Zoological Society, and was worried sick about his poorly labeled bird specimens from the Galápagos. Only a week earlier, Darwin had turned over his bird collection to John Gould, a leading ornithologist at the London Museum. Gould had begun examining the collection and was immediately struck by the unusual characteristics of the Galápagos birds. Six days later, on January 10, the Zoological Society held its usual biweekly meeting, which was soon dominated by news of the unusual specimens the young naturalist, Charles Darwin, had recently returned with. A reporter from London's *Morning Herald* attended the meeting, little realizing that the small story he was about to file would one day become a footnote in a much larger discovery:

> ZOOLOGICAL SOCIETY—The ordinary meeting was held on Tuesday evening . . . On the table was part of an extensive collection of mammalia and birds, brought over by Mr. Darwin, who accompanied the *Beagle* in its late surveying expedition in the capacity of Naturalist, and at his own expense, a free passage only being allowed by the Government. Of the former there were 80, and of the latter 450 specimens, including about 150 species, many of which are new to European collections. . . . Several species of the mammalia were explained by Mr. Reid, amongst which was a new variety of Felis [cat], named F. Danvinnia, with several opossums. Mr. Gould [the ornithologist] likewise described 11 species of the birds brought by Mr. Darwin from the Galápagos Islands, all of which were new . . . [species], none being previously known in this country.

The eleven Galápagos bird species, it turned out, were all finches, but of a kind that neither Gould nor any other ornithologist had ever seen. By the end of January, Gould had identified two more finches among Darwin's collection, or a total of thirteen. Gould next examined Darwin's mockingbirds, which Darwin believed to be four different varieties of the same species, although he'd had his doubts. Gould quickly identified three of the four specimens not as varieties but as separate species. Fortunately, Darwin had labeled them according to the island where they'd been found. With Gould's help, Darwin could now list the mockingbird species—all of them completely new to science—according to their island habitats:

> *Orpheus trifasciatus* (Floreana Island) (Floreana mockingbird)
> *Orpheus melanotis* (San Cristóbal Island) (San Cristóbal
>   mockingbird)
> *Orpheus parvulus* (Isabella and Santiago Islands) (Galápagos
>   mockingbird)

Clearly, Darwin now realized, a number of the islands he'd visited seemed to have their own similar yet distinct species of mockingbird. But why was that? Why wouldn't God have created just *one* species on *all* of the islands? Why would He have created three similar yet different ones?

The ornithologist Gould, meanwhile, having completed the identification of the finches, now asked Darwin an obvious question: *which islands had these unusual finches come from?* This was when Darwin looked through his notes and realized the great error he'd made. As mentioned at the beginning of this chapter, Darwin—mortified and now desperate to rectify his error—quickly sent out messages to the three other members of the *Beagle*'s crew who had also made collections: Captain Fitz-Roy, FitzRoy's steward, and Darwin's servant. After they'd delivered their collections, Darwin worriedly searched through them, comparing the crew's specimens to his own and doing his best to determine which islands his finches had come from. Unfortunately, however, the information he sought was often lacking and, in the end, Darwin was forced to guess. It would ultimately take decades and the efforts of subsequent scientists to properly identify which islands "Darwin's finches" originally had been collected on. Yet even though he'd made a royal mess of it, it was nevertheless clear to Darwin that the Galápagos finches appeared to follow the same pattern as the mockingbirds: each island seemed to have its own distinct yet similar species. His lack of precise data, however, prevented him from ever proving this during his lifetime.

Gould's classification of Darwin's bird collection nevertheless marked a turning point for the young naturalist, one that would forever alter his thinking on the mutability of species. Of the twenty-six land birds Darwin had collected on the Galápagos, Gould now informed him that *twenty-five* were species completely new to science. Eventually, it became clear that most of the Galápagos' inhabitants—more than 90 percent of its reptiles, 50 percent of its land birds, and 45 percent of its higher plants—were species found *nowhere else on Earth*. Yet all were related to—although different from—species found in nearby South America. Darwin was completely stunned by this news, later noting that

> I never dreamed that islands, about fifty or sixty miles apart, and most of them in sight of each other, formed of precisely the same rocks, placed under a quite similar climate, rising to a nearly equal height, would have been [so] differently tenanted. . . . [B]ut I ought, perhaps, to be thankful that I obtained sufficient materials to establish this most remarkable fact in the distribution of organic beings.

What Darwin didn't mention in this passage is that, in reality—at least as far as finches were concerned—he personally hadn't "obtained sufficient materials" to establish anything of the kind. Instead, he'd been forced to pore over the collections of three other members of the ship. That was because during the entire, nearly five-year-long voyage, Darwin fully believed that God had created immutable species. That deeply ingrained belief had thus prevented Darwin from *seeing*, on the Galápagos Islands at least, evidence of the mutability of species: that one species could change into another through natural forces and not because of the hand of God.

Four months after learning about the islands' unusual number of unique species and after having absorbed more information given to him by other taxonomists, Darwin purchased a new notebook, opened its cover, then carefully began to write out a title on its first page:

Notebook on the Transmutation of Species

The evidence from his voyage—and in particular from the Galápagos Islands—had by now convinced Darwin that nature must somehow be able to forge new species. There was no other explanation for what he had belatedly seen on the Galápagos Islands and in other parts of the world. Like the biblical deluge, which he no longer accepted as literal fact, Darwin now realized that species were *not* immutable, as the Bible implied. For more than two thousand years, much of the Western world had believed that God had created animal and plant species and that those species had remained fixed for all time. Darwin now began to suspect that a different set of forces must somehow be responsible for the origin of species and that that process must in some way be linked to changing environments. Darwin was twenty-seven years old when he opened his notebook and first began jotting down his thoughts on the subject. It would take him another twenty-two years of diligent thinking, experimentation, and research, however, before he would publish in book form the explanation of a mechanism—natural selection—that could explain how new species could be formed.

Although Darwin was never able to use the finches he had collected as evidence supporting his theory, he *was* able to theorize that a single ancestral finch species must have long ago arrived in the Galápagos and that members of this same species must have eventually distributed themselves on islands with slightly different habitats. Like the hummingbird with two-inch beaks described earlier, "adapting" themselves mindlessly through natural selection to their habitat, the finches, too, underwent the process of natural selection. Eventually, the different island environments so altered the original finch's form that by the time Darwin arrived it was not clear that some of its descendants were even *finches* anymore. Much later, and as Darwin suspected but never had the data to prove, these same finches would be held up as classic examples of the results of "Darwinian" evolution.

In *On the Origin of Species: Races in the Struggle for Life,* which Darwin published in 1859 when he was fifty years old, he referred back to his time on the Galápagos Islands and recalled the unique birds he had stumbled upon there as a young man:

The most striking and important fact for us in regard to the inhabitants of islands, is their affinity to those of the nearest mainland, without being actually the same species. [In] the Galápagos Archipelago . . . almost every product of the land and water bears the unmistakable stamp of the American continent. There are twenty-six land birds, and twenty-five of these are ranked by Mr. Gould as distinct species, supposed to have been created [by God] here; yet the close affinity of most of these birds to American species in every character, in their habits, gestures, and tones of voice, was manifest. . . . The naturalist, looking at the inhabitants of these volcanic islands in the Pacific, distant several hundred miles from the continent, yet feels that he is standing on American land. Why should this be so? Why should the species which are supposed to have been created in the Galápagos Archipelago, and nowhere else, bear so plain a stamp of affinity to those created in America?

There is nothing in the conditions of life, in the geological nature of the islands, in their height or climate, or in the proportions in which the several classes are associated together, which resembles closely the conditions of the South American coast: in fact there is a considerable dissimilarity in all these respects. On the other hand, there is a considerable degree of resemblance in the volcanic nature of the soil, in climate, height, and size of the islands, between the Galápagos and [Africa's] Cape de Verde Archipelagos: but what an entire and absolute difference in their inhabitants!

The inhabitants of the Cape de Verde Islands are related to those of Africa, like those of the Galápagos to America. I believe this grand fact can receive no sort of explanation on the ordinary view of independent creation [by God]; whereas on the view here maintained, it is obvious that the Galápagos Islands would be likely to receive colonists, whether by occasional means of transport or by formerly continuous land, from America; and the Cape de Verde Islands from Africa; and that such colonists would be liable to modification;—the principle of inheritance still betraying their original birthplace.

Since Africa's Cape Verde Islands and the Galápagos Islands shared much more in common environmentally than either archipelago did with their nearby continents, Darwin was arguing, why would God not put the same species He had created for the Galápagos on the Cape Verde Islands—or vice versa—rather than create completely new species for each one? The Galápagos Islands' species, however, were clearly related to those on mainland South America while Cape Verde Islands' species were just as clearly related to those on mainland Africa. So, surely, the only explanation was that each group of islands was first inhabited by creatures from their nearby continents, and that these original inhabitants had then somehow "evolved" into new yet related species.

In the last paragraph of *On the Origin of Species*, and after more than a quarter of a century of ruminations, Darwin wrote a final reflection on the strange and mutable world he had just introduced to the world:

> It is interesting to contemplate a tangled [stream] bank, clothed with many plants of many kinds, with birds singing on the bushes, with various insects flitting about, and with worms crawling through the damp earth, and to reflect that these elaborately constructed forms, so different from each other, and dependent upon each other in so complex a manner, have all been produced by [natural] laws acting around us . . . Thus, from the war of nature, from famine and death, the most exalted object which we are capable of conceiving, namely, the production of the higher animals, directly follows. There is grandeur in this view of life, with its several powers, having been originally breathed by the Creator into a few forms or into one; and that, whilst this planet has gone circling on according to the fixed law of gravity, from so simple a beginning endless forms most beautiful and most wonderful have been, and are being evolved.

"So, have you read the book?" the elderly gentleman asks me. "*Darwin On Trial?*"

It's evening, and he has joined me on the deck of the *Eden*. We are still moored off Puerto Ayora, on Santa Cruz Island. Earlier, we had returned to the ship at dusk, traveling on the small Zodiac, riding past boats lit by yellow lamps and with names from around the world stenciled on their sterns. Water taxis darted between the boats, carrying crews to and from town, the sky a deep indigo blue. With the yellow lamps, the last light and the silhouettes of the masts and ships, it was easy to imagine the *Beagle* moored here, too, with Charles Darwin in his breeches, stretching and yawning on deck after a long day of collecting, perhaps examining one of his newly found pet tortoises, almost ready to turn in for the night.

"Yes, I read some of it," I tell him.

"What did you think?"

Rachel comes out to join us, pulls up a chair, and looks out at the twinkling lights.

"It was written by a lawyer. And lawyers aren't specialists in evolution," I answer. "Nor do they necessarily look for the truth. Lawyers are all about winning cases. They'll suppress evidence if it helps them win a case. They'll have evidence tossed out if it suits their purpose."

"But he makes a very good *case!*" the elderly gentleman protests. "That the science is simply not there!"

There are different kinds of people with religious beliefs, I have long since realized. Some, like the elderly gentleman, believe in a literal interpretation of a religious text, as did Captain FitzRoy of the *Beagle*. Others believe that, while evolution exists, God created its laws and simply used evolution as a kind of Rube Goldberg method of creating what is presumed to be the end product, man. The author of *Darwin On Trial*, who states at the outset that he is a Christian and a "philosophical theist," falls into the latter category. So, too, does the modern Catholic Church and most Jewish and Muslim theologians. With the by-now overwhelming evidence supporting Darwin's theory of evolution, most religions have retreated back to first causes—stating that, whatever else science may discover, God nevertheless created the universe and the original life within it. Thus, God's intention was to ultimately "create" the world as we know it—a process that eventually led to the appearance of humans.

In 1878, four years before Darwin died and nineteen years after the publication of *On the Origin of Species*, an Anglican priest named Edward

Pusey gave a sermon attacking Darwin's theory that was subsequently published in London's *Guardian* newspaper. A friend sent Darwin a copy and, while waiting for a train in a railway station outside of London, the elderly Darwin—by now resembling the classic, white-bearded, beetle-browed scientist that the world would forever remember him as—penned the following reply:

Nov 28 [*1878*]

Dear Sir,

I just skimmed through Dr. Pusey's sermon as published . . . but it did not seem to me worthy of any attention. As I have never answered criticisms excepting those made by scientific men I am not willing that this [present letter I am writing to you] . . . should be published . . . Dr. Pusey was mistaken in imagining that I wrote the Origin [of Species] *with any relation whatever to Theology. I should have thought that this would have been evident to anyone who has taken the trouble to read the book, more especially as in the opening lines of the Introduction. I specify how the subject arose in my mind . . . I may add that many years ago when I was collecting facts for the* Origin, *my belief in what is called a personal God was as firm as that of Dr. Pusey himself, & as to the eternity of matter I have never troubled myself about such insoluble questions.*

Dr. Pusey's attack [however] will be as powerless to retard by a day the belief in evolution as were the virulent attacks made by divines fifty years ago against Geology, & the still older ones of the Catholic church against Galileo, for the public is wise enough always to follow scientific men when they agree on any subject; & now there is almost complete unanimity amongst Biologists about Evolution, tho' there is still considerable difference as to the means, such as how far natural selection has acted & how far external conditions, or whether there exists some mysterious innate tendency to perfectibility.

I remain dear Sir,
Yours faithfully,
Charles Darwin

Darwin characterized his own religious beliefs perhaps most clearly in his posthumously published autobiography: "The mystery of the beginning of all things is insoluble by us," he wrote, "and I for one must be content to remain an Agnostic." In other words, Darwin was a scientist first and foremost but left room for the possibility of God. He simply felt that the origin of the universe was quite possibly beyond the capability of man's intellect, as far beyond his own intellect, in fact, as Sir Isaac Newton's calculus would be for an ant or for one of his beloved beetles to comprehend.

"Why do you think you and I look different from one another?" I ask the elderly gentleman, continuing the conversation. "And why do we both look different from black Africans? Why don't we all look more or less the same?"

"We are all children of Adam and Eve," he says. "And God made of one blood all nations of men," he says, quoting the Bible, "and for those men to dwell upon the face of the Earth."

"Yes, but why are *you* Asian and why am *I* Caucasian, and why do other people have black skins?"

"Why do *you* think?" he asks.

"Because sixty-five thousand years ago humans left Africa," I say. The elderly gentleman begins to shake his head. "Some of us went north," I continue, "where there was little sun and we needed our skin to produce vitamin D, so our skins gradually became pale. Others stayed in Africa with lots of sun and remained black. Others went to Asia, where the environment was different, and people changed there, too. Our populations were small, we were cut off from one another. We couldn't interbreed. Just like the tortoises on the Galápagos. We were separated from one other geographically, as if we were all living on islands. It took the original finch millions of years to become thirteen different species here. We've been out of Africa for only sixty-five thousand years or so. And look how much we've *changed*! We became different *races*—just like the original Galápagos tortoise became different subspecies. Eventually, with enough time, those tortoises would have become separate species, too."

The elderly gentleman continues to shake his head.

"No," he says. "I don't believe it. You leave no place for God."

"Do you know the story about the hobbit?" I ask. "The tiny humans that lived on that island in Indonesia?"

He shakes his head.

"They found three-foot-tall versions of humans on an island in Indonesia less than ten years ago. They used stone tools and went extinct only about ten thousand years ago. It's like the story of the finch— a species of human ended up on a tiny island, cut off from the rest of the world, with a different environment, and gradually changed and became a different species."

The elderly gentleman looks at his watch and then stands up. He's still shaking his head. He bids us good night and thanks us politely for our good company during the cruise.

He shakes my hand warmly, then peers at me.

"We did *not* come from monkeys," he says.

"I respectfully disagree."

"Good night, then," he says, walking slowly away and shaking his gray head.

Rachel and I remain on the deck, transfixed by the shimmering lights and by the outline of a two-million-year-old volcanic island called Santa Cruz, rooted thousands of feet below us and bathed by the final vestiges of the Humboldt Current.

"So have you decided on what you're going to do when you're back in Miami?" I ask.

"I'm going to raise my child," she says quietly. "I don't know if it's a boy or a girl. But no matter what happens—things will work themselves out."

"God willing?" I ask.

She smiles.

"*B'ezrat Hashem*," she says in Hebrew.

"God willing."

3

DEATH IN THE ANDES: THE CAPTURE OF SHINING PATH LEADER ABIMAEL GUZMÁN (PERU)

Their burning conviction that there must be a new life and a new order is fueled by the realization that the old will have to be razed to the ground before the new can be built. Their clamor for a new millennium is shot through with a hatred for all that exists, and a craving for the end of the world.

—Eric Hoffer, *The True Believer*

The philosophers have only interpreted the world . . . the point is to change it.

—Karl Marx, *Theses on Feuerbach*, 1845

Revolution is not a dinner party, nor an essay, nor a painting, nor a piece of embroidery; it cannot be so refined, so leisurely and gentle, so temperate, kind, courteous, restrained and magnanimous. A revolution is an insurrection, an act of violence by which one class overthrows another.

—Mao Tse-tung

From the moment the people take up arms to overthrow the old order, from that moment, the reaction seeks to crush, destroy and annihilate the struggle . . . we are seeing it now, and will continue to see it even more until the outmoded Peruvian State is demolished.

—Shining Path leader Abimael Guzmán, 1988

May 1987

The two Guardia Civil, one a corporal, the other a simple guard, were traveling on a bus by night through Sendero Luminoso [Shining Path] guerrilla territory, high in the Peruvian Andes, when suddenly boulders appeared in the headlights. The guards were dressed as civilians and carried forged civilian IDs—common among police who worked in the emergency zones. Both knew what a roadblock meant. Shots exploded outside, then a voice ordered the driver to open the door. The corporal moved quickly beside a woman with a baby and put his arm around her. "Say you're my wife," he whispered. The other guard tried hiding in the rear.

Armed Senderistas got on, wearing black ski masks, or pasamontañas, then began checking documents by flashlight. They came to the corporal and checked his papers. Satisfied, they moved on. They were almost done when they found at the end of the bus the other guard hiding behind a seat.

"You're guardia, aren't you!" one of them demanded. The guard, so frightened he could hardly speak, nodded. He was quickly escorted off.

In the cold chill of the altiplano, the lone guard stood outside with the Senderistas as the bus prepared to leave. The corporal's window was open.

"Mi cabo," the frightened guard suddenly called out to him, "bajamos." ("My corporal, let's get off.") The Shining Path guerrillas lost no time in correcting their error.

The two guards' bodies, lying side by side, were found a day later.

I arrived in Lima, Peru, for the first time in 1986, around midnight in the airport, during the height of the Shining Path's guerrilla war. The Peruvian government had recently imposed a *toque de queda,* or curfew on the capital, which began at 10:00 p.m. and lasted until 5:00 a.m. During that time, the city streets were deserted except for the occasional army truck patrolling or the odd tank parked straddling the sidewalk on some corner. Inside the army trucks sat soldiers wearing black ski masks, their M-1 rifles pointing out at the streets. Civilians were allowed to venture out during curfew only if they possessed a *salvo conducto,* or "safe conduct," pass; without one, arrest was automatic. If someone tried to flee, then the police and army routinely opened fire. Each morning, as the mist rose from the lugubrious city and the long, cold Pacific breakers rolled in below it on the coast, Lima's inhabitants would awaken to find a front-page story in their papers about a car or taxi full of revelers trying to return home from a party, inevitably during curfew and without a pass. The story always contained a picture of a car whose windows had been blasted out, its occupants dead. None of the cars I ever read about were carrying guerrillas.

On this particular evening, as I rode from the airport outside of Lima through the rings of shantytowns that surrounded it, the streets were deserted. Our small van with passengers carried a white flag from its antenna to signal that it had a safe conduct pass. We passed truckloads of soldiers on the way, their dull green uniforms illuminated by the streetlamps' yellow pools of light. The soldiers peered at us through the eye slits in their black hoods. The hoods were worn so that the Shining Path could not identify them for later retribution. The attire, however, made them look like phantom dragoons patrolling a city that was dead.

"They shoot at anything," the middle-aged Peruvian beside me said, shaking his head. "Because they're afraid of an attack."

He meant an attack by Sendero Luminoso, the Shining Path guerrillas, a movement that had begun high up in the Andes and had spread the length and breadth of Peru's massive mountain chain and into the lowlands like some rapidly advancing cancer. Having launched their guerrilla war in 1980, the Shining Path had recently begun to surround and infiltrate Peru's ultimate prize: its capital city of Lima, where one-third of Peru's population lived.

By the time of my arrival, Peru and its inhabitants were experiencing something similar to a scene from *Invasion of the Body Snatchers*. The country lay like a somnambulant body, convulsing as it tried to fight off the ever-increasing infiltrations of the guerrilla movement, the latter wrapping its tendrils tighter and tighter around the stricken form, knocking out power pylons high in the Andes that paralyzed vast swaths of the country, gradually morphing Quechua-speaking civilians into Quechua-speaking guerrillas, "liquidating" government representatives such as police, mayors, and politicians with bullet holes in their heads, while slowly replacing Peru's body—cell by cell and membrane by membrane—with a structure of its own.

As the Shining Path continued to gain momentum, Peru's government held increasingly desperate meetings, eventually turning the army loose in the Andes, where wholesale genocide began to occur. Yet still the cancer spread. The army, unable to distinguish between Quechua-speaking peasants and Quechua-speaking guerrillas, soon began wiping out whole villages, using guns, torture, and terror as weapons. Meanwhile, the Shining Path's attacks continued to increase in size and sophistication, while the area where those attacks occurred continued to spread. The government's antiguerrilla strategy was clearly not working.

On many nights during my first year in Peru, the entire city of Lima would suddenly go black, a message to its inhabitants that a group of guerrillas in the Andes had dynamited yet another power pylon. I soon learned to store candles as other Limeños did, ready to light them and work by candlelight until, some hours later, the power would inevitably come on again. Like the rest of Lima's seven million inhabitants, I stayed inside during the military curfews. On only a few occasions did

I get caught out after the witching hour; I was then careful to keep to the shadows on the deserted streets until I finally arrived home.

Even in the latter half of the 1980s, few really had any idea who the Shining Path were or why they had launched their war. While the guerrillas were not shy about setting off explosions, they made no proclamations. They issued no communiqués like other guerrilla groups did. They simply went about their business, selectively annihilating those who stood in their way and developing a plan that was clear only to themselves.

Occasionally graffiti scrawled in bold red appeared on city and village walls: "Develop the Popular War!" or "Long Live the Communist Party of Peru!" On the day they began their war in 1980, some of the inhabitants of Lima actually woke to find dead dogs strung from lampposts. No one knew what kind of message was intended, although the dogs slowly twisting from their cords didn't seem to augur well for the future.

One of the Shining Path's biggest mysteries was the man who founded it—an ex-professor of philosophy named Abimael Guzmán. Although Guzmán had disappeared from sight and gone underground back in 1979, he was still presumed to lead both the party and the war. Some believed the white-skinned, thickset man with black-rimmed spectacles lived in a remote part of Peru. Some believed he lived in a nearby country. Still others believed he was dead. In a similar manner, little was known about the movement's members other than that many of them seemed to speak Quechua, the Incas' ancient language, and that most were from the Andes.

From captured documents, however, it gradually became clear that the ideology of the movement was not indigenous, but Maoist. The Shining Path were apparently trying to emulate the example of Mao Tse-tung, the Chinese leader who carried out the Cultural Revolution, an internal purge during which more than a million people died. Some of the Shining Path prisoners who were captured and tortured admitted their Maoist strategy and goals: first to take over Peru's countryside and then to surround and take over its cities. Gradually, both Peru's police and its army came to the realization that, from the growing number of emergency zones the government had declared in the Andes and from the increasingly frequent attacks in the cities, the members of the strange Peruvian-Maoist–style guerrilla movement were well into the second phase of their strategy: the conquest and assumption of power.

In 1989, three years after I arrived in Peru, where I worked as a writer and anthropologist, a journalist friend told me that one of Peru's better-kept secrets was that some two hundred Shining Path guerrillas, both men and women, were currently incarcerated within Lima's Canto Grande prison. The prisoners had broken the locks on their cell doors, my friend said, and had virtually taken control of certain sections of the prison. Increasingly curious about what the guerrillas were like and where the country was headed, I decided that the only way to learn more about the movement was to visit the guerrillas in prison.

It's Sunday, April 30, 1989, and I'm standing in a line of visitors outside the high walls of Canto Grande, the maximum-security prison located in the bleak slums in the northeastern section of the capital.

"Be careful which cell block you go into," an old man tells me helpfully, while standing in a line of visitors outside the prison walls. He makes a twisting motion with his hand and thrusts it forward—sign language for being knifed or robbed—then shuffles away. Murderers, rapists, and thieves are held in certain prison blocks; the Shining Path guerrillas—designated as political prisoners—are held in two others.

Republican Guards in purple uniforms, berets, and leather jungle boots stamp my forearm with several purple and gold medallions, adding to this a series of numbers printed in ink. One by one the line I'm in is carefully searched; we then pass beyond the walls and past six checkpoints to where the eight cell blocks, each four stories high and with narrow barred windows, stand in a semicircular ring. Between the bars protrude the hands and arms of some of the worst of Peru's poverty-wracked society.

Before each cell block stand two guards. Their job is to count visitors as they go in, making sure that the same ones come out. The guards' post represents the last bastion of state-instituted order. Inside, it's the prisoners who have control.

Since the inmates have long since broken the locks on their cell doors, they're free to roam about within the cell blocks at will. Here the guards rarely enter, and a strict jungle law reigns: homemade knives, weapons, and drugs are common; gang wars and violent death, a mere routine.

It's difficult to know at this point whether my reception among the members of the Shining Path—housed according to sex in two separate prison blocks—will be any better than that among the common prisoners. According to the local and international press, it's not likely.

The US political journal *The Nation*, for example, refers to them as "Peru's enigmatic killers." France's *Le Monde,* as "the continent's most fanatical and mysterious subversive movement." *America's Watch* says simply that "Sendero Luminoso is the most brutal and vicious guerrilla organization that has yet appeared in the Western Hemisphere."

In June of 1986, Sendero prisoners took several hostages and staged a simultaneous riot in three separate Lima prisons. Asking basically for better prison conditions, the riot coincided with a Socialist International conference. After a brief attempt at negotiating, Peru's president, Alan Garcia, turned the situation over to the military.

What followed was perhaps one of the most brutal resolutions to a prison conflict anywhere. More than 250 prisoners were killed, many of them shot in the head at close range after they had surrendered. The riot quelled, the few remaining survivors—vowing to kill ten government officials for every prisoner massacred—were transferred to the new maximum-security prison of Canto Grande. It's into that prison that I enter now.

Since visitors cannot visit a cell block without a specific prisoner's name, I ask a prison trustee and am given the name of a woman. Two guards open the metal gate to the block where the female Senderistas are kept. I enter; the door clicks and is locked behind.

Inside I find myself in a large room with cement beams across the ceiling. Each beam has a sign stenciled across it in red. "Welcome to the Luminous Combat Trench of Canto Grande!" proclaims one. "Long Live the Communist Party of Peru!" reads another. The room is decorated with red pennant flags, each with an embroidered white hammer and sickle. Young women mill about, all of them with dark eyes and dark hair.

The women are representative of Sendero Luminoso's successful recruiting strategy: in a predominantly class-conscious society Sendero has offered to three strongly disadvantaged sectors—Indians, women, and youth—an alternative, albeit a violent one, to endemic and often fatalistic poverty. Estimated to have between two thousand and five thousand armed guerrillas in a nation of twenty one million, over 75 percent of Senderistas are under the age of twenty-five; at least a quarter of those are women.

Traditionally, Sendero has relied on the poor indigenous peasants of Peru's Andes for support. Exploited since the Spanish conquest, Peru's Quechua-speaking peasants—heirs of the Inca Empire—have spent the last five centuries scratching out meager existences on tiny plots of land. The average life expectancy in many parts of the Andes is forty-nine years. Literacy is 50 percent; running water, electricity, and medical care in many Andean villages are virtually unknown.

Most observers agree that half a millennium of Western "progress" has only widened the gap between rich and poor, leaving Peru's southern Andes—the birthplace and stronghold of the movement—as a fourth-world enclave marooned in the midst of the third.

It was into such an environment that Sendero Luminoso moved in the early 1970s, offering an alternative solution (that of armed conflict) and an alternative vision (orthodox Marxism-Leninism-Maoism) to the often ignored and disenfranchised poor. Sendero's leaders saw Peru as a sort of prerevolutionary China: a colonized, semifeudal country whose peasants have long been relegated to producing wealth for the country's notoriously non-Indian elite.

Viewing the increasing polarization of wealth—between metropolis and countryside, between the "imperialistic" Northern Hemisphere and the "exploited," underdeveloped south—as the inevitable consequence of the conflict of classes, Sendero Luminoso began a patient, ten-year period of proselytization. Led by Guzmán—the fifty-six-year-old Peruvian philosophy professor who founded the movement in 1970—their idea was to create a strong party on the one hand and to organize rural peasant support bases on the other. Once achieved, they would launch the revolution's second stage following Mao's successful strategy in China: armed struggle followed by the takeover of the countryside and the eventual encirclement and overrunning of the cities.

In 1980 a committee meeting of Sendero leaders, headed by Guzmán—who renamed himself Comrade Gonzalo (a name derived from the Germanic Gundisalvo: meaning "genius of the struggle") for the occasion—declared that the party was ready to "begin demolishing the walls and unfurling the dawn." The war on the "bourgeois" Peruvian state was on.

Inside Canto Grande prison and surrounded by mixed-blood women and hanging red flags, I stand inside the cell block until a smiling, older woman comes up to me. The woman has gray hair pulled back into a bun and wears a sweater and a long skirt. She could easily be mistaken for someone's grandmother, but she is the widow of one of Peru's greatest novelists, Jose Maria Arguedas. Arguedas, born in the city to mestizo (mixed-blood) parents yet raised by Quechua-speaking maids, committed suicide in 1969. Many attribute his death to his inability to reconcile Andean and Western cultures, a problem that continues to plague Peru to this day. His widow, Sybila Arredondo, is suspected of being one of the leaders of Lima's suburban guerrillas.

"Good afternoon," she says pleasantly. "Whom do you wish to see?"

I tell her that I'd like to speak with a representative of the party; she nods, and I follow her out of the room. Young Indian women in their late teens or early twenties and many of whom are from the Andes stare at me with mildly curious eyes. Several smile shyly as I pass.

Outside is a large cement patio of at least a thousand square feet, surrounded by high brick walls. The Senderistas have strung lengths of string with red streamers that crisscross the yard. In its center stands a high makeshift wooden pole attached to which is a large scarlet-colored flag. The flag is emblazoned with a white hammer and sickle and flaps lazily in the breeze.

Large slogans are prominently stenciled on the high walls:

DEVELOP THE POPULAR WAR SERVING THE WORLD
    REVOLUTION!
UNDERSTAND THAT THERE IS ONLY ONE IDEOLOGY THAT
    CAN SAVE US—MAOISM!
A SINGLE FORM—THE POPULAR WAR!
A SINGLE PARTY CAN DIRECT US—THE COMMUNIST PARTY!

"Won't you have a seat?" Arguedas's widow asks pleasantly. I take a seat beside two "delegates," or Party representatives, on a low cement wall. A young Senderista soon arrives and offers us a tray of fruit drinks. Arguedas's widow then politely departs.

I tell the two women I'd like to ask them some questions about their politics, military strategy, and tactics. They smile and nod. They first want to know, however, what I think about what I've seen so far. I look about at the neatly dressed women, the flags and slogans, the carefully swept patio, and remember the faces of the common prisoners, leering at me from between the bars of the other cell blocks. Quite frankly, I say, I'm somewhat relieved.

The women's image here, in fact, is difficult to reconcile with Sendero's known actions. In the Andes, Sendero has been known to round up peasants, ostensibly those who have "sided" with the government, and then to hack them to death with machetes and knives. One of their trademark execution styles is a bullet in the back of the head or the slitting of an opponent's throat from ear to ear.

I look at the women, these two in about their midtwenties, with brown skin and black, almost almond-shaped eyes. They both lean forward patiently, wearing polite smiles.

"Why the government officials?" I ask. "Why do you kill them?"

"The way to take power," one of them says, "is by conquering the vertical hierarchy of government. We are merely attacking the hierarchical structure." The other Senderista leans forward. "Look at how the price of milk has gone up," she says. "The officials' lives are worthless."

The women's answer points out one of the overriding character-istics of Sendero's war—it is ideological to the extreme. In Sendero's Marxist-Leninist-Maoist worldview, human beings are classified into the rigid categories of peasants, proletariats, and bourgeoisie. To find oneself labeled as a bourgeois "exploiter of the people"—which in the bitterly poor zones of the Andes can simply mean owning a few too many cows or employing a few too many laborers—is to find oneself arbitrarily tried, judged, and sentenced to death.

Another of Sendero's common targets are members of the security forces such as the Guardia Civil, or Civil Guards. The guards are often young mestizo males, miserably paid, with a wife and children to sup-port. Only recently in the Andean town of Huancayo, several women struck up a flirtatious conversation with two guards standing before a bank. While the guards were so occupied, two men came up abruptly behind them and fired point-blank into the bases of their skulls. As one of the guards sank down, helplessly clutching onto a pole, the two women—actually Senderistas—quickly took the guards' guns and fled.

"What about the policemen?" I ask. "Why kill them?

"It's not against the person," one of the women says, "it's against the institution. We have nothing against them personally."

"They wear the uniform of the reactionaries," says the other. "When the authorities give them the order, they will kill us. Besides," she adds, "we need their guns."

Before I can ask any more questions, I notice that most of the ninety-seven women prisoners are beginning to line up in the large square in files beneath the large hammer and sickle flag, each one of the "combatants" standing a pace apart from the next.

The representatives ask to be excused. Would I mind terribly watching with the combatants' families and friends? Today is special, they say: there will be a speech and then a four-act play. I can ask them more questions afterward.

I walk across the spacious square, led by a young female guerrilla who acts as an usher. Beneath a huge, brightly painted mural of Marx, Lenin, and Mao, I'm seated on blankets laid out on the ground with about forty visitors—mostly the prisoners' families and friends.

There is a speech denouncing the "revisionism" of the Soviet Union and China, followed by a play in which a young man (played by a woman) joins the Senderistas over his mother's objections. Later he is brought home fatally wounded and expresses happiness that he gave his life to the party and revolution. Despite her loss, his mother now endorses his decision.

While several Senderistas clear away the theater props and others visit with family and friends, I strike up a conversation with a group of Senderista women next to me. Given their present situation, the subject quite naturally turns to Peruvian law. Currently, they say, a recently detained terrorist suspect can be held incommunicado for interrogation by the special anti-terrorist police (Dircote) for fifteen days. I ask about the interrogation. One of the Senderistas, a short, stocky woman wearing her Sunday best—a bright green dress and pink high-heeled shoes—begins to tell me quietly how she was tortured. Her name is Marta.

Marta's interrogation began, she says, on the first night and continued for the fifteen nights that she was there. The guards put a black hood over her head and took her to a room where she was made to stand in the middle. With the hood on and her hands tied, about eight Dircote police, both men and women, stood around her.

"They talked to me and asked me, 'Don't you love your mother? You have betrayed her! Do you want her to *suffer?*' They knew all about me, that my mother suffered from rheumatism, et cetera," she says.

They next began to beat her in the head, the chest, and ears—especially where there was hair so that the beating didn't show. They boxed her ears so many times, she says, that her eardrums burst. This lasted from around seven to ten o'clock in the evening.

Marta pauses for a moment as the three other Senderista women nearby nod in agreement. They say the same thing happened to them.

After the initial beating, Marta continues, she was kept standing without a restroom, with her head covered, and without food or water. At around two o'clock in the morning, the guards returned.

"They next tied a rope to my hands, which were tied behind my back, and pulled me up to the ceiling. The pain was very severe. They wanted me to admit that I had done something, to give them names and addresses. They questioned me while I was hanging from the ceiling."

This went on for an hour or so until she couldn't stand it anymore, Marta says. After some of these sessions, they rubbed her wounds with a medicine that reduced the hemorrhage marks.

Marta says the sequence was repeated each night, carried out in a room in the downtown area of Lima that lies perhaps only fifteen blocks from the former dungeons of the Spanish Inquisition. Marta says they next tried to drown her.

"I was tied up completely, blindfolded, and my head was pushed into a bathtub while I was strapped to a bench. I couldn't move. They left me there for a few minutes, then pulled me out while I spit up water. They asked me whether I was going to talk or not." The guards didn't stop, she says, until she lost consciousness.

This was followed by electric shocks. Guards fastened copper electrodes to the most sensitive parts of her body: the vagina, anus, and breasts.

"You can't help but scream," she says, using her brown fingers to try to straighten a wrinkle in her dress.

The torture/interrogation went on every day, every night, for the fifteen nights that she was there. Marta says that the Dircote members have raped other women, not once but repeatedly, each of the agents taking turns. She says that almost all of the women taken recently have been raped.

I ask if these methods succeed; that is, do they give up information?

"In the beginning, it was successful," Marta says. "Now, however, Sendero is too powerful. We don't violate the golden rule, which is 'to say nothing.' The majority of us now keep the golden rule."

I stand up and shake hands with the women and then watch as
Marta, in her green dress and high heels, walks somewhat clumsily
away. I later learn that she is accused of having killed two policemen.

As it is now late in the day, and the visits are nearing an end, I leave
the women's block and cross over to that of the men's.

A welcoming committee of six slender young Sendero guerrillas greet
me as soon as the guards close the door to the men's prison block.
Standing three in a line on either side of the door and all wearing faint
smiles, the men begin to clap in unison, first slowly, then gradually
faster and faster. I am later told that this is their "revolutionary clap,"
which is to show their pleasure at having visitors. All of the Senderistas
wear shy, eager-to-please expressions; at first glance, one would think
them the friendliest people in the world.

I see the same slogans on the walls: DEVELOP THE POPULAR
WAR SERVING THE WORLD REVOLUTION! LONG LIVE PRESI-
DENT GONZALO! all stenciled neatly in blood red. I'm then led out into
the patio, where a delegate sits with me. He introduces himself and says
his name is Javier. Javier looks to be about thirty, was arrested twice, and
on his first arrest spent three years in the island prison of El Frontón,
off the coast of Lima. He was released shortly before the 1986 massacre
and the prison's subsequent closure. Javier was born in Lima and studied
economics at Lima's highly politicized San Marcos University.

Most of what Javier knows, he says, he learned outside of the university. Inside, he says, he basically learned isolated subjects, not in
a unified context such as with Marxism. Javier thoroughly believes in
Hegel's dialectical theory, in the intrinsic correctness of the Marxist
maxims. Sentenced here for twenty years without the possibility of pa-
role, he seems certain that Sendero possesses the one correct theory,
that Sendero possesses the truth. It's the same unshakable faith that
one encounters again and again when talking with Senderistas; it's the
faith of the true believer.

"They say we're messianic, fanatics, but this isn't true," Javier begins. "Rather, we're people who have a total comprehension of things,

of the whole historical process since primitivism. If war is a continuation of politics by other means, as Clausewitz said," he continues, "then we're conscious that there is no other political form of taking power than through armed struggle."

They are political prisoners, Javier says, not common ones. Theirs is a struggle to end hunger, oppression, and misery. Terrorism, he says, is the reactionary's word, the term the Peruvian government uses. In reality they are "combatants in the popular army of the Communist Party of Peru."

Our conversation is interrupted by a group of inmates who begin forming up with various musical instruments—guitars, pan pipes, tambour drums—and begin to play. Every Sunday, Javier says, the Sendero prisoners and their visitors dance and sing. As they launch into their first number, a relyricized Andean folk piece entitled "Long Live Maoism," he continues.

"He who controls the Andes," Javier says, "controls Peru." Already Sendero Luminoso has bases of support from one end of the Peruvian Andes to the other. In addition, Sendero is continuing to move into the coast and the jungle.

"The reactionaries can't defeat us in such a large territory," Javier says. "Instead, they try to attack us at our weakest link—here as prisoners of war."

Javier mentions the Paris Commune, the Bolshevik and Chinese Revolutions. Sendero conducts daily classes inside the prison, and Javier is one of the teachers. "We use the laws of history," he says emphatically. "There are laws—if not, then why does history exist?"

In the center of the square, most of the men are dancing to the pan pipes and to small Andean guitars called *charangos*, arm in arm and in two long lines. The music picks up gradually, and the dance gets faster. Javier points at the men, all of whom are smiling.

"What you see here is what you see in the Andes where we have our power!" he says, having to shout now to make himself heard. "There is a necessity to transform the world and to do it correctly! We are willing to give our lives! Beyond death there *is* nothing else!" He looks at the dancers and then back at me, his face lined and somewhat tired.

"Within the next two years," he shouts, as the music makes his voice almost inaudible, "we will have decided the issue of power!"

With the square full of dancing revolutionaries and the hollow, raspy sound of Andean flutes and drums, I pick my way through the weaving lines, past a part of the Andes now under lock and key. Inside the prison block, Javier pauses before a large mural painted on the wall and facing the entryway. It's a visual rendition—a decidedly apocalyptic one—of Sendero Luminoso coming to power. It's a portrait of Peru in convulsion, a portrait of Peru on fire.

In the forefront of the mural and charging up a hill toward the spectator are three men waving machine guns and soundlessly screaming; they represent Sendero's idea of the three motive forces of the revolution: the wage-earning class, or proletariat; the peasants; and the small businessmen, or petit bourgeoisie. Behind them surges a giant sea of arisen masses carrying machine guns, their mouths opened in a silent yet deafening roar. Towering over them like a Goyan Cyclops is Sendero's founder and leader, Abimael Guzmán, frowning sternly, with dark wavy hair and wearing thick, black-rimmed glasses and a brown suit. In his right hand, Guzmán holds a red flag with a white hammer and sickle and in his left a book across which is written "Develop the Popular War Serving the World Revolution!"

Javier points at the three hills, each spiked with a Communist flag, which rise behind the seething masses and represent stages of the revolution Sendero has already achieved: the formation of the party; the initiation of armed warfare; the spread of warfare throughout the country. In the background and on the sides, the mural's atmosphere writhes and crackles in flames.

Javier points at the screaming masses and chuckles. "Everyone is participating," he says. He then points out an enraged Peruvian holding aloft a gun. "Everyone is armed."

At the gate, I stop and shake hands while behind us, the Andean music continues in a frenzy. "Mao said it would take five hundred to a thousand years to install Communism worldwide," Javier says. "In Peru it will take less. Within the next two years," he says again, "we will have defined the question of power."

The truck of peasants jerked to a stop, raising a cloud of dust just short of an unexpected pile of boulders, high in the Yanaquilca Pass. Within seconds, eight hooded Senderistas surrounded the truck, on its way to Chalhuanca, a small city in the southern Andean state of Apurimac. Riding with the peasants was a Guardia Civil, dressed like a peasant.

"You're guardia, aren't you!" the masked Senderistas demanded, as they made the man lie on the ground. "No," the guardia protested. He had a family in Chalhuanca, he said. He was a laborer, nothing more.

The Senderistas checked the guardia's false papers suspiciously, then seemed satisfied. They gave a brief lecture to the frightened peasants, appealed for a "collaboration" of money, then the truck and the passengers were allowed to leave.

Arriving in Chalhuanca that night, the guardia went directly to his captain. A convoy was mobilized.

The police found them the next morning at dawn on a high grassland in a solitary house of adobe. A conscripted peasant led them there. The police split into two groups, surrounded the house, then called out, demanding that the guerrillas surrender.

From the house there was no sound. A rooster crowed. The guardia opened fire.

Inside, they found all eight Senderistas sprawled out besides overturned bowls of breakfast. Lying among them was an old woman who had been cooking for them over a fire.

The founder of the Shining Path, Abimael Guzmán Reynoso, was born in 1934, the son of a small-time provincial businessman, who was married, and an unwed maid. For a time, Guzmán's mother lived near her lover's home in Arequipa, a resplendent colonial city whose cathedral and buildings are made of white volcanic pumice stone and which sits high up in Peru's southern Andes. When Guzmán was just a few years old, his mother decided to move, eventually leaving young Abimael with the family of a brother in Lima, on the coast. For all intents and purposes, by the time Guzmán was eight his mother had abandoned him. "My son, take care of your mother's child," his mother wrote to him in one of her last letters, "for you are in the best position to do so." In other words, it was up to Guzmán now to take care of himself. That was the last time he ever saw her.

By all accounts, Guzmán was quiet and introverted, stigmatized by his companions due to his illegitimate status yet nevertheless a good student. Abandoned and with neither brothers, sisters, nor friends, the young boy soon found escape through reading. He also liked to listen to the radio and go to the cinema. Guzmán's father, meanwhile, continued with his accounting practice in Arequipa, while keeping up a string of affairs. His illicit liaisons eventually produced a brood of at least ten half brothers and half sisters—all with different women—in addition to the children he had with his wife. Somehow Guzmán kept in touch with his distant patriarch and wrote to him sporadically. Then, when Guzmán was fifteen, one of his letters inadvertently fell into the hands of his father's wife. Rather than destroy it, however, she did the opposite: inviting her husband's illegitimate son to come live with them. Eventually, she did the same with Guzmán's other half siblings.

In Arequipa, Guzmán enrolled in a private school and kept a low profile. He enjoyed chess, he enjoyed reading, and he played a little soccer, but he was generally shy and kept his feelings to himself. When in groups, he gave the impression that he wanted to melt into the background. As his half sister Susana later said, "When I met him he [behaved] as if he thought . . . [his father's] family would be disappointed or as if he were a nuisance that people would prefer to sweep aside."

In 1950, when Guzmán was sixteen and during the dictatorship of General Manual Odría, students from a nearby *colegio* accused their director of misappropriating funds and then seized the school in protest.

When the mayor ordered a military attack with tanks, the students threw bricks in return. One of the students, a young Communist, was wounded and his compatriots carried him to Arequipa's central plaza. A mob of students soon gathered and entered the cathedral, ringing its bronze bells. As townspeople began to gather, some seized the military barracks while others pushed a piano from the second story onto the square. They then burned the barracks to the ground. Frustrated by the two-year-old dictatorship, the protestors next declared their independence from the government and began electing their own provisional council. What had begun as a student protest had metastasized into an uprising against the Peruvian state.

The dictatorship, alarmed by the events, quickly sent in troops. The army soon surrounded the city, then advanced toward the square. When the protestors sent a delegation to negotiate, the troops opened fire. A massacre ensued with the soldiers shooting many of the protestors and jailing the rest. At the time of the rebellion, Abimael Guzmán and his family lived only a few blocks away. As he later recounted:

> A lot of blood was shed . . . I saw the fighting spirit of the people . . . how the masses fought with uncontainable fury in response to the barbarous slaughter of the youth. And I saw how they fought the army, forcing them to retreat to their barracks. And how forces had to be brought in from other places in order to crush the people. This is an event that . . . has been imprinted quite vividly in my memory. Because there . . . I understood how the people . . . when they take to the streets and march, can make the reactionaries tremble, despite all their power.

Four years after the insurrection, Guzmán enrolled in Arequipa's *Universidad Nacional de San Agustín*. The bespectacled youth with the white skin and dark, wavy hair soon met his first love: the beautiful daughter of neighbors who were schoolteachers. Guzmán, by all accounts, fell for the girl head over heels. She reciprocated. Unlike in the Hollywood movies Guzmán so enjoyed, however, their love story did not end happily.

The girl was beautiful but had no money. Guzmán, although the son of a respectable, middle-class businessman, was illegitimate. The girl's parents thus feared that their daughter's suitor would inherit nothing. In a Peruvian version of *The Great Gatsby*, the girl's parents insisted that their daughter set her sights higher. The last time Guzmán saw his beloved was at the wedding of one of his cousins. The girl was attending with her parents, although the parents had forbidden her to see him. Guzmán bided his time, however, then asked her to dance. Out in the middle of the floor the couple danced for a while as the father looked on disapprovingly. Then the girl leaned forward toward Guzmán and told him something. According to Guzmán's sister, Susana, "I don't know exactly what happened, but she stopped dancing, her feet stopped in the middle of a song, and he had to leave her politely at one end of the room. . . . when the party was over, he went to his room, saw himself in the [full-length] mirror, and gave it such a kick that it shattered." That was the last time Guzmán ever mentioned her name. As Guzmán's half sister Susana later wrote,

> This girl . . . actually decided the current history of Peru. At that time . . . [Abimael] was still half Catholic, and if they had married at the time he would now be a rich lawyer. He loved her a great deal and he would have been careful to give her and their children everything they needed. Without her he had more time to think about what he called "the unjustness of life." He lost interest in himself, in his own safety and well-being. They say that in college he became a leftist, but I believe that ever since childhood he had always been one. Sofía was the only one who could have steered him away from that path, but she could not or would not. Because if she had wanted, her parents' orders would not have mattered. Well, such are the things in life!

The future leader of a guerrilla war that would eventually rip Peru in two, Guzmán was heartbroken—and single once again. He now poured himself into his twin majors of law and philosophy. Peru was still controlled by General Odría, and, like many university students, Guzmán joined the Communist Party, becoming part of a revolutionary cell that was made up of workers and intellectuals. Unlike most who joined, however, Guzmán was a philosophy student—he had thus read in depth the writings of Marx, Engels, and the other German philosophers. By the time Guzmán was twenty-seven, he'd graduated with a doctorate and a law degree. His twin dissertations were titled "About the Kantian Theory of Space" and "The Bourgeois-Democratic State." The latter title confirmed the obvious: that Guzmán was by now a confirmed Marxist.

"He was one of the best students in an epoch that was known for having brilliant ones," noted his mentor, the Arequipeñan philosophy professor Miguel Ángel Rodríguez Rivas. "He was a theoretician of the highest level."

Abimael Guzmán, now twenty-eight years old, accepted the job of philosophy professor in the small city of Ayacucho, a provincial Andean capital of seventeen thousand located in one of the poorest provinces in Peru. Many of the students at the local university were the sons and daughters of Quechua-speaking peasants, those who labored in the surrounding countryside on land they did not own. At the time of Guzmán's appointment in 1962, some four centuries after a group of Spanish conquistadors had brutally seized control of Peru, 0.1 percent of Peru's population owned 60 percent of the arable land, and 25 percent of Peruvians had no elementary school education while only 30 percent began secondary school. A whopping 30 percent of Peruvians were completely illiterate. Conditions in Ayacucho—one of twenty-five "states" or "regions" in Peru—were even worse. For Guzmán, whose access to higher education had been assured by his status as the son of a petit bourgeoisie businessman, his first contact with Peru's rural peasantry came as a shock. As he later wrote,

> Their reality opened my eyes and my mind . . . The peasants from
> Ayacucho are very poor . . . I saw people working as slaves on
> ranches, people who even had to provide their own food. I met

people who had to walk tens of kilometers, taking their own food with them, to work. I saw the peasants' struggles and the strong repressions. I could sense the plight of the poor Peruvian peasants who have struggled and worked in the communities for centuries. But the centuries have not managed to exterminate them. They are vigorous and fight against all odds. They are the cornerstone of the land. I saw that the peasants are the cornerstone of Peru.

Guzmán soon began instructing the sons and daughters of those same peasants—who somehow against the odds had managed to get into the university—in Greek and German philosophy, and especially in the philosophy of his favorite German philosopher, Karl Marx. Guzmán, without a doubt, was passionate about philosophy, and his students quickly discovered that he was an equally passionate teacher. As they had years earlier, philosophical discussions helped to bring Guzmán out of his shell. Slowly, the young professor began to gather a student following, often conducting informal discussions late into the night. Many of his students eventually took jobs as teachers in rural schools, passing on what they had learned from their professor to small classrooms of sandal-footed, Quechua-speaking students. Marx's philosophy thus began to spread slowly out from the university, like a dye staining wool, across the rugged terrain of Ayacucho.

In his spare time, Guzmán devoted himself to Peru's Communist Party, gradually rising in its ranks to secretary general. Although a philosophy professor dedicated to teaching, Guzmán was inevitably confronted by the "end game" of Marxian logic: "The philosophers," Marx wrote, "have only interpreted the world . . . the point is to change it." Marx had analyzed history and society and had concluded that violent revolution was necessary in order to achieve the "utopia" of Communist society. Marx himself, however, had lived most of his life in exile. The revolutionary battle he carried out was therefore theoretical, not physical. It was only after Marx's death that others—such as Lenin and Mao—carried out successful socialist revolutions.

During his incubation period in Ayacucho, nine thousand feet up in the Andes, Guzmán slowly came to the realization that his own destiny was no longer to teach, but to *act*—to put into motion the philosophy that so fascinated him. For most scholars, Marx's view of the "inevitable" evolution of society from primitive-to-capitalist-to-communist was a theory. For Guzmán, Marx's theory had become in his mind a natural *law* of human development. If the definition of a true believer is someone who "is strongly attached to a particular belief, depreciates the present, and glorifies the future," then Guzmán had clearly become a true believer. Like Marx, Guzmán began to believe that a glorious, stateless future awaited humanity—although that future might have to be prodded into existence with the help of guns. As Guzmán later declared,

> Let's remember, that . . . only the revisionists and opportunists are pessimists, the proletariat and communists are always optimists, because the future is ours—it is historically determined so long as we keep to our course.

Poverty was endemic in Peru, Guzmán believed, because the capitalists—beginning with the arrival of the Spanish conquistadors—owned everything and kept the masses oppressed. The only way to remove poverty, he reasoned, was to remove the capitalists from power. Shifting from the profession of teaching to that of a revolutionary leader, however, was a mental Rubicon that Guzmán could cross only with enormous personal consequences. He was a university professor, after all, a law-abiding wage earner. He was a member of the proletariat. Guzmán could easily continue to teach comfortably until the day he retired, with the satisfaction that he had taught his beloved Marxism to a large number of students. Perhaps one of these might someday become a revolutionary leader and set the Andes on fire. Sometime in the 1960s, however, Guzmán gradually shifted from seeing himself as a college professor to viewing himself as a future revolutionary leader. He already had a coterie of students who not only believed in what he was teaching but, just as important, believed in *him*. If he really *believed* what he was teaching,

Guzmán eventually realized, then the only logical conclusion was to put his words—that is, his *beliefs*—into action.

"The intellectuals: What can I say about them?" Guzmán later said, obviously distancing himself from the mere armchair philosopher. ". . . All they did was talk. It seems there are people for whom words are enough . . . [Yet] words can be easily crushed, no matter how right they may be."

In 1965, while Guzmán was still settling into life in Ayacucho, an insurrection erupted in Peru. Two armed bands of guerrillas began attacking haciendas and police posts in different areas of the Andes. The guerrillas belonged to the Movement of the Revolutionary Left (MIR), a group that believed in Che Guevara's theory that a small, armed band of revolutionaries, or *foco*, could gain the support of impoverished, local peasants and ignite a popular war. MIR was comprised mainly of middle-class students and professionals from Lima, however, who had no ability to speak Quechua and even less experience living in the Andes. Peru's armed forces—supplied with napalm and counterinsurgency advice by the United States—soon wiped out both groups, killing their leaders.

Two years later, in 1967, Che Guevara himself tried to test his *foco* theory in Bolivia, relying mostly upon a small group of Cuban revolutionaries and also a few Peruvians who had survived the 1965 disaster. Like the Lima-based, middle-class Peruvian guerrillas, however, Che's forces failed to incorporate even a single rural farmer into their group. Guevara and his troops knew little about the surrounding culture and had spent little if any time preparing the local population for armed warfare. The result was that the locals viewed the Cubans as foreigners and soon became informants. As with the guerrillas in Peru, the Bolivian army quickly isolated Guevara and his men from the local population, hunted them down, and exterminated them. Guzmán, an ardent student of guerrilla movements, studied the results of these insurrections carefully, later referring disdainfully to Guevara's aborted efforts as those of a "weekend guerrilla."

Che Guevara's failure, in fact, highlighted a number of perceived mistakes that Guzmán was determined to avoid. Clearly, it was important to base a revolutionary movement on guerrillas who understood the local conditions and culture. Inserting guerrillas from outside had proved to be a disaster. It was also important to prepare the local population for guerrilla warfare—to begin capturing the peasants' "hearts and minds" before the first shot was even fired. Only when the local population had been prepared politically, Guzmán concluded, should armed revolution begin. Guzmán therefore patiently continued his efforts of slowly spreading Marxist ideas throughout the Ayacucho area, confident that they would one day bear fruit. In 1976, after fourteen years as a university instructor and after having taught thousands of students, Guzmán quit the university and began to organize his movement full-time. Four years later, in 1980, on the eve of launching his war, Guzmán exhorted his small group of future revolutionaries at a final meeting, steeling them for what lay ahead:

> Comrades, we are entering the great rupture . . . the hour has arrived . . . We will be the protagonists of history: responsible, organized, and armed . . . we will be the makers of the last new dawn . . . the international proletariat and the peoples of the world, the working class, and the people of the nation, the Party with its committees, cells, and leaders: all of the great actions of the centuries have culminated at this moment in history. The promise unfolds, the future unfurls . . . What has been given to us as a future must be fulfilled with our lives, for the sake of the people, the proletariat, and Marxist-Leninist-Mao Zedong Thought. Comrades, the effort invested will reward itself by its accomplishments . . . The future lies in guns and cannons! The armed revolution has begun!

Less than a month later, on May 17, 1980, and after nearly two decades of carefully preparing the minds of his students for battle, Abimael Guzmán and a few hundred of his followers launched their revolution.

I meet Benedicto Jiménez Baca, a former lieutenant colonel in the Antiterrorism Police, in a quiet café in Surco, an upscale neighborhood of

Lima, in January 2011. Until recently, few in Peru or abroad really knew how Abimael Guzmán had been captured. Or, if they thought they did, they were wrong—as many stepped forward to take the credit for it afterward. "Success has a thousand fathers, and failure is an orphan," the saying goes. Only recently has it emerged that Benedicto Jiménez, now sixty-two years old, was the mastermind who actually defeated the Shining Path by capturing its leader. The reality is that it took three years of intense, high-stakes, mano a mano combat before Benedicto finally brought down the philosophy professor turned revolutionary Guzmán. And it was all done in secret.

Benedicto is tall and heavyset, with white curly hair, dark eyebrows, and light, coffee-colored skin. No one in the noisy café recognizes him. Yet, like Guzmán, he too changed the recent course of Peruvian history. Peru and Lima, in fact, have morphed profoundly since my first visit in the 1980s. The shantytowns of the city's exterior have shrunk, the economy is booming, and international aid organizations have recently reclassified Peru as a "middle-class" country, with an average per capita income of over $10,000. Even the region of Ayacucho, which helped to launch Sendero Luminoso's guerrilla war, has improved. None of this was due to the Shining Path having come to power and having implemented a communist utopia, but instead was the result of the movement's defeat, the resulting stabilization of the economy, and the end of the huge economic drain of the war.

"Peru, in 1990, was in a shambles," Benedicto tells me, sipping an espresso from a small cup, his eyebrows furled in a frown, his voice resonant and deep. "The government had used the same antiterrorism policy for ten years, and it was a complete disaster. Each year the Shining Path was getting stronger."

At the time the forty-eight-year-old Guzmán launched his war, Benedicto was a twenty-seven-year-old policeman, only four years out of the police academy. But if Guzmán was no ordinary philosophy professor, then Benedicto was no ordinary policeman. Born in 1953 in Peru's southern port town of Pisco, Benedicto was the son of a Greek woman who'd fled Europe during World War II and a black Peruvian laborer. The boy grew up in a series of poor neighborhoods, attended public schools for low-income families, and upon graduation from high school wanted to become an engineer. Benedicto couldn't afford to go to the university, however, so he applied for officer-training school at the police academy instead. If accepted, he knew he'd receive not only an education but also room and board.

Benedicto entered the academy in 1972, then rose to the top of his class for each year of the four years he was there. Upon graduation, he was taken under the wing of a retiring general who, a year later, asked the young officer if there was anything he could do for him. Benedicto immediately replied: he wanted to undergo commando ranger training. The young officer's answer surprised the general; it was like a newly minted police officer in the United States asking to undergo Navy SEAL training. The general granted his wish, however, and a year later Benedicto finished commando school. Of the thirty-three who began it, only seventeen finished. Benedicto is still the only police officer in Peru to have completed the rigorous training.

In 1978 Benedicto was assigned to work in an elite antinarcotics intelligence group that worked with the US Drug Enforcement Administration, or DEA. For several years he and his fellow officers learned to follow drug traffickers patiently, to uncover their networks of contacts, then to abruptly seize the entire network, dismantling the operation. It was training that Benedicto never forgot. By the time Benedicto had worked his way up through the system to the rank of major, he was working for Dircote, the antiterrorist police. Yet he felt constrained by the antiquated methodology they were using. "Dircote was fighting a 'reactive war,' " Benedicto explains to me, "not a 'proactive' war. It was exactly the opposite of the strategy we'd used against the narcotics traffickers."

In 1990, frustrated by the growth of the Shining Path and by the ineffectual methodology of both the Peruvian army and the police, Benedicto visited the police director, General Reyes Roca. If the general would allow him, Benedicto offered, he would set up a unit that would apply the same surveillance techniques he had used in the drug war—yet this time against the Shining Path. Only if they understood how the Shining Path functioned and how its leadership worked, he said, could they hope to defeat them. And the only way to do that was to start identifying and dismantling their clandestine networks. Benedicto did not mince words: either the general would allow him to start using these new techniques—or else he'd like to be transferred out of the antiterrorist police altogether.

General Roca listened carefully. He knew Benedicto and liked him. After the explanation, he nodded his head. A few months later, on March 4, 1990, Benedicto launched GEIN, the Peruvian acronym for "special intelligence group." Unlike the rest of Peru's police, they would not arrest Shining Path suspects. Instead, they would follow them. Benedicto and his agents would place suspects under surveillance, would keep track of whom the suspects visited and who visited them, and thus would start to gather information about the Shining Path's networks. Amazingly, after ten years of counterguerrilla warfare, no such system had ever been put into place.

"Guerrillas do not operate in isolation," Benedicto tells me. "They all receive orders and give orders." The Shining Path operated through a clandestine network, like a spiderweb, he says, a spiderweb that had been spun across Peru. The job of his unit was to find some of the web's threads and then to follow them. Hopefully, the threads would lead to the web's center—and there they might finally discover who was running the Shining Path.

Instead of simply trying to capture the inevitably low-ranking guerrillas immediately after an attack, who belonged to secret cells anyway and who knew little beyond their purposefully restricted universe, Benedicto's plan was to begin piecing together an organizational chart of Sendero's leadership. Once he understood how Sendero was organized and who its leaders were, he could then begin to dismantle the organization bit by bit, with the goal of taking down the entire superstructure.

"No one really knew who ran the Shining Path," Benedicto tells me. "No one had a clue as to who its leaders were or how the organization was structured. It was presumed that Guzmán was its leader, but no one had seen him in eleven years. Meanwhile, all of the counterinsurgency operations were 'search and destroy.' They seized terrorists, got no information out of them, then threw them into prison. The Peruvian government was simply lashing out—it was like a body reacting without a brain."

In his 1984 novel *The Real Life of Alejandro Mayta*, the Peruvian novelist Mario Vargas Llosa imagined a near future in which a revolutionary group resembling the Shining Path seized Peru's ancient Inca capital of Cusco, the next-to-last step before seizing Lima and coming to power:

> Amid the smoke and pestilence, you could make out the columns of people fleeing from the destroyed city, tripping over the broken pavement, covering their mouths and noses. The dead, the badly wounded, the very old, and the very young remained among the ruins. . . . From the heights, the survivors, parents, wounded, the fighters, the internationalists, all of them, with a minimum of fantasy, could hear the anxious tearing, the febrile pecking, the abject beating of [vultures'] wings, and smell the horrifying stench.

Six years after the novel's publication, when Benedicto Jiménez began to form his group in 1990, more and more Peruvians believed that Vargas Llosa's apocalyptic vision was about to become reality. Attacks were increasing. Shining Path assassination squads roamed the country's capital, almost at will. Blackouts were commonplace. Whole stretches of the Andes were now war zones. Peru was like a body in the midst of convulsion.

"We had very few resources to start out with," Benedicto tells me, "compared to the other agencies." His intelligence unit was given a tiny office that had one broken chair, a borrowed typewriter, and a single lightbulb that hung from the ceiling. At the end of the day, the lightbulb had to unscrewed, as there was no switch. Plywood had been nailed over the office's windows, which had no glass, thus light did not enter. Benedicto had asked for twenty agents. He was given five. They had no car. No phone. All surveillance, at first, was carried out on foot.

Not surprisingly, the new unit soon became the butt of jokes made by the other police groups, who called them disparagingly the "ghost busters." After all, the new unit supposedly followed guerrillas but made no arrests. To the rest of the police, the "special agents" appeared to spend their days reading Shining Path literature. They made curious diagrams on the wall. They often appeared ill shaven and unkempt.

Benedicto had a plan, however, and his handpicked agents—all of whom had worked for him before—followed it. They would use intelligence, not force, he told his agents at their first meeting. They would learn to outwit the Shining Path guerrillas, who until now had outwitted *them*. They would follow their operatives, they would diagram their networks, and then—and only when they were ready—they would dismantle those networks. They would work seven days a week, not five like the rest of the police. There would be no vacations. They would all be expected to work long hours. Their goal, Benedicto said—striding about in the small room with its single bulb as one agent sat in its only chair and the rest stood—was to uncover the networks until they reached the Shining Path's leaders.

"I had four small children at the time," Benedicto tells me, tapping the café table for emphasis. "I knew that if we failed, then Peru as I knew it would cease to exist. If the Shining Path came to power, I knew that I'd have to take my family into exile."

If you want to reach the top of a mountain, Benedicto told his agents over and over again, then you have to start by taking the first step. The intelligence group's "first step" was a small one—it was following up a lead Benedicto had received two years earlier but was not then in a position to do anything about. In 1988 a detective had handed him an anonymous letter that had been passed around the police department but that no one thought was important enough to follow up on. The letter was written by an anguished mother, a retired schoolteacher. The woman was worried about the future of her son, an excellent university student, she wrote, but one who had fallen in love with a girl whom she believed belonged to the Shining Path. Despite the mother's anger and tears, her son refused to break up with the girl. The mother was so distraught that he, too, might become a guerrilla that she took a drastic step: she arranged for her and her son to leave the country. Before she did so, however, she wanted to divulge the name of the girlfriend to the police: her name was Judith Díaz Contreras. She lived on the 400 block of Lunes Pizarro Street, in the poor Lima neighborhood of La Victoria. Soon after writing the letter, the woman and her son left the country.

Peru's police had not followed up on the tip because they had larger fish to fry: they were busy investigating ("reacting to," as Benedicto would say) a variety of bomb blasts, terrorist attacks, and assassinations. They had no time to investigate whether someone's girlfriend was a member of the Shining Path. They were interested in *attacks*—not in potential attackers.

In March 1990, Benedicto's agents tracked down the address the mother had left and found that her son's ex-girlfriend, Judith, was still there, living with her parents. They soon tapped the family's phone and began transcribing the conversations. Meanwhile, when the girl went out, an agent would follow her, pretending to be a pedestrian. Each day a different agent would follow her, then they would rotate. At first, everything seemed to be normal. The girl, it turned out, was an administrative employee at Lima's National Agrarian University. Later, however, Benedicto's men discovered something curious. When the girl was out, her father routinely answered the phone and wrote down orders that were placed for his daughter. The orders were for soap, detergent, toothpaste, nails, screws, and other commonplace items. What attracted the agents' attention, however, was that they never saw the girl carrying any of these things. They soon began to suspect that the orders were some kind of Shining Path code.

Following the girl was difficult, especially since Benedicto's unit had no automobile. Two weeks after their surveillance began, however, Benedicto discovered a broken-down Volkswagen Beetle in the garage of the technical police. Benedicto asked if he could use the car if he got it fixed. The technical police agreed. He then took it to a mechanic friend who fixed it for free. The special police intelligence group now had its first automobile. Not long afterward, Benedicto scrounged a video camera and two bulky portable radios. The agents following Judith now began compiling video of their suspect.

Judith's movements soon led them to a second suspect, a girl who lived nearby named Miriam. Unlike Judith, Miriam was well trained in how to avoid being followed. She often climbed in and out of crowded buses, walked a block or two, reversed her tracks, then promptly jumped into a taxi and disappeared into Lima's congested traffic. Slowly, however, the agents became more adept at following both suspects. With their new portable radios, video camera, and car, they began coordinating their surveillance activities. If Miriam exited her house and jumped onto a crowded bus, an agent would get on the same bus. Two other agents would then call headquarters and soon Benedicto would arrive, driving the recently salvaged Volkswagen. The two agents would then pile into the car and the three would try to follow the bus as best as they could.

Because there were so few agents, Benedicto's men gradually began to adopt disguises so that they wouldn't be recognized. They would frequently change their clothes and jackets, put on false beards or mustaches, put on or take off hats, and would adopt different walking styles, all so that their quarry would be unable to detect them. Some agents became especially adept at posing as garbagemen, street sweepers, or the homeless—returning to their own homes at night with a disgusting stench yet unable to explain to their wives what they had been doing.

On June 1, 1990, after nearly three months of surveillance, Benedicto ordered the arrest of the Shining Path network they had uncovered.

"Unfurl the storm," he commanded via his radio and in his deep, baritone voice.

It was a code phrase for his agents to begin making the arrests.

By the end of that day, thirty-one Shining Path suspects had been captured, including Sybila Arredondo, the widow of the Peruvian novelist José María Arguedas—the same woman I had met briefly in Canto Grande prison two years earlier. In another house that Benedicto's agents raided, in the wealthy suburb of Monterrico, the intelligence team hit pay dirt. After arresting three women inside the two-story home, they began exploring its various rooms.

"Chief, come here quickly," one of the agents soon radioed Benedicto.

"What's happening?" he answered.

"Just come here quickly—we need your help!"

Shortly after he arrived, Benedicto was amazed by what they had found.

"It was Sendero's archive," he tells me, draining the last of his coffee. "Books, papers, documents—even Guzmán's private library." In a small bedroom upstairs, they found a single bed, thick eyeglasses, a man's well-worn boots, and even medicine for a skin condition that Guzmán was known to suffer from: psoriasis.

"It was at that moment that we knew that Guzmán was still alive— that he was still leading the Shining Path," Benedicto says. "We had found a 'safe house' that he sometimes used."

More important, the documents they'd seized allowed Benedicto to begin to understand Sendero's unusual structure—and why it was so difficult to disrupt. As Benedicto and his detectives pored over each document and began to draw organizational diagrams on the walls of their office, a picture slowly began to emerge. At the top of the Shining Path's organization was the Central Committee, or Comité Central, composed of Guzmán and eighteen others. Below the Central Committee were a number of organizations that the Central Committee directed: the Political Bureau and the departments of organizational support, logistics, propaganda, legal support, and so on. Each region in Peru where Sendero operated had its own subdepartments, reaching all the way down to the smallest clandestine party cells. Abimael Guzmán, meanwhile, was not only the president of the Central Committee but was also military commander and president of the organizing committee. The latter was the network that made up the New Democratic and Popular Republic of Peru—the name the Shining Path leadership had decided that Peru would be called in the future.

What was both unusual and brilliant about the Shining Path's structure, Benedicto realized, was the fact that not only was the Shining Path operating as a kind of clandestine "shadow government" as it patiently worked to demolish the Peruvian state, but each of its departments and substructures had their own "mirror copies." If the police or army succeeded in liquidating one of Sendero's structures, an identical structure had already been preformed and was ready to spring into place. Like a shark whose teeth, once lost, are immediately replaced from rows behind, Sendero Luminoso had created a structure designed to withstand the brutal exigencies of guerrilla warfare. If Sendero's soldiers in the front line went down, new ones were ready to leap into action. The same was true for its larger structures—the equivalent of platoons and even regiments. After piecing together its organizational structure and marveling at how well it functioned, Benedicto eventually realized that the Shining Path was not perfect, however—and that in fact he may have just stumbled across a fatal organizational flaw.

"They had no replacement for the Comité Central," Benedicto says, seemingly still surprised by his discovery.

"We realized that if we could just reach Guzmán and his group," Benedicto tells me, "then we could capitalize on a colossal mistake: they had forgotten to organize replacements for *themselves.*"

One day in early July 1992, in the upscale Lima neighborhood of Los Sauces, the front door of a well-appointed, two-story home opened, a young architect with a black goatee emerged carrying a briefcase, while the young man's wife—a pretty, white-skinned ballet dancer—kissed her husband good-bye, then closed the door as he went off to work. The young ballet dancer was Maritza Garrido Lecca, a twenty-seven-year-old upper-middle-class woman from Lima who ran a dance studio on the first floor of her home. The man's name was Carlos Inchaustegui, thirty-two years old, a graduate of Lima's Ricardo Palma University. The couple had been together for four years. Neither had ever been arrested or had any police record.

As the young man walked to work, past a small convenience store next to his home and past the row homes on his block, all of which had

small gardens surrounded by ornate, wrought-iron gates out front, neither her nor his wife had any idea that their home had recently been put
under police surveillance. Just one block away, on the third story of a
similar-looking house, a group of Benedicto's men had begun watching
the couple's home based on a tip that the two belonged to the Shining
Path and just might be connected to its leadership.

By this time, Benedicto managed a group of fifty agents, all of
whom were better equipped than they had been at the beginning two
years earlier. They now had portable radios and electronic surveillance
equipment, and they had received training and some financial support
from the Central Intelligence Agency of the United States. After their
first successful roundup of the thirty-one Shining Path members in
June 1990, Benedicto's men had continued to score more successes. On
December 19, 1990, the team "rolled up" most of the Shining Path's
propaganda division. A month later, they raided a house in the upscale
neighborhood of San Borja, only to discover that Guzmán had left this
particular safe house just three days earlier.

"We were getting close," Benedicto tells me. "We were breathing
down Guzmán's neck—and he knew it. We also knew that he was based
in Lima—and not in the jungle or the Andes. He was right here in the
capital. We were all operating in the same city."

During the raid on Guzmán's safe house, Benedicto's men discovered another treasure trove of Sendero material, packed into card-
board boxes that the guerrillas intended to transport elsewhere but
that the raid had prevented. In one of the boxes, inside a small plastic
bag, an agent found a small collection of videotapes. Benedicto arrived shortly afterward and soon radioed a request for a video camera.
When it arrived, he put a tape in and began watching images on the
camera's tiny screen. He was stunned by the images that appeared.
After twelve years in clandestinity, Abimael Guzmán could be seen in
a series of video clips, dancing at a party with the highest members
of Sendero's leadership—the Comité Central. Guzmán was by now
fifty-six years old, bearded, heavyset, and wore thick glasses. He also
wore a kind of dark, Chinese-style tunic. As Benedicto peered at the

screen, he watched speechlessly as Guzmán raised a hand over his head, his arm arched, while the rest of the Comité looked on, smiling and clapping. The music was from the soundtrack of the movie *Zorba the Greek.*

"Chief, what are you watching?" one of the agents asked.

"Pornography—pure pornography," Benedicto answered.

"No one had seen him in twelve years," Benedicto tells me. "Now here he was—dancing. Suddenly we not only had his image but also the images of the rest of the Central Committee. They were celebrating the end of their Third Congress."

The next day, Peruvians woke to find on their television screens the images of the Shining Path leader, Abimael Guzmán, broadcast for the first time, and quixotically dancing to a Greek tune with the rest of his Peruvian entourage. Despite the raid, however, Sendero's attacks on Lima continued to increase. On July 16, 1992, a car bomb exploded in an upscale area of Lima, killing twenty-four people and wounding two hundred more. The blast destroyed or damaged four hundred local businesses. Guzmán was purposely stepping up his attacks on the capital, certain that he was now close to seizing power.

"Guzmán was beginning to get worried, however," Benedicto says. "We'd had some successes, had made some important captures. He knew that a special group of police had been formed and that we were getting closer and closer."

Soon after the seizure of their archive, the Shining Path directorate sent out warnings to all of its members. They were to tighten up security procedures and use all of the counterintelligence measures they had developed over the years. Each one of them should behave as if he or she were being watched and followed.

By the time Benedicto's group received the tip on the ballet dancer and her presumed husband, the intelligence group was conducting surveillance on numerous suspects in a variety of locations. They were also continuing their patient methodology of collecting as much information on a specific Sendero network before abruptly "disarticulating" it. At first, the agents assigned to the young dancer, whom they nicknamed Lola, and her partner, whom they nicknamed Lolo, saw nothing suspicious. Each morning, the young man walked to work and each afternoon he came home. Young dance students, meanwhile, appeared regularly at their house to receive dance lessons from Lola. The visiting dancers, too, were followed—but nothing seemed out of the ordinary. At the same time, agents posing as trash men began collecting the trash in front of the couple's home, which they nicknamed the "castle." Nothing seemed amiss. The trash contained exactly what one would expect from a young couple living together.

Always short of agents, Benedicto finally ordered that surveillance on the "castle" be suspended. Two of his agents, however, following their instincts, continued anyway, including the collection of trash. Eventually, something odd caught their attention: cigarettes. Picking through the couple's trash, the agents realized that eight to ten cigarette butts were showing up each day. Yet after watching the couple carefully, they never saw either of them smoking. The detectives then discovered something else: all of the cigarette butts came from only two brands: Winston Lights and Yves Saint Laurent. On a hunch, they reviewed the video tape of Guzmán dancing *Zorba the Greek*. In one video clip, on a small table, they noticed two cigarette packs. The two detectives peered closely at the images and then looked at one another: one pack was Winston Lights; the other was Yves Saint Laurent.

The detectives quickly alerted Benedicto and overnight a full surveillance team was reinstalled. One day not long afterward, while out shopping and unaware that she was being followed, Lola threw a piece of crumpled up paper into a sewage drain. Reaching his arm into the smelly hole, the agent was able to retrieve the paper. It was a receipt from a drugstore for medicine. The agent then peered at it more carefully: it was a medicine used to treat psoriasis. And Abimael Guzmán, the agent knew, had suffered from psoriasis for years.

The following week, on September 8, 1992, a night attack by Shining Path guerrillas cut the electricity to Lima, blacking out most of the city. While a pair of Benedicto's agents observed the "castle" from their darkened room, they watched through binoculars as Lola lit candles on the first floor of her home. A few moments later, a single candle appeared in one of the upstairs rooms. As the city lay in darkness and the detectives peered through the night, a silhouette appeared on the thin curtain of the upstairs room. It was a silhouette—like a phantom, the detectives later said—of a heavyset man with a large beard, standing between the curtain and the candle.

"I can't believe what my eyes are seeing," whispered one agent to the other.

In the late afternoon of Saturday, September 12, 1992, twenty undercover GEIN agents in various disguises infiltrated the neighborhood around the home where Maritza Garrido Lecca and Carlos Inchaustegui lived. Only hours before, Benedicto Jiménez, leader of the Special Intelligence group that he had formed just two and a half years earlier, had issued his coded radio command: "Unfurl the storm." On this occasion, however, his objective was different from previous ones. Today was a day in which there was a very real possibility that—unless their analysis of the evidence was mistaken or they arrived too late—they might finally be in a position to capture the leader of the Shining Path, Abimael Guzmán Reynoso.

"We were on edge," says Benedicto, who remained in his office with radio contact that day. "Many of us believed that Guzmán was always accompanied by a kind of 'suicide guard,' special Shining Path members who were ready to sacrifice their lives to protect him."

At 5:30 in the afternoon, just as dusk was falling and before all of the agents were in place, an unknown couple arrived in a car, got out, and knocked on the young couple's door. Maritza opened it and the couple went in. Had their cover been blown, the agents wondered? Had the pair been tipped off?

"Wait for movement," Benedicto ordered, following his policy of not breaking down doors but instead of waiting for someone to enter or leave

a residence so that access and surprise were easier. His method, however, required that an agent be as close to the residence as possible, as timing was critical and often a quick decision had to be made.

Yet on the isolated residential street where the young Shining Path couple lived, keeping an agent close to the house without being noticed was difficult. On this particular evening it was decided that two young officers, themselves a couple, would pretend to have a romantic rendezvous in the small, open-fronted convenience store located beside the suspects' home.

The two plainclothes agents, Becerra and Cecilia, ordered Cokes, then stood chatting and embracing each other while the rest of the agents listened to their radios nervously, waiting for something to happen. Was Guzmán inside? And if he were, would he be surrounded by a retinue of fanatics with guns? No one knew.

Finally, at 8:40 p.m., the door of the suspects' house opened. The visiting couple began walking out, followed by Maritza and her husband. The two officers, Becerra and Cecilia, meanwhile, quickly abandoned the store and began running toward the house, drawing their guns. It was now or never. Their job was to force their way inside, making sure that the door of the house stayed open until the other agents arrived. Becerra was twenty-four years old. Cecilia was twenty-two.

Four people had by now emerged from the house: the two visitors along with Maritza and her husband. The group formed a small circle in front of the house, near the open door, unaware that they were in danger. As they were smiling and saying good-bye to one another, they suddenly saw a woman sprinting toward them, her gun drawn, and shouting:

"Halt! We're police! You're under arrest!"

The foursome froze, turning to face the unknown man and woman running toward them with guns in hand. The two clearly did not look like police. The first to react was the architect, Inchaustegui, who lurched toward Becerra, grabbing him and trying to wrestle away his gun. Maritza, the ballet dancer, meanwhile, started to shout. As the two men grappled and Maritza shouted as loudly as she could, a gun suddenly exploded. It was Cecilia—she had just fired her revolver into the air, and the sound made the suspects freeze. Becerra now wrenched himself free of the architect and rushed toward the open door, leaving Cecilia to watch over the suspects. As Cecilia shouted for them to get on the ground, Becerra burst through the door, his gun ready to fire.

Inside, the young detective found himself in a large room. To the right was a stairway, and he immediately ran toward it, then began taking giant steps up the stairs. His orders had been to secure the second floor, which was presumably where Abimael Guzmán was located. Halfway up the stairway he saw a middle-aged woman's face above look at him briefly through the gap in a partially opened plywood door. She then quickly slammed it shut.

Reaching the top of the stairway, Becerra threw his shoulder against the door, breaking it open just in time to see the woman disappear down a hallway and into a room. Becerra ran after her, aiming his gun, then raced into the room.

Inside, a heavyset man with a thick beard and glasses sat in a leather chair. Standing next to him was the woman Becerra had seen as well as two other women, all facing toward the strange intruder who had suddenly invaded their home. The heavyset man stood up as Becerra trained his gun on him. The women began shouting.

"Shut up, God dammit!" Becerra yelled. "You're under arrest! I'm police!"

The heavyset man froze, his eyes opened wide.

There was no doubt about it: standing before Becerra was Abimael Guzmán, the leader of the Shining Path.

It's a twenty-minute bus ride from the upscale neighborhood of Los Sauces, where Guzmán was captured, to the more middle-class district of Chorrillos, a busy neighborhood that sprawls alongside the sea. On a bright Sunday afternoon in January—Lima's summer—I get off at the stop for the Penal de Santa Monica, the women's prison. Incarcerated within its high walls is Maritza Garrido Lecca, the former ballet dancer who, nearly twenty years after her capture on September 12, 1992, still remains in prison. Maritza was twenty-seven the night she was arrested. Now she is forty-six. In captivity with her are some forty political prisoners, including Guzmán's wife, Elena Iparraguirre, and the other two women—all part of Sendero's Comité Central—who had tried to form a protective ring around their leader the night of his arrest. Guzmán himself remains in isolation in a naval prison across the city in the port of Callao, serving a life sentence. He is not allowed to receive visitors.

The women's prison with its brick walls, barbed wire, and guard towers contrasts strangely with the busy motorway before it and with the pedestrians in shorts and T-shirts going about their weekend activities. In a nearby supermarket, I purchase a large plastic container of shampoo, a large container of hair conditioner, three tubes of toothpaste, four bars of soap, skin-softening cream, detergent, and a large sweet cake, or *paneton*. I then cross the street to the squat, drab, olive-colored prison and join a line of men and women visiting their relatives inside. Most of the pedestrians walking along the boulevard here have little knowledge of those incarcerated within the prison's walls. Many, however, have heard of the story of Maritza, the ballet dancer, who was captured while hiding the leader of the Shining Path. In 2002 the American actor John Malkovich directed a movie, *The Dancer Upstairs*, based upon a 1995 novel of the same name. The film is a fictionalized portrait of a dancer, a guerrilla leader, and the police officer trying to hunt down the guerrilla leader. Javier Bardem plays the officer, who ultimately falls in love with the dancer. At the time the novel was written, however, its author, Nicholas Shakespeare, had no idea who Benedicto Jiménez was, nor any idea of how Guzmán had actually been captured.

On that particular night, Benedicto was actually sitting in his office with General Ketin Vidal Herrera—the director of the investigative police—and with a CIA agent whom Benedicto's men referred to as "Superman," due to the agent's large size and build. "He looked like [the actor] Christopher Reeve," Benedicto told me. When Benedicto's agents rushed into the room to find Becerra pointing a gun at Guzmán, one of them quickly radioed their chief that they had found the Shining Path leader, whom they had code named *el cachetón*, or "Chubby Cheeks."

"*Tenemos el cachetón!*" the voice came through ("We have Chubby Cheeks!").

Benedicto and the other two men immediately leapt from their chairs and high-fived each other. Then the CIA agent "Superman" made a quick phone call to the president of the United States, George H. W. Bush.

"He [Bush] was the first person to find out," Benedicto told me. "Before Fuji [Peru's president, Alberto Fujimori], before anyone."

Guzmán, who had lived clandestinely for more than a dozen years, was removed from the house he had been hiding in that same night. The agents took him to Benedicto's headquarters, where they interrogated him for fifteen days—the limit allowed by Peruvian law at the time. The Shining Path leader was composed and relaxed, Benedicto said. Benedicto's men were also respectful, addressing him as *Doctor*. "We found that if we treated him as a professor, then he was the most comfortable and was the most inclined to talk." And Guzmán, Benedicto said, was quite a talker. Although the Shining Path leader wouldn't give the agents' names or other kinds of actionable information, he *would* discuss politics, ideology, and history. It was perhaps no surprise that a man who'd spent most of his life in rooms reading books, who had limited contact with outsiders yet had been running the largest guerrilla operation in the history of Peru, had a great deal to say.

As Benedicto later recounted,

> You had to know quite a bit simply to be able to hold a conversation with him. He could talk a whole day about Simón Bolívar. Then about Beethoven's *Ninth*. Then about Mozart. Then about history and about [Peru's] Armed Forces. Or about philosophy. He was an encyclopedia.

At one point, Benedicto said, Peru's minister of the interior, Juan Briones Dávila, stopped by to visit the onetime academic and now infamous revolutionary leader.

"Doctor," the minister asked Guzmán, with furrowed brow, "why so many *deaths*?"

"Why are you so surprised?" Guzmán responded. "How many children die in this country each year from hunger? From malnutrition? Who are the *real* assassins? I have already calculated that," the bearded revolutionary said emphatically, "and it's the [Peruvian] state."

According to Benedicto, the minister soon shrugged his shoulders and left. (Ironically, both the minister and Peru's president, Alberto Fujimori, would later be thrown in prison themselves for carrying out a coup d'état and abusing their powers.)

One thing that surprised Benedicto was a story Guzmán told about how he'd had close run-ins with the police twice before his capture. For health and logistical reasons, Guzmán had lived in Lima ever since launching his armed struggle in 1980. Yet before Benedicto's men discovered the video of Guzmán and his cadres dancing to *Zorba the Greek*, few in Peru had seen the revolutionary leader's image. Occasionally, Guzmán would travel across the capital or to nearby cities. To do so, he would dress up in an elegant three-piece suit, and then would take a seat in the back of a well-appointed car with tinted windows. His wife, meanwhile—the second-in-command—would often drive him, acting as a chauffeur. On such occasions Guzmán carried fake identity papers stating that he was an engineer.

One day in the late 1980s, Guzmán recounted, his wife drove off the road while traveling outside of Lima and their car became stuck in a ditch. A police car soon pulled up and an officer got out. Walking over to their car, the officer asked them what the problem was. Guzmán's wife calmly explained what had happened while Guzmán remained in the backseat. Eventually, the officer helped them get their car out, then waved as the two most wanted fugitives in Peru quietly drove away.

Another time, Guzmán said, he was similarly being driven in a car when they were pulled over by the police. Although he and his wife had fake documents, they were missing some legal papers for the car. The policeman bent over by the driver's side, looked through the window, took stock of the well-dressed passenger, then demanded a small bribe in order to forget about the lack of a permit. Guzmán's wife paid the money, the policeman returned to his car, and the two Shining Path leaders once again quickly disappeared.

Two weeks after Guzmán's capture, the military removed him from Benedicto's control and took the revolutionary leader to the nearby island of San Lorenzo, just off the coast of Lima. Although Peru's constitution prohibited capital punishment, President Fujimori and his secretive head of intelligence, Vladimiro Montesinos, wanted Guzmán dead, and as soon as possible. Fujimori quickly signed a presidential decree ordering the execution, a firing squad was selected, and the final arrangements were made. The plan called for Guzmán's wife to be brought in front of him. She was to be offered life in prison if she revealed everything she knew. If she refused, then she would be shot. Guzmán, who was to witness either his wife's death or betrayal, would then be shot. Peru's Council of Ministers, however, refused to sign the decree, and Guzmán's life was spared. Eventually, Guzmán and his wife were sentenced to life in prison. The former ballet dancer, Maritza Garrido Lecca, and the architect, Carlos Inchaustegui, were sentenced to twenty-five and twenty-two years, respectively. Nineteen years into Maritza's sentence, I pass through the prison doors in Chorrillos and give the guards her name.

Inside the second floor of prison Block B, I wait in a large cement visiting room that has an assortment of aqua blue tables and chairs. Visitors sit with inmates and converse. Most of the prisoners in Block B are Shining Path members, although some are also common prisoners. No guards circulate within the block. Here, it is the prisoners who have control, yet the atmosphere is quiet, like a women's social club. Everyone is friendly and polite.

Maritza arrives, wearing pants and a checkered shirt. Her shoulder-length dark hair is flecked with gray, and she has dark eyebrows, a bright white smile, and green eyes. Although she's been in prison now for nearly two decades, she's slender as a dancer and still pretty. What sets her apart from the prison setting is her skin color. While the other Shining Path members in the room are all brown-skinned, of mixed Spanish-Indian ancestry, Maritza is white and looks Iberian. Rare among Sendero, she grew up among Lima's upper middle class.

"I used to run away from interviews and journalists," she says, sitting beside me on a bench and smiling. I hand her the bag of toiletries, and she thanks me. She is neat and clean, wears no makeup, and has small freckles or age marks. "The journalists had their agenda, and I was pilloried in the Peruvian press. They painted me as this 'rare bird.' I am *not* a rare bird," she says, shaking her head.

"You're from the middle class, you were a ballerina, and you were living in the same house as the leader of the Shining Path," I tell her. "So you *are* a rare bird." She thinks about this for a moment, then nods resignedly.

I ask her what happened after she was captured. She was held by the antiterrorism police for fifteen days, she tells me. "Did they torture you?" I ask. "No," she says. Her case was so high profile that they didn't dare. After fifteen days of interrogation, she was sent to a military base in Lima. At first, she received a life sentence, under the military courts. The judge and the prosecutors wore hoods. Then, when civilian rule returned, she was retried in a civilian court. A jury found her guilty, and she was sentenced to twenty years. The prosecutor then asked for five more, she says, and the court granted him that. After her first sentence, she was transferred to a prison in Puno, located thirteen thousand feet up in Peru's southern Andes.

"It was very hard," says the woman who grew up in one of Lima's toniest beachfront neighborhoods. The weather in Puno was very dry, very cold. Her skin cracked and opened. She was kept in isolation. No books, no papers, no anything. She remembers pounding through ice to get water, the same icy water she bathed with. Maritza remained in that Andean prison for seven and a half years. I do a quick mental calculation: that was where she spent the years from age twenty-seven to thirty-five.

In 2001, after she was transferred to another prison, the authorities decided to return her to Lima, to the prison in Chorrillos where we now are, not far from where she grew up. Her father visits her every two weeks. He is eighty-four, she says. Maritza feels badly because she realizes that her parents will probably die before she is to be released, in 2017. Her father had a heart attack after she was arrested. If she is released on schedule, she will be fifty-two years old.

I ask about her upbringing. She was very religious when she was young, she says. Her parents were and still are Opus Dei, a secretive branch of the Catholic Church. Opus Dei members generally do not admit their religious affiliation in public. It was her Catholic education, she says, that made her conscious of the poor and the downtrodden, who were abundant outside her neighborhood. I ask if she is religious now. She says she isn't.

A week earlier I'd spoken with one of Maritza's relatives in the relative's posh home in Miraflores. She and her family were gathered around a large wooden table with an intricate spread of Peruvian cheeses, olives, fresh bread, slices of ripe guava, cherries, grapes, smoked trout, white wine, and Porto. It's the kind of lifestyle that Maritza—given her upbringing, social standing, and education—would have been enjoying if her life had mimicked those of her peers.

"She was very curious, very open as a young girl," her relative, who is in her sixties, said. "Dance was the most important thing to her." When Maritza was sixteen, the woman said, she backpacked around Peru on her own—an almost unheard of thing for a young upper-middle-class girl to do. Around six years before her capture, when she was twenty-one, Maritza left home, began teaching dance, and putting on recitals, which she elaborately choreographed. Her recitals, however, gradually became more and more political as the war with the Shining Path intensified and stark headlines filled the newspapers.

"She would choreograph things so that some dancers lay on the floor, like dead bodies," her relative said. "She covered them in newspapers with headlines about [Shining Path] bomb attacks and army massacres. Her parents became more and more concerned."

"Do you believe in armed revolution?" I ask Maritza suddenly. She looks at me with open green eyes and says that she does, "at the right time and place." We dance around the subject of armed revolution for a while. She is, after all, serving a lengthy prison sentence and has never admitted to aiding or abetting the Shining Path or to helping its leader,

Abimael Guzmán. Her legal stance is that she had no idea the president of the Shining Path lived on the floor above her. Benedicto, however, has assured me privately that the only way that anyone upstairs could have left the house was to descend the stairway and walk through the downstairs. The upstairs rooms where Guzmán and his cadres lived had no separate entrance. Maritza, Benedicto said, was in charge not only of helping to hide Guzmán but also of transporting high-ranking Shining Path members to and from Guzmán's safe house, so that they could hold meetings. "She was one of Guzmán's inner circle," he told me simply.

It's noontime, and a woman arrives bringing us two plastic plates of food, heaped with rice and chicken. "I don't believe that if there is a civil war going on in your country that you can remain on the fence," Maritza tells me quietly, picking at the rice with a fork. "You have to choose. You can't say 'I don't know.' "

"Is your belief based on Marx?" I ask.

Marx made it clear, Maritza says, that man's problems began with private property. Thus private property has to be done away with. I tell her about how I once lived with an Amazonian tribe (the Yaminahua) and about how they would attack and kill members of other tribes in order to steal their possessions. In my opinion, man coveted property long before there were police forces or capitalism. The problem lies perhaps not in capitalism, I tell her, but in the human condition.

She thinks about this for a few moments, then turns to me: "Then we have a real problem!" she says. We both laugh. "What are we going to *do*?" she asks rhetorically.

In speaking with Maritza, I can see that she still has faith, as Che Guevara did and as many religious groups still do, that man can be perfected, that he can be imbued with the spirit of solidarity, of community. And that that solidarity can somehow transcend one group dominating another. I tell her that I have my doubts, that when Che visited the Soviet Union, he was taken aback by how the Soviet leadership clearly coveted material things. Soviet leaders had more access to material goods, and they quickly formed their own elite.

"When did he visit?" she asks.

"In the early nineteen-sixties."

"Ah, yes, it [the Soviet Union] had already changed."

She asks what my opinion is, and I tell her that no one has yet figured out how to equably govern mankind, and that *all* societies, after agriculture was invented, have ended up with an elite on top, whether the Chimu or the Incas or the US or the Soviets.

"Look what happened to the Bolshevik Revolution after Stalin took over," I say.

"Stalin has been greatly distorted," she says.

"But he killed *millions!*"

"Yet look at the circumstances he was laboring under," she says. "Like World War Two!"

"But the pact he made with Hitler," I say, "was *before* the war."

"I think there has been a lot of distortions made about him," she says firmly.

Talking to Maritza I think at times she is lively and open and completely normal; at other times, I think she is crazy. When she speaks about something she is passionate about, she uses her arms and hands for emphasis and she has the habit of showing her lower teeth, making almost but not quite a grimace. At other times, she breaks into a nice, easy, and relaxed smile. Clearly, like Guzmán, Maritza believes in the infallibility of Marxism-Leninism. Marx's predictions about social evolution are not theories for her, but ineluctable *laws*. First as an Opus Dei Catholic, then as a Shining Path revolutionary, she was and still is a true believer. Guzmán, I have read, admires Stalin. So does Maritza. Guzmán hates the "revisionists"—the Chinese and Soviets who destroyed Communism. So does Maritza. Like Guzmán, Maritza believes that capitalism and the United States are the world's biggest problems. I mention that both China and Russia are now capitalist. She is aware of that, she says. But that is because of the revisionists.

"Why do you think we failed?" she asks me suddenly.

"Because they caught Guzmán."

She nods.

"It's like riding in a car without a driver," she says quietly.

I mention that before Guzmán's capture, Sendero seemed to be on an upward trajectory, that Peru's military didn't seem able to stop it.

Not true, she says. There had been important setbacks. She is referring to various guerrillas and safe houses captured by Benedicto's men. Things were getting hot for the leadership, she says. That's when the Shining Path asked her a very important question.

"They knocked at my door and said they needed help," she says, turning to look at me. "So I had to decide, 'yes' or 'no'? When they knock at your door," she says quietly, "what do you *do?*"

I can't help but think that the answer she delivered will ultimately have kept her behind bars for twenty-five years.

Our conversation at an end, Maritza accompanies me downstairs. At the exit to the cellblock, she gives me a hug and a kiss on the check, then returns to the cell she is staying in, where she is scheduled to spend another six years. I walk out of the block, turn to the right, then right again. I show the guards the number they had written on my arm in ink earlier; they check it against their notebook registry, then hand me back my passport. I exit the prison's metal doors, out into the sunlight and onto the Avenida Huaylas, past the lines of visitors waiting to go inside, then take a bus headed to the neighborhood of Miraflores. The air is humid, and the streets are full of people, some dressed for the beach, others in shorts, the whole area lively with people enjoying themselves. As I gaze out the window, something the Peruvian historian Nelson Manrique wrote drifts into my mind:

> The armed insurrection of the Shining Path is the clearest and crudest expression of the deformed social order that has reigned in Peru for centuries, since its formation as a state during the colonial era. To overcome this situation will require very profound structural changes. *Sendero Luminoso* placed on the agenda the unpostponable necessity of carrying out radical social reforms. The defeat of this group does not mean that the factors that generated it have been eliminated. The causes of the Peruvian crisis have not [yet] been radically attacked.

"The conditions of poverty, corruption, misery, and hunger still exist," Benedicto had told me the week before. "They have not been overcome. As long as these conditions exist, the possibility of terrorism continues."

I reflect on the fact that, although the percentage of Peruvians living in poverty has declined during the last ten years from more than 50 percent to roughly 30 percent, that is still a lot of people living in poverty.

"The only thing missing [to ignite things again]," Benedicto said, "is the ideology—nothing more." Revolutionary ideology is like a lighter fluid, I muse. But it evaporates unless it's poured onto the hard-burning fuel of thwarted expectations. If a society is purring along smoothly and its citizens are well fed, then revolution is an impossibility—Marx or no Marx.

During one of Abimael Guzmán's last days in Benedicto's custody, several agents took the Shining Path leader to a large room. Inside was a kind of museum where the agents had assembled many of the objects and papers they had captured during their numerous raids. Guzmán followed the agents quietly inside, his uncuffed hands clasped behind his back. He then began to wander around. Rows of metal tables held thousands of objects including photos, notebooks, flags with hammers and sickles, drawings from Shining Path prisoners, ceramic *retablos*—tiny bas-relief scenes of Shining Path attacks—portraits of a stern Abimael Guzmán looking much younger, his fist in the air, as well as documents commemorating various milestones in the Shining Path's trajectory, from a small band of ideologues to a clandestine network that nearly toppled the government of Peru. In sum, Benedicto's agents had inadvertently created a museum that portrayed the life of Abimael Guzmán, a record of his achievements when he was at the height of his power.

"All I was ever interested in was becoming a revolutionary," Guzmán once said, who had no children. As the leader and creator of the Shining Path slowly wandered the aisles, his hands clasped in the attitude of a professor, one of the agents eventually intruded upon his reverie. "*Doctor*, it's time to go."

On the way out, Guzmán's hands were plunged into his pockets. His head hung down. One of the agents peered closely at his face. The Shining Path leader's cheeks were wet with tears.

The man who had been abandoned by his mother fifty years earlier—and who had never been seen to cry since—now wept silently over the collapse of his movement, a movement that had cost the lives of more than seventy thousand Peruvians. As he walked down the corridor, destined to spend the rest of his life in prison, Guzmán wept over the failure of his dreams and illusions—and over the loss of what he believed could and should have been a glorious and miraculous future.

4

THE RISE AND FALL OF HIRAM BINGHAM, "DISCOVERER" OF MACHU PICCHU (PERU)

Yesterday I had a glorious flight. Flying [in France] in between the high . . . and fleecy clouds below was a wonderful experience. I could see the great white sea of clouds below me for miles and miles. Occasionally the sun broke though the upper layer and made the upper surface of the lower layer look like snow fields and peaks in the Andes. I flew for an hour and a half and haven't enjoyed anything so much in months.

> —Lieutenant Colonel Hiram Bingham, pilot and commander of the (World War I) Third Aviation Instruction Center, France, 1919

I warn you . . . you must follow a course midway between earth and heaven, in case the sun should scorch your feathers if you go too high, or the water make them heavy if you are too low. Fly halfway between the two . . . and pay no attention to the stars.

> —Daedalus to his son, Icarus, from the *Metamorphoses*, Ovid, 8 A.D.

"**S**o you're saying that professor Hiram Bingham, who discovered Machu Picchu, was a *thief*?" Jonah asks incredulously.

"Maybe more of a smuggler," I say.

"But isn't 'thief' and 'smuggler' the same *thing*?"

"I suppose. All I'm saying is that he wasn't the great American hero most people think he was. Or that he was a *flawed* American hero. Who just happened to have stumbled upon Machu Picchu."

"But that's *why* he *was* a hero," Jonah insists.

Jonah is twenty-five. He's clearly annoyed and is shaking his head. Bingham is one of Jonah's biggest heroes, and Jonah is carrying one of Bingham's books, *Lost City of the Incas*, during our hike on the Inca Trail. Jonah likes to underline passages and read them to us in the morning, in the eating tent. His fiancée, Sarah, is also twenty-five. Both have dark curly hair, are in PhD programs in economics at Stanford, and, perhaps because of their future professions, both like to have all of their *i*'s dotted and their *t*'s crossed. Every evening, they put their boots neatly outside of their yellow tent, under the rain flap with their toothbrushes set out in blue and green plastic cases, and they are picky with their meals. Both are vegetarians, and both are driving our guide, Eduardo, a little bit nuts. Jonah has the additional habit of carrying a small yellow GPS with him. He's eternally calling out the elevations and directions.

Altogether there are seven of us and our guide. We've met only the day before on a four-day hike run by a company called Amazonas Explorer that began near the Inca town of Ollantaytambo; the hike will end at the ruins of Machu Picchu. This is day two, the long—some would say "death march"—slog up and over Dead Woman's Pass or, in the Incas' Quechua language, *Warmiwañusca*. The pass is at nearly 14,000 feet, our guide tells us, and this is the most difficult day of the trip.

We remain sprawled on our backs in a grassy area at an elevation, according to Jonah, of precisely 11,933 feet. In the distance, mountain peaks stretch off to the horizon, some capped with ice and snow. At least one, Salcantay, rises over twenty thousand feet. Ahead and behind us winds the Inca tail—a narrow ribbon of cut stones, ancient bridges, and phenomenal native engineering, a wonder of the world, really.

It turns out, however, that the classic "Inca Trail" is only a minuscule, 27-mile section of the vast, 26,000-mile road network the Incas constructed, which once linked southern Colombia with central Chile—a distance of nearly three thousand miles. The reason some seventy-five thousand people now hike this portion of the Inca roadway each year is because it ends at Machu Picchu—the spectacular, abandoned Inca citadel discovered by the Yale University historian Hiram Bingham in 1911. I look at my wristwatch. It's still two hours to lunch.

"Do you know the story of Icarus?" I ask Jonah, as we lie on our backs, our faces to the sun.

"What?"

"The Greek story about Icarus."

"The kid who got burned?" Jonah's fiancée says.

"Right. His father gave him wings of wax but told him not to fly too close to the sun."

"And he didn't listen," the fiancée says.

"That's what happened to Bingham," I say. "He was so ambitious to get ahead that he broke a lot of rules, got burned, and his whole career came crashing down."

"Bingham was a *dick*," Eduardo says quietly. Eduardo is the only Peruvian in the group, not counting our twenty porters, who outnumber us roughly three to one. Eduardo is twenty-nine, speaks good English, and lies sprawled out on his back as well. He's a good guide, has his head propped up on his daypack, and is wearing a purple baseball cap with the name "Cusco" stitched in orange on the front. He has wraparound sunglasses and is putting coca leaves, one by one, inside his left cheek, to give himself some extra pep.

"Bingham ripped us off. He ripped off the whole country," he says.

"It doesn't say anywhere in his book that he stole *anything*," Jonah says.

"But who *wrote* the book?" Eduardo asks.

Jonah is silent.

"Bingham! That's who," Eduardo says.

"He was *excavating*," Jonah retorts. He's fiddling with his GPS and making sharp stabs at its buttons, his fingers full of nervous energy. "He was an explorer. He wasn't a *thief*."

"So if he stole the artifacts, how did he steal them?" Margaret asks in a wheezy voice, cutting to the chase. Margaret's from England. She's here with her friend, Beth. Both are in their early sixties, are short and a bit thick around the waist. Although the two had practiced hiking with some gusto on the flatlands at sea level in Cornwall, they quickly discovered that they were almost totally unprepared to be hiking at 9,000, let alone 14,000 feet. I'm actually encouraged that she can speak. Beth lies beside her, stretched out as if she's in an advanced stage of rigor mortis, stuck to the ground but looking as if she is about to levitate. She hasn't said a word since we stopped for a break.

"And *why* did he steal those things?" Margaret asks. "Why not do it legally?"

"Yes, *do* tell," Jonah asks me, a bit sarcastically.

You have to go back to 1913, I tell them. Back to when Hiram Bingham was an assistant professor at Yale University. Or maybe even further back than that. Bingham's parents were strict, second-generation Protestant missionaries in Hawaii. So he grew up in an atmosphere of school, church, Bible translation, getting whacked on the hands for doing anything wrong, and wearing ties and blazers. All the while he was living in an island paradise where the natives liked to have a good time and went around in shorts. Bingham's family life was so suffocating, in fact, that when Bingham was twelve he bought a ticket on a ship and tried to run away. But his parents discovered his plans and soon packed him off to a prep school on the mainland. To study with rich kids. In Massachusetts. Bingham didn't have any money, so he'd had to work in the school kitchen to make ends meet. The other students therefore looked down on him. And it wasn't any better for Bingham at Yale. He studied history there as an undergrad, but no one invited him to join any of their secret clubs—Skull and Bones and all of that kind of thing. Bingham was an outsider—a poor, skinny, six-foot-four-inch kid from Hawaii with uptight missionaries for parents. He was always on the outside looking in.

"Sounds like [your President] Obama," says Margaret. "*He's* from Hawaii, isn't he? He wasn't poor, but he was black—so I do imagine it was a similar kind of thing."

"Bingham and Obama actually went to the same high school," I say. "On land that Bingham's grandfather had donated."

"But none of that makes Bingham a *thief*," Jonah counters. "And besides, he *married* money. So what you're saying makes no sense."

Jonah is partially right. Bingham married one of the heirs to the Tiffany fortune. He had seven kids with her, all boys. Bingham got a PhD from Harvard in Latin American history and became a part-time professor at Yale, but professors were poorly paid back then. And although his wife received an allowance from her family and used that allowance to pay for some expenses, if Bingham wanted to go exploring, he had to raise the money himself. He did so by asking wealthy friends and sponsors. Bingham made a couple of trips down to South America in his early thirties, and then, when he was thirty-five, he stumbled upon Machu Picchu.

"But what about the stealing? When did he do that?" Margaret asks.

Three years after finding Machu Picchu, I tell them. Bingham was sitting in his house in Connecticut. It was a large colonial home in New Haven that his wife's parents had bought for them. So he gets this letter from a Peruvian "antiquities dealer," which back then meant a looter. And still kinda does, come to think of it. And the dealer tells Bingham that he's got more than three hundred Inca artifacts to sell. Pots, vases, jugs, trepanned skulls, bones, all kinds of stuff, most of which was looted from Inca tombs. Bingham knows it's illegal to export any of these things without a permit. But the dealer tells him that with enough money he can bribe customs officials and get everything out of Peru without anyone finding out. The catch is that the dealer wants the equivalent of a couple of hundred thousand dollars. So he asks Bingham if he's interested.

"And where," asks Margaret, "was he supposed to get that kind of money?"

"From the Tiffany fortune. But the artifacts were for Yale. That is, for Yale's museum. The dealer wanted to know if Bingham wanted to buy Inca artifacts that had been looted from graves. He knew that Bingham had discovered Machu Picchu, so he figured Bingham must have plenty of money—and that he might be interested."

"And was he?" Margaret asks.

"He bought the whole lot. Then had it shipped illegally out of the country to Yale."

"I told you he was a dick," Eduardo says.

"And did anyone find out?" Margaret asks.

"Not at the time. But within three years, Bingham's career was over. Kaput. He was finished as an explorer and finished as an archaeologist. Peru basically barred him from doing any more research."

"Serves him right," Margaret says, looking over to see if her friend is still alive. She pokes her with a walking stick.

Beth grunts but doesn't move. Her arms are stretched out flat besides her, palms down, as if she's on her deathbed. Both she and Margaret are wearing floppy blue hats whose brims are turned down. Beth has hers over her face, keeping off the sun.

"Okay," Eduardo says. "Time to go."

We get back to our feet and head out slowly, breathing in the thin air and continuing our plodding steps up the trail, many portions of which are formed by steps cut out of sheer bedrock. Other sections curve around the sides of steep hills, with long drops on the side. No handrails are evident anywhere; it would be easy to plummet over an edge.

Ferns poke out of crevices. Water trickles in rivulets down rock sides, wetting the stone, turning it black with algae. We scatter out in a ragged line, tiny dots moving slowly over a crested ridge of the Andes, sucking in oxygen with deeper and deeper breaths. Margaret gradually drops behind, followed by a nearly catatonic Beth. Both plod slowly with a walking stick in either hand, as if they were making the final push to the summit of Everest: step, pause, step, pause, step, pause, step, rest. Eduardo hangs back with them, keeping the two buoyed up with cheerful stories while dutifully bringing up the rear.

Bingham's story has always fascinated me, ever since I first visited

Machu Picchu several decades ago. How did he "discover" a city hidden on top of a mountain saddle covered in cloud forest vegetation and invisible from the deep canyons below? How did he know where to look for it? Why did he basically get kicked out of Peru—and why was he later censured by the US Senate? Bingham had accomplished so much—becoming a Yale University professor, discovering Machu Picchu, and then going on to become a US Army lieutenant colonel, Connecticut governor, bestselling author, and US senator. So how had he fallen so low?

As Jonah had mentioned, in 1900, when Bingham was twenty-five, he married Alfreda Mitchell, the heiress to part of the Tiffany fortune. Five years later, at the age of thirty, he obtained a doctorate in history. It was three years after that when Bingham first encountered a story that would completely change the direction of his life. A turning point, perhaps, came in 1909, when Bingham was thirty-three. He traveled to Cusco, Peru, the former capital of the Inca Empire, while on his way back from an international science conference in Chile. It was while visiting Inca ruins outside of Cusco that Bingham first heard about a remote Inca capital explorers had been seeking for at least a century. Almost four hundred years earlier, Bingham learned, the Incas had abruptly abandoned their capital of Cusco after the Spaniards had seized their empire. A renegade Inca emperor had then headed down the eastern side of the Andes, followed by a large retinue of followers. Together, they had founded a new capital in the wild Antisuyu—the mostly jungle-choked eastern quarter of the empire. The Incas called their capital Vilcabamba. For the next four decades, the city would serve as the headquarters of a fierce guerrilla war the Incas carried out against the European invaders. Eventually, the Spaniards discovered Vilcabamba, captured the last Inca emperor, then yoked him in chains and dragged him back to Cusco. There, they beheaded him in 1572, thus putting an end to the largest indigenous empire ever to have existed in the New World.

In the decades and ultimately centuries that followed, the Incas' rebel capital gradually became engulfed by the jungle and its whereabouts forgotten. Yet the more Bingham learned about the story, the more determined he became that *he* would be the one to find it. Months later, after he'd returned to his lecturing job at Yale, Bingham spent countless hours scouring the historical archives and searching for clues in old Spanish manuscripts. He was determined to use everything in his power—his education, his connections, and his drive—to achieve his newly appointed goal. If only he could discover Vilcabamba, the Incas' ancient capital, then Bingham was certain that he'd have finally made his mark upon the world, both as an explorer and as an historian.

In June 1911, Bingham arrived back in Cusco, this time leading a team of scientists hoping to find the lost Inca city. The expedition soon headed out on mule-back toward Peru's Sacred Valley, then began making its way down the Urubamba Valley, which ultimately led to the Amazon jungle. Paying local guides to help him investigate rumors of local ruins, Bingham hit pay dirt on July 24, 1911, only two weeks after his actual exploring had begun. It was then that a local farmer led him up a sheer mountainside in a little-inhabited stretch of cloud forest along the Urubamba River, toward a ridge that stretched between two peaks covered in tropical vegetation. When they arrived on top, Bingham was stunned to find an entire abandoned Inca city composed of immaculately cut granite stones, some the size of automobiles. Many of the stones were so perfectly fitted together that their joints were flush—without the slightest trace of mortar. These must have been Inca palaces and temples, Bingham realized—but why had they been created in such a remote and inaccessible area? Who had lived here? Although he didn't realize it, Bingham had just made the discovery of a lifetime: the ruins would soon become known throughout the world as Machu Picchu.

Bingham, however, was confronted with a few problems. Three families of Peruvian farmers already lived among the ruins, so he really couldn't claim to have "discovered" this site. The families, in fact, had already cleared a substantial number of the buildings in order to grow their crops. Only a portion of the ruins were overgrown and looked like the kind of "lost" city Bingham had been searching for. Bingham was also faced with the fact that he'd been led here by a farmer who lived below in the Urubamba Valley and who had already visited the site. To make matters worse, while exploring the ruins and taking photographs on a large Kodak camera set on a tripod, Bingham discovered a third and potentially even more serious problem. Written in charcoal on one of the Inca temples, someone had written:

LIZARRAGA, 1902

Had a previous "explorer" already discovered the site—and published the fact? Bingham wondered. Was the city he'd just stumbled upon already known to the world?

Bingham was relieved to discover that the inscription belonged to that of Agustín Lizarraga, a local muleteer who'd lived on the nearby valley floor for more than thirty years. He was hardly someone who would publish anything about his explorations. Lizarraga was also a mestizo, or "half-caste," as Bingham later referred to him. Bingham clearly used that term with the belief that a poor, mixed-blood muleteer was hardly anyone to take seriously. Lizarraga, however, had obviously felt the ruins of sufficient importance to have written his name in charcoal on one of the walls *nine years* before the arrival of the tall, lanky North American. The muleteer, however, wasn't leading a scientific expedition at the time. Nor did he have any way of contacting the media—and perhaps had no desire to do so. In addition, Lizarraga died in 1912, the year after Bingham's first visit.

Bingham solved his first problem—that of stumbling upon ruins that had already been partially cleared—by eventually publishing photos of only those ruins that on his first visit had *not* been cleared. Instead, he published photos that reflected the romantic quest depicted in one of his favorite poems by Rudyard Kipling:

Something hidden! Go and find it!
Go and look behind the ranges—
Something lost behind the ranges.
Lost and waiting for you.
Go!

Bingham solved his other two problems—that of people actually living among the ruins and the inscription and date on the temple wall—in a more roundabout fashion. While Bingham initially gave full credit to the man who had affixed his name to Machu Picchu before him—"Agustín Lizarraga is the discoverer of Machu Picchu," he wrote in his field notebook—in his later publications he was not nearly so generous. In his 1922 book *Inca Land*, Bingham included only Lizarraga's last name: "From a crude scrawl on the walls of one of the finest buildings," Bingham wrote, "we learned that the ruins were visited in 1902 by Lizarraga, lessee of the lands immediately below the bridge of San Miguel. This is the earliest local record." In this version Lizarraga has no first name, he is a renter, not an owner of nearby lands, and his inscription is "crude." By the time Bingham published his last book on the subject, however, his 1948 account, *Lost City of the Incas*, Bingham made no mention of Lizarraga whatsoever. Instead, he flatly stated in the book's preface, referring to the discovery of Machu Picchu, "I found it." Thus, with some judicious editing carried out over a period of decades and not a little bit of racism, Hiram Bingham ultimately excised Agustín Lizarraga's name from history, playing down any local knowledge of the ruins because its first discoverers were "half-castes," while simultaneously magnifying his own "discovery."

Bingham had another substantial problem to deal with, however, that particular day in July 1911, as he stood among the mysterious ruins perched two thousand feet above the valley floor. The significance of the Incas' remote city—festooned with vines and ferns and seeming to erupt organically from atop a high mountain spur—puzzled him completely. Superficially, the citadel sandwiched between two, sugarloaf-like mountains called Machu Picchu and Huayna Picchu—which in the Quechua language mean "old peak" and "young peak"—didn't seem to match the descriptions Bingham had unearthed about the lost city of Vilcabamba he had been searching for. In addition, he had never encountered the names "Machu Picchu" or "Huayna Picchu" in any of the old Spanish chronicles he had studied. After a mere five hours amid the ruins, therefore, and during which time he busily took photos, Bingham left the site and returned down the mountainside to his camp. For the next month, Bingham continued searching for Vilcabamba, locating more Inca ruins along the way. None of those he discovered, however, compared with the citadel he had found at Machu Picchu. Was it possible—just possible—that Machu Picchu was actually Vilcabamba?

Back in the United States, the National Geographic Society soon agreed to cosponsor Bingham's next expedition to Peru,* in return for Bingham writing an article for its magazine about his discoveries. But what *was* this "lost city"? Bingham wondered. Was it Vilcabamba—the rebel capital that he had been searching for—or something else entirely? Bingham began to pore through the old Spanish chronicles again, trying to compare the site he'd stumbled upon at Machu Picchu with the various sixteenth-century descriptions of Vilcabamba. Were they the same? Bingham couldn't be sure. Eventually, he realized that there was only one way to find out: he needed to return to Machu Picchu and study the citadel in greater detail. Only through further exploration could he discover, once and for all, whether Machu Picchu and the Incas' rebel capital were one and the same—or whether the ruins he'd discovered were "something lost behind the ranges" and hence completely new.

"The Incas—they worshipped the mountains," Eduardo tells us. He's strolling about, using one walking stick as a sort of pointer while his "troops"—our exhausted group—lie sprawled about Dead Woman's Pass. "They called the mountains *apus*, which means 'gods' or 'mountain spirits.' They worshipped the mountains because the mountains were gods—and they still are to the local farmers." Eduardo spits a little coca juice onto the ground, adjusts his baseball cap with one hand, then continues. His left cheek is bulging with a wad of the pale green leaves, the same leaves from which the alkaloid cocaine is distilled. "The mountains controlled the rivers, they controlled the weather, they controlled

---

*Bingham's 1912 expedition, in fact, would be the National Geographic Society's first sponsored scientific expedition. Since then, they have sponsored more than eighty thousand.

the fertility of the farmers' crops and herds. So people worshipped them and made offerings. When things were really bad," Eduardo says, adding a few more leaves to his mouth from a plastic bag, "then they even sacrificed children on the mountaintops."

Margaret holds up a hand. She is wearing a purple fleece and her floppy blue hat.

"But *why*? Why children?"

"Because they were the best sacrifice," Eduardo says. "*El mejor sacrificio*," he repeats in Spanish. "A more important sacrifice than llamas. Better than alpacas. People thought that these sacrifices pleased the gods, no?"

Eduardo puts his coca bag in one jacket pocket and pulls a small bottle out of the other, uncaps it, then pours a small dribble of *pisco* (alcohol) onto the ground. "To Apu Salcantay, on whose flank lies Machu Picchu," he says, nodding and pouring in the direction of Mount Salcantay, a jagged white peak that rises to 20,574 feet. Eduardo turns first in one direction and pours, then in another, then in another. Salcantay is the highest and most powerful mountain in the entire region, he says. Its glaciers hold vast reservoirs of water. In 1912 Bingham named one of them Grosvenor Glacier, in honor of the editor and director of the National Geographic Society, Gilbert Grosvenor. Within a year of Bingham's magnanimous gesture, Grosvenor made Bingham famous by devoting an entire issue of *National Geographic* magazine to Bingham's discoveries at Machu Picchu. No other explorer or writer has received so much space in the magazine since.

"To Apu Veronica," Eduardo concludes, nodding and pouring alcohol in the direction of Salcantay's 18,635-foot sister.

A few of us follow Eduardo's movements, but for the most part we lie about as if we have already been sacrificed, trying to regain our energies.

"This is the highest pass of the trip," Eduardo continues. "Almost fourteen thousand feet, no? But the Incas," he says, pointing in the direction of Salcantay, "climbed mountains more than twenty-two thousand feet high. And they made stone temples on top of them, in the ice and snow. Imagine," he says.

It's hard for any of us to conceive, actually, of anyone wearing open sandals and dressed in nothing more than loose-fitting robes climbing so high, let alone building anything there. Most of us are wearing stiff hiking boots with Kevlar soles, nylon pants, polyester long underwear, polarized sunglasses, sunblock, and lip screen. We also have compasses and wristwatches. Most of us carry smart phones—the modern electronic equivalent of the old Swiss army knife with its multiplicity of stainless steel tools. Our own tools are now electronic and include voice recorders, cameras, music players, and a plethora of easily downloadable "apps." How is it that the Incas were able to transit and climb this hard-ribbed, thin-aired landscape, then create—in areas that are almost inaccessible—cities of stone with only stone and bronze tools?

"The Incas were, undeniably, lovers of beautiful scenery," Bingham wrote in 1913, in his first article for *National Geographic*'s special edition, which he titled "In the Wonderland of Peru." "Many of the ruins of their most important places are located on hilltops, ridges, and mountain shoulders, from which particularly beautiful views can be obtained."

"Remarkable as is the architecture of Machu Picchu, and impressive as is the extent of the stone-cutting done by a people who had no steel or iron tools," he continued, "neither of these things leaves more impression on the mind of the visitor than the inexpressible beauty and grandeur of the surroundings."

Most of us on this expedition would agree, although to be honest, the beauty of our surroundings sometimes gets lost amid the struggle to find enough oxygen and energy to continue moving.*

In 1912, just a year after discovering Machu Picchu, Bingham returned to Peru, bringing with him another team of scientists. He had a new problem, however. In August 1911, the Peruvian government had

---

*According to medical studies, it takes an average of forty-five days for the human body to adapt to an altitude change of roughly ten thousand feet. Most of us on this hike have bodies that are adapted to life near sea level, so we're feeling the effects of the equivalent of a strenuous aerobics class lasting all day long, plus our bodies trying to adapt simultaneously to an abrupt shift in altitude, along with the subsequent lack of oxygen.

issued a presidential decree stating that all archaeological antiquities belonged to the Peruvian state. No archaeological excavation could take place, therefore, without a representative of the government being present, nor could any antiquities be exported. Anyone caught exporting antiquities from Peru without a permit would be treated as a smuggler.

Bingham, however, had already promised Yale he would bring back a sizeable collection of Peruvian antiquities and had received funding to do so. He thus found himself in a quandary. How could he bring back a collection of antiquities now that doing so was illegal?

Soon after his arrival, Bingham hurried to Peru's capital of Lima, enlisted the aid of the US State Department, and desperately tried to wrangle a deal. In the end, he was successful: Peru's new president agreed that Bingham could export the antiquities he planned to excavate. There were two important conditions, however. One was that Bingham could export only whatever he found *before* December 1, 1912, which would allow Bingham only one more month to excavate. The other was that Peru had the right to demand that everything Bingham exported would one day to be returned—*if* Peru asked Yale to do so. Bingham agreed to the provisions and signed the document. Once back in the United States, however, he carefully kept the second condition of the agreement quiet. Yale, Bingham knew, would from now on be unable to "own" any of the Machu Picchu artifacts he might deliver and thus would be unable to place them in any kind of permanent collection. Clearly, according to the agreement, whatever Bingham exported from Peru to the United States was still owned by the Peruvian government; it was only temporarily on loan to Yale.

In the end, Bingham shipped 136 wooden crates to Yale, stuffed with what he had excavated during the first part of his 1912 expedition. During that time, his team had rapidly disentombed 107 graves at Machu Picchu and had extracted the skeletal remains of 173 individuals, along with their associated offerings of stone implements, ceramics, and bronze tools. In addition, two years later, and as noted at the beginning of this story, Bingham purchased a collection of 366 Peruvian antiquities. These he illegally exported and added to his on-loan collection at Yale. Because the Peruvian government was unaware of Bingham's purchase, however, there was no inventory conducted. Thus, there was little chance the illegal collection would ever be traced.

When Bingham departed on a third expedition to Machu Picchu in 1915, however, he left this time without having obtained permission to excavate at Machu Picchu. Once in Peru, Bingham informed the authorities that he was going to carry out "geographical surveys," not archaeological excavations. Peruvian officials soon discovered, however, that Bingham had in fact been excavating bones and artifacts and had packed them into wooden boxes. They immediately seized four of Bingham's seventy-four crates as evidence that he had broken the law. Soon, the local press in Cusco broke the story and began running bold headlines such as the following:

THE CRIMINAL EXCAVATION OF MACHU PICCHU
Members of the Yale Commission Are Taking Our Treasures
The Denunciations of [the newspaper] EL SOL Completely Proven

Bingham was now in serious trouble: his illegal excavations had been publicly exposed while his reputation and that of Yale University were now at stake. The Peruvian government was unaware that Bingham had already smuggled antiquities out of Peru. Nor did it know that he had smuggled the remains of an Inca mountaintop burial—complete with silver, gold, and bronze sun idols—by hiding those things in the expedition doctor's private trunk. If any of these actions came to light and were added to his present transgression, then Bingham's reputation would be ruined. Holed up in Cusco, unable to excavate or leave the country, Bingham wrote to a friend that he was suffering from a "considerable amount of mental depression." All he could do now, however, was to wait and see what the Peruvian authorities would do.

Within weeks, the authorities convened an inquest in Cusco that required the attendance of Bingham, his American team, and their accusers. After carefully examining the contents of some of Bingham's crates, the officials concluded that Bingham had indeed been excavating illegally and had broken Peruvian law. The material was confiscated, and Bingham was ordered to cease his activities. Crestfallen, Bingham cut short his expedition and soon departed for Lima. While he waited for a ship to return to the United States, however, Bingham nevertheless found himself unable to resist a further temptation: a new dealer offered to sell him a large collection of Peruvian antiquities, this time looted from the Nazca culture. Bingham quickly agreed to terms and bought the collection outright. Because of the controversy now associated with Bingham's name, however, the dealer suggested shipping the collection under a pseudonym so that the shipment would not be flagged by customs officials. It was, after all, illegal.

"It seems to me a strange thing to do," Bingham wrote in a letter shortly afterward, "to consign the goods to a fictitious character like J. P. Simmons, but I suppose they thought it was necessary under the circumstances. The question is, how is Yale University to get hold of the shipment, when it has been consigned to J. P. Simmons?"

The shipment of looted Nazca artifacts did, in the end, arrive at Yale successfully. Altogether, Bingham had spent approximately $480,000 in today's dollars to purchase and smuggle ancient artifacts for Yale's Peabody Museum. On August 19, 1915, Hiram Bingham finally departed from Peru, three months earlier than scheduled. He was forty years old. Although he didn't realize it at the time, his archaeological and exploring careers—begun so spectacularly only four years earlier—were over.

"Listen to this," Jonah says. It's now our third night on the Inca Trail, and we're huddled in our eating tent at *Phuyupatamarca*, a Quechua name meaning "the place over the clouds." Earlier in the evening, we'd witnessed a spectacular sunset, the clouds stretching out below us like an iridescent carpet with Andean peaks poking through from below. But now the cold has descended, and we're suitably outfitted in down jackets, ski hats, gloves, and long underwear, waiting for a first course of hot soup. Outside, the porters, cooks, and camp workers are getting ready for dinner too and speak to one another in Quechua. It's their job to carry our belongings and the camp equipment, bundled into giant, rainproof backpacks. Wearing only tire sandals, or *ojotas*, the porters routinely race past us every day on the trail, even though we begin each morning well ahead of them and are carrying only day packs. Even with such a handicap, however, the porters arrive hours before the fatigued gringos and have the camp ready long before our arrival.

Meanwhile, according to Jonah, we are dining at 11,936 feet. Jonah's been reading an article Bingham wrote for *National Geographic* after his last expedition. A kerosene lantern sits before him, burning steadily with a hiss and throwing yellow light onto his sunburned face.

"This is the part where Bingham starts searching for the Inca Trail," Jonah says.

> "The most thrilling moment in my four expeditions into the interior of Peru was at Machu Picchu, on the 24th of July, 1911, when I first saw the Temple of the Three Windows and the Chief Palace. In order to reach them, it had been necessary to follow an Indian guide through a dense jungle, and finally along precipices where one literally had to hold on with one's fingernails. Clearly this was not the way that the builders of Machu Picchu had approached their city . . . Later we located part of an ancient road leading back from the city up the mountain side and across the face of one of the towering precipices on Machu Picchu Mountain. It appeared to proceed in a southerly direction into a region of high mountains, deep valleys, and well-nigh impassable jungles. In 1915 it was my privilege to penetrate that unexplored country back of Machu Picchu, visit its ruins, and follow its ancient trails."

"So four years after discovering Machu Picchu," Jonah says, as camp attendants begin to bring one steaming soup bowl after another into our tent, "Bingham started trying to figure out how the Incas used to travel to Machu Picchu. They didn't climb up from the valley floor like Bingham did, because there was no trail. So Bingham started looking around for Inca roads up on the ridges. This is where he mentions Patallacta, where we began our hike":

"Not far from Patallacta, in the Huayllabamba Valley, we located the remains of an old Inca road leading out of the valley in the direction of Machu Picchu. It was with mingled feelings of keen anticipation and lively curiosity that Mr. Hardy and I, with a gang of Indian bearers from Ollantaytambo, in April, 1915, set out to discover how far we could follow this ancient road."

"So he had porters too, just like we do" Elizabeth says, hovering over a large bowl of cream of mushroom soup. Her friend, Beth, is so tired that she's already asleep in her tent.

"He had both porters and mules," I add.

"So Bingham was the first outsider to walk the Inca Trail—he discovered it, and described all the ruins along it," Jonah says. "Man, wish I'd been there with him!"

The next day, late in the afternoon, we walk down a final ridgeline and approach the Sun Gate at approximately eight thousand feet, the classic entryway the Incas used to enter Machu Picchu. The gateway is made from stone and is approached by climbing up a flight of stone stairs. Through its rectangular portal one catches one's first glimpse of the citadel, often wreathed in clouds, that still offers spectacular views over the valley and distant mountains.

Eduardo leads Jonah to just before the gate, where he stops. He then blindfolds Jonah and leads him to a spot in the center of the gateway, facing the citadel below. Eduardo finally pulls off the blindfold theatrically, revealing the sacred city in all of its splendor, now etched with late-afternoon sunlight.

"Wow," Jonah says, shaking his head. "Incredible."

Eduardo next does the same with Margaret. She's wearing jeans and her purple fleece, her blue hat, and the blindfold. Margaret stands expectantly until Eduardo removes the blindfold, then is left to take in the city for the first time. After a few moments, tears begin to roll down her cheeks. A bit later, Beth also begins weeping. I'm not sure, however, whether the two Englishwomen are overwhelmed by the sudden sight of the miraculous ruins, stretching out so splendidly before them, or if they are crying simply because they have survived the trip.

"Gracious," is all Beth says. "Gracious me."

We begin to wander through the ruins, which are now visited by a million people a year, most of whom arrive by train to the valley below and then take a bus up to the ruins. As we do so, I can't help but think of the man who once camped here nearly one hundred years earlier and who had such high hopes for his future. Although Hiram Bingham eventually claimed that Machu Picchu was the lost Inca capital of Vilcabamba and that the Incas had founded this as the very first city in their empire, he was ultimately proven wrong by archaeologists on both counts. Another American explorer, Gene Savoy, eventually identified Vilcabamba in 1964, some four thousand feet farther down in the jungle and about one hundred miles away. Machu Picchu, it turned out, was also not the Incas' first city, but was apparently a royal retreat for one of their greatest emperors, Pachacutec, who had Machu Picchu built to commemorate his conquests in the area in roughly AD 1450–1470.

Since the Inca Empire was a theocracy, meaning that its emperor was both a secular ruler and a god, it is not surprising that 30 percent of Machu Picchu's buildings had a religious function. In addition, the citadel overlooked a series of sacred peaks in the distance and was nearly surrounded below by the sacred Urubamba River, while some of its temples were constructed so that splinters of sunlight marked the winter and summer solstices. Other temple windows marked the pathway of the stars—such as the Pleiades and Southern Cross. Inca architects thus incorporated into their design both the sacred and profane—blending their emperor's desire to commemorate himself and his conquests with the simultaneous desire to worship and acknowledge the multiple gods and spirits that imbued the very landscape around them. Without paying deference to the gods, the Incas realized, there could be neither life nor empire.

After Bingham's hasty departure in 1915, the rest of his story continued to follow the pattern of an ancient Greek tragedy in which the hero, although brave and fearless, is eventually felled by a fatal flaw in his character. In 1917, two years after returning from Machu Picchu, Bingham learned to fly, joined the army, and served in World War I in France as the commander of a flight instruction school. He quickly rose to the rank of lieutenant colonel. In 1922 Bingham ran for and was elected governor of Connecticut as a Republican and then, from 1924 to 1933, served in the United States Senate. In 1929, however—the very week of the stock market crash—Bingham's latest string of successes once again came crashing to the ground. A fellow senator accused Bingham of having secretly placed a manufacturing lobbyist on the congressional payroll, a clear breach of Senate rules. Bingham, it turned out, had also arranged for the lobbyist to attend tariff negotiations, while having him pose as an innocuous "aide." Although Bingham later denied that he had done anything wrong, in the end he finally admitted that "my judgment in the way in which I endeavored to use this tariff expert may have been at fault." The Senate agreed. It censured Bingham in 1929 for having behaved contrary "to good morals and Senatorial ethics." Bingham thus became one of only nine senators to have been censured in more than two hundred years of US history.

The Senate's action, it soon became apparent, proved to be a mortal blow. Three years later, Bingham lost his reelection bid and retired from politics at the age of fifty-seven. It had been eighteen years since he'd left Peru under a similar cloud of controversy—and now another lapse in moral judgment helped to end his second career. Hiram Bingham never again held political office, nor did he ever again explore or carry out any excavations. In 1937 Bingham's wife divorced him, citing "cold indifference" and an "attitude of superiority," and she accused him of carrying on a longtime affair with the wife of a former congressman. Bingham was sixty-two years old at the time, and, after the divorce, he promptly married his mistress.

Hiram Bingham did, however, write another book after his retirement, revisiting his discovery of Machu Picchu and the excavations he had carried out there so many decades earlier. Initially, Bingham had agreed to cowrite the book with a young Harvard archaeologist and Inca specialist, Philip Ainsworth Means. When Means eventually delivered a completed manuscript to Bingham, however, Bingham delayed publishing it for a number of years. Eventually, Bingham kept the structure that Means had created but rewrote much of the text. The book, *Machu Picchu, A Citadel of the Incas*, was finally published in 1938. Bingham, however, hadn't included Means's name on the title page, nor was there any mention of Means in the book. In Bingham's final book, *Lost City of the Incas*, published in 1948, the former explorer and ex-senator took full credit for having discovered Machu Picchu, as mentioned earlier.

> I suppose that in the same sense of the word as it is used in the expression, "Columbus discovered America," it is fair to say that I discovered Machu Picchu. The Norsemen and the French fishermen undoubtedly visited North America long before Columbus crossed the Atlantic. On the other hand it was Columbus who made America known to the civilized world. In the same sense of the word, I "discovered" Machu Picchu—in that before my visit and report on it, it was not known to the geographical and historical societies in Peru, nor to the Peruvian government. It had [only] been visited by a few Indians and half-castes.

Bingham's logic was essentially correct—he *was* the first to make Machu Picchu known to the rest of the world. However, he also made sure that he wasn't going to share any of the limelight or prestige surrounding the "discovery" of Machu Picchu with any "Indians" or "half-castes"— or with any Harvard coauthor either.

Hiram Bingham made one final visit to Peru in 1948, at the age of seventy-four, to witness the inauguration of the Hiram Bingham Highway, the corkscrew-like road that leads up to the ruins from the Urubamba Valley and which tourist buses use to this day. The still thin and now gray-haired former explorer also witnessed the installation of a bronze plaque bearing the following inscription, which still remains:

CUSCO IS THANKFUL TO HIRAM BINGHAM, THE SCIENTIFIC
DISCOVERER OF MACHU PICCHU IN 1911
—DECEMBER, 1948

Like the Inca emperor who had ordered Machu Picchu's construction, Hiram Bingham, too, had achieved a slice of immortality. Little could he have known as a boy in Hawaii that it would be here, on this remote mountain saddle in the cloud forest of Peru, that he would ultimately make his mark.

Hiram Bingham died in 1956, at the age of eighty-one, and was buried in Arlington National Cemetery. Most of his legal and illegal Machu Picchu collections, meanwhile, some still wrapped in 1911, 1912, 1914, and 1915 Peruvian newspapers, remained after their arrival from Peru in old wooden crates at Yale for the next seven decades. In 1918 Peru's diplomat in Washington requested that Yale return to Peru the objects that Bingham had exported under the 1912 agreement. Yale deferred the request. In 1920 Peru's consul in the United States again asked for the artifacts' return, and Yale ultimately returned forty-seven boxes. This was only a fraction, however, of the hundreds of boxes that Bingham had exported. The boxes they relinquished contained mostly "duplicate" artifacts.

In 1952 the future Argentine revolutionary Che Guevara, while on a motorcycle trip through South America, visited Machu Picchu. Guevara noted that

> All the ruins were cleaned of underbrush, perfectly studied and described and . . . totally robbed of every object that fell into the hands of the researchers, who triumphantly brought back to their country more than two hundred boxes containing invaluable archaeological treasures. . . . Bingham is not the culprit . . . nor are the North Americans guilty in general. . . . But where can we admire or study the treasures of the indigenous city? The answer is obvious: in the museums of North America.

In 2008 the Peruvian government sued Yale University, demanding that Yale return Hiram Bingham's Machu Picchu artifacts after a "loan" of nearly a century. Yale fought the lawsuit until 2010, at which time Peru upped the ante by privately threatening to file a lawsuit against Yale's president, Richard Levin. Such a move could have rendered the president of one of America's most prestigious universities an international criminal and subject to arrest. Within weeks of the threat—and after a century of stonewalling—Yale agreed to return the 1912–15 Machu Picchu artifacts, putting an end to the controversy. Yale also promised to return some of the material to Peru by the centenary of Machu Picchu's discovery, in July 2011. In 2012, the last of Bingham's material was quietly returned to Peru.

Today, at the foot of the mountain that Bingham scrambled up, a small museum houses artifacts from Machu Picchu. Some 250 objects are displayed, most discovered in the last few decades by archaeologists working in the area, which is still littered with magnificent Incan ruins. Although all of the 5,000-plus "lots" or "groups" of artifacts (some 40,000-plus individual pieces) that Bingham excavated were finally returned to Peru, none of Bingham's smuggled collections of Inca and Nazca artifacts were ever requested as no inventory had ever been conducted. Like the Greek Elgin marbles in London or the Egyptian antiquities looted by Napoléon now in the Louvre, Bingham's smuggled collections continue to be housed in Yale's Peabody Museum.

More than one hundred thousand archaeological sites, meanwhile, exist in Peru, only 10 percent of which have been excavated. When new sites are discovered, it is often only after treasure hunters and professional looters have already done their grisly work. In 2007 US Customs officials returned 412 looted ancient Peruvian artifacts, worth millions of dollars, to the Peruvian government. Seized from an Italian antiquities thief living in Miami, among the artifacts were silver masks, Inca quipu cords, gold jewelry, and ancient burial shrouds. It was the largest seizure in the United States since the two countries had signed an accord in 1997 to help prevent the theft of pre-Columbian art from Peru. Worldwide, the systematic looting of ancient artifacts is a multibillion-dollar business.

Hiram Bingham's bones meanwhile, remain in Arlington Cemetery, while the bones he discovered buried at Machu Picchu, along with their votive funerary offerings, have finally been returned to their homeland after a circuitous, eight-thousand-mile journey to North America and back. They now lie in a museum within a former Inca palace in Cusco, called the Casa Concha, about fifty miles as the condor flies from their original, cloud-wreathed burial site.

In 1943, some thirteen years before Bingham's death, Chile's great poet Pablo Neruda visited Machu Picchu and later composed a poem inspired by the site. In one of his stanzas Neruda summed up the experiences of those natives who, long ago, had visited the sacred citadel of the Incas and then had unexpectedly met their ends there, never dreaming that their mortal remains would one day endure such a strange, peripatetic fate:

> to the sharp iron edge I came, to the shroud of farms and stone,
> to the stellar void of the final footsteps . . .
> but wide sea, oh death!, you don't come wave afer wave
> but like a gallup of nocturnal clarity
> or like the absolute numbers of the night.

5

ICE MAIDENS, VOLCANOES, AND INCAS (PERU)

These children [to be sacrificed to the mountain and other gods] would be collected from all over the land and would be carried in litters together . . . They should be very well dressed, paired up female and male.

—Juan de Betanzos, 1551

Some females included in the sacrifices were . . . maidens . . . kept in the enclosures or convents of the mamaconas. They could not have any blemish or even a mole on their entire body [before they were sacrificed].

Human nature would not allow them to kill their own children . . . if they did not expect some reward for what they were doing or if they did not believe that they were sending their children to a better place.

—Bernabé Cobo, 1653

*Juanita was just ten years old and only four short years from death as she hurried to keep up with her mother.** The two walked quickly down a street lined by perfectly cut stone walls in the Inca capital of Cusco. Sparkling water so cold it made your hands turn purple gurgled down a channel in the middle of the stone-flagged street, the water from snowmelt funneled into the city from the sacred mountains nearby. Men and women passed by them, the men wearing sandals and clothed in colorful alpaca tunics, or unqo, the women, like Juanita's mother, wearing equally colorful tunics and cloaks. Juanita loved to peek at visitors to the capital and guess where they were from. Her mother could tell which part of the empire they lived in simply by looking at the colors and patterns of what they wore: some were nobles from the north, from recently conquered areas; others, from the far south, beyond the great lake of Titicaca; still others were part of the local hanan nobility, to which she and her mother belonged. On the right, up ahead, two warriors stood guard in front of a large, trapezoidal door bordered by smoothly cut stones and set within a massive wall that seemed to stretch along the street forever. Although Juanita couldn't possibly have known it as she and her mother hurried through the capital of the newly created, 2,500-mile-long Inca Empire, fate would soon transform her from a "p'asña," or ordinary girl, into an "aclla capacocha"—or human sacrifice. In less than a handful of years, Juanita would be led up to the top of a 20,700-foot volcano overlooking the great, majestic sweep of the Andes, and there would be sacrificed to the gods.*

"Mama, what do they do inside the acclawasi [the house of the virgins]?" Juanita asked, as she and her mother passed by the two guards and the trapezoidal door. Juanita spoke in her native tongue of Quechua, the lingua franca of the Inca Empire.

"Hush," her mother said in a low voice, then seemed to walk even faster. "Hurry, child." Juanita would have given anything to enter the doors of the acclawasi, the secretive enclosure run within by priestesses and where hundreds of aclla cuna, or Chosen Women, led their mysterious lives. But doing

---

*The life story of "Juanita," who lived briefly in the late 1400s, is an imaginative reconstruction based upon historical, ethnographic, forensic, and archaeological evidence.

so was forbidden to unauthorized visitors: any man found inside would immediately be put to death.

Up ahead, Juanita could see a group of Rucana natives smoothly carrying an Inca nobleman on a litter. The man sat on a low wooden stool, a canopy over his head and with the bright green feathers of jungle parrots interwoven into the canopy's cloth. The man had the specially elongated earlobes bearing large golden plugs signifying his noble status; he also wore golden amulets on his arms. Juanita caught herself staring, first at his clothing, which was sumptuously dyed and woven, and then at his face. As the procession moved toward them up the street, Juanita saw the nobleman turn and look at her, causing the skin on her face to flush. Juanita then cast her eyes down, but not before she saw the nobleman point at her and say something to one of his attendants. As Juanita and her mother hurried along, she glanced back and saw the attendant turn, and then quickly begin running after them. The attendant ran past Juanita, then touched her mother's shawl, causing her to stop. He said something, but Juanita couldn't make out the words. The young girl only saw her mother's eyes on the ground and her mother's face, which suddenly seemed to lose all its color. Her mother listened, nodded solemnly, then looked over at her. Neither the cold mountain air nor the dampness from the recent rains but rather something in her mother's eyes caused Juanita's skin to tingle. With just that single, somber look, Juanita knew that her life and that of her mother's would never again be the same.

Abby Franquemont was just five years old when she, her sister, and her parents were stricken with severe hepatitis in Peru. The year was 1977, and the American family had arrived in the country only about four months earlier. Falling ill in their home in the small rural town of Chinchero, about twenty-five miles by dirt road from Cusco, Abby's parents decided to move the family to the former Inca capital, where they could be close to a hospital. Their problem was that they were freelance anthropologists, work was scarce, and they had only a few dollars' worth of Peruvian *soles* left to their name.

Abby's parents were in their late twenties and had come of age during the 1960s. Her mother, Chris, had graduated from Radcliffe while her father, Ed, had graduated from Harvard. The two had then moved to a commune on a rural farm, where Abby was born. When the elderly owner of the farm passed away and his heirs wanted no part of the commune, Abby's parents moved to a small tract of land her mother had inherited in New Hampshire. Their idea was to build a small cabin. Abby's father was strong and bearded and had wrestled in college. He was a natural leader, was good with his hands, and had a decisive, can-do attitude.

Chris Franquemont, Abby's mother, had begun college at sixteen and had graduated cum laude by the time she was twenty. She was pretty, brown haired, and slender and had met Ed while on an archaeo-logical dig in Ancón, on the coast of Peru. The two had sifted sand together, pulling out bits of bones and scraps of two-thousand-year-old tapestries while gradually falling in love. Abby's mother dreamed of one day becoming a professional ethnologist, of researching cultures, and of living abroad. Her father was especially fascinated by ancient tex-tile techniques and had begun learning how to weave. Years later, now married in New Hampshire and with a young family, Abby's parents realized that the cabin they intended to build would never be finished before the onset of winter. They then made a fateful decision: throwing their possessions into some suitcases, the couple bought four round-trip tickets and boarded a plane for Peru. Ed and Chris, five-year-old Abby, and her two-year-old sister soon arrived in Cusco. They had a total of $200 that remained.

The family soon made their way to Chinchero, a sleepy, rural com-munity of whitewashed adobe buildings, red tile roofs, and scattered Inca ruins, located on a high *pampa*, or plain, at an elevation of 12,400 feet. It took three hours' riding on the back of a cattle truck to get there, even though it was only a few dozen miles from Cusco. Surrounded by steep hills sown with potatoes that were grazed by sheep and alpacas,

Chinchero's biggest attraction was that it was renowned for the quality of its traditional weavings.

"We settled in Chinchero because of its active community of weavers of all ages," Ed and Chris later wrote, "but our primary goal at the time . . . was to unlock the 'meaning' of the complex textile patterns woven by Chinchero women." The two freelance anthropologists hoped to research weaving and somehow make a living by writing articles about it.

News of the young gringo family with the two small, blonde-haired girls and of their strange request to settle there soon spread throughout the community. The town council held a meeting, the request was considered, and, after much deliberation, it was decided that the family could stay. The council placed the family under the care of the *cuper ayllu*, one of thirteen subcommunities the inhabitants of Chinchero were divided into. *Ayllus* are an ancient Andean survival strategy in which communities are divided into groups comprised of extended family members. The tightly bound groups function as workforce organizers and human social nets, helping to mitigate the impacts of frost, drought, earthquakes, and other kinds of calamities. Occasionally an *ayllu* will allow nonfamily members to join. For Abby and her family, the *cuper ayllu* made just such an exception.*

Four months after they had arrived, Abby and her father fell very ill. They soon suspected hepatitis, a virus that attacks the liver. When Abby's sister and mother also began to get sick, the family set off on a cattle truck to Cusco in search of medical care. They soon moved into a room an American archaeology student had rented but didn't occupy while out conducting fieldwork. Abby's parents, who'd been expecting a check to arrive in Cusco for an article they'd written, arrived only to find that no check was there. Now they had only pocket change left.

---

*Like any group of people, *ayllus* are competitive, hence in Chinchero they had derogatory nicknames for one another. Three of the largest *ayllus* in town are the Yanacona, Cuper, and Ayllupunqu. The nickname given to the *Yanacona ayllu* by the others is *Yana Qhuna*, or "black snot." The *Cuper ayllu* is known as the *Woqcha Cuper*—the *ayllu* of the "impoverished" or "orphaned"; finally, the third *ayllu* is nicknamed *Kullu Papa Suqsuq*, or the group with potatoes so small they can easily be swallowed whole—meaning of negligible worth.

"I'd been really really sick," recalls Abby, who is now forty-four and lives in Ohio. "I remember waking up in the room and it being cold and my dad having been very sick and my mom and little sister were starting to get sick."

A few days after arriving, Abby and her father went out in search of food. They had just five *soles*—a little over a dollar—left to spend.

"That was all the money we had, and I remember my dad having to make the decision about what we were going to buy," Abby remembers, "either powdered soup, which we could cook on a hot plate, or bread, because that was all we could afford. And my dad said, 'Well, I think it's going to have to be the powdered soup because I have a whole sick family and the soup will go further.' "

In the end, Abby's father bought the soup, and the two of them walked back to their room. Abby remembers watching her father pour the powder into a pot full of near freezing water and then putting the pot on a hot plate. She also remembers how, at precisely that moment, the power in Cusco went out.

"The power was out for a day," Abby said, "and I remember this particular moment and me running around and shouting 'I'm hungry! I'm hungry! Why can't we *eat*!?' I remember my father sitting there with his head in his hands and saying 'You know, it's one thing to lead a hippie lifestyle when you don't have a family, when you don't have responsibility. But, boy, does it change when people are counting on you!' "

Abby recalls that she and her father went back outside to walk around a bit. Her father wanted to clear his head and try to figure out what next to do. They were now literally penniless—without even so much as a Peruvian *sol* remaining. Then, while crossing a street, Abby spotted something crumpled up in the gutter. She went over and picked it up: it was a ten-*sol* bill.

"I was ecstatic," Abby remembers. "That was enough for us to go to the [covered] market and buy something to eat."

Cusco's central market in the 1970s was much as it still is now: a huge, cavernous building with Quechua-speaking women inside wearing bowler hats and dressed in long ankle-length skirts, or *polleras*, minding tiny booths and stands. Surrounding the women stood piles of potatoes, mottled plantains, scaly onions, *ocra*, squash, *lúcuma*, papayas, onions, and other vegetables and fruits. In one section women hovered over cooking stations replete with small tables, wooden benches, and steaming kettles of soup.

By the time Abby and her father entered the market, holding on to their ten-*sol* bill, they were obviously the worse for wear, both having only recently recovered from hepatitis and having lost considerable weight.

"We saw a food vendor lady," Abby recalls. "She took one look at us and insisted that we sit down and eat. She then fixed a whole big meal and gave us food to take back to my mom and sister. All for free. That's how Peruvian people have always been—that's indigenous Peruvian generosity. They don't want to see anyone go hungry on their watch. So we ended up spending the money I found on medicine instead of for food."

The Franquemont family ultimately survived their illness and eventually returned to Chinchero, where Abby and her sister began to learn Spanish and all four of them began to learn Quechua, which was routinely spoken in town.

"I remember consciously studying Spanish," Abby remembers, "but Quechua I learned simply by soaking it up."

On one particular evening, Abby says, she woke suddenly in the middle of the night. Outside, a group of men were returning from a celebration from somewhere in the fields. They had obviously been drinking and were talking loudly in Quechua as they passed by the Franquemonts' small adobe home.

"I remember waking up and hearing them—and I remember suddenly realizing that I understood every word they were saying," Abby says. "That's how it happens when you're a child—language kind of gradually sinks in and then suddenly—bam!—it's there."

Every Sunday in Chinchero, the townspeople held a large open market, just as they do today. The market took place on a square lined on one side by an Inca wall with large trapezoidal niches and on the others by adobe buildings. On such mornings women dressed in colorful handwoven shirts, or *aymillas*; snug jackets, or *juyunas*; wide-brimmed hats, or *monteras*; and long skirts. There, they would throw down sheets of blue plastic or woven blankets in rows and then pile onto them heaps of woven textiles they hoped to barter or sell. Beyond the town and past the sixteenth-century church set upon an ancient Inca palace rose terraced hills. To the north lay the Sacred Valley, and even farther out rose the sharply etched, snow-covered mountains of the Cordillera Vilcabamba.

In the late 1970s, when the Franquemonts arrived in Chinchero, market days were still largely based on barter, with farmers exchanging corn for potatoes, potters exchanging ceramics for alpaca wool, herders from the highlands exchanging dried meat for coca leaves from the jungle, and so on. Some tourists occasionally arrived, despite the difficult road from Cusco, and paid for the women's weavings in cash. The weavers then used the cash to buy items that couldn't be so easily bartered for—medicines, for example, or books, pens, and pencils for their children attending the local school.

For five-year-old Abby, the market with its piles of pungent herbs, vegetables, and meats, the people from nearby towns wearing their own distinctive, handwoven clothing and speaking Spanish or Quechua, the wandering sheep and goats and the live guinea pigs for sale, were all something out of the pages of *Alice in Wonderland*:

> As a child I'd seen pictures that my parents had taken in Peru, and I'd heard all of these stories, and so I was dying to go to Peru, I was just desperate to go. I thought it sounded like some kind of fantasy land. So when we went, I was really thrilled. It just seemed like a great place to be, the people were fantastic . . . I was useful, it didn't take that long to learn to speak the languages, I had jobs, I had value to my family and to my peer group and my community— I loved it there. In fact, I didn't want to go back to the US.

Ed and Chris Franquemont, meanwhile, didn't waste any time in trying to pick up local weaving techniques, the complexity and beauty of which completely fascinated both of them. Not long after moving to Chinchero, Ed began asking the town's weavers, who were all women, if they would teach him to weave. Most thought the request quite comical—after all, everyone knew that weavers began weaving when they were very young. Girls (and many boys) typically learn to spin yarn from alpaca or sheep's wool when five or six years old. By the time girls reach ten, they begin to learn to weave thin strips of cloth, called *hakimas*, on simple backstrap looms. At fourteen, girls have advanced to weaving complexly patterned *chumpis*, or belts. At eighteen, a common age to marry, a young woman is fully capable of weaving *llicllas*, *q'ipirinas*, ponchos, and other types of complexly woven cloths. And now here was this bearded, twenty-seven-year-old man—a foreigner whose own weaving skills were rudimentary at best—who wanted to learn how to weave! It was enough to make the women laugh.

One Sunday morning, however, Ed saw a young, teenaged girl on the square selling her own weavings and stopped to inspect them. He was immediately impressed with their quality. The girl was seated and wore the typical, black, white, and scarlet *montera* hat that women in Chinchero wear. Ed watched as the girl deftly wove a small textile, only half finished, on a small loom.

"I'd like to buy that from you," Ed told her. The girl looked up at him, not understanding.

"So that I can finish it," he said.

The girl smiled, shrugged, and eventually sold Ed the unfinished weaving. As she watched the strange gringo walk away, she shook her head in wonder.

A week later, Ed returned to the market. He'd spent the first part of the week carefully examining the weaving, which still had its spools of colored thread attached to it. Eventually, he'd figured out how to finish it. Now he wanted to find the girl who had sold it to him, so that he could show her. Ed didn't know the girl's name, however, and was unable to find her. So he asked around, describing the girl to other women and showing the weaving he'd bought.

"Ah, that's Nilda," a woman finally told him. "Nilda Callañaupa." The woman said the girl lived on a certain street, in such and such a house, and the door of the house was of such and such a color.

Ten minutes later, Ed knocked at the door and Nilda opened it.

"I finished your weaving," Ed said, matter-of-factly. "Will you teach me more?"

The girl at first didn't believe the gringo had finished it. Then, as she listened, she finally smiled and nodded. "Yes," she said. "I will teach you."

And thus it was, on a certain Sunday morning in 1977, as the jagged peaks of the Vilcabamba Range glistened in the distance, llamas strolled the hills, and people haggled over exchanges in the nearby market, that a meeting occurred between Ed Franquemont and Nilda Callañaupa. It was a meeting that would not only change both of their lives—but would also change the future of traditional weaving in Peru.

Juanita was by now fourteen and had been living in Cusco's acclawasi—the House of the Chosen Women—for about four years. She still remembered the day when she and her mother had been walking down the street outside, the day when the apupanaca, or imperial official, had seen her and had chosen her to be an accla, or "chosen woman." Not long afterward, her parents had accompanied Juanita to that same street, to that same imposing trapezoidal doorway she had once tried to peer through, wondering what lay within. Her mother had wept as they stopped before the door where an older priestess stood waiting. Her father, with his long earlobes and golden plugs, simply said he was proud that his daughter would now serve the Sun, but Juanita could see the sadness in his face. Juanita stared hard at both of them, fighting back tears, and then turned and followed the attendant inside. Juanita had already been told that neither she nor any of the other girls would ever be allowed visitors, so she knew upon entering that

she would probably never see her family again. That night, trying to sleep on a pile of alpaca blankets in a cold stone room with other new girls beside her, Juanita quietly wept.

Life in the acclawasi, however, hidden as it was from the rest of the city, soon became routine. Juanita and other first-year girls would wake early to follow the instructions of the older temple priestesses, or mamaconas. The mamaconas taught them how to prepare various soups and stews, such as motepatasca (a corn soup flavored with chili peppers and herbs), locro (a stew made of fish, potatoes, vegetables, and peppers), and corn bread, or çancu, which Juanita learned to bake. She and the other girls also began the long process of learning how to use the various looms on which to weave cumpi, or royal cloth, the finest cloth that Juanita had ever seen. It was this cloth—made either from the finest alpaca or from pure vicuña wool*—that the Inca emperor and his family wore. Cumpi cloth, too, was often burned in sacrifices for the gods or used to clothe the sacred idols made from gold or silver.

Juanita and the other girls soon began to learn about the numerous religious rituals—so many that it sometimes made her head spin—and were instructed in the nature of the various gods and the sacrifices needed in order to please them. Every morning, when the Sun God woke, His first rays struck the large golden punchao, or sun idol, that had been placed prominently in a patio of the Sun Temple. The rays illuminated the glistening metal and immediately bathed the entire area in a rich golden light.

Meanwhile, Juanita and the other acllas placed the food they'd prepared before the idol. As they made their offerings, the priestesses in attendance chanted, "Sun, eat this food that your wives have prepared for you!" The rest of the food was for the priests and the numerous temple attendants, or was offered in sacrifices to other gods such as Viracocha, the creator god; Illapa, the god of lightning; Pachamama, the earth goddess; or to Mamaquilla, the goddess of the moon.

Juanita soon discovered that there were about two hundred girls and

---

*The vicuña is a wild relative of the llama that bears the finest wool in the world.

priestesses living in the compound, most of them, like her, having been chosen when they were about ten years of age. All of them—here in Cusco at least—were the daughters of Inca nobles or native chiefs from the conquered territories. Juanita and the other girls had been selected because of their physical beauty and also because of their noble status. It was here that they were to be trained to become either priestesses or wives who would be given away to Inca nobles or valiant warriors. A small number of the new acllas, Juanita was told, her eyes no doubt opening wide upon hearing this, would join the Inca emperor's harem—there to be bedded by the son of the Sun God himself—perhaps to bear some of the emperor's children. A small number of new acllas, Juanita also learned—and this time from whispered comments made by some of the older girls who had already become priestesses—would be sacrificed to the gods. Juanita was told not to worry, however, for if that were to happen (and it was the Inca emperor himself who would decide this, she was told), then those sacrificed would be the most fortunate, for their reward would be to join the gods and to enjoy with them a life of ease and abundance in the afterworld.

When Juanita first heard this story, she trembled. The different possibilities for her future both fascinated and frightened her. As her nimble fingers practiced weaving a belt from fine alpaca fiber, Juanita fervently hoped that her own fate was not to become a sacrifice or to join a harem or even to become a temple mamacona, but rather to one day become a nobleman's wife. Only in that way, Juanita realized, would she ever be able to see her family again. She greatly missed them. Then, one morning, when Juanita was fourteen years old, she learned that this year—just after the great sun festival of Inti Raymi—she and the rest of the royal virgins would be presented to the emperor. It would be during that meeting, Juanita was told, that the emperor would decide their fates.

When Nilda Callañaupa was about four years old, her mother began to take her to the fields. There her family raised some of the 880 different varieties of potatoes in the Chinchero area as well as *ollucu* and *oca* and other root crops. By the time Nilda was six, her family trusted her to watch over their sheep flock. Nilda would walk long distances every day, nimbly climbing the rugged hillsides around Chinchero, the town sprawled out below, its market square visible along with the white rectangular tower of the seventeenth-century adobe and stone church, *Nuestra Señora de Monserrat*, the bells of which would periodically ring out over the hills. It was during her wanderings that Nilda met another shepherdess, this one not a girl but rather an ancient woman named Doña Sebastiana. The elderly woman, too, tended a flock of sheep during the day and, like the other women in the area, wore the typical long *pollera* skirts and the flattened black, red, and white hat with its up-turned rims that all Chinchero women wore, hats that both protected them from the sun and also clearly communicated which village they were from. Nilda often used to visit Doña Sebastiana's adobe home. There, she would sit and watch as the woman's gnarled hands spooned out *locro* stew into two bowls, one of which she invariably set down for her inquisitive visitor. In a corner of the small living area, the woman had an old wooden loom and on it was always strung a partially finished weaving—a *manta* cloth or a *chuspa* bag or a shawl—weavings invariably so beautiful that even as a young girl Nilda was taken aback by the old woman's dexterity and skill.

"Her spinning was so fine, and she spun so quickly, that I dreamed at night of spinning," Nilda later wrote, who is now fifty and divides her time between Chinchero and Cusco. "That is where my love of hand-made cloth began and my desire to learn from my elders."

Nilda's own mother could weave, but Nilda's grandfather was Spanish and her grandmother had thus taught Nilda's mother only to weave simple patterns for making generic cloth. As Nilda recounted:

When I was growing up in Chinchero in the 1960s, traditional cloth had little value to the people in my village. The country folk still spun and wove, and the older and more traditional women of Chinchero as well. But in families with Spanish heritage, the men put on modern trousers to go to their jobs, and all the children wore modern clothes to school. To do otherwise would be looked down upon.

Four hundred years earlier, Spanish conquistadors had conquered the Inca Empire and had seized not only the land but also the Quechua-speaking peasants. The Spaniards divided the peasants up among themselves like so many cattle, demanding that they pay "tribute" to their new masters. It wasn't until the 1960s—more than four long centuries later—that the Peruvian government finally undertook an agrarian reform that tried to redress some of the many injustices created by the original conquest. The Spanish language was by now dominant, having displaced Quechua, while other European institutions—such as the Catholic Church, a monetary economy, and European jurisprudence—were firmly implanted, like foreign grafts spliced onto thick indigenous roots. Countless generations of Catholic priests, meanwhile, had done their best to exterminate the local religion, a practice referred to euphemistically as "the extirpation of idolatries." While doing so, Spanish priests smashed idols, destroyed temples, razed sacred monuments, and built Spanish-style buildings on top of what remained. Other aspects of indigenous culture also gradually disappeared: such as how to read the knotted *quipu* cords, an information storage system that had been used in Peru for thousands of years; or how to cut, score, and position giant blocks of stone so deftly and without mortar that the resulting structures still astound visitors to this day.

Even as late as the 1970s, when Andean children such as Nilda mandatorily attended state-run schools, students had to be careful not to make the mistake of speaking their own native language in classrooms—even in whispers—otherwise they were literally beaten by their teachers with sticks until they switched back to Spanish.

In 1968 the Quechua-speaking Peruvian novelist José Maria Arguedas* won the Inca Garcilaso de la Vega literary prize. The award was

---

*This is the same man whose Shining Path guerrilla widow, Sybila Arredondo, I met in Lima's Canto Grande prison in 1987 (described in chapter 3).

named after a sixteenth-century indigenous chronicler who wrote the first account of the Spanish conquest from a native point of view. In his acceptance speech, Arguedas made it clear that he was accepting the prize not only for himself, but also on behalf of

> the art and wisdom of a people who were considered to be degenerate and debilitated, or "strange" and "impenetrable," but instead were really doing nothing less than becoming a great people, oppressed by being scorned socially, dominated politically, and exploited economically on their own soil, where they accomplished great feats for which history considered them a great people: they had been transformed into a corralled nation (isolated in order to be better and more easily managed) about which only those who had walled it in spoke, while viewing it from a distance with repugnance or curiosity.

Despite centuries of Spanish dominance, however, native Quechua and/or Aymara continued to be spoken by family members in homes scattered throughout the Andes. Meanwhile in the nooks and crannies of Peru—and especially in the remote highlands—numerous indigenous practices continued, such as the worship of sacred mountains and other gods, the maintenance of social structures such as the *ayllu*, and even the practice of traditional spinning and weaving.

Yet by the late 1960s, even as the novelist Arguedas was delivering his speech, this last practice was also falling into disuse, as inexpensive synthetic yarns and cloth manufactured on machines continued to infiltrate the Andes. Village men especially—who often had to travel to the cities in order to get jobs—were eager not to be viewed as "country bumpkins" and thus began wearing Western clothing instead of their traditional attire, the latter handwoven and replete with the symbols and motifs of their ancestry. Faced with hanging on to traditions or shedding them in order to blend in better with the dominant culture, native Peruvians were increasingly at a crossroads. There was no reason, however, the novelist Arguedas pointed out, that the route followed [by indigenous people in Peru] had to be, nor was it possible that it should solely be, the one imperiously demanded by the plundering conquerors, that is: that the conquered nation should renounce its soul . . . and take on the soul of the conquerors, that is to say, that it should become acculturated. I am not an acculturated man; I am a Peruvian who, like a cheerful demon, proudly speaks in Christian and in Indian, in Spanish and in Quechua . . . In technology they [the Western world] will surpass us and dominate us, for how long we do not know, but in art we can already oblige them to learn from us and we can do it without even budging from right here.

As Arguedas well knew, ancient South American coastal and Andean artists had produced some of the finest weavings ever created. Weavings fashioned on looms over two thousand years old on the coast of Peru, for example, had thread counts of more than six hundred threads per square inch—a feat not duplicated anywhere else until Europe's industrial revolution in the nineteenth century, and then only with machines. A typical burial ceremony among the Paracas culture, on Peru's southern coast, included wrapping a deceased relative in exquisite weavings that equaled some three hundred square yards of cotton cloth—a quantity that required two acres of cotton plants to produce.

More than a thousand years later, when the first Spanish conquistadors arrived in Peru, they quickly discovered that the Incas, too, produced enormous quantities of cloth, some of the finest the Spaniards had ever seen. Pedro Pizarro, a young cousin of the Spanish leader Francisco Pizarro, wrote:

There were vast numbers of storehouses in Cusco when we entered the city, filled with very delicate cloth and with other coarser cloths; and stores of stools, of foodstuffs or coca [leaves] . . . There were also cloaks completely covered with gold and silver chaquiras [very delicate little beads], with no thread visible, like very dense chain mail, and there were storehouses of shoes with soles made of sisal and . . . [the upper part of the shoes] of fine [alpaca] wool in many colors.

By the time the Incas rose to power, in the mid-1400s, woven cloth was as integral to their empire as coinage was to Rome. Inca citizens—both male and female—not only wove clothing for themselves but also produced cloth for the Inca state, as a required labor tax. The Incas wove three basic kinds of cloth: *cosi*, which had thread counts of roughly 120 threads per square inch, was coarsely woven from llama wool, and was mainly used for blankets; *awasqa*, a grade used for most clothing and fashioned from native cotton or alpaca wool; and *cumpi*, which was made from specially bred alpacas with very fine wool or sometimes from vicuñas. It was Inca citizens who harvested the cotton or sheared the flocks, spun the thread, and wove. It was also from their labor that cloth and other goods filled the state warehouses to the ceilings. Especially fine weavings were produced by male weavers called *cumpikamayuq*, or "keepers of fine cloth"; the latter wove one of the highest grades of *cumpi* cloth, worn by the nobility. Finally, the richest cloth of all—with thread counts surpassing six hundred and almost exclusively woven from vicuña wool—was woven by the Chosen Women of the Sun, who lived as Juanita did in their nun-like *acclawasi*, or convents. It was the Chosen Women—instructed in the arts of weaving since they were young girls—who wove the finest embroidered clothing for the emperor and the emperor's principal wife, or *coya*.

The Chosen Women often interwove into the cloth tiny beads of gold or silver, iridescent hummingbird feathers, or other precious materials. According to the seventeenth-century priest and chronicler Bernabé Cobo,

> The [Inca] king . . . wore a cloak and a shirt, with . . . [sandals] on his feet. In this respect he followed the custom of the common people, but his clothing was different from the usual in that it was made of the finest wool and the best cloth that was woven in his whole kingdom, with more brilliant colors and finer-quality weaving. The *mamaconas* [the older Chosen Women] made this clothing for him, and most of it was made from vicuña wool, which is almost as fine as silk. Some of his clothes were ordinary and simple . . . other clothing was very colorful and showy with very small feathers

woven into it, and [still] other clothing was covered with ornaments of gold, emeralds, and other precious stones; this was the finest formal attire and corresponds to our embroidery, cloth of gold or silver, and brocades.

Within eighteen years of the conquest, however, Spanish chroniclers wrote that the production of *cumpi* cloth—as fine as the finest European silk—was already a dying art, as such cloth was destined for the noble classes and the noble classes themselves were quickly disappearing.

And yet, even as the power and influence of the Inca rulers gradually faded, the traditional art of weaving continued in hamlets and villages across Peru. Peasants continued making clothes for themselves down through the centuries, just as they had long before the emergence of the Incas. It wasn't until the appearance of synthetic thread and inexpensive, manufactured cloth in the mid–twentieth century, however, that the production of traditional cloth for the first time began to falter. Connected to a cash economy and wanting to earn money more quickly, Peruvian weavers began to abandon the more time-consuming ancient traditions and instead began adopting styles and methods that produced more goods, although of lower artistic quality.

The Quechua-speaking community of Chinchero was inevitably caught up in the midst of these great tidal sweeps of globalization and modernity, as was young Nilda Callañaupa. Nevertheless, Nilda continued to teach herself how to spin and weave in the ancient tradition, the movements of her fingers mirroring the fingers of thousands of her ancestors, guided in the present by the influence of the elderly shepherdess Doña Sebastiana.

After several years of full-time herding, Nilda had finally begun school at the age of eight. The state-run school consisted of a series of rectangular adobe buildings whose classrooms had wooden desks and a single lightbulb that hung from the ceiling. From the very beginning, Nilda proved to be an excellent student, applying herself to her studies while continuing her independent study of weaving. As she later wrote,

My father was insistent that I study hard and spend time on my homework. I enjoyed learning in school, but at the same time, I was developing my interest in traditional weaving. My father would come back from trips bringing cloth from distant villages, and each piece was unique. "How was that made?" I would ask myself. I experimented, trying techniques I had seen older women doing. I did this late at night in my room, when my father thought I was studying. My mother knew what I was doing and did not discourage me. [But] My father would say, "Weaving will never make you prosperous."

Nilda persisted, however, and by the time she was a young teenager, she'd begun to sell her weavings at Chinchero's Sunday market. "I continued learning to weave [in the traditional style] like a crazy person," she said. "Not because I was thinking about money but just because I was so interested."

One would have thought that Chinchero's older generation of weavers—those who were witnessing the gradual decline and disappearance of their craft—would have approved of a young girl's interest in their old-fashioned methods. Yet the encouragement of Doña Sebastiana proved to be the exception.

"You would think the grandmothers would have been the very people to have said 'Oh, how marvelous, look at her learn to weave!' " Nilda said, "but instead they told me that weaving was something to do on the side, that 'this is never going to make any real money'—that at best it would merely allow me to survive. They acted like it was almost stupid for a young person to be spending so much time learning to do this. That I should be thinking of other things."

For Nilda, however, weaving had long since become a passion. She loved the feel, she loved the textures, she loved the challenge of it. Now a young teenager, Nilda was not only a quick study, but she also soon realized that Chinchero's Sunday market was a kind of natural laboratory. There she could experiment with whether the skills she was learning had any effect on tourists or not. Instead of using synthetic yarns,

Nilda continued to make ever more complex weavings from alpaca or sheep's wool, mostly using ancient designs. And on Sundays she sold them.

It was while she was at the market square one Sunday when she was fourteen that Ed Franquemont approached her with his unusual proposition.

"A week later," Nilda says, "he knocked on the door of my house and said 'Look, I finished your belt!' At first I didn't believe him. I said 'No, it's impossible that you finished that—I don't believe you!' None of the tourists I'd met knew anything about weaving and besides, he was a man. But he finally convinced me and asked me if I would teach him. And that's how I met Ed Franquemont."

Conch shells blasted the air, signifying the emperor's arrival on Cusco's packed square, the square filled with nobles and priests wearing colorful tunics, golden bracelets, and ear spools. Beneath everyone's sandaled feet lay fine white beach sand, brought up from the coast on the backs of llamas, inside woven sacks, then emptied and spread out over the square. The sand symbolized the connection between the mountains and Mamacocha, the mother sea. Here and there on the sand lay embedded sacred pink Spondylus shells from the northern seacoast, as if they had washed up into the Andes. Also scattered about were gold and silver figurines of llamas, alpacas, foxes, and other animals that craftsmen had created in smoldering forges on the outskirts of the capital.

Juanita and the other acllas of her age group strained to see over the crowd and catch a glimpse of the emperor, Topa Inca Yupanqui, son of the Sun God and conqueror of so many distant peoples and lands. Juanita strained, too, to look in the direction of the adjacent streets that led onto the square. These were crowded with townspeople—men, women, and children. Juanita was hoping to catch a glimpse of her father or mother or members of her family. Last year, at this same festival, she had seen her *father in the distance, for the first time since she'd entered the acclawasi. Her father had held his hand up, but Juanita had been commanded along with the other acllas not to make any gestures in return. In any case, today, Juanita knew, her fate was to be decided, and since the last full moon she and the other girls had wondered aloud in whispers among themselves as to what might become of them. Which among them might be wedded to the emperor? Which to the Sun, as a temple priestess? Which to a royal noble or to a renowned warrior? And which among them, they asked one another, in even lower whispers, would become an accla-capacocha, or sacrifice?*

Juanita stood on her toes and tried to see over people's heads. She was just able to see the Sun Priest, or Willaq-Umu, who stood near the emperor. During this month of Inti Raymi, when the days were shortest and the Sun God farthest in His sacred journey to the north, the priest held his hands up toward the glowing orb in the sky and beseeched Him to return, to warm their fields and crops, to give them life, sustenance, and blessings.

"O Sun . . . [our] father," the priest cried out, as the crowd hushed and the emperor, wearing his royal lluncu tassel over his forehead and clothed in a sumptuous vicuña cloak, stood alongside. "[Our] father, who said 'Let there be Cusco!' and by your will it was founded and it is preserved with such grandeur! Let these sons of yours," he said, gesturing toward the emperor, "the Incas, be conquerors and despoilers of all mankind. We adore you and offer this sacrifice to you so that you will grant us what we beg of you. Let them be prosperous and make them happy, and do not allow them to be conquered by anyone, but let them always be conquerors, since you made them for that purpose."

Juanita watched as incense and smoke rose into the air and then as a priest led six pure white alpacas, with woven red tassels hanging from their ears, through the crowd toward the high priest. Juanita could also see four previous Inca emperors, desiccated now and sitting in an upright fashion and still richly clothed, carried on litters by attendants. The mummified emperors seemed to look out over the square, which was lined on all sides with massive gray stone palaces. Servants with whisks stood by the former emperors, making sure flies didn't bother them.

"They're sacrificing the alpacas," Quispe, her best friend, whispered. Quispe had entered the acclaswasi the same year she had. "Then they'll make the selection."

As the alpacas disappeared, one by one, pulled to the ground and sacrificed by the priests with bronze knives that quickly turned red, Juanita turned again to scan the crowds in the streets, staring hard at the faces. Then, just as she had about given up, she saw a familiar figure. There was no mistaking it. Their eyes locked. It was her father.

It's a half-hour bus ride from Cusco to the town of Chinchero, where a paved road eventually shortened the journey in 1982. It's November, which is simultaneously springtime and the beginning of the rainy season in the Andes. The bus winds its way past fields where farmers still slice the earth with wooden plows pulled by oxen or else punch holes in the ground with Inca-style foot plows called *chakitaqlla*. November is also potato planting season, so the fields are brown now with furrows and also with tiny expectant tubers that lie in wait for the rains.

An old woman on the seat across from me clutches a woven blue bag of small, lilac-colored potatoes. The potatoes are rumpled in texture and are almost as wrinkled as her brown hands. I ask her what kind they are. Potatoes originated in the Andes, and Peru has a mind-numbing five thousand varieties of them. It's difficult for most foreigners, including myself, to tell them apart.

"*Chuño*," the woman says, smiling and revealing two gold-capped upper teeth. "For soup."

Chuños are potatoes that have been left outside to alternately freeze and dry in the sun, a process that is repeated over and over again until a nearly waterless tuber remains. The technique was invented in the Andes thousands of years ago and has subsequently been exported as the "freeze-drying" process known to the rest of the world. After a week of such treatment, the potatoes and other tubers can be stored for decades. The old woman hands me a three-inch-long *chuño*. I cup it in my hand. It's as light as a piece of Styrofoam.

A half hour later, I arrive in Chinchero, the ancient Inca settlement and political province located on a high plain near the Sacred Valley. Chinchero was once the site of the Inca emperor Topa Inca Yupanqui's royal residence, which he had built sometime in the late fifteenth century. When the Spaniards conquered the area, two peasant communities lived near the cluster of finely hewn royal buildings and terraces, each belonging to a different *ayllu*. The Spaniards quickly built a Christian church on top of the remains of Topa Inca's royal palace, then forced the two native communities to join together and relocate nearby, so that they would be easier to control. It was from those two relocated communities that the town of Chinchero was born.

Today is Sunday, Chinchero's market is in full force, and the strong tropical sunshine splashes everywhere. Men wear black *ojota* sandals; brown, black, or gray pants; and jackets or colorfully woven *ponchos*. Some older men wear knitted *chullos* on their heads that look like ski hats, a tassel hanging from their tops. Women are for the most part dressed as they have dressed for at least a century, with multiple *pollera* skirts, woven shawls of alpaca, and—depending on which village they are from—a variety of hats. The streets of the town are narrow, cobblestoned, and bordered by row houses of adobe or brick, the walls of which have been plastered over with lime. Inca ruins emerge here and there alongside the streets, and the nearby hills are scored with Inca terraces still in use.

At the entrance to the market stands an old colonial portal, and on either side women are gathered. The women have long black hair woven into two braids with a tassel of black yarn tying the braided ends together. They sit or stand beside knee-high stacks of fresh green barley, which they are selling. Barley is an Old World import, and its color contrasts sharply with the oranges, reds, and ochres of the women's clothing. The ancient cereal is used to make beer and is also fed to one of the New World's few domesticated animals, the Andean guinea pig, or *cuy*. The small rodents are often served on a plate roasted and splayed, with their arms and legs stretching out, looking like road kill. *Cuy* live in people's homes, scavenging about on the floor for scraps of food and emitting occasional squeaks. Ancient Andean peoples domesticated the tasty rodents at least seven thousand years ago. The *cuy*— easy to breed—were later used in lab experiments in the eighteenth and nineteenth centuries before scientists ultimately switched to mice and rats. Hence the expression of not wanting to be used as a "guinea pig."

On Chinchero's market square I ask a young girl selling weavings where I can find the *Centro de Textiles Tradicionales,* or weaving cooperative, founded by Nilda Callañaupa—the same woman who as a young girl once sold her own weavings here. I'm interested in the story of Juanita, the Inca Ice Maiden, and Nilda, I'm told, has some unusual knowledge about the girl, specifically about the clothes she was wearing when she was discovered. But first I have to find her. Nilda should be at the *Centro,* the girl tells me, pointing in the direction I should go. She then returns to weaving a small belt.

Unlike most girls in Chinchero, Nilda not only finished grade school and middle school, but she also finished high school. She had then gone on to do the unthinkable: she enrolled in college in Cusco and graduated. Nilda was the first woman in Chinchero to do so. Her old friends, the Franquemonts, meanwhile, had by this time returned to the United States, although the two families had remained in contact. As soon as Nilda graduated from college, Ed and Chris Franquemont told her about a travel grant she could apply for that would allow her to spend six months in the United States and teach weaving there. Nilda was, after all, not only a college graduate but also a master weaver who specialized in traditional Andean techniques. At the time, Nilda applied for and got the grant, she spoke only Quechua and Spanish and had never traveled beyond Cusco.

"I didn't speak English," Nilda later told me, "not a word. It was my first time in an airplane, my first time in Lima, my first time for *everything.*"

In the United States, Nilda was surprised to find such intense interest in her weaving, a fact that only served to reinforce her belief in the value of studying local weaving traditions. Traditions that were continuing to fade as, one by one, the older generation of weavers passed away.

"Young people were not learning to weave," Nilda says. "The only good quality weavings you could find in markets were used ones, forty, fifty, or sixty years old."

Nilda's trip to the United States—coupled with her own understanding of the tourist market in Chinchero—got her to thinking: What if she taught a group of young weavers in Chinchero how to weave in the ancient style? And what if they wove using traditional dyes, threads, and looms and tried selling high-quality weavings—like those created a generation ago? What if together they formed a cooperative and shared their earnings with one another?

"Creating a cooperative became my dream," Nilda says. "But everyone I spoke to about it—except for Ed and Chris [Franquemont]—said it was impossible. [Only] Ed volunteered to help."

As I walk across Chinchero's square, women have set out their weavings and sit patiently beside them, ready to bargain. Tourists mill about, some haggling, others walking off with brightly embroidered bags meant to carry coca leaves or else with square weavings called *mantas*, used as a shawl to protect against the Andes' often bitter nighttime cold. Without clothing, of course, the Andes could never have been inhabited in the first place. And what better material to use than wool fibers that evolution has taken millions of years to produce?

A few blocks away, up a stone-lined street, I find a sign on a wall beside a large double door:

CENTRO DE TEXTILES TRADICIONALES

Inside I discover a large grassy courtyard. Perhaps a hundred people are milling about: weavers and weaving aficionados from around the world. Some come from Bolivia; others, from Ecuador, Colombia, Guatemala, the United States, Canada, and various European countries. Sprinkled among them are Quechua-speaking women from nine local villages who sell their weavings through the cooperative. The women wear traditional long skirts and broad flat hats, the colors and designs distinctive to each village. This week the center—run by Nilda Callañaupa—is hosting a semiannual *tinkuy*, which in Quechua means "encounter." Attendees have found their way to this weavers' gathering from all over the world.

Buildings with tile roofs and stuccoed exteriors surround the courtyard. The stucco is ochre colored, and the buildings house offices, storerooms, and additional rooms for visiting weavers. Under a portico squats the cooperative's retail store, a large, rectangular shop stacked with high-quality weavings, fresh off the loom.

In an adjacent area, I find Nilda Callañaupa standing before a large, steaming cauldron. She's in the middle of giving a demonstration in natural dyeing techniques to a group of foreign weavers. Nilda is short and stocky, with black hair pulled back in a single braid. She's fifty but looks about forty, with not a trace of gray hair. In the distance, the Urubamba Mountains rise up, some of their jagged peaks ice capped. The highest, Mount Salcantay, reaches over twenty thousand feet. The word *salcantay* comes from the Quechua word *sallqa*, which means "wild," "uncivilized," or "savage." Salcantay, perhaps not surprisingly, is the most sacred peak in the region and is home to a powerful local god, or *apu*.

"You can make a dye in any quantity," Nilda is saying, in Spanish-accented English, "but just be sure to use the same proportions. Once it's heated, the dye is ready."

Nilda takes a bundle of spun white alpaca wool and places it into a waist-high metal vat filled with a bubbling black liquid. The dye's color comes from a fungus that Nilda is teaching the crowd how to use. About forty weavers from around the world watch carefully, taking notes or filming on small video recorders or phones. As Nilda stirs the vat, she tells her audience the story of how she discovered this black dye in a remote community in the cloud forest.

"There was only one elderly man," Nilda says, stirring the black brew with a long wooden pole, "who remembered how they used to make this. He took me out into the forest and showed me a tree that had a black fungus growing on it. They hadn't used the fungus in years."

Out in the courtyard, during a break, the women from the cooperative begin serving lunch. One of them, wearing a bright, colorful, red-and-black outfit that is typical of Chinchero, hands me a plate of roasted guinea pig with a side of small, freeze-dried *chuño* potatoes. The potatoes have been rehydrated.

"Would you like a *mate de coca* [coca-leaf tea]?" she asks.

I nod, and she returns with a steaming cup and a big smile. The feeling here is of a big family reunion, the colorfully dressed women milling about the more drably dressed foreigners, like so many brightly plumaged birds. A pair of obviously foreign women walk over and occupy two empty chairs next to me. One is lean and gray haired, in her sixties; the other, blonde and Rubenesque, about forty. They both have plates of guinea pig and potatoes, and both are from the United States. They introduce themselves.

"I'm Chris," says the elder one, the mother.

"I'm Abby," says her daughter, smiling.

Their last name, it turns out, is Franquemont.

At 12,400 feet, as we work our way through plates of guinea pig, a rodent that's tasty yet full of small bones, the Franquemonts fill me in on their lives since leaving Peru. Abby now lives in Ohio, has a son, and owns a weaving studio. Chris lives in Connecticut and is retired.* Ed Franquemont, they tell me, was diagnosed with bone cancer in 2002. He passed away in 2004, at the age of fifty-nine.

"I miss him every day," Abby says.

In the last year of his life, Abby says, Ed was working hard to help raise funds to purchase the store the cooperative now owns in Cusco on the grounds of the old Inca Sun Temple, or Qoricancha. The man who'd once bought an unfinished textile from a teenaged Andean weaver

*Christine Franquemont passed away from natural causes in her hotel room in Cusco on November 12, 2013, within a day after arriving for the latest *tinkuy* and a week before launching a book she co-wrote with Nilda Callañaupa, *Faces of Tradition: Weaving Elders of the Andes.*

ultimately shared that girl's dream of not allowing an ancient weaving tradition to die.

"He didn't live to see the cooperative's inauguration," Abby says, "but he was pretty confident it was going to work out. He would've loved to have seen it and how it's grown. It's funny how things come full circle," she says, looking around. "If my parents hadn't met on an archaeological dig in Ancón—I don't think any of this would ever have happened."

We speak for a while of sickness and losing fathers. I tell Abby that until my own father died, I never understood what anyone else went through when something as tragic as that occurs. She agrees:

"At first, I couldn't understand why some people's condolences bothered me and why others really mattered," she said. "Until I realized that the ones that really mattered were from people who had experienced the same thing."

Abby's father had suffered from "bum knees," she says, reminiscing. It was a condition she believes she inherited from him. One day, when she was a girl in Chinchero, she wrenched one of her knees. Her neighbors quickly took her to a local *curandero*, an older man named Lorenzo.

"I dislocated my knee so badly that it bent forward toward me," Abby says. "Lorenzo was this fantastic bone and joint guy who people from all around came to visit. He was a *curandero*, so he had this whole spiritual realm thing going as well. They brought me in, he took a big swig of cane alcohol and coca leaves and chewed them all up together into a paste and spit it onto my knee. It went numb pretty quick. Because that's basically like morphine. Then he put my kneecap back in place. My dad was there and he'd had surgery for this same problem. In his case, he couldn't walk for weeks. But Lorenzo got me back walking again within days. My dad was amazed."

Lorenzo was not only a talented physical therapist, Abby says, but he was also able to foretell people's futures and could rid their bodies of evil spirits. He did so with coca leaves.

Did Lorenzo ever read leaves for *you*? I ask.

Pablo Escobar dressed as one of his heroes,
the American gangster Al Capone.

Foreground, left to right: Major Hugo Aguilar, Colonel Hugo Martínez, and his son, Hugo Martínez Jr., two days after their final operation against Pablo Escobar. *(Hugo Martínez)*

Roberto Escobar at his home in Medellín. Behind him, a wall-sized photo of the entrance to *Hacienda Nápoles*, with a replica of the small plane that flew Pablo's first load of cocaine to the US.

Charles Darwin at thirty-one years of age, four years after his return to England on the HMS *Beagle*.

Robert FitzRoy, captain of the HMS *Beagle*. His religious views ultimately led to a falling out with Charles Darwin, whom he had hired. *(Getty Images)*

The Shining Path leader Abimael Guzmán had prepared for every possibility but one: his own capture. Ten days after his arrest, he was shown to the public for the first time, on September 24, 1992, in Lima, Peru. *(Getty Images)*

Professor Hiram Bingham at Machu Picchu in 1912, a year after his discovery.

(National Geographic)

The 15th century Inca ruins of Machu Picchu, Peru.

The first, second, and third place winners of the "Ice Maiden of Ampato" weaving contest. Olga Huamán, who won first place, is on the right.

Nilda Callañaupa (left) demonstrating the use of natural dyes to color alpaca wool at a *tinkuy* in Chinchero, Peru.

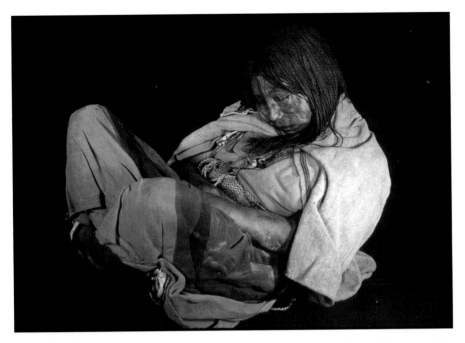

A 15-year-old sacrificed Inca girl, called the "Llullaillco Maiden," discovered by archaeologist Johan Reinhard in 1999. The girl was found on Mount Llullaillco, which straddles the border of northern Chile and Argentina. She had been frozen for more than five centuries and had ingested both alcohol and coca leaves before her death. *(Johan Reinhard)*

The ten-ton megalithic "Gateway of the Sun," carved from a single block of andesite, at Tiwanaku, Bolivia.

Master *totora*-reed boat builder Paulino Esteban, in Huatajata, Bolivia.

The Norwegian explorer Thor Heyerdahl, surveying thousand-year-old pyramids in 1988 at Túcume, Peru.

The floating Uros Islands on Lake Titicaca near Puno, Peru.

A bust of Che Guevara
in La Higuera, Bolivia,
the same village where
the revolutionary was
executed.

The iconic image
of Che Guevara by
Alberto Korda.

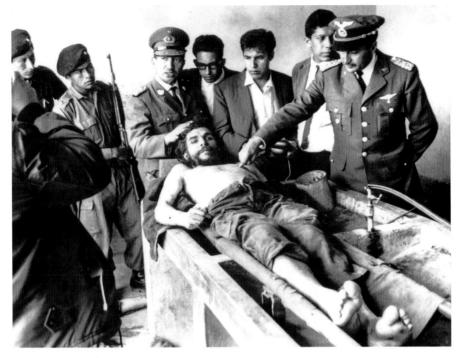

Che Guevara after his execution in a laundry room in Vallegrande, Bolivia, on October 10, 1967. A Bolivian officer examines one of his bullet wounds. *(Getty Images)*

Julia Cortez was a 19-year old school teacher when she met and conversed with Che Guevara on the final day of his life. Here, she is at her home in Vallegrande, Bolivia.

The Wild Bunch posing for a photo in Fort Worth, Texas, in 1900. Sitting, left to right: The Sundance Kid, the Tall Texan, and Butch Cassidy. Just a few months later, Butch and Sundance would leave for Patagonia. All five men would die violent deaths within the next eight years.

Judge Felix Charlar at his home in Tupiza, Bolivia.

Froilán Risso's father was a young boy living in San Vicente, Bolivia, when Butch Cassidy and the Sundance Kid arrived in town. Froilán claims to know where the bodies are buried.

Ushuaia, Argentina, where Thomas Bridges built his mission among the Yámana.

The HMS *Beagle* sailing on what would later be known as the Beagle Channel. Two canoe-loads of Yámana Indians are in the foreground *(painting by Conrad Martens)*.

The missionary Thomas Bridges founded Harberton Ranch in 1886 on Tierra del Fuego Island. His descendants still run it today.

Portraits of three native Patagonians—Fuegia Basket (top), Jemmy Button (middle), and York Minster. Darwin first met the trio in England, then accompanied them to Patagonia. *(Darwin Online)*

Cristina Calderon in Ukika (on Navarino Island, Chile), the southernmost city in the world. She is the last speaker of the Yámana language.

"He did, when I was fourteen," Abby says, referring to the process of casting a handful of coca leaves onto the ground and carefully studying their arrangement.

"In the end he said—and I remember this very distinctly—he said, 'You know, I have to tell you something that's going to be hard, hard for you to hear and hard for you to accept, but it's going to be okay.' "

Abby had looked at him, not comprehending.

" 'I have to tell you that you will have only one child and it will be a son,' " he said, gathering the leaves up and replacing them in his bag. He then looked at her carefully:

" 'But the son will *live*.' "

Abby looks at me and laughs. "So the bad news was that I was only going to have one child. But the *good* news was that he would live."

Years, later, on a visit to Chinchero with her son, who was ten years old at the time, Abby ran into Lorenzo. The old *curandero*, although aged and stooped, immediately recognized her. Abby introduced her son to the old man, who nodded knowingly.

"And you still have just the one, no?" he asked.

Abby nodded.

"But don't worry—he will live," the old man said, remembering.

Lorenzo passed away five or six years ago, Abby says, taking his gift of prophecy with him.

I ask Abby if she knows the story of Juanita, the Ice Maiden, and Abby nods.

"Do you remember making offerings when you lived here?" I ask.

"Yes, you would always share your food and your drink with *Pachamama* [the Earth Mother]," she says. "That was just a part of the way of thinking about things. Like on All Saints' Day, when you take food to your dead family members in the graveyard and leave it there for them. People would make offerings—it's kind of like Catholics burning candles. Asking for this and that. It's very personal. There's this sense of sharing what you've got with the whole surroundings, with the mountains you live with. I mean, everyone sort of has a mountain that 'owns' them," Abby says. "And of course I have one, too."

I ask her how she first discovered that.

"Well, you just *know*," she says. "You just know. Mine is called Quilca and it's here in Chinchero. If you stand looking at the old church, it's right behind it in the distance."

When she was a young girl living here, Abby explains, she used to have dreams of being abandoned by her parents and of being separated from the people she cared about. In her dreams, she visited the far side of Quilca Mountain, where she'd never been before, and it was there that she was reunited with her parents and friends. The strange thing is, when she eventually visited the far side of the mountain, it was *exactly* like what she had seen in her dreams. At the time, she'd told her Quechua-speaking girlfriends about this. They immediately knew what her dreams meant: "Well, it's obvious!" they said. "You belong to Apu Quilca. The *apu* [mountain spirit] owns you now."

Abby finishes her plate of guinea pig and sets it down beside her. "Auntie Quilca still shows up in my dreams," she says matter-of-factly.

I ask Abby what struck her most about growing up in this small Andean town. She thinks a bit before speaking.

When I think of being homesick for a place, it's for this town and this community. It's where I feel like I'm *from*, even though clearly I'm not. But this is where the formative things happened to me, where I used to hang out in the hills with the other [shepherd] girls, and where I learned how to weave. Even now, living in Ohio and an "American," my loyalty is to this town and to my community. It "owns" me to a great extent. And I think it's partly because this is a culture of people who never looked at anybody based on how they appeared or how they looked and made all of these judgments— everybody was just a person, with the same needs. I feel comfortable in saying that our family would not have made it here were it not for the people of Chinchero and their belief that we were a young family in need of help and that we were in their community and thus "belonged" to them. They felt a responsibility to bring us up to speed. And we felt a responsibility toward them. They shared what they had with us. I don't know anywhere else that's like that. So this is the place and these are the people I get homesick for. Chinchero is where I feel "at home."

I ask Abby if her father felt the same way—or if it was different for her parents as adults.

"My dad was pretty good at learning languages and getting along with people. He was remarkably charismatic. He could get along with anyone, from any walk of life. But it was my mom who had the obsession for Peru. My dad always liked to say that he just went along for the ride. But he fell in love with Peru, too."

Her father was a doer, she said. For some reason, he always ended up in a leadership position. People relied upon him. Abby remembers how surprised she was at the sheer number of people who showed up at his memorial service and who said that, when they were undergoing extremely stressful moments, they would ask themselves silently, "What would *Ed* do?"

Abby particularly remembers a man who showed up who'd lived on the commune with them as a "troubled teen." As a young man he'd later joined the merchant marine and had worked his way up to captain. There was many a time, he told the audience, that as a captain guiding his ship through heavy seas he would suddenly stop and say, "Now, what would *Ed* do in this situation?" And he would do exactly what he thought Ed would have done.

"The funny thing," Abby says, "is that my dad was never *in* the merchant marine. Nor did he know a *thing* about sailing!"

"He was decisive," Abby says, "He didn't spend a lot of time sitting around wondering if something could be pulled off. My father was the kind of guy who would pack up and move his family to Peru with a few hundred dollars in his pocket. And he would say, 'We can swing it. We can figure it out.' And that's exactly what he did," she says.

"You know, it's amazing how interconnected so many things are in life. It's amazing to see all these things come together and work out. It's just remarkable."

She looks around at the people milling about, chatting with one another, sharing their passion for weaving, all of them from a kaleidoscope of backgrounds.

"I mean, how much more in life can people really ask for," Abby says, "than to know that what they did made a *difference?*"

Juanita could scarcely believe what she'd seen. Already, standing in Cusco's great square, she'd watched as a small group of acllas had knelt before the emperor and the sun priest had bidden them to rise. "For the temple," is all the emperor had said, and the girls had immediately realized that they would spend the rest of their lives in the Acclawasi, where they had already spent the last four years. The priests had then brought another group of girls forward, the audience silent the length and breadth of the square. Once again, the emperor had lifted his hand, his robe shimmering with the tiny feathers of hummingbirds that had been sewn into the immaculate cloth.

"For the nobility," he'd uttered, his eyes gazing down upon girls, now destined to become the wives of various nobles and warriors. Juanita found it difficult to breathe, and her skin felt cold. Already, the emperor had selected acllas to become temple priestesses and others to become nobles' wives. Now all that was left were those who would be selected for the emperor's harem—and those who were to be sacrificed. Juanita stared hard at a small seashell lying in the beach sand next to her sandals and uttered a silent prayer to Mamacocha, goddess of a vast sea she'd heard of yet had never seen. Juanita's friend Quispe stood close beside her, wearing her woven tunic of burnt-umber colors. Juanita could clearly feel Quispe's body trembling. Juanita wanted to look back, to look over the crowd, to see if she could see her father again. There was no doubt that he was here, watching. Was her mother here somewhere, too?

"Here he comes," Quispe whispered, referring to a temple priest who somehow seemed to know which girls were to be formed into which

groups. Juanita watched as the priest held out his arm, parting the remaining acllas into two groups. On whichever side his arm pointed, the girls moved to the left or right. Quispe tried pushing against Juanita, but the priest approached, and his arm pointed directly between them. Reluctantly, Juanita's friend moved away, then stole a fearful glance backward toward Juanita as her group approached the emperor. It was all Juanita could do not to look left, over the crowd, in the direction of her father. Before the emperor and the high priest, Quispe and the other girls knelt. The emperor gazed over the crowd, swept his eyes over their bent heads, then looked up at the sky. Juanita stole a glance at the emperor's royal headband, which only he wore. It had a fringe of scarlet-colored alpaca fibers dangling from it, each interwoven around a small golden ornament that glistened in the sun. Juanita held her breath as the emperor stretched his arm out toward the group of acllas kneeling before him. Silence descended once again upon the square.

"For the harem," the emperor said.

Juanita's eyes opened wide. She looked hard at the back of Quispe's head. Several girls around her let out deep sighs. Juanita's head spun and suddenly she felt weak as she watched Quispe's group head off. Her own group, quite small and the only one remaining, was now led forward. In a daze, Juanita knelt with the others before the priest and the emperor, as the other groups had done before.

"Aclla-capacocha," the emperor said simply, his eyes dark and solemn, "Chosen women sacrifices."

The crowd was hushed before the high-altitude tableau of the small knot of girls now destined to join the gods, wordless before the presence of their emperor and the newly appointed offerings. The sacrifices to the Sun had been dutifully made. The Accla-capacochas had been selected. The world was as it should be, as it had always been, ever since the first Inca emperor had brought forth the world from darkness and had given civilization to the world. The son of the Sun God, having spoken, now stepped onto his royal litter, seated himself on his duho, then was lifted up and borne away toward his palace. Juanita, walking across the square with the other girls and through a crowd that now parted respectfully before them—the *specially chosen ones—felt her legs growing weak. And then, suddenly, blackness overcame her.*

"Weaving in this way is beautiful," says Nilda Callañaupa. She's seated in an office at the *Centro de Textiles Tradicionales* in Chinchero, which is now one of nine centers, each run by a local community of weavers.

"It's not solely about weaving and making money," she says. "It's about staying in one's own community, it's about bringing alive traditions of all types, including languages. It's about relearning things that have been lost in agriculture and in the arts. It's all of those things. What we do is not going to make anyone rich—but what we do *is* rich in traditions, rich in knowledge, rich in art."

In 1979, when Nilda was nineteen, Ed and Chris Franquemont helped the Chinchero community establish a local museum dedicated to promoting traditional Chinchero culture. Four years later, the Franquemonts, with the help of Earthwatch volunteers, began a systematic, multidisciplinary study of all of the Chinchero district's flora, assembling in the process a team of international botanists (among them Harvard ethnobotanists Timothy Plowman and Wade Davis), anthropologists (Ed and Chris Franquemont), and native Quechua speakers from Chinchero. The study ran off and on for nearly a dozen years and ultimately became the largest of its kind.

Nilda, meanwhile, after graduating college in Cusco, began leading tours of foreign weavers visiting Peru, as a way of earning a living. She also continued to visit nearby communities to learn local weaving techniques. In some communities, she discovered, weaving traditions were literally hanging by a thread—with only one or two elderly people who knew how to weave in the traditional manner. There had to be some way to create an organization, she realized, to help preserve these traditions before they completely disappeared.

The time was not right, however, as beginning in 1980 a fierce guerrilla war had broken out between the Maoist Shining Path guerrilla insurgency and Peru's government, a struggle centered in the south-central Andes. Many of the guerrillas were native Quechua speakers. At least some of them fought believing in the Andean myth of Inkarri, the resurrection of the Inca state. That myth began to emerge after the execution of the Inca emperor Atahualpa by the Spaniards in 1533. According to legend, Atahualpa was said to have vowed to avenge his death, and the Spaniards were said to have buried the Inca emperor's body in different parts of the empire in order to prevent that from occurring. They thus buried the emperor's legs in the Andes in Ayacucho, his head beneath what is now the presidential palace in Lima, and his arms under the Waqaypata, or "Square of Tears," in Cusco. One day, the legend proclaimed, the parts would reassemble themselves, and Atahualpa would rise from the ground, reestablishing the rule of the Inca and restoring the preinvasion harmony that had ended with the conquest.

"The war was brutal," Nilda says, "and it touched everybody. People's friends disappeared. Some were captured by the Shining Path and forced to fight, others were killed or captured by the army. Everyone was afraid."

Given the increasing negative publicity, foreigners were afraid of visiting Peru. The normal flood of tourists to Cusco soon shrank to a mere trickle. In 1992 the government finally captured Abimael Guzmán, the guerrilla movement's leader—but by then more than seventy thousand people had died in the struggle. Slowly, ever so slowly, Peru's economy began to recover, and with it, tourism began to flow again. It was time once more for Nilda to think of realizing her dream.

In 1995 Cultural Survival—a UK-based organization dedicated to helping indigenous people defend their lands, languages, and cultures—sponsored Nilda to help protect and revive the backstrap loom traditions in the Chinchero and Cusco areas. Called the Chinchero Culture Project, the idea was for Nilda to begin researching and documenting the various weaving techniques that were quickly disappearing. Nilda had only recently returned from a trip to the United States, where she had worked with the Peabody Museum at Harvard University, the Museum of Textiles in Toronto, the Center for International Studies at the University College of Cape Breton, and the Museum of Fine Arts in Boston. By now she was a university graduate, fluent in English, Spanish, and Quechua, and a master weaver. And she possessed several additional qualities that would serve her well during the coming years: she was a born leader and organizer. Abby Franquemont, in fact, remembers Nilda chastising Abby and her other eight-year-old girl friends when they had tried to sell their small weavings at Chinchero's Sunday market. Nilda, Abby says, who was perhaps fifteen or sixteen at the time,

> would come over when girls were thinking about cutting corners and doing something half-assed to make a sale, and she would quietly say something like, "You know, is that *really* work that you feel good about?" Then she'd walk away. Or she'd come over and say, "Oh really—you're going to sell that for *how* much, to make a sale? If you sell all of your weavings for that price, then you won't have enough money to buy material and you'll be out of business! Does that seem like a good long-range *plan*?" And we would all look at one another and say, "Uh oh!" She had that kind of presence as a girl. In fact, we all looked up to her and wanted to be how Nilda was and wanted to be able to do the things that Nilda could do. We used to say, "Well, I hope that *I'm* going to grow up to be as good a teenaged girl as Nilda."

Years later, when Abby worked for a stint in California as a software developer, before she turned full time to weaving, she was always amazed at how well Nilda fit into any given situation.

> When I was at my Silicon Valley job, Nilda once called me up and said, "Meet me at the Stanford Alumni Center for lunch." And I would say, "Oh, I didn't realize that you were here!" And then at other times she'd take me to the most remote, fifteen-thousand-foot

mud hut you could possibly find and would sit around and hang out with people. She's equally at home in either of those settings. She's inspirational and empowering, and a lot of the time you don't even think about whether what she's suggesting you do is feasible or not—you just *do* it. And somehow it works out.

Tim Wells, a sixty-two-year-old weaver and artist, first met Nilda at an Andean textile workshop Ed Franquemont was teaching at the de Young Museum in San Francisco in the late 1990s. Nilda had been in the area for other purposes and decided to stay a few extra days, in order to help out Ed. Recalls Tim,

> So for the three days she was there, helping people learn to do Andean weaving. Mainly belts and things like that. Nilda had already begun her project to preserve traditional techniques in Chinchero, and Ed wanted her to tell the class about that. So on the last day, Ed gave this introduction and Nilda basically thanked him and walked away. She just kept helping with the class. Nilda was too humble. She had no intention of mentioning the project. She said she was there to help people weave, and that was it.

Wells, however, was interested in the project and introduced himself. The more he heard, the more he wanted to volunteer to help out. First, however, he called up two seasoned community organizers who had recently accompanied Nilda to some remote Andean communities. Nilda had been there to discuss the idea of the communities forming a weaving cooperative and joining together in a common effort. Different villages, Wells says, have different histories, and their inhabitants belong to different *ayllus*, so the politics involved can be quite delicate.

"The two organizers had already worked in Chile and Ecuador," Wells said, "but when they returned, they were flabbergasted. They told me in a nutshell that Nilda was the most effective community organizer that they had ever met." Wells soon traveled to Peru and volunteered—and has been doing so off and on for the last twelve years.

It wasn't until 1996, however, that Nilda's ideas finally jelled and she decided to establish a weaving cooperative not in Chinchero, but in Cusco, which the vast majority of tourists visited on their way to Machu Picchu. As Nilda later wrote in her book *Weaving in the Peruvian Highlands,*

> I had been going out into other communities in the Cusco Department for some time to look at textiles . . . I realized that in some areas textiles were disappearing or changing, and that these traditional techniques should be preserved. I believed that locating a museum in Chinchero would limit that effort. So I thought, "What if I dream of a bigger project? What would be the next step?" And these questions led to the idea of locating a center in Cusco, one that would represent the weaving of many parts of the Department of Cusco. We called it the Center for Traditional Textiles of Cusco.

The center's overall purpose, Nilda envisioned, would be to help preserve and celebrate Andean textiles, a tradition that has been carried on for thousands of years. At the same time, she wanted to help improve the economies of the different villages that participated. Rather than have young women leave their communities and emigrate to large, deracinated cities such as Lima, what if they could supplement their income substantially by carrying on an ancient tradition right in their own villages, among their friends, families, and *ayllus*?

Nilda began in Chinchero, gathering a group of women and encouraging them to begin making high-quality, traditional textiles made from handspun fibers and natural dyes. There had to be an incentive, however, and that incentive was being able to sell their weavings for a price commensurate with the added time and labor invested. Nilda provided the venue through the cooperative's store in Cusco. She then sought to expand the market by soliciting museums and other institutions to place orders. Slowly, the orders began to trickle in. Eventually, Nilda visited other communities whose weaving traditions were in danger of disappearing and pitched them the idea of forming their own cooperatives.

At first, Nilda tells me, there were just a few villages. Then there was a handful. Today there are nine communities, each with its own cooperative. Together, the cooperative employs about eight hundred master weavers. The weavings they produce currently find their way into local stores, into the Center for Traditional Textiles's store in Cusco, and, through the center's website, into museums and collectors' hands around the world.

For young women (and some men) who have not finished their public schooling, a requirement of joining the cooperative is to do just that—to complete their schooling. "It's not an 'apprenticeship,'" says Tim Wells. "And that comes from Nilda. Because she realizes that the future lies in education."

Each cooperative can do what it wants with the members' earnings. The cash produced can thus be divided individually or else used for communal purposes, which is an ancient Andean tradition.

In one of the participating communities, Accha Alta, Wells was stunned by the village's location: "It's five thousand feet up from the valley floor," he says. "They grow incredible potatoes and herd alpacas. It's an extremely harsh climate—all their water is glacial runoff." In this particular community, the villagers use a supplementary warp technique and create weavings in various shades of reds and ochres, all from natural dyes. "They took their extra income," Wells says, "and set up an education room so that they could learn to read and write. That's how much education means to them."

One of the other things Nilda began through the center was to create a weaving competition, complete with prizes and awards, offered to weavers in the participating villages. Nilda, who is always encouraging the weavers to strive for the highest quality possible, set up the competition in order to encourage the creation of truly virtuoso weavings—weavings as good as any the women's Inca ancestors had ever produced.

In 2006 the center created an unusual competition that reached into the very heart of the weavers' past. Eleven years earlier, in 1995, an American high-altitude archaeologist, Johan Reinhard, along with his Peruvian climbing partner, Miguel "Miki" Zárate, had climbed to the top of Ampato Volcano, outside of Arequipa in southern Peru. There, at an elevation of 20,700 feet, the two could clearly see the nearby volcano of Sabancaya, which was regularly erupting, and also the long chain of ice-covered Andean peaks. Reinhard and Zárate had been searching the summit for possible Inca offerings and had found two gold and silver female figurines dressed in miniature textiles and wearing feather head-dresses. They discovered the figurines near portions of a sacrificial plat-form that had recently collapsed. When the pair began searching for the rest of the platform below, Reinhard's companion suddenly called out, "I see something inside the crater! It looks like a [mummy] bundle!" As Reinhard later wrote,

> [An Inca] mummy bundle was simply lying on top of the ice. This seemed so unlikely that we couldn't believe our eyes. For fifteen years I had visited dozens of sites on peaks in the Andes and had never even seen a mummy bundle on a mountain, let alone one lying out in the open. Only a couple of intact mummy bundles had ever been recovered from high mountains, and only one by an archaeologist . . . The outer [intricately woven] cloth wrapping had stripes typical of Inca textiles . . . This could mean only one thing: The Incas had performed a human sacrifice . . . I took photos as Miki used his ice axe to cut the ice beneath the bundle to free it. He turned it on its side for a better grip, and as he did so the bundle revolved in his hands. Suddenly, we froze and time seemed to stop. We were looking straight into the face of an Inca [girl].

The girl was completely frozen, Reinhard discovered, and had remained in that state for at least five hundred years. She'd been sacrificed on top of the volcano. Wearing sandals and the perfectly preserved clothing she'd worn on her final day, the young girl had lived briefly sometime during the mid-fifteenth century.

Reinhard's team later nicknamed the frozen girl "Juanita," as a tribute to Johan, the leader of the expedition that had discovered her. The girl's own name, of course, was unknown. Juanita appeared to be from the nobility, as she'd been wearing beautifully woven clothes of spun alpaca wool, clothes that either she or others had made for her. Women from the Cusco area, it was known, had especially beautiful and stylish dress. The Spanish chronicler Pedro Cieza de León had marveled that

> Some of the women wear the very graceful dress of those of Cusco, with a long mantle extending from the neck to the feet, having holes for the arms. Round the waist they fasten a very broad and graceful belt called *chumpi*, which tightens and secures the mantle. Over this they wear another fine mantle falling from the shoulders and coming down so as to cover the feet, called *lliclla*. To secure their mantles they wear pins of gold and silver rather broad at one end, called *topu*. On the head they wear a very graceful band, which they call *uncha*, and the *usutas*, or sandals, complete their attire. In short, the dress of the ladies of Cusco is the most graceful and rich that has been seen up to this time in all the Indies.

The chronicler's description could have been a description of the dress of the young, four-foot-two-inch-tall Inca girl found on the mountaintop, born presumably in the Cusco area sometime in the 1400s. On her head, Juanita wore a head cloth frequently used by noblewomen. She also wore a brilliantly colored, rainbow-hued dress, or *acsu*, which consisted of a rectangular piece of cloth wound around her body and under the arms, fastened with silver pins, or *tupus*, one over each shoulder. Juanita also wore an elaborately woven belt, or *chumpi*, around her waist while over her shoulders she wore a bright red-and-white striped shawl, or *lliclla*, fastened with a silver pin. All the clothing was of course woven from handspun threads colored with natural dyes. And it was precisely this discovery of a nearly perfectly preserved Inca girl and her clothing—which *Time* magazine hailed in 1995 as "one of the world's top 10 discoveries"—that caught the attention not only of the press, but also of Nilda Callañaupa.

"Johan is an old friend," Nilda tells me in her office, pulling out some aged photos and showing me two of them. "We used to work together as guides at a travel agency." When the news hit about the discovery of the Ice Maiden of Ampato [Volcano], as Juanita came to be called, Nilda and Johan got in touch. Nilda remembers the shock of seeing the first photos taken of Juanita's clothing. "Beautiful, of very high quality," she says, shaking her head slowly. Some years later, after Nilda had established her center and had begun carrying out yearly weaving competitions, Johan suggested an idea: Why not see if any of the women in the different village cooperatives could reproduce the clothes that Juanita had been wearing? Why not have them examine the girl's clothes and see if their present skill level approached that of their ancestors?

And so began the 2006–07 Lady of Ampato weaving competition, a challenge open to any of the weavers belonging to one of the cooperatives. The women who participated ultimately were not able to visit Juanita herself, who remained in a glass-lined, ice-cold chamber in Arequipa, but they did closely examine photos of what Juanita had been wearing. Then, working from these same photos, they slowly began the process of deciphering what Inca hands some five hundred years earlier had created—weavings so fine that there was little doubt that they had been produced by Chosen Women who, like Juanita, had once lived in Cusco's *acclawasi*.

"The weavers asked themselves, 'How was this done?' " Nilda recalls. " 'Were these made on a [backstrap] loom—or were some tapestries [weavings hiding the warp threads and made on vertical looms that fell into disuse after the fall of the Inca Empire]?' " Finally, after close examination, the women determined that the girl's clothes had been made on backstrap looms such as those they themselves used, and set to work trying to duplicate the Inca women's feat.

"You know, the winner is here today at the *tinkuy*," Nilda tells me. "Her name is Olga Huamán—and she's from Chinchero."

I find Olga tending a vat of dye on the courtyard, surrounded by other weavers from her community. She has her hair done up in multiple braids, in the Chinchero style, is decked out in resplendent woven clothing, and smiles shyly when I mention the Lady from Ampato competition. Olga was worried at first, she says, that she couldn't figure out how the weavings were done: it's difficult to study a weaving just by looking at it, and even harder when only looking at a photo.

How did it make her feel, I ask, reproducing the clothing of a young girl from Inca times?

"Privileged," she says, and smiles again, stirring the bubbling liquid dye before her.

Because the women and men who belong to the cooperatives are mostly from small, isolated communities and have traveled very little, the center has sponsored trips for them, so that they can see for themselves some of the heritage that millions of tourists visiting Peru each year get to see. In 1996 a group of them traveled for the first time to the citadel of Machu Picchu, once the royal residence of the greatest Inca emperor, Pachacutec. There Olga and the rest of the women, dressed in their characteristic clothes, explored the citadel surrounded by giant crags and swirling clouds, a city assembled from thousands of stones cut and carved by their ancestors.

"What was your impression?" I ask her.

"It was like a dream," she says. "I felt like I was dreaming."

It strikes me that, had Olga been transported five hundred years into the past and had she met people living in Machu Picchu, she no doubt would have understood both their language and the intricate manner in which they were dressed.

"Proud," she continues, remembering her visit. "It made me proud."

Early in the morning on the seventh day of her journey from Cusco, at 16,200 feet on the lower flank of Ampato volcano, Juanita woke suddenly with a start. She'd slept only fitfully ever since she and the rest of the procession of llamas, priests, and assistants had left Cusco the week before. Four months after learning that she'd been chosen by the emperor as an "aclla-capacocha," whose destiny was now to be joined with the gods, Juanita was told by a priestess that she was to prepare herself for a journey the

following day. That night, Juanita had not been able to sleep. It had been months since she'd last seen her friend Quispe, who was now married to an Inca noble and could no longer visit the Acclawasi. It had also been four months since she'd last glimpsed her father, on Cusco's sacred square. It had been a year since she'd last seen her father, a brief interlocking of the eyes when she'd spotted her in a crowd.

The morning of her departure, Juanita had said good-bye to those acllas she had lived with and also to the mamacona, or head priestess. The mamacona had placed both hands on Juanita's bowed head and had whispered for her to be strong—for she had been chosen and was blessed to be with the gods. Juanita's memory of the following week was blurred—sometimes she'd ridden on a litter, borne by members of the Rucana tribe up and down stone roadways that twisted like snakes along sheer cliffs. At other times, when the ground was not so steep, she'd walked in the middle of the procession, through valleys rimmed by ice-topped mountains and past small villages whose inhabitants bowed or sometimes fell to their knees when they saw the procession pass.

Just yesterday, Juanita had glimpsed for the first time the mountain that was their destination—a sheer black, upswept cone with a white cap of ice on top. When they'd first came in sight of it and a priest had told her what it was, her heart had seemed to stop beating. The procession of priests and the train of llamas carrying supplies had come to a stop, and the priests had stretched out their arms and bowed. There, besides Ampato, rose another cone-like mountain, but from the top of this one a stream of gray-white smoke rose skyward and then flattened and formed a gray mantle above. "Apu Sabancaya," one of the priests had told her. It was the god who dwelled within this volcano who had shaken the whole region. Even now, Juanita could feel his sudden movements through the ground.

That night, the volcano had glowed red in the distance, and they could hear the apu roaring and grumbling, the mountain god enraged, with flames sometimes bursting from the volcano's mouth. Because of the roars and the red glow and because of everything that had happened since her meeting with the emperor, Juanita had been unable to sleep. Now, in fact, *she ate very little: some roasted corn and a few other vegetables. A priest wearing a golden amulet and carrying a staff had given Juanita a small woven bag full of sacred coca leaves, instructing her how to place the leaves in her mouth, just inside her cheek. The leaves helped numb her body and took away her hunger. They made her feel stronger. Yesterday, climbing up Ampato's flanks and leaving their footprints finely etched in a layer of gray ash, they'd arrived at a camp on the volcano's lower flank. A group of small stone houses had awaited them, with roofs of thatched ichu grass. The attendants had taken off the llamas' packs and had enclosed the animals in a small stone corral.*

This morning, Juanita had woken with a start. Outside the stone house a number of priests had already left, beginning the climb above her and toward the volcano's crown. Juanita soon joined them. At this rarefied height, she could look out over at Sabancaya, which continued to rumble and growl and pour out smoke. Sometimes, the angry god shook the ground, as if threatening them; at other times, a fine veil of gray ash fell, as delicate as the smallest snowflakes Juanita had ever seen. Now, and almost in a daze, Juanita climbed up the volcano's side, followed by several priests. Behind them followed the llamas and attendants. The going was steep and Juanita frequently had to stop. A priest offered her more coca leaves, directing her to place fresh ones in her mouth. Another gave her chicha, a strong, fermented corn drink that made her head feel light. The chicha was so cold it almost seemed to freeze in her mouth.

Snow now appeared beneath their feet as Juanita pulled her alpaca shawl closely around her, clutching at the cloth. Her bare legs beneath her tunic felt cold, nearly frozen. She was unused to the altitude, unused to climbing, and was so numb with tiredness and cold that she found it difficult to think. Juanita felt fear, she felt awe; she also felt a strange mixture of both exhaustion and anticipation.

Late in the afternoon, they arrived near the summit. Juanita's breathing was difficult. Her lips were cracked from the sun and the thin air. The priests instructed Juanita to walk with them to a stone platform. There, before her, spread a line of white-capped mountains—each the home of a powerful apu, or mountain god. These were the same gods who provided them with streams and rivers and water for their crops, who provided them with abundant herds of alpacas and llamas, who provided them with life itself. Juanita was surprised to see that now, slightly below them, she could clearly look down upon angry Sabancaya. A tortured river of smoke still poured out of its mouth, at times obscuring the sun. Stones occasionally shot straight up, and Juanita could see the apu's angry red lips of fire.

The priests now poured offerings of chicha onto the ground, each in one of the four sacred directions. They then bowed and offered a stream of golden chicha to the angry volcano. "Apu Sabancaya," the eldest priest said, gesturing toward it, "have mercy on us—and behold our offerings." Juanita, eyes wide, pulled her cloak even more tightly around her, gazing at the smoke pouring forth so violently, as thick and convoluted as a coil of writhing snakes.

A priest poured chicha into a small golden cup and handed it to her. "Prepare yourself," he said.

Two hundred and eighty miles south of Cusco lies Arequipa, a sunny, resplendent colonial city hemmed in by ice-capped volcanoes, flamingo-dotted blue lakes, and high plains with yellow tufts of *ichu* grass. Arequipa is sometimes called *la ciudad blanca,* or "the white city." Depending on whom you speak to, this is either because its first inhabitants were white-skinned Spaniards or else because its colonial buildings were fashioned from a pale, lilac-colored stone called *sillar.* The stone is a soft volcanic rock full of holes made from volcanic gases. Because of the *sillar,* the buildings lining the central streets of Arequipa appear as if they've been sprayed by machine gun fire or else hit by shrapnel, giving the appearance that great battles once raged here. Some of the holes, however, *are* actually from bullets, as Arequipa is also a city of coups and revolutionaries. Mario Vargas Llosa, the Peruvian Nobel laureate, was born here, his career launched by his first novel, *The City of the Dogs*, an exposé about life in a Peruvian military academy, which the government promptly banned. Abimael Guzmán Reynoso, the imprisoned leader of the Shining Path, is also an *Arequipeño*, and frequently took coffee as a young law student in a small café off the Plaza de Armas. During the Shining Path's ten-year "millenarian" war, the guerrilla group never launched an attack on the city. Many say that this was due to the fact that Arequipa was Guzmán's hometown.

Most of the battle scars on Arequipa's colonial façades, however, are not the result of human but tectonic forces. Arequipa sits in the midst of a region that has long served as a crucible for the ancient conflict between man and nature—a *real* millennarian war that is sometimes quiet, sometimes simmering, and occasionally catastrophic. House walls here are purposely built thick—often as much as three to seven feet—as earthquakes and volcanic eruptions are common. Seismic events frequently decapitate one or both of the city's high cathedral towers, collapsing bridges, arcades, and porticos at the same time. It was on top of a volcano not far from here that the body of Juanita, the Inca Ice Maiden, was found.

On the city's outskirts rises another majestic, nearly 20,000-foot-tall volcano called Misti. The volcano's cone-like outline resembles that of Mount Fujiyama in Japan, or the outlines of the nineteenth-century Krakatoa volcano, before it exploded into smithereens. All three of these volcanoes—Misti, Fujiyama, and Krakatoa—as well as more than 430 others, form part of the Pacific Ocean's Ring of Fire, a 10,000-mile diameter volcanic circle that surrounds the Pacific Ocean. The friction arising from two enormous continental plates grinding their way eastward across the Pacific has ultimately created a kind of giant flaming hoop around the ocean's edges—a band of volcanoes that periodically belch fire and smoke into the atmosphere and often incinerate their surroundings.

At 7,600 feet, Arequipa sits midway in a line of more than a dozen volcanoes that form part of this ring, in a region that is one of four major volcanic zones in South America. One of these zones lies along the coast of Colombia, another stretches through the Andes of southern Peru and Bolivia, while two more extend farther south into Chile. All are the result of the Nazca Plate slowly smashing into the South American Plate, sliding and grinding its way beneath the latter in a subduction zone that forms the Peru-Chile Oceanic Trench, just off the coast. Where the angle of that collision zone is steepest—some thirty degrees or more—earthquakes are common and volcanoes emerge, the latter forming giant vents that help release some of the immense heat generated below.

On February 19, 1600, one such volcanic release took place, about forty-three miles southeast of Arequipa. Three days after the initial eruption, as many of Arequipa's inhabitants crammed themselves into the cathedral, repenting and wondering if the End of Days and the Apocalypse had begun, another violent earthquake struck the city. The new cathedral abruptly collapsed upon the worshippers.

In 2001 the most recent earthquake struck the region, measuring 8.1 on the Richter scale. It brought down the cathedral's southern tower and damaged other buildings in the city. Especially hard hit was Arequipa's sixteenth-century Santa Catalina Convent, which is surrounded by high *sillar* walls and lies in the heart of the city.

"The entire convent was destroyed," my guide, Carmen, a young, Quechua-speaking woman, says to me as we tour the four-century-old convent one afternoon. Wrought-iron grills fit like bird cages over the windows where once lived the nuns wearing black or white habits and living in seclusion. Over one archway is stenciled a command that is still followed by the two dozen nuns who presently live here and who will spend their lives within these cloistered walls:

SILENCIO

"Everything collapsed," Carmen says, as we walk down an azure-colored alleyway lined with wooden doors leading into nuns' cells. "Many were killed."

Ever since it was founded in 1579, Carmen says, Peruvian families have been bringing their daughters to the convent named after Saint Catherine, a fourteenth-century Italian woman who experienced a vision of Jesus Christ at the age of six. By tradition, Spanish descendants living in Peru commonly selected their second eldest sons to become priests and their second eldest daughters to become nuns. Thus, ever since the convent's founding, young girls of a certain birth order have entered—usually around the age of twelve to fourteen—and then have spent the rest of their lives in seclusion, devoted to God. Like the Inca girls cloistered in the *acclawasi*, these young Christian girls entered the convent knowing full well that their future lives of abstinence and devotion would ultimately benefit their families and the rest of society. They were, after all, now "married" to God, just as the Inca girls had been "married" to the Sun; they thus had one foot on Earth and another already in heaven.

Once inside the convent, nuns were not allowed to leave, while the newest entrants, known as novitiates, were sequestered from the rest of the convent and allowed no contact with family or friends. Once the three-year novitiate period had ended and a girl took her vows, family members could visit, but the visits took place in almost prison-like conditions: the nun's family would enter one room, while the nun, seated in an adjacent corridor, "visited" her family by speaking through a double wooden grill that allowed no physical contact. Once fully "betrothed" to Christ and now wearing a ring symbolizing their "marriage" to Him, the nuns were exposed to as little temptation as was humanly possible, their lives carefully supervised and regulated. When they died, the nuns were buried in a cemetery within the convent's walls.

In a courtyard nearby, I watch as a brown-skinned woman in a broad-rimmed hat and long *pollera* skirts walks carefully up the steps besides a cupola and places a small stone, the size of a potato, on a wall. A gray-haired man in a black jacket waits for her below. The scene reminds me of the fact that, for thousands of years, native Andeans have placed similar small stones, or *apachetas*, on sacred places, offerings to the earth goddess or other deities. Even today, Christianity in the Andes remains infused by native beliefs, the natives having dutifully added the Christian God to their own abundant pantheon of indigenous gods and spirits, along with the hundreds of lesser Catholic saints.

Just four blocks down from the convent, past the cathedral with its two white *sillar* stone towers, past the Plaza de Armas with its two-story arcades, and down Santa Catalina Avenue rises the bloodred façade with white pilasters of the Catholic University of Santa María. The locale was virtually unknown outside of Peru until September 13, 1995, when several men carried a freezer through the university's doors and then placed it in a hastily cleared room. Inside the heavy box crouched Juanita, the Ice Maiden, discovered on the summit of Ampato volcano, some sixty miles to the northwest. The nearby volcano of Sabancaya had been erupting on and off for some time, sending up ash that had coated the snow-and-ice-covered summit of Ampato. The darker ash had absorbed the sun, had melted the snow, and then suddenly, a portion of the summit's ridge had collapsed, carrying down with it a mixture of ice and rock and also a strange, alpaca-wool bundle that contained the frozen body of Juanita. Around her, amid the snow and ice, lay small gold and silver figurines, a feather headdress, and scraps of woven cloth.

Stunned by his first encounter with an intact Inca sacrifice, the archaeologist Johan Reinhard had been immediately faced with a difficult decision: Should he leave everything as he had found it, possibly to be looted by grave robbers or destroyed by the elements? Or should he try to move the mummy bundle and the artifacts down the volcano and take them to Arequipa, where they might be secured? As he later wrote,

> My mind raced with all the implications of the discovery. What was the next best step? If we left the mummy behind, the sun and volcanic ash would further damage it. Also, at this time of year a heavy snowfall could cover the summit any day and make recovery impossible, perhaps forever. I knew that obtaining an archaeological

permit could take weeks, if not months, as could obtaining the funding to organize a scientific expedition. Nor could we save time by flying in with a helicopter. Most helicopters could not land safely even at the [16,700-foot] altitude of our base camp [let alone at the summit].

Eventually, Reinhard decided he had no choice. He had to get the mummy down off the mountain. To do so, however, would require a quasi-Herculean effort as he and his companion were by now tired and hungry, standing on a volcanic peak at 20,700 feet, and had no one to help them. What's more, Juanita was frozen and weighed more than eighty pounds. Below them, meanwhile, stretched a dangerous section of slippery snow and ice. As Reinhard later recounted:

> I couldn't hoist the pack [with the mummy inside] directly off the ground, so I sat down, put the straps around my shoulders, and Miki pulled me to my feet. I could hardly stand up, let alone navigate an ice-covered slope . . . In the fading light the [nearby Sabancaya] volcano's cloud of ash seemed to take on a sinister aspect. Having a dead body on my back added to the surreal scene. Images of Incas struggling through the same terrain ran through my mind. For a moment, I was transported back in time, and I had the eerie feeling that I was rescuing someone who was alive.

Later examination revealed that Juanita had died from blunt force trauma that had cracked the side of her skull near her right eye, no doubt inflicted by a stone hammer or club. In full view of an erupting volcano, and no doubt with the hope that her sacrifice would calm the mountain god responsible for the eruption, Juanita had been sacrificed. "According to the chroniclers," Reinhard later wrote,

> [Inca] children were selected because their purity made them more acceptable to live with the gods. After being sacrificed, these children became messengers or representatives of the people to the gods

and could intervene on their behalf. The children became, in effect, deified and worshipped together with the gods with whom they were believed to reside. They would be honored for all time, unlike the majority of common people, who only received offerings for a few generations [after their deaths].

It was considered an honor for the parents of the children selected, and some were known to have offered their children willingly. The parents were not supposed to show sadness, and it was even said to have been a major offense if they did. Not all parents felt the honor worth the price, however. Thus they were not opposed to their daughters losing their virginity, since in this way they avoided being taken away.

The next day and now farther down the volcano, Reinhard transferred Juanita from his backpack frame to a burro. Once a road was reached, he then placed the still-frozen girl in the storage area of a bus bound for Arequipa. The following morning, at six forty-five, the bus arrived in the city, a freezer was located, and Juanita was placed inside. Eventually, the Catholic University of Santa Maria created a permanent exhibit, placing Juanita in a glass chamber whose temperature was lowered to 10 degrees Fahrenheit.

By the time I arrive at the Catholic University, Juanita has been sitting in her icy crypt for more than sixteen years. I enter the *Museo Santuarios Andinos* (Andean Sanctuaries Museum) through an arched entryway with a Moorish-style, wrought-iron grill covering the upper arch of the portico, then pass through to a sunny courtyard set amid rust-colored walls, white pilasters, and red geraniums. I buy a ticket, and then pass between thick wooden doors and into a series of rooms inside. A sign at the entryway announces that one is about to step into a world some 550 years in the past. Inside, Inca offerings from various mountaintop burials rest quietly beneath glass cases, including miniature gold and silver alpaca figurines that symbolized the Incas' flocks. A large Inca *lliclla* weaving, in rich burgundy colors and bordered with black, stretches across one wall, the colors of the alpaca fibers so rich the weaving looks like it was made only yesterday. As I penetrate into the museum's inner sanctuary, the atmosphere darkens, and the lights dim. Finally, I enter a room that is lit in perpetual twilight. Against one wall, on a waist-high stand, rests a large glass cubicle. Because of the chill air, goose bumps rise on my skin.

Through the frosted glass, I can make out the outlines of an Inca girl, still covered in a finely woven tunic and shawl, her hair coiffed in an almost Gorgon's coil of finely woven black braids. Juanita sits in the same crouching position she has remained in for half a millennia, until recent global warming and nearby volcanic activity suddenly broke open her icy crypt, spilling her abruptly outside. Juanita's face has a remote look; her eyes are slightly open. She seems to be squinting into the face of eternity.

Not long after her discovery, Mario Vargas Llosa visited her new crypt, wishing to examine this sudden apparition from his country's distant past.

"She was the age of Shakespeare's Juliet," Vargas Llosa wrote afterward,

> fourteen years [old]—and like her, she had a romantic and tragic history . . . I was convinced that the spectacle [of seeing her] would turn my stomach. It was not like that. It takes nothing else than to see her . . . Her exotic, lengthened face, with high cheekbones and large, somewhat slanted eyes, suggest a remote oriental influence. She has her mouth open, as if challenging the world with the whiteness of her perfect teeth that purse her upper lip in a coquettish expression . . . I was moved, captivated by Juanita's beauty.

In May 1996, museum technicians loaded Juanita onto a jetliner within a specially made freezer. The plane took off, flying first past Misti and then Ampato volcanoes, the latter still crowned with the ice on which she had been discovered. The plane then turned northward, reaching an altitude of thirty thousand feet, before heading toward Washington, DC. For the next month and at a specially made exhibit at the National

Geographic Society's headquarters, Juanita received a steady stream of visitors. One of those was Peru's president, Alberto Fujimori, who happened to be in the capital at the time. Moved by his visit, Fujimori spoke to a small crowd of gathered dignitaries:

> On behalf of the people of Peru, I am proud to be here to introduce Juanita, the Princess of Ampato. Hers is a tale told across half a millennium, one that might have remained buried forever, but has emerged suddenly to astound the world. The story of her discovery is known to you—her long journey from the top of Mount Ampato to . . . here today. The lessons we, and all the world, may learn from her are beyond today's calculations. We are proud to share with you, our neighbors and friends to the north, this great and precious treasure—lifted by nature herself from the very depths of the ground atop one of the highest peaks on Earth. Juanita's awakening—and her long journey to this time and place—leave us mindful of the great distance the world has traveled in these centuries. The princess could not have known that one unimaginable day fate would give her a new and conspicuous place on the global stage of the future. May she teach us lessons, bring us to look into our hearts, our history, and our conscience. And may the soul of Juanita rest in peace.

"Riqch'ariy sonq'ollay," a voice said into Juanita's ear ("wake up").

It was morning. Juanita opened her eyes and saw the eldest priest's face quite near hers, his dark eyes peering at her intently. At first she stared at him, uncomprehending.

"Wake up," he said again, shaking her lightly.

Somehow, Juanita had fallen to sleep the night before, covered in alpaca blankets beneath an alpaca cloth tent. The priest held out a small bowl of cooked vegetables and Juanita ate them, grateful, but still so bone-shakingly cold that her arms and legs shivered. A few moments later, she stumbled outside.

The sun had not yet come up, and Juanita was soon surrounded by the priests, who began helping her up the last stretch of mountainside to the volcano's crest. The ground was now pure ice, in spots layered with gray ash, and in places her sandals had trouble gaining a foothold. The air was so cold and thin it took her breath away.

Once on the summit, Juanita and the priest waited for the Sun God, Inti, to emerge. Finally, almost miraculously, He did so, bathing them now in a sharp yellow light that also etched the edges of the funnel of gray smoke that was still pouring forth from Sabancaya below them, filling up the sky. Juanita could feel a priest's hands adjusting her shawl, making sure her silver tupus were correctly fastened, adjusting her acsu as well around her, straightening her hair, and fastening her long braid behind her to her chumpi belt, with a cord of black wool. In a daze from the thin air, lack of sleep, and the biting cold, Juanita watched as a group of priests crouching beside her readied small figurines of gold and silver llamas and alpacas, fitting them with small woven clothes.

Juanita followed the line of priests to a small platform on the volcano's icy summit, stumbling at times, the rainbow colors of her acsu dress bathed in the early-morning sun. On a small stone platform, a priest bade her to kneel, and Juanita knelt, dutifully doing as she was told. Before her, arms stretched horizontally out toward the Sun, two priests stood and poured golden-colored chicha from a vase onto the volcano's crown, the liquid cord of their offering glimmering in the sunlight. Another held his arms out-stretched toward the erupting apu, pleading with it to spare their crops, to spare their fields, to spare their villages and towns.

Juanita knelt silently in the snow and ice, on top of an apu on the very summit of the world.

"Apu Sabancaya," she heard the priests' voices say, rising together in unison, "have mercy on us. Behold our offerings."

A strong hand then pushed her head down.

Juanita waited, her breath heaving, the sound of the chanting and the volcano's eruption in her ears.

On her tunic, she saw fine flakes of freshly fallen ash, gray against the rich ochre colors of her dress, the tunic's bright colors almost blinding her because of the dazzling sun.

Two hands held her strongly from behind and another pushed her head down even farther as the chanting grew louder.

And then, like a sudden clap of thunder, Juanita knew no more.

6

THE *KON-TIKI* VOYAGE, WHITE GODS, AND THE FLOATING ISLANDS OF LAKE TITICACA (PERU AND BOLIVIA)

I asked the Indians what this [creator god] Viracocha looked like when the ancients saw him, as far as they have information. They told me that he was a tall man dressed in a white garment that reached to his ankles and was belted at the waist. His hair was short and he had a tonsure like a priest . . . I asked them the name . . . and they said his name was Contiti [Kon Tiki] Viracocha . . . which means "God, maker of the world . . ."

—Juan de Betanzos, *Narrative of the Incas*, 1564

I was no longer in doubt that the white chief-god Sun-Tiki, whom the Incas declared that their forefathers had driven out of Peru on to the Pacific, was identical with the white chief-god Tiki, son of the sun, whom the inhabitants of all the eastern Pacific islands hailed as the original founder of their race. And the details of Sun-Tiki's life in Peru, with the ancient names of places round Lake Titicaca, cropped up again in historic legends current among the natives of the Pacific

islands . . . my theory was complete. I must go to America and put
it forward.

—Thor Heyerdahl, *Kon-Tiki: Across the Pacific by Raft*

"Did you know we found a dead rooster and a dead dog inside
our wire fence just a few days ago?" Thor Heyerdahl, the Norwegian explorer, asks me. It is May 1987, and we are driving in a Jeep
on a dirt road on the northern coast of Peru. Two-thousand-year-old
adobe pyramids from the Moche culture loom around us, and Heyerdahl, seventy-one years old, with white wispy hair and wearing a blue
jumpsuit, looks over at me, all the while trying to dodge the occasional
barking dog or surprised chicken.

I shake my head.

"Witchcraft," he says, then swerves past a dog that races after us,
fangs bared. The dog reminds me of some of the palm-sized, golden
faces with fangs that have recently been unearthed near here, buried
within the tomb of a Moche king called "the Lord of Sipán." Looters had
stumbled upon the grave, so full of copper and silver and gold artifacts
that it was soon dubbed the New World's version of King Tut's tomb.
Within days of the discovery, the police arrived, shot one of the robbers, and confiscated some of the golden images. A few of the gold figurines later smuggled out of Peru sold for nearly a million dollars each.
All of this occurred just thirty miles north of where we are driving. The
local people are now understandably nervous, apprehensive, and angry.
They know that pockets of fabulous treasure could lie anywhere within
the crumbling pyramids around them. And at least some of them want
a portion of that treasure for themselves.

Adobe homes with thatched roofs appear, and a few people with
dark brown skin and black hair and wearing tire sandals, emerge to look
at us. Heyerdahl waves genially. Not all of them wave back.

"We want to dig in their ancestors' burial grounds," he says. "Within
their temples and pyramids. And the witchdoctors don't like it."

To counteract the witchdoctors' spells, Heyerdahl and I are off to a local market to search for some hot peppers and other secret ingredients that a friendly shaman has instructed us to buy. They'll help ward off any evil spells, the shaman said. Heyerdahl parks his Jeep near an open-air market. Although I'm more than four decades younger, Heyerdahl's invited me to spend a few days with him. He knows that I've been working in Peru for the last year as an anthropologist in the Amazon.

We climb out of the Jeep and enter the market, then begin exploring the stalls stocked with bags of quinoa, *aji* peppers, star fruit, *granadilla*, *lúcuma*, and other produce.

Years ago, when I was a child, I'd read Heyerdahl's first book, *Kon-Tiki: Across the Pacific by Raft*. I remember being completely captivated. This is how he began his book:

> Once in a while, you find yourself in an odd situation. You get into it by degrees and in the most natural way but, when you are right in the midst of it, you are suddenly astonished and ask yourself how in the world it all came about. If, for example, you put to sea with a parrot and five companions, it is inevitable that sooner or later you will wake up one morning out at sea, perhaps a little better rested than ordinarily, and begin to think about it. On one such morning I sat writing in a dew-drenched logbook:
>
>> "May 17. Norwegian Independence Day. Heavy Sea. Fair wind. I am cook today and found seven flying fish on deck, one squid on the cabin roof, and one unknown fish in Torstein's sleeping bag."

The fish, it turned out, was a wonderfully rare snake mackerel—which had never been seen alive before. And the voyage—4,300 miles across the Pacific Ocean on a small balsa-wood, Inca-style raft—had also never been seen before, at least not in modern times. Heyerdahl and his companions—some of whom, like himself, were Norwegian resistance fighters who'd fought against the Nazis during World War II—eventually sailed their craft from Peru to the Tuamotu Islands in French

Polynesia, where they crash-landed on a coral reef. Heyerdahl called his raft the *Kon-Tiki*—after an ancient god once revered by the Incas and by the ancient Tiahuanaco people who lived near Lake Titicaca, twelve thousand feet up in the Andes. His book eventually sold more than 20 million copies and was published in sixty-seven languages. Now financially independent, Heyerdahl continued to research and excavate the remains of ancient cultures—on the Galápagos Islands, on Easter Island, on the Maldives, and on the Canary Islands—all in an attempt to prove that indigenous people not only had developed seagoing rafts, but that they had also once used those rafts to cross entire oceans. Heyerdahl believed that rafts had allowed contact between ancient civilizations such as those in Peru and Polynesia and between the Old World and the New.

"Have you been to Egypt?" Heyerdahl suddenly asks me, as he makes a purchase from an old woman of some peppers. I shake my head.

"The [Egyptian] pyramids at Sakkara look much like the ones around here," he says, referring to the ancient Moche pyramids in the area, so eroded that they look like crumbling hills.

"You think there's a connection?" I ask.

"Yes."

"But how?"

"Reed rafts," he says. "Similar to those on Lake Titicaca."

The woman places the cluster of withered maroon-colored peppers in a small bag and hands them to Heyerdahl.

"Have you been there?" he asks.

I shake my head again.

"Fabulous place," he says.

We climb back into the Jeep and take off.

"They still use reed rafts on Titicaca, just like they used to in Egypt and ancient Mesopotamia," Heyerdahl says. "On Titicaca, people still live on islands made from reeds. The Uros Islands, that's what they're called. There was a connection, between the Old World and the New."

The weathered explorer turns to look at me. His face is lined, but his blue eyes are as fresh and sparkling as the open ocean on a sunny day. More than forty years after he and his five companions crash-landed the *Kon-Tiki* onto an atoll in the Pacific, Heyerdahl is still deeply passionate about this work.

"If you haven't been to Titicaca," he says, "then by all means go. The boatbuilders who built my ship, the *Ra II*, still live there. That's what I sailed on, from Morocco to Barbados [in the Caribbean]. The two continents weren't separated—they were once connected by rafts."

Nearly a quarter of a century later, I arrive in Puno, Peru, a city on the edge of the world's highest navigable body of water, Lake Titicaca. Although I'm no longer in my twenties, I did take some of Heyerdahl's advice. After my visit with him among the Moche pyramids, I eventually visited the pyramids of Egypt, traveled among Greek and Roman ruins around the Mediterranean, investigated various ancient temples strewn across India, explored the ruined temples of Angkor Wat, lived with a recently contacted tribe in the Amazon, visited isolated areas of Papua New Guinea and now, while on a north-south journey from the northern edge of South America to its southernmost tip in Patagonia, I can't help but hear Heyerdahl's questions come back to me: "Have you visited Lake Titicaca? Do you know about the *Uros*?"

I *had* visited the lake after our encounter, but only briefly. Since then, I've read that at least one of the boatbuilders Heyerdahl mentioned— the man who had designed and built the *Ra II*—still lives on an island in the Bolivian part of the lake. Heyerdahl's Titicaca boatbuilder, I calculate, must by now be in his eighties. Since the Uros Islands are quite near Puno, and since I'm on my way south to Bolivia, I decide to visit the islands, and then to try to find the man who built Heyerdahl's boat.

Along the base of hills that rim the northwestern corner of Lake Titicaca, the city of Puno spills like a river down the hillside until it reaches the shore. There, a cement quay squats, lined with small boats. Puno has a population of one hundred thousand and sits at 12,500 feet, or more than two miles, above sea level. I soon discover that any main avenue you follow either runs down to the lakeshore or else tilts up from the lake's edge and heads back up through town. Bicycle-pedaled, three-wheel taxis ply the roads, with plastic roofs overhead to keep the frequent rains off the passengers. The tricycles have rubber-bulbed horns on their handlebars that the drivers use to bleat their way in and out of traffic.

Puno itself is rather drab and roughly hewn. Around the main plaza women sit on stone benches wearing shawls and bowler hats, knitting or tending children, while elderly men dressed in worn and creased suits sit beside them, holding canes, their heads nodding forward in slumber. A few policemen stroll about in uniforms of dull green, past homes and buildings that are made from red brick. Most buildings in Puno have sprouts of iron rebar sticking up out of the upper corners of the roofs, like insect antennas. The rebar is for adding another floor to a building or house. Eventually, when a building reaches completion— and in this area of Peru, that means four or five stories high—the owners plaster over the brick exterior and paint the building blue, green, or some other color. Most buildings in Puno are thus creeping slowly skyward, one floor at a time.

Although Puno has little in the way of sights to recommend it, ironically, the city sits on the shores of one of the most beautiful lakes in the world. Imagine a giant swimming pool over one hundred miles in length, 50 miles wide, and more than a thousand feet deep lifted into the air and suspended two miles above the sea. Imagine a line of mountains, the Cordillera Real, complete with 20,000-foot peaks, ranging along the lake's eastern border while another mountain range, the Cordillera Occidental, ranges to the west. To the east, beyond the sacred, ice-capped mountains, lies the Amazon rain forest, which stretches for 3,000 miles; to the west lie the shores of the Pacific Ocean, about 150 miles away and two miles down. Viewed from above, Lake Titicaca sits like a glistening blue jewel in the midst of the brown *altiplano*, its southern half in Bolivia, its northern half in Peru.

Down on Puno's concrete wharf I meet Juan, a thirty-six-year-old Aymara Indian who lives on one of Titicaca's floating islands, *Los Uros*.

These are the same islands Thor Heyerdahl had told me about years ago. Juan—who wears tire sandals and a knitted *chu'ullu* hat of brightly colored alpaca wool and speaks Spanish with a thick Aymara accent—tells me that he'll be departing for his island home later in the afternoon. He invites me to go along. When I tell him that I'd like to spend a few nights on the islands, he quickly assures me that not only does he have room—he has a *hotel* made entirely from reeds.

"Of reeds?" I ask.

"*Sí, sí sí. De totora*" ("Yes, yes yes. Of *totora* reeds").

Late in the afternoon, we take off in a small wooden boat powered by an Evinrude motor and head out into Puno Bay.

Juan is short and stocky, has high cheekbones and short black hair. He was born on a floating reed island, as were his father, his grandfather, and all of his ancestors as far back as he can remember. His wife, Elsa, was also born on the Uros, floating mats of reeds that are manmade, are moored to wooden stakes, and are about ten feet thick. Like Juan's, his wife's mother tongue is Aymara.

The Uros, it turns out, have a rather complicated history. Although archaeologists believe that the first Americans walked across the Bering Land Bridge sometime between twenty-two thousand and fifteen thousand years ago, with their descendants arriving in the area around Lake Titicaca by 8,000 BC, no one really knows when people began to live on floating reed islands. What archaeologists *do* know is that people began inhabiting some of the natural islands in Lake Titicaca by 2,000 BC and presumably arrived there by rafts made from *totora* reeds. Sometime after that, although the exact date is unknown, people began fashioning islands from reeds and started living on them.

It wasn't until the sixteenth century that Europeans visited Lake Titicaca for the first time and wrote of a people they referred to as the Uros. The first Spanish chroniclers spoke of these unusual lake dwellers disparagingly because, unlike people who lived a settled existence on land, the Uros lived on floating islands, subsisting on fish, ducks, and even on the reeds themselves. Wrote the Augustinian monk Antonio de la Calancha,

These Uros are barbarous . . . [they are] blackened, unclean, are enemies of language, and have no affection for the worship of our faith. . . . the Uros Indians are born, reared, and live on the lake among the reeds, which are called totora and are very thick [reed beds] . . . they live here without any more clothes or cover (although this land is very cold) than a mat of [reeds] . . . Their language is the most obscure, short and primitive of all the guttural ones in Peru. . . . their religious practices are to worship the sun and the lake; they adore the latter and make it offerings of [sacred] corn.

Forty years later, another Spanish priest, José de Acosta, poured further scorn on the islanders by writing:

They raise a large amount of reeds, which the Indians call Totora and which is useful for a thousand things because it's food for pigs and horses and men; they make houses from it and fire and boats and when it's necessary the Uros [Indians] can be found in the Totora [reeds]. These Uros are so brutish that they themselves do not consider themselves men. It is said that when they were questioned, they responded that they were not men, but Uros, as if they were another kind of animal. Whole villages of Uros have been found, [the inhabitants] in their reed boats [that were] bound to one another and tied to a bluff, and if it became necessary to move, they would move the entire [floating] village to another site, so [if] searching for them today where they were yesterday [you would find] . . . no trace of them or of their village.

What seemed to annoy the Spaniards greatly and no doubt the Incas before them was the fact that the Uros people were so difficult to find and keep track of. Both the Spaniards and the Incas ran empires based upon the taxation of their citizens. But how do you tax a people who, at the drop of the proverbial bowler hat, can simply vanish from one day to the next, taking their entire village with them?

Anthropologists continue to debate whether the Uros referred to by the chroniclers were actually a distinct ethnic group with a separate language or were simply Aymara Indians who specialized in making a living on and about the lake. In any event, if there ever *were* a separate Uros language, it has long since vanished, as have many other languages in South America. The people living on the Uros Islands today speak Aymara, a language spoken by more than two million people in the Andes of Peru, Bolivia, and Chile. It was the Aymaras who created the great civilization of Tiahuanaco and its renowned capital of the same name, which lies at the southern end of Lake Titicaca in Bolivia.

Knifing out through water that is as pure and blue as the sky, we motor away, leaving the city of Puno shrinking in our wake. Titicaca is the largest lake in South America, and its average temperature hovers between 50 and 57 degrees Fahrenheit. Because of its elevation and the tropical sun, evaporation rates are high; thus the skies around the lake are often full of giant cumulus clouds that boil up and rise to tremendous heights, periodically exploding with rain, lightning, and thunder.

The vast, low reed beds among which the Uros live begin only about three miles from the city, so within a short time I can see the islands, at first a line of low green reeds and then, poking out above them, the rounded tops of reed houses, like clusters of strange, sprouting yellow mushrooms. An Andean gull spins overhead, white with a black head, through air that is fresh, well scrubbed, and chilly. Our boat then turns as Juan motors it into a large blue channel in the reeds.

The floating islands of the Uros soon begin to appear, forty-two of them, no longer obscured by the reeds but now out in the open, the islands floating on either side of the reed channel. The islands appear like flat, low spits of land with dried yellow reeds strewn on top of them, although there is no land but instead layers of reeds and nothing but lake water that extends for sixty feet below. On top of the islands, small reed houses with curved roofs squat clustered together. From one island rises a high wooden watchtower, the kind used centuries ago to warn of danger. The mustard-colored homes with their rounded roofs are the kind you might think that hobbits lived in, or at least an unusual people who have a fantastic sense of craftsmanship and style.

"The Uros!" Juan shouts, guiding the boat down the middle of the channel and gesturing with one arm. Other small boats ply the channel or are docked against the islands. Women on one island wear bowler hats and bright lime green or pink *pollera* skirts and are hanging out laundry to dry; on another island, a couple of small kids kick a soccer ball around. Moored to some of the islands are large *totora*-reed ships with curved prows that have been fashioned into puma heads. The whole area looks like some kind of fantastical, mythical world, as if it were lifted directly out of a page from *The Travels of Marco Polo.*

Life among the Uros Islands, Juan tells me, is literally based upon the *totora* reed, a subspecies of *Schoenoplectus Californicus. Schoenoplectus* is Latin and means "plenty of grass material." Although long and cylindrical, *totora* reeds are not grasses but a type of bulrush—a flowering plant related to the papyrus reed in Egypt. The *totora* subspecies grows only in the shallow waters of Lake Titicaca and along Peru's northern coast, where local fishermen bind them together to make small fishing craft. The reeds also grow, strangely enough, on Easter Island, nearly two and a half thousand miles away.

Beneath the water, the *totora* reeds' roots interweave with one another in a thick buoyant mass, rather like a giant cork. Natives learned most likely eons ago to cut the living roots into blocks that they found growing along the shallow lake edge, which they then bound together with rope that was also made from *totora*. After a few months, the roots in the blocks intermesh and the inhabitants cover them with a layer of dry *totora* reeds equal in thickness to the root layer. If the root mass is three feet thick, then the islanders lay down three feet of harvested reeds on top. Small foundations—consisting of another foot of dry *totora*—are then laid down, and houses are built upon them. The raised *totora*-reed foundations become the floors.

The houses are all one-roomed with walls made from woven *totora*-reed mats, one mat forming each of a house's four sides. The roofs are fashioned from two large *totora* mats woven even more tightly together, so that water cannot penetrate. The mats are then joined carefully together at the top and are pulled out and down so that they form large rounded eaves that project around the walls like a *totora*-reed tent. In a sense, a reed house is like an overturned boat: the roof is the equivalent of the hull, while the walls are like a ship's bulwarks. The upside-down "hull" is fastened into place to keep the rains from dribbling through the house and wetting the inhabitants. Instead, rainwater drains off the reed roofs onto the island, filtering down through the reeds before rejoining the lake and then evaporating again and beginning the cycle anew. Lake Titicaca's rainy season occurs during the Andean summer, from December to March. During the heavy rains, the islands are often soggy. Extra attention must then be taken to lay down fresh *totora* on the island's floor.

Juan motors into a reed inlet, cuts the engine, and our boat glides through the water until it nudges softly against the stiff *totora* edge of his island home. His wife, Elsa, is there, wearing a typical ankle-length *pollera*, bright blue in color, a black bowler hat on her head, and a sweater the color of rouge. Elsa smiles, revealing two front teeth rimmed in gold. Juan's children are here, too—Sarah, fifteen, and Leonardo, thirteen. Leonardo is playing on the edge of the island, pulling a three-foot-long *totora*-reed boat along with a string.

I step onto their island home, expecting it to sink like a waterbed underneath. It doesn't. Although the island is spongy and walking on it is a bit like walking on a stiff, giant marshmallow, a visitor's feet actually sink only a few inches each time. Juan's island is about one hundred feet long and half as wide; it is surprisingly stable, moving only when a motor boat's wake washes against it. When that occurs, you can feel a dull lifting and sinking as the waves pass smoothly underneath, like an underground ripple. The island is really a giant raft, and the houses are the raft's tiny cabins. The islanders' homes have a fresh, clean *totora* smell to them—like a hayloft or barn.

"What about storms?" I ask, looking at a bank of threatening clouds that seem to be approaching. "Do they affect the islands?"

They do, Juan says, but the islands themselves are anchored with long ropes—nylon now, *totora* in the past—that are tied to eucalyptus stakes planted firmly in the mud. The stakes are pounded into the shallow reed beds, and each island has at least eight or ten stakes anchoring it. When a storm comes, the islands shift on their moorings like floating ships attached to buoys, but they don't drift away.

Gradually, Juan says, the *totora* layer on the top of the island becomes water laden and rots, so the islanders are constantly refurbishing them, paddling off into the *totora* beds, cutting fresh reeds with metal scythes attached to wooden poles, then laying down fresh *totora* again. It takes roughly eight months to a year for several families to create an island, Juan says. They vary in size and may have from two to ten families on each of them. To weave the roof of a house takes one person a month. Three people can build the walls of a house in a day. During the wet season, they lay down a fresh layer of *totora* every two to three weeks.

"We can't live without the *totora*," Juan says, walking to the edge of his island to a grove of the dark green reeds. He reaches for one, then begins to carefully pull it up, root and all.

"We eat it, we sleep on it, we make our houses from it, we make our furniture with it, we use it to make boats, we use it as tea, we even use it as fuel," he says, stripping the white, root-like rhizome at the bottom of the six-foot plant.

A foot-tall, mottled gray, black-crowned night heron walks up to us, one hesitant leg at a time. The bird is young and has intense orange eyes with black pupils—the eyes of a predator. Its name is "Martin" (Mar TEEN)—from the bird's Spanish name, *martin pescadero*. It's one of the family's pets.

"We took it from its nest as a chick," Juan tells me. "If you do so before the chick is a few days old, the chick will imprint on whichever human has taken it—and not on its mother." The orphaned heron pecks at the freshly cut *totora* in front of us, looking for food. I'm surprised to see a cat walking toward us, about twenty feet away. "We have no mice," Juan says. Every island has cats and thus are vermin-free, he explains. When the cat approaches too closely, the heron lunges toward it, pecking aggressively. "He can take care of himself," Juan says as the cat runs away.

Juan hands me a short section of *totora* root. The Aymara word for the root is *chullo*; it's white and clean and looks like the end of a giant green onion. I bite into it. The taste is slightly sweet, and the sensation is like biting into a piece of white asparagus. I suddenly realize that living amid the vast maze of *totora* reeds—which supply mats and houses and rope and twine and boats and furniture—is a bit like living in the middle of a lumberyard, except that here you can even eat the tips of the lumber.

Juan's wife shows me the cooking area, about ten feet from their house. She does all of her cooking in a small clay oven about two feet high that sits on a large stone placed on the reed floor. The stove has a foot-wide cavity for the fire and two small holes above on which to place pots. A metal pot hangs nearby, suspended from a piece of twine made, of course, from *totora*.

Juan's wife, who smiles frequently, gets up at four in the morning, she says, unless it rains. If it's raining, she stays in bed. On most days, however, Elsa emerges from their house while it's still dark, lights a fire in the clay oven, and feeds the fire stalks of dry *totora*. The *totora* burns well, she says, but it's difficult to find dry *totora* in the rainy season.

Living on the island requires a lot of upkeep, Juan says. They're constantly repairing and refurbishing their *totora*-reed houses, boats, and the islands themselves. Still, I can't help but think that the islanders here pay no rent for their homes, have no mortgages, have plenty of free building materials (*totora*), can transport themselves on *totora* boats if necessary, have an abundant supply of fresh, drinkable water beneath their feet, can hunt ducks and grebes, and can find plentiful amounts of fish, which they catch in nets. Having visited new settlements on Peru's barren desert coast, where people live in shacks made from whatever materials they can find and where they must find a job in order to buy basic things like food and water, I find the Uros islanders to be far better off. They've clearly mastered their watery environment.

Juan takes me to my "hotel," basically an extra house on the island. He opens the *totora*-reed door and turns on a light. Juan has installed power here in the form of a small solar panel and a low-wattage bulb. He purchased the solar panel with a five-year loan from the government. Two wooden beds adorn my room, with mattresses and thick woolen blankets. It's neat and clean, and Elsa has decorated the walls with weavings bought on the mainland. Juan leads me to a smaller *totora* house and indicates that this is the bathroom. He's installed a sink and a commode toilet that is glistening white. The islanders themselves maintain tiny "outhouse" islands nearby, where their waste is absorbed by the *totora*-reed roots.

The guesthouse and bathroom have electricity, Juan says, but there is none in the larger house where they live next door. Electric power is only for the tourists, he says. Juan and his wife charge ten dollars a night. "I hope to eventually be able to house twenty people," he says. Juan's been working on his hotel project for ten years and has three other small "hotels" under construction.

Later in the evening, after the family has gone to sleep, I wander about. It's dark and quiet among the floating reed islands; few of the inhabitants have lights of any kind, and most people are in bed by seven or eight o'clock. The air is cold and still, and in the distance, beyond the reed beds, I can see the lights of Puno glimmering, spreading up into the hills and rimming the black lake like a wash of jewels. Overhead stretches an almost equally intense, glimmering Milky Way, the stars etched into the night sky and with even some galaxies visible, like faint puffs of smoke. I return to my *totora*-reed room, climb under the covers, and try to go to sleep, but the intense cold keeps me awake. After about an hour, I pull out my down sleeping bag, put it on the bed, climb inside, and fall immediately to sleep.

Early the next morning, Juan and I take a small wooden boat out to check on the fishnets he set the day before. Juan stands and oars the boat through the reed canals. Yellow-winged blackbirds flit about the *totora*, calling in raucous-melodic voices, as do sparrow-sized, many-colored rush tyrants, fittingly colored green, black, yellow, and blue. Long, flowing water plants, looking like bottle brushes, undulate in the translucent water below us.

As we pass by stands of reeds, we begin to see plastic bottles bobbing on the surface. Juan says they're floats attached to nylon nets. Juan has set his own translucent green net closer to a certain patch of *totora*—the edges of the reed beds are the best place to catch small *carachis*, the preferred native fish, bony yet tasty.

Although more than fifteen thousand species of fish live in the world's oceans, and more than two thousand live in the Amazon River Basin, the lake we are gliding on at 12,500 feet has a mere twenty-six native species. Around three million years ago, a small fish related to the pupfish somehow worked its way up the Andes' River systems and finned its way into Lake Titicaca. Like Charles Darwin's ancestral finch species that, blown out to the Galápagos Islands, eventually gave rise to thirteen separate species, so too did Titicaca's first finned visitor give rise to twenty-four of the lake's twenty-six native species. The other two species are closely related catfish.

Juan has set his floatless net with small stones, so that the net is invisible from the surface. He finds it easily, however, by recognizing the *totora*-reed outlines, similar to how city dwellers recognize landmarks while driving down a street. On market days, Juan says, the villagers retrieve their nets at 1:00 a.m., in the dark, using no lights. Juan says that they can find their way to their nets simply by following the topography of the reeds and with the light of the stars or moon.

Finally, Juan stops, puts down the oars, reaches over, and finds the rim of his net underwater. He then begins to pull it in, bit by bit, the thin green filaments piling into the bottom of the boat, with an occasional silver-yellow *carachi* emerging as well, snared by its gills and flapping. Juan extracts each *carachi*, only about four or five inches long, and places it squirming inside a small ceramic bowl. After about a half an hour, he has retrieved perhaps twenty of them. Blackbirds squawk and fight nearby. In the distance, I can see other lone fishermen pulling in their nets, hand over hand. Like Juan, they use wooden boats, not *totora* ones, although Juan says the older Uros islanders, such as his father, still use the small *totora*-reed boats they call *balsas*.

"Do you want to see the goddess of the lake, the Mamacocha?" Juan asks suddenly while pulling the last arm length of net into the boat. I nod my head.

We now head out on another excursion, this time through the maze of natural canals that slice and wind their way through the reeds toward shore. We pass other small boats, a man often standing and oaring, a woman wearing a bowler hat in the prow, and between them a huge pile of freshly cut green *totora* stacked chest high. The crews call out to one another in Aymara, everyone seeming to know everyone else, even though there are some two thousand people who live on the Uros Islands.

Although people here have mostly stopped using small *totora*-reed boats, they haven't given up building large ones. In 1912, a year after discovering the Inca ruins of Machu Picchu, Hiram Bingham ventured out onto Lake Titicaca. He later wrote,

> Ages ago the lake dwellers learned to dry the . . . [*totora* reeds], tie them securely in long bundles, fasten the bundles together, turn up the ends . . . and so construct a fishing-boat, or balsa . . . large balsas constructed for use in crossing the rough waters of the deeper portions of the lake are capable of carrying a dozen people and their luggage. Once I saw a ploughman and his team of oxen being ferried across the lake on a bulrush [*totora*-reed] raft . . . One of the more highly speculative of the Bolivian writers, Señor Posnansky, of La Paz, believes that gigantic balsas were used in bringing ten-ton monoliths across the lake to [the ancient city of] Tiahuanaco.

"My ancestors used to live on reed boats," Juan tells me matter-of-factly, continuing to oar our boat down a canal. "When the Incas arrived in this area, my ancestors moved out onto the lake with their boats. That's when they began living in the reeds.

"Look there," he says, jutting out his chin and pointing with it. In the distance, a small island begins to loom, an island seemingly made up of massive round gray boulders. "That's Foroba," he says. The oars dip and drip water, then dip and drip water again, the boat gliding smoothly ahead. A flightless grebe, dark brown with a white neck and rust-colored head, flushes from the *totora* ahead of us, propelling itself like a skipping torpedo across the lake before sinking into the water again. This grebe lives only on Lake Titicaca and nearby lakes. Long ago, it lost its ability to fly.

"My grandparents used to call Foroba 'the Island of the Devils,' " Juan says. "It had sirens that lured people there. No one went near it."

We touch ground on the island's edge, stepping off onto dry land. Massive gray boulders like Noguchi sculptures loom above us. A long wooden dock protrudes from the island out toward the shore. Because the lake has sunk nearly twenty feet in the last quarter century, most likely due to global warming, the dock now sits stranded high in the air and forty feet from the lake's edge.

In 1978 the Peruvian government declared the entire sweep of *totora* wetlands in this part of Lake Titicaca a national reserve, much to the disappointment of the Uros islanders. Few of them wanted the state controlling natural resources that they had used and taken care of for centuries.

"My father fought against it," Juan says. When the Peruvian government went ahead with the reserve anyway, Juan's father and the rest of the islanders promptly chased the reserve guards out of the area. The *Reserva Nacional del Titicaca* exists more on maps in Lima than amid the labyrinth of reed beds on Lake Titicaca.

On one side of Foroba Island, two white buildings with A-frame corrugated tin roofs protrude from the ground, built by the government as guardhouses for the reserve. Both are empty when we arrive. A local watchman from the Uros Islands is supposed to be here but is absent. One of the buildings is open and contains a dilapidated museum. Inside we find a few photos and posters of other reserves in Peru hanging from the walls. The photos are badly faded.

Juan and I hike up a trail to the top of the island. From its summit, we discover a panoramic view over the vast beds of *totora*, with the Uros Islands and their houses a splash of green and yellow in the distance. To the west, the city of Puno spreads out along the bay, some of its tin roofs sparkling in the sun. A sweep of brown hills rises like a mantle behind it. Beside us, in a small enclave formed by two massive gray boulders, sit a couple of clay pots, two small woven tapestries, and a small pile of burnt ashes.

"Offerings to the Mamacocha," Juan says, the goddess of the sea and lakes. "On land, they make offerings to the earth mother, the Pachamama," he tells me, "here we make them to the water mother, the Mamacocha."

It's the Mamacocha who controls the waters in the oceans and the lakes. It is she who is responsible for making the waters calm or rough, and whether fish and *totora* and waterfowl will be abundant or scarce, Juan tells me.

Juan looks out over the lake and points to the signs below of a much higher water level before.

"Ever since 1986, the lake water has been falling," he says. "There is less rain and rain feeds the lake. Without rain, the *totora* dies."

"We pray to the Mamacocha," he says, "so that she'll make the *totora* grow again."

On another boulder nearby, someone has set up several small piles of hand-sized rocks. The rock piles are offerings called *apachetas*. Burnt sticks lie in front of the piles, and a piece of worn clothing hangs nearby. "It's the work of the shamans," Juan says.

More than four hundred years ago, a Jesuit priest named Bernabé Cobo observed that

> The [Andean] Indians, [worshipped] the sun, water, earth and many other things that they held to be divine. In each of these cases, they believe that these things had the power to make or preserve what was necessary for human life, and this was always their main interest . . . These Indians used two names to designate their gods; one of the names was *vilca* and the other *guaca* [*huaca*]. Both of them are used in the same way and mean not only any god or idol, but also all places venerated and where sacrifices were made.

It's clear that Foroba Island, an outcrop of bedrock, is a living *huaca*, or shrine. Rocks, rock outcrops, and mountains were sacred places to the

Incas and continue to be with many Andean natives. Ironically, the Peruvian state tried to implant its own symbol of authority on this ancient site, by locating a park outpost here. Their attempts, however, seem to have been largely ignored. The locals continue to make offerings to the Mamacocha and to other spirits, ignoring the state and its demands, just as the Uros islanders ignored the demands of the Incas and the conquistadors five centuries earlier.

We row back toward Juan's home, down a labyrinth of canals that wind their way through the reeds. The beds themselves are alive with waterfowl. Juan points out a black *gallina de agua*, a squat, Andean coot the islanders like to eat. Even though they live in a reserve, some of the islanders hunt with shotguns made by a man who uses old water pipes for gun barrels. The islanders mix saltpeter, charcoal, and sulfur together, and then test a bit with a match. If the handmade gunpowder burns quickly, Juan says, it's good to use.

Plastic bottles and other trash bob in some of the canals. Juan says they have a service on the islands that takes trash to the mainland. He blames the trash on national (Peruvian) tourists. Farther along, we pass two small A-frame buildings, isolated in the reeds, each painted bright green and bearing a cross on the top of its corrugated metal roof.

"They're for the saints," Juan says, who is Catholic.

I ask which ones.

"Santiago," he says, but seems uncertain. "Pedro?" he then asks himself rhetorically. He shakes his head, unsure. Like elsewhere in the Andes, Catholic saints here must wait in line behind a long line of gods, goddesses, and spirits.

A priest comes out from Puno, Juan says, and gives Mass at each of these small chapels on that particular saint's day. Juan says there are also Adventists here.

"How many?"

"Fifty."

"The rest are Catholics?"

"Yes," he answers, and continues pulling on the oars. But the Catholics on the Uros are Catholics similar to himself. Juan doesn't go to Mass. Instead he makes offerings to the Mamacocha. He says there are about eight shamans on the islands. Each learned from their fathers and took over shamanic duties when their fathers died. There are also *brujos* [witches], he says. The witches can cause you harm or can cause harm to your island or possessions.

"If you could have anything in the world, what would it be?" I ask him.

Juan thinks a minute, still rowing. *"Una chosita,"* ("a small house") he says finally, meaning on the mainland. Juan and his wife have only elementary school educations, he says. He wants his two children to go to college. Thirteen-year-old Leonardo already wants to be an engineer. It's difficult to find work on the mainland, without an education Juan says. Right now, his two children row forty minutes each morning to Chulluni, the nearest town on shore, then take a bus to Puno to go to school. They require books and clothes and other things, he says. Juan and his wife want to secure their futures.

That is the reason for Juan and Elsa's hotel, I realize. The reed hotel is a net set not for fish but for tourists, which Juan hopes will one day power his kids into good professions.

"The people who are most content on the islands are those who have never been to school," Juan says, meaning anything above elementary school, or *la primaria*. Juan hopes that his kids will one day have houses on the mainland and a life filled with all the advantages and amenities that mainland life has to offer.

In the meantime, as their hotel business searches for its footing, at six o'clock every Sunday morning Juan's wife arrives at Acora, after rowing to shore and taking a bus, in order to attend the weekly market. There she sells or trades dried fish and fresh *totora* for potatoes, wheat, barley, quinoa, and anything else she might need. It's an exchange the Uros Islanders have carried on for centuries, capturing the resources of the lake and trading those resources to the land dwellers who cultivate the soil and tend the herds. The land dwellers eat the *totora* roots and feed the rest to their sheep, guinea pigs, alpacas, and cattle.

We turn into the main canal and suddenly see the sweep of blue water and the sky boiling with muscular white cumulus clouds in the distance. A breeze kicks up, and Juan mentions that everyone on the islands knows where the winds will come from. They know how the wind routinely shifts on the lake and when that is most likely to happen, like sailors. If the families on one island decide they want to move, they wait until the wind and currents are right, pull up their stakes, and then drift toward the new location. Juan, in fact, is thinking of moving his own island. "There are too many people around here," he says, although his island seems quite isolated to me.

"Do families on the same island ever have conflicts?" I ask.

"Sometimes," he says. He continues rowing and then asks me, "Do you know about the *juez*" (the judge)?

I shake my head.

He oars the boat a little farther along and points. On a small island with a number of houses, a large tree saw, perhaps ten or more feet long, stands on end against a storage shed with a conical roof.

"That's the *juez*," Juan says.

If two families really begin to get on each other's nerves, then the final arbiter of any dispute is not a jury but the long saw, or "judge." In a very short while, islanders can cut their island in two, then the two halves can take their differences elsewhere.

We pass by a giant, twin-hulled catamaran docked to one island and made from *totora* reeds. A number of Uros Islanders have recently begun building the catamarans in order to take tourists out for cruises. Most tourists arrive on larger, motor-driven boats, stop off at one or two islands, buy some trinkets, take some photos, then return to Puno after a few hours' visit. Some spend more time and take a tour on the large reed boats. A few spend the night. A giant catamaran, perhaps thirty feet long, travels down the canal with the benefit of a small outboard, the dried yellow reeds bound tightly together with cords and formed into giant, cigar-like pontoons—firm, sleek, and curved. A group of tourists snaps pictures of the islands as Juan oars our boat along, which soon begins to bob in the catamarans' wake.

The islanders, Juan says, carefully regulate the tourist trade, charging each tourist a fee for entering the island area. On carefully designated days, the islands moored along the southern edge of the canal are visited and the islanders sell their trinkets—small, foot-long boats made from *totora* or else fairly rudimentary weavings. On alternate days, the tourist boats visit the islands on the northern side. As we watch a boat disgorge a group of tourists onto an island, I realize that they are the real harvest now of the Uros Islanders. For centuries the islanders have relied upon the resources of the lake and have maintained their independence through the specialized knowledge it takes to make a living here. Now, the tourists are the choicest catch, their visits generating the largest source of income on the islands.

"Are there any master *totora*-reed boatbuilders left on the lake?" I ask, as we pass by another twin-hulled ship whose prows have been fashioned into puma heads. "Old craftsmen who can make fine ships?"

"In Bolivia," Juan says. "On Suriqui Island. Suriqui is famous for its reed boatbuilders."

In order to get to Suriqui, which lies in the southeastern portion of the lake, you must first pass near the ancient city of Tiahuanaco, located just south of the lake. It was the Tiahuanacan culture, Thor Heyerdahl believed, that had spread down from the Andes, reached the Pacific Ocean, and then diffused its culture throughout the Pacific islands by raft. Eventually, Heyerdahl stated, the Tiahuanacans had reached Easter Island, some 2,500 miles away. The enormous stone monolithic heads found on Easter Island, Heyerdahl had told me, greatly resembled the famous stone statues found high in the Andes, at Tiahuanaco.

To get to the ancient city, I travel to La Paz, in western Bolivia. Early one morning I board a bus that stops at various hotels in the city, picking up small clumps of tourists in twos, threes, and fours. A light drizzle falls on the black stone streets while 21,000-foot Mount Illimani, partially hidden in the distance, shows only its lower black flanks. The mountain's crown of blue and white ice lies hidden beneath sullen gray clouds.

In 1546 a small group of Spanish conquistadors founded *Nuestra Señora de La Paz* on Bolivia's high *altiplano*, about twenty miles north of here. Three days later, after discovering that farther south an enormous, protected bowl offered better shelter from the cold, they refounded their capital city there. During the next four centuries, La Paz gradually spread up the sides of what, geologically speaking, was an enormous erosional bowl. Eventually the city filled the bowl and crept up over the edge onto the *altiplano*. The outer flanks of the city are now spreading rapidly outward, straight across the high plains.

The bus grinds gears as it labors through the city, up the glistening cobbled streets and toward the sodden *altiplano* above. After about a half hour we reach the edge of the bowl, flatten out, and then begin lumbering past the four- and five-story, raw brick buildings of El Alto, a city of immigrants from the countryside. While the nine hundred thousand inhabitants of La Paz live snuggly fitted within their protected erosional bowl, more than a million inhabitants of El Alto live on the exposed, flat plains above. At 13,615 feet, it's one of the highest major cities in the world.

El Alto is also the fastest-growing city in Bolivia; the ground floor of nearly every building on its main streets, in fact, seems to have been converted into a *ferreteria*, or hardware store, the doors open to the streets and overflowing with construction materials. Bolivian women in bowler hats and long pleated skirts push wheelbarrows piled with hardware goods, such as rolls of blue and green plastic or bales of wire. Sacks of cement lie piled on top of one another on the sidewalks, covered now in blue tarps. Because of today's drizzle, some of the women wear white plastic bags over their bowler hats, which were introduced by English railway workers in the nineteenth century. Other than their covered hats, the women go about in the rain unprotected.

Sixty miles north of La Paz we arrive at the outskirts of Tiahuanaco, the ancient capital of a culture that sprang up upon the *altiplano* in the first centuries after Christ. Gradually, by harnessing increasingly intensive forms of agriculture, the Tiahuanaco culture grew in size, power, strength, and complexity. The civilization then entered a classic period, during which the empire extended its range southward into what is now northern Chile and northward into southern Peru. At its height, the city of Tiahuanaco had a population of 100,000 people with an additional 300,000 inhabitants living in the nearby countryside. At the time, it was one of the largest cities in the world. For roughly a thousand years, the Tiahuanaco culture flourished, until by AD 950, its builders' hard-wrought empire abruptly disappeared. Left behind were giant pyramids of adobe and stone, towering, enigmatic standing figures, and a residue of myths about the civilization's origins, rise, and collapse. According to the Spanish chronicler Cieza de León, who wrote in the 1550s,

> Tihuanaco . . . is famous for its great buildings, [and for its] stone idols of human size and shape, with the features beautifully carved, so much so that they seem the work of great artists or masters. They are so large that they seem [like] small giants . . . Some of the stones are very worn and wasted, and there are others so large that one wonders how human hands could have brought them to where they now stand.

The Spaniards who visited the ruins and who had only recently arrived in the New World had no understanding of South America's history. They *were* familiar with the Incas, whom they had conquered, but they knew nothing about this ancient city, who had constructed it, or why it had been abandoned. Both genetic and linguistic evidence supports the theory that the languages spoken by the first inhabitants of South America eventually separated into the multitude of tongues (about fifteen hundred) that were spoken there when the first Europeans arrived. Like the first meandering fish to arrive in Lake Titicaca, the cultures of South America's first inhabitants—along with their languages—gradually evolved into a bewildering variety of new forms.

Roughly ten thousand years ago, the first evidence of agriculture appeared in the South American archaeological record. By 3000 BC (roughly the same time as the Egyptians were building their first pyramids), people on Peru's northern coast had begun building ceremonial architecture and terraced mounds. By AD 100, the first state, or kingdom, arose, that of the Moche (AD 100–800). It was the highly stratified Moche society that constructed the adobe pyramids I had visited during my stay with Thor Heyerdahl on Peru's northern coast. Meanwhile, two miles up in the Andes, along the high plains bordering Lake Titicaca, the Tiahuanaco culture gradually emerged, nearly a thousand years before the Incas. The Tiahuanacans most likely spoke Aymara and, near the southern shores of Lake Titicaca, they erected a beautiful city of stone, with soaring stepped pyramids, sunken courts, stone temples, and large, enigmatic stone sculptures of humans whose eyes seemed to stare blankly at the heavens. By AD 950, however, the Tiahuanacan culture suddenly disappeared.

By the time the Incas extended their own empire southward five hundred years later, the local Aymara farmers could no longer tell them who had created the giant monuments. When the Spanish chronicler Pedro de Cieza de León showed up in the 1550s, he too queried the local inhabitants:

> [When] . . . I asked the natives . . . if these buildings had been built in the time of the Incas . . . they laughed at the question . . . However, they had heard from their forefathers that all that are there appeared overnight. Because of this and because they also say that bearded [white] men were seen on the island of Titicaca . . . I say that it might have been that, before the Incas ruled, there were [white] people . . . in these kingdoms, come from no one knows where, who did these things, and who, being few and the natives many, perished in the wars.

Another Spanish chronicler, Bernabé Cobo, who visited roughly a hundred years later, was told that when the Inca emperor Tupac Inca Yupanqui first visited the Titicaca area in the late 1400s,

> he tried to find out, by asking the natives of that town [of Tiahuanaco], from where the stone for that . . . [ruined city] had been brought and who had been its builder. The Indians answered that

they did not know nor did they have any information about when it had been built.

Various chroniclers gradually continued gathering the receding fragments of memories and tales, trying to decipher the ruins' origins. The Spanish chronicler Pedro Sarmiento de Gamboa, for example, was told that a subsequent Inca emperor, Huayna Capac, visited Tiahuanaco in probably around 1500. The emperor, it was said, had

> received news that the [northern] provinces of [the Inca Empire] . . . had rebelled. He, therefore, hurried his return and came to Tiahuanacu, where he prepared for war against the Quitos and Cayambis, and gave orders how the Urus [people] were to live, granting them the localities in which each tribe of them was to fish in the lake. He [then] visited the Temple of the Sun and the *huaca* [shrine] of Ticci Viracocha on the island [of the Sun] . . . and sent orders that all those provinces should send troops to go to that war which he had proclaimed.

The Island of the Sun the natives referred to is located in nearly the center of Lake Titicaca. According to this account, the Inca emperor visited the island on a fleet of rafts made from local *totora* reeds, which were no doubt piloted by the Uros Indians, now vassals of the Inca Empire. It's not surprising that the busy emperor took the time to visit the island as it was one of the most sacred sites in their realm—the very birthplace of the sun and stars, and which had been brought into existence by the creator god, [Kon] Tici Viracocha. According to another chronicler, Juan de Betanzos, the creation had taken place in the following manner:

> In ancient times . . . the land and the provinces of Peru were dark and neither light nor daylight existed . . . During this time of total night, they say that a lord emerged from a lake in this land of Peru . . . and that his name was Contiti Viracocha . . . When he had emerged from the lake [Titicaca] he went from there to a place near the lake

where today there is a town called Tiahuanaco . . . [then] they say
that he suddenly made the sun and the day and ordered the sun to
follow the course that it follows.

On the Island of the Sun, wrote another chronicler,

> Viracocha . . . [then] ordered that the sun, moon, and stars should
> come forth, and be set in the heavens to give light to the world, and
> it was so . . . This done, Viracocha made a sacred idol in that place,
> as a place for worship and as a sign of what he had there created.

Wrote still another:

> In [the city of] Tiaguanaco, the Creator [Viracocha] used clay to
> form all the nations that there are in this land; he painted each one
> with the clothing to be used by that nation, and he also gave each
> nation the language they were to speak, the songs they were to sing,
> as well as the foods, seeds, and vegetables with which they were to
> sustain themselves.

After creating mankind and bestowing upon him the arts of civilization, Viracocha next journeyed north to Cusco, then along the Andes,
and finally down to the coast of Ecuador, "working his miracles and
instructing his created beings." There, with the Pacific Ocean as a back-
drop, Viracocha stopped to make one final and dramatic speech, to the
people he had created.

> He told them that people would [one day] come, who would say that
> they were Viracocha, their creator, and that they were not to believe
> them; but that in the time to come he would send his messengers
> who would protect and teach them. Having said this he went to sea
> with his two servants, and went travelling over the water as if it were
> land, without sinking. For they appeared like foam over the water
> and the people, therefore, gave them the name of Viracocha which is
> the same as to say the . . . foam of the sea.

According to Inca myth then, it was Viracocha who had created the sun and the stars on the Island of the Sun, and it was he who had created the moon nearby. The Incas thus venerated the northern part of the island where they believed this miracle to have occurred. The Incas built an important shrine, and the shrine thus became a great pilgrimage center, with penitents arriving from throughout the empire.

What the Spanish chroniclers didn't know, however, was that long before the arrival of the Incas, the same island had already been considered sacred by the Tiahuanaco culture. The Tiahuanacans, too, had built shrines on the island, and the site had similarly been a great pilgrimage center. No doubt the Tiahuanacans' myths had described a similar story: that something miraculous and powerful had occurred here—perhaps the origin of their world.

When Inca armies finally arrived at Lake Titicaca's shores five hundred years after Tiahuanaco's collapse, they not only physically appropriated the former empire's territory, but they also appropriated the former empire's most sacred island, incorporating it into their own mythology. For although the Tiahuanaco culture may have disappeared, the Island of the Sun had remained a sacred center for the local inhabitants. By physically and figuratively incorporating the island into the fabric of their own culture, the Incas were thus able to increase both their own ruling legitimacy and also their mythological power.

Amid the ruins of Tiahuanaco, I walk with a small tour group and our guide, climbing up the stone steps of the Akapana, a pyramid six stories high. A Japanese couple is also on the tour; the fortyish husband has a Nikon camera slung from his neck and carries a small notebook. He scribbles furiously when our Bolivian guide says anything and closely shadows the guide to make sure he misses nothing. During a pause in the guide's speech, I ask the man if he's taking notes for any particular reason.

"I have been to over fifty countries," he tells me in broken Spanish. "I try and tie everything together."

His name is Hiroshi, and he's a firm believer that South American and Central American cultures once had contact in the past. Our

Bolivian guide is in agreement: North, South, and Central America, he assures us, all once had contact. The British Columbian totem poles look very similar to the giant stone statues the Tiahuanacans left, the guide says. Hiroshi scribbles furiously, nodding his head. Both the Aztecs and the Tiahuanacans carved similarly in stone, our guide continues, and it's not a coincidence. The only problem with that theory, I reflect, is that at least five hundred years separate the collapse of the Tiahuanacan culture and the rise of the Aztecs. If the Aztecs *had* arrived here, they would have had to have traveled three thousand miles from their homeland, and even then would have found only ruins. And then they would have had to find their way home.

Tiahuanaco *is* an unforgettable site, however, and would have impressed any visitor, no matter from what region of the globe. The Akapana pyramid has seven terraces, like the step pyramids of Egypt. A thousand years ago, visitors ascended the pyramid by walking through a stone gate that had a crouching stone figure on either side, each holding a severed human head. On top, where priests apparently once sacrificed llamas and alpacas and even humans, one can look out over the layout of the ancient city below, with its walled compounds, subterranean temple, massive stone gates, and giant standing figures.

The whole complex is apparently laid out with astronomical designs. Archaeologists, for example, have excavated humans who were sacrificed and then buried in an area where, at sunset on the day of the winter solstice, a beam of sunlight appears through a temple doorway. Buried in a corner of the Akapana, beneath where I am standing, archaeologists also discovered the skeletons of seventeen humans, all without heads, the majority of them young males in their twenties. Fragments of Tiahuanacan ceramic pots, meanwhile, often depict warriors wearing puma skull masks, decapitating various enemies and holding their severed heads aloft. The warriors' belts are adorned with more human heads—all of which have had their tongues torn out.

At its height, in AD 600–800 and while Europe languished in the Dark Ages, Tiahuanaco contained a core of large, sumptuous buildings that could be seen for miles. In the distance rose the sacred peaks of the

Andes, the two pyramids here possibly mirroring those peaks, while the city itself lay studded with stone portals and enormous statues, both of which were carved in intricate detail—as finely as medieval stained glass—displaying for all to see the stories and symbols of the Tiahuanacan religion.

At the height of the empire, vast herds of llamas and alpacas roamed the *altiplano* while beyond the city's core extended the residential neighborhoods, dotted with gardens and separated by well-traveled streets or by artificially constructed canals and ponds. At one point, Tiahuanacan engineers designed and built an ingenious water system that allowed water to flow to the top of the Akapana pyramid, then to emerge suddenly and rush down its sides. The water disappeared mysteriously into each level before emerging again at the next, possibly symbolizing the waterfalls and water cycle on the nearby mountains. The pyramids themselves are thought to have been covered in metal sheets or else with finely embroidered and colored cloth, rich in symbols and imagery.

On the high plateau surrounding the lake, engineers dug canals and created raised earthen beds that allowed 40 percent more crops to be grown than with previous methods. Meanwhile, llama trains headed from Tiahuanaco down the Andes to bring back seafood and other goods from the coast. Pack trains traveling down the eastern side of the Andes, meanwhile, visited the Amazon rain forest, returning with large quantities of coca leaves, jaguar skins, resins, oils, and hallucinogenic plants, such as ayahuasca.

Mummies recently disinterred here, in fact, were found accompanied by snuff trays, once filled with finely ground hallucinogenic plants. The plants induced not just trances but allowed the imbibers to enter a three-dimensional spirit world that would have rivaled the best animated films currently shown in IMAX 3-D. Priests, astronomers, engineers, potters, metallurgists, weavers, stone masons, soldiers, peasants, road and canal builders, and tax specialists all congregated in the city. This was a highly stratified, state-level society, one of only six such areas where state-level societies have emerged in the world. (The others were Mesoamerica, northern China, Mesopotamia, the Indus Valley, and Egypt.)

Not surprisingly, making a pilgrimage to Tiahuanaco was like visiting another world. For the first time, a visitor would have glimpsed the fabled city lying beside the sacred blue lake of Titicaca, with the Mecca-like Island of the Sun set like a jewel in its center. Gold-colored reed boats would have ferried pilgrims to the sacred island while the whole area was surrounded by ice-topped mountains whose summits were inhabited by gods. With one's visit enhanced by the use of hallucinogenic drugs, this would have been an unforgettable, mind-bending, once-in-a-lifetime experience.

From on top of Akapana pyramid, we descend and walk onto a stone-lined square. An acoustic amplifier has been cut into one of the large blocks, a kind of stone trumpet with a narrow opening on one side and a wide opening on the other. Our guide addresses us from one side and his voice booms at us.

Attention, all pilgrims! I can imagine a priest shouting. The Tiahuanacans once played music on clay trumpets, so perhaps they once blew their trumpets into the "amplifier" orifice as well.

We walk over to a large stone figure, its sightless eyes still peering into the distance and towering over us. Incised into its stone body are all kinds of carved symbols. On its right side, the stone around its neck has rough hack marks. Spanish priests once tried to sever the head, our guide says, as they had done with many "pagan" monuments throughout the conquered Inca Empire. Carved from hard andesite, however, the ancient god withstood the priests' blows and the bewildered clergymen had obviously been forced to rethink their strategy. On the god's right shoulder the priests subsequently carved a Christian cross into the stone, defiling the natives' religious symbols by superimposing their own.

The priests who came to Peru were sent to root out "false beliefs," a process they called "extirpating idolatry." They took seriously their own god's command (Psalm 81:9) "You shall have no foreign god among you; you shall not bow down to an alien god" and (Exodus 34:14) "For thou shalt worship no other god: for the Lord, whose name is Jealous, is a jealous God." As a result, priests physically destroyed as many of the natives' "false idols" as they could, doing everything in their power to wipe out the local religion. What the Spanish priests had a difficult time rooting out, however, was the pan-Andean belief that powerful spirits controlled the natives' resources—the rains, the water, the fertility of animal flocks and fields, the lightning, the earthquakes, the movements of the sun, the moon, and stars—and that these spirits were embedded in the very landscape itself. Tiahuanaco—one of the most famous and renowned shrines in the Andes—was purposely built near a sacred body of water that mirrored the sky and resembled the ocean. Its inhabitants purposely erected pyramids that appear to have imitated the sacred Andean peaks, the same peaks whose glaciers provided water to the rivers, lakes, and crops below. The city's creators designed Tiahuanaco as a sacred center dedicated to guaranteeing the continued fertility and abundance of the surrounding crops and animals, and thus guaranteeing the very existence of life itself. To the Tiahuanacans' descendants and to those who lived in the now-ruined Inca Empire, the Christians' god might be powerful, but their own gods were equally so: those of the sun, moon, lightning, water, stars, mountains, and earth. *All* of these gods—not just one—had to be honored in order for the world to continue as it was, so that the often precarious hold that humans had on life could be maintained and protected.

I wander past the Gateway of the Sun, whose massive portal bears a skull-like face thought to be that of Viracocha, the god of creation. The doorway is ten feet high, the entire frame thirteen feet wide, and the whole is cut from a single enormous block of hard andesite stone. Andesite is an igneous rock known to be formed by the tremendous friction that occurs when two continental plates—such as those that formed the Andes—meet far beneath the ocean. It is also the main ingredient of the crust on Mars. The stone that the Sun Gateway was carved from was thus originally created beneath the sea, was then lifted through geological processes 12,500 feet up into the Andes, only to be subsequently cut by Tiahuanacan stone masons at a quarry across the lake, near the modern town of Copacabana. Ancient craftsmen then transported the block ninety miles to Tiahuanaco. The gateway portal weighs ten tons, which is about the same weight as two adult elephants;

it was most likely transported across the lake by a gigantic reed boat, then dragged for roughly six miles to its present location.*

I look up at the face of Viracocha, whose head protrudes in a bas relief from the smooth stone fronting: the face looks something like a cross between a human skull and a puma—the eyes are hollow sockets, the snout protrudes, and writhing snakes have been carved for hair. The decapitated heads of enemies hang from Viracocha's belt while the friezes of thirty-two more gods surround him, covering the portal. Clearly, this was a god to fear. Like the Old Testament god, Viracocha required offerings and demanded to be worshiped. He was a god to be obeyed and feared, yet no doubt also adored.

Two days later, a bus deposits me one morning on the southeastern edge of Lake Titicaca, near the town of Huatajata, alongside a lonely two-lane highway. The road runs along the lake's eastern side and is bordered by tall eucalyptus trees. I'm on my way to Suriqui Island, in search of Heyerdahl's boatbuilder, a man whose name, I've found out, is Paulino Esteban. By now he must be at least eighty years old.

The bus I arrive in from La Paz was a local one, full of women with derby hats and men with gnarled and weathered hands from working in the fields. I watch the bus head north, then walk across the highway to a small, plain white restaurant that overlooks the lake. A girl is out in front, cleaning the restaurant's aging sign. I ask her about boats leaving for Suriqui Island.

"It already left," she says.

"Will there be another one?"

"If there are enough passengers."

"Are there any other passengers?"

"Just you."

---

*In 2002 Dr. Alexei Vranich, an anthropologist from the University of Pennsylvania, led an expedition that transported a nine-ton andesite stone from the ancient Tiahuanacan quarry near Copacabana to the shore near Tiahuanaco. Vranich's team did so using a fifteen-meter (fifty-foot) *totora*-reed raft constructed by the Bolivian boatbuilder Paulino Esteban. The raft was built using approximately 1.8 million *totora* reeds.

"Will there be another boat today?"

"I don't know."

The owner of the restaurant comes out, carrying a towel and wiping his hands. He has no clients. He is small and affable and introduces himself: his name is José. I ask José if he's heard of a boatbuilder named Paulino Esteban. He immediately brightens.

"Yes! He lives over there!" he says, pointing back down the highway. "A ten-minute walk." Jose tells me that Paulino has a sign out on the highway, that I can't miss it.

I start walking back down the road, the lake on my right, low hills and occasional houses on the left. After about five minutes I come upon an elderly couple hoeing potatoes in a field. The woman has gray hair and wears a typical pleated skirt, or *pollera*, the color of dull maroon. They both grip short wooden hoes and are bent over like pretzels, working the earth slowly. The scene reminds me of Van Gogh's *Peasant Man and Woman Planting Potatoes*, a portrait of a similar couple sowing New World potatoes outside a small village in Holland. Van Gogh painted it nearly four hundred years after the humble tuber had traveled from the Andes to Europe, where it eventually became an essential crop.

It begins to drizzle, so I take refuge under a tall eucalyptus tree. The couple never stops hoeing. When the rain lets up, I move on, leaving the old potato planters bent over their field, slowly dragging their hoes through the soil.

Clouds hover over the lake, etched by sun, the lake's water silver and expansive. Eventually I arrive at a large white sign on the right side of the road that reads in Spanish,

PAULINO ESTEBAN
EXPERT BUILDER OF THE RA 2, TIGRIS, URU,
MATARANGI I, II, AND III EXPEDITIONS

A dirt path runs down beside the sign toward the lake. Near the shore squats a giant *totora*-reed boat covered with blue plastic to protect it from the rain. On the right side of the path and in a row sit several one-story houses made from *totora* reed but with glass windows, tin roofs, and wooden frames. I walk down toward the dock. A middle-aged Bolivian man with a small potbelly and closely cropped hair approaches me. He is one of Paulino's sons, Porfirio, and is thirty-five years old. Porfirio says his father is in one of the small houses nearby. A few minutes later, Paulino comes out. He's short, lean, and handsome, eighty-two years old, with gray hair, high cheekbones, worn pants, tire sandals, and a brown jacket. His handshake is soft, and his hands are slightly swollen. His fingernails are as thick and curved as the prows of wooden boats.

I tell Paulino how I met Thor Heyerdahl many years ago, amid the pyramids of Túcume, on the northern coast of Peru. He smiles, turns, then waves for me to follow him. We walk down to the reed boat, and he begins to pull off the blue tarp that covers it. The raft is sleek and elegant; its tightly bound hull is thirty-three feet long and is freshly made. A low *totora*-reed cabin sits on its center. It looks ready to cross an ocean.

"It's going to Norway," Paulino tells me, running one of his thick hands over the reeds.

One of Heyerdahl's relatives has commissioned the boat, he explains. When it's finished later this month, workers will load it onto a truck and take it down the Andes to a port in Chile. There it will be loaded onto a ship and sent on its way.

Paulino leads me to one of the low buildings where he has a small museum set up. In the main room sit two, six-foot-long *totora*-reed rafts, as well as two other miniature rafts about three feet long, all with diminutive masts and *totora*-reed sails. They are all beautifully built, as painstakingly put together as the raft outside. Paulino opens a drawer beneath a table and withdraws a thick, well-worn binder. It's bulging with plastic leaves of photos of Paulino and Heyerdahl in Morocco, in Egypt, in Iraq, and on Lake Titicaca. Underneath one of his fingers he taps a faded images of the *Ra II*, which he and three other Bolivians from Lake Titicaca built in Morocco.

Porfirio walks in and says that he last saw Heyerdahl on Tenerife

Island in 2000. Heyerdahl was excavating mysterious stone pyramids that he was certain were linked to Egypt. I ask Paulino how he met the Norwegian.

Forty years ago, he says, Heyerdahl took a boat out to Suriqui Island, where Paulino was born and lived at the time. Heyerdahl gathered the boatbuilders together and offered them a job. There was only one catch: Heyerdahl was looking for only the best boatbuilders. So he suggested a competition: whoever could build the best small *totora*-reed boat, Heyerdahl would hire and take to Africa. There the winner would be asked to build a much larger raft that Heyerdahl wanted to sail across the ocean. None of the boatbuilders listening to him had ever seen an ocean. Most had never been farther than a few miles from Lake Titicaca. There were fifteen of them, Paulino says. They all wanted to go—but it was he who won the competition.

"What's your name?" Paulino says Heyerdahl asked him.

"Paulino Esteban."

"What's the biggest boat you can build?"

"Five, six meters [fifteen, eighteen feet]."

"Can you build a much larger boat? A boat that is *fifteen* meters [fifty feet]?"

"Yes!" Paulino answered, although he had never built such a large raft before.

"Thor was very aware, very intelligent," Paulino says. "He didn't want to take someone who didn't know how to build a good balsa."

True to his word, Heyerdahl flew Paulino and also three other Aymara boatbuilders from Suriqui Island to Morocco, where an enormous quantity of papyrus reeds had been gathered. There they began work on a reed boat, using the same techniques they used for the smaller boats they commonly made on Lake Titicaca.

One of his three boatbuilding companions has died, Paulino says. Another is sick. "Me, I'm okay," he says, grabbing my arm in a strong grip as proof.

Thus, in 1970, in a garden compound in the ancient Phoenician port of Safi, Morocco, Paulino and his compatriots fashioned a thirty-nine-foot reed ship from papyrus reed, a bulrush that is closely related to *totora*. Only ten months earlier, Heyerdahl had attempted to cross the Atlantic on a papyrus raft, the *Ra I*, built by boatbuilders from Chad. The raft had traveled more than two thousand miles before it sank due to storms and structural problems. Now Heyerdahl was taking no chances. He'd assembled a team of the best reed boatbuilders in the world, all of whom just happened to be from Lake Titicaca.

"They knew how to build reed boats with a perfection no engineer, no model builder, no archaeologist in our modern world could emulate," Heyerdahl later wrote.

Launched in May 1970, the *Ra II* ultimately journeyed 3,270 miles and landed on the shores of the Caribbean island of Barbados. By the time it arrived, however, Paulino was already back on his tiny, two-mile-long island of Suriqui.

"My grandfather taught me how to make *totora* boats," Paulino says. "My father had died—so my grandfather taught me."

"Did he make very big boats?" I ask.

"No! Four, five meters [twelve to fifteen feet]—not big ones."

"With sails?"

"Yes, with *totora*-reed sails."

"Do your children know how to build big boats?"

"Yes, my son. It's he who is going to Norway, to teach them."

"And you? Are you going?"

"Me? No! I'm staying here! (*Aquí no más!*)"

We both laugh. Paulino has trouble with one of his knees, he says, so doesn't want to take an airplane flight. He begins to flip through the photos, leaning forward and examining faded Polaroids of himself among the three-thousand-year-old pyramids of Egypt, in Iraq, in Morocco, and in a host of other countries.

"Have you been to Norway?" I ask.

"I know the whole world—Norway, Egypt, Israel, Damascus, Denmark, Spain, India. All for work. I made a reed boat and took it to Seville for the Expo in '92. Last year, to Denmark I went."

"Which country did you like the most?"

"Denmark."

"How about Norway?"

"A little bit," Paulino says, flipping through the photos. "*Dinamarca es de lujo* (Denmark is luxurious), a very nice country," he says. "Good food, good people. Not like other countries."

"What about India?" I ask. It happens to be one of my favorite countries.

"No! Too much smoke [from exhaust]! Bad food!" he says.

Paulino's wife comes in and he says something to her in Aymara. A bit later, she returns with cups and a pot of *mate de coca* tea. Ten years ago, the family moved from Suriqui Island to Huatajata, where we are now, to be closer to the highway. Nowadays on Suriqui, Paulino says, the inhabitants no longer make *totora*-reed boats, but wooden ones, which cost money to build but last for years.

The old boatbuilder takes out a weathered copy of Heyerdahl's book *Aku-Aku*, about the Norwegian explorer's excavations on Easter Island, 2,500 miles off the coast of Chile.

"Beautiful place," Paulino says, running his hand over a photo in the book. "For six months I was there."

A Spanish adventurer, he says, invited him to build a giant reed raft on Easter Island in 1996. The adventurer's name was Kitin Muñoz and he, inspired by Heyerdahl, wanted to sail the raft from Easter Island to Australia. Eventually, Paulino built a 120-foot (40-meter) ship, called the *Mata Rangi*, using the same subspecies of *totora* that is found at Lake Titicaca but that also grows in Easter Islands' lakes.*

"The *totora* is bad there," Paulino says. "It's much better here."

Perhaps as a consequence, the *Mata Rangi* sank after only twenty days, when it was only 180 miles out to sea. Paulino constructed a second boat for Muñoz three years later, the *Mata Rangi II*. It sailed from Arica, a port in northern Chile, and was initially bound for Asia, some

---

*Although Thor Heyerdahl was certain that the *totora* reed must have been brought to Easter Island by ancient South Americans, the island was not inhabited before AD 700. Archaeologists subsequently discovered that the *totora* reed on the island dates back as far as thirty thousand years, long before the arrival of humans.

eight thousand miles away. Muñoz, however, lost half of the ship in the Pacific. Eventually, he limped into a port on the Marquesas Islands, where he ended the trip.

The idea for Muñoz's attempt to sail from Easter Island on a reed raft came from Thor Heyerdahl, of course. Heyerdahl had led a multidisciplinary team to Easter Island in 1955 in order to try to solve the mystery of who had built the enormous stone figures there, some of which stand over thirty-three feet high and weigh more than eighty tons. By contrast, the largest stone monolith at Tiahuanaco, called the Bennett Monolith, is twenty-four feet high and weighs twenty tons. Heyerdahl was convinced, however, that ancient South Americans on rafts had discovered and populated this remote, seven-mile-wide outpost. But not just any South Americans.

The seafarers who arrived on Easter Island, Heyerdahl theorized, were led by none other than the pale-skinned, bearded god Viracocha who, according to Inca legend, had created mankind. After founding the civilization of Tiahuanaco and disappearing "over the water" from the shores of Ecuador, Viracocha and his followers, Heyerdahl believed, then traveled 3,500 miles on rafts made of balsa logs or *totora* reeds before arriving at Easter Island. It was Viracocha, Heyerdahl thought, who brought the arts of "civilization" to Polynesia, which for Heyerdahl meant the mastery of agriculture, stepped pyramids, the worship of a sun god, and the possession of rafts that could navigate across the seas.

From Egypt, where the oldest civilization had originated, Heyerdahl believed that ancient mariners had carried the embers of that civilization across the Atlantic to the New World. The mariners or their descendants had then somehow traveled to the other side of South America, had climbed 12,500 feet up into the Andes, and had bestowed the blessings of Egyptian civilization upon the local people living on the high plateau around Lake Titicaca. As a result, the ancient Tiahuanacans soon began constructing stepped pyramids and cities of stone similar to those halfway across the world. The descendants of these mariners—whom Heyerdahl believed possessed Caucasian features and were pale skinned—then departed on rafts across the Pacific Ocean. Viracocha and his fellow "white gods" eventually traveled amid the inhabited and uninhabited islands of the Pacific, disseminating their knowledge of stone carving, agriculture, and raftbuilding all of the way to New Zealand, some seven thousand miles from the shores of Lake Titicaca.

Viracocha, Heyerdahl believed, was thus not a god but rather the leader of a group of bearded white men who had somehow arrived in Bolivia a thousand or more years before Columbus made landfall in the New World. It was they—and not the local Aymaras—who had introduced the knowledge of how to cut and carve stones, how to build cities and empires, and how to construct oceangoing rafts from the slenderest of reeds. As Heyerdahl explained in his 1971 book, *The Ra Expeditions,*

[Reed] boats of this distinctive type are still built in their hundreds on every side of this enormous inland sea [Lake Titicaca] . . . They were built exactly in this way by the Aymara and Quechua Indians' fathers and grandfathers. This is exactly how they had looked four hundred years ago also when the Spaniards came to this lake and discovered Tiahuanaco's deserted ruins with their stepped platforms, pyramid and stone colossi, abandoned vestiges which according to consistent traditions among the primitive Aymara Indians were not the work of their own ancestors. They [the Aymaras] firmly believed the spectacular constructions to have been left since the morning of time by the *viracocha* people. These were described as white men with beards, whose priest-King was Con-Ticci-Viracocha, the sun's representative on earth. At the outset, the *viracocha* people had settled on the Island of the Sun out in Lake Titicaca. Legend has it that it was they who built the first reed boats. The white and bearded men, it was claimed, had come forth in a flotilla of reed boats when first appearing to the local Indians who at the time were ignorant of sun worship, architecture, and agriculture. These legends, which the Spaniards wrote down four hundred years ago, are still alive among the lakeside Indians.

Many times I was addressed as *Viracocha*, still the word for "white man."

Although some Spanish chroniclers copying down the oral histories of the Incas did write that Viracocha was "pale" or "white," other informants made no mention of this characteristic. Most anthropologists today believe the myth of a "white god" was more an artifact of the sixteenth-century Spaniards writing down these stories and introducing their own biases from their European backgrounds. And while it is true that various ethnic groups in the Andes referred to the Spaniards at various times as *viracochas*, it is more likely that this was due to the fact that the Spaniards—who had just conquered the vast Inca Empire with guns, horses, and steel—were perceived as extremely powerful and exotic beings, just like the natives' idea of Viracocha and his followers. Meanwhile, sun worship, architecture, and agriculture go back at least eight thousand years in Peru—long before the emergence of the Tiahuanaco culture and the stories of bearded gods. According to Heyerdahl, however, Paulino Esteban was one of the last purveyors of an ancient raft-building tradition that had originally arisen in Egypt, but had been reduced to a tiny island in the middle of Lake Titicaca, some eight thousand miles distant from Egypt's shores.

"Do you think they used rafts to travel from Peru to Easter Island, in ancient times?" I ask Paulino, who continues to examine old pictures of he and Heyerdahl in different parts of the world.

"Yes," Paulino says, but by the tone of his voice, I can sense that he is equivocal. He is quiet for a moment and is obviously thinking.

"I like the ocean," he says finally, "but it doesn't have sweet water. You can't drink it. Here on Titicaca the water is clean."

As Paulino continues flipping through photos from the past, I can't help but wonder why Heyerdahl, who was so impressed by the great detail Egyptian artists lavished on their tomb paintings, didn't notice the most obvious trait of all. While some of those paintings depicted the Egyptians' reed ships down to the minutest details of their rigging and oars, why did they not show traces of the white, bearded gods Heyerdahl so firmly believed carried civilization from Egypt to the New

World? I had seen plenty of Egyptian tomb paintings myself—every single one depicted people with dark brown or black Nubian skin, dark eyes, and black hair.

Fixated on his Old-World-to-New-World theory, Heyerdahl with his *Kon-Tiki* voyage had planted himself smack in the middle of a long-standing anthropological debate involving various theories about the origin of civilizations.

During the latter half of the nineteenth century and the first four decades of the twentieth, for example, the idea of "diffusionism" had dominated anthropological thought. The theory hypothesized that most civilizations had a common origin and, in its extreme form, later called "hyperdiffusionism," the theory held that *all* civilizations had derived from a single source: Egypt. Adherents of the theory believed that by natural "diffusion"—the physical transmission of culture from one area to another—basic inventions had gradually spread across the world only to be "rediscovered" in the New World by early European explorers.

Heyerdahl, who was trained as a zoologist, was born in 1914. He thus grew up in a Europe where "diffusionism" was widely accepted. By the time hyperdiffusionism had become discredited in the late 1950s, however, Heyerdahl had already carried out his 1947 *Kon-Tiki* voyage. Unfazed by the theory's collapse, the explorer and amateur anthropologist would spend the rest of his life trying to prove that South American civilizations had derived from the Egyptian civilization. In 1971, nearly a quarter of a century after his *Kon-Tiki* expedition, Heyerdahl wrote in his book *The Ra Expeditions,*

> Who were right, the isolationists or the diffusionists? . . . The jump from Morocco to [the Mayan civilization in] Mexico was not as startlingly absurd as the distance between the farthest points, Egypt and Peru. [So] I decided to build a reed boat [to prove the possibility of contact between the Old World and the New].

Since Heyerdahl was essentially a "hyperdiffusionist," then it made perfect sense that if other civilizations later cropped up in Peru, Bolivia,

Mexico, Central America, Easter Island, or on Hawaii, they must *all* have somehow had contact with the cultural traditions that arose in the Middle East thousands of years earlier. In Mexico's southern rain forest, for example, is an archaeological site called Palenque, which is studded with Mayan pyramids. Heyerdahl visited the site and not surprisingly was soon convinced that the Mayans must have had contact with Egypt. As he later wrote,

> Here was a large pyramid in the deep [rain] forest. Had ordinary Indians put it [the pyramid] there? Or had people other than primitive hunters from Siberia mixed with the aboriginal population in Mexico's primeval forests?

To Heyerdahl, the answer was clear: Mexico's Mayas and Aztecs, Peru's Incas, and Bolivia's Tiahuanacans all owed the existence of their advanced cultures to the same source: Egypt. It was that simple.

While Heyerdahl continued to search for evidence that would support his theory, diffusionism itself was gradually replaced by the American school of anthropological thought, which was heavily influenced by evolutionary biology and was dubbed "ecological anthropology." According to this new school, just as dissimilar organisms often evolved similar adaptations when confronted with similar environments (an example would be the snow-white coats of certain rabbits, mink, and mice in the Arctic), so too did people at different places and times invent similar cultural adaptations (in clothing, architecture, social organization, and so on) when confronted with similar environmental challenges.

According to this school of thought, civilizations in the New World arose only after lengthy independent gestation periods and entirely removed from contact with the Old World. If early agrarian societies in Peru and the Middle East utilized similar hydraulic works, social structures, and sun-dried adobe houses, these analogous traits were due to similar strategies adopted in order to solve similar problems of survival—not because of contact with one another.

The Uros people around Lake Titicaca, for example, confronted with figuring out the best way of making a living around a body of water filled with abundant fish, waterfowl, and extensive reed beds, ended up making reed boats and artificial islands. So too did the Buduma people living halfway around the world under similar conditions on Africa's Lake Chad. Similarly, if people in hot, humid climates—such as in central Africa and the Amazon—tended to go about nearly naked, it didn't necessarily mean that these widely distant cultures had once had contact with one another. Instead, these groups were simply meeting similar environmental challenges in similar ways—in this case, by not wearing clothing in hot, humid environments.

Although Heyerdahl clung stubbornly to his belief in diffusionism, he did successfully pioneer an entirely new field: the experimental use of ancient-style sailing rafts. Heyerdahl also pioneered the practical, hands-on testing of these rafts—often risking his own life in the process. Since his first trans-Pacific crossing on the *Kon-Tiki*—a balsa-wood replica of an Inca-style raft—Heyerdahl had subsequently crossed or nearly crossed the Atlantic on the papyrus rafts *Ra I* and *Ra II*, then had sailed another papyrus raft, the *Tigris* (also built by Paulino Esteban) in 1978 from Iraq to Pakistan. The goal of the *Tigris* expedition was to show that contact between the Tigris-Euphrates and Indus civilizations could have occurred by sea. In Heyerdahl's opinion, the seas were not barriers to civilizations, as had often been presumed, but instead could be used as *highways* by cultures that had oceangoing rafts and the requisite knowledge to use them.

Heyerdahl's pioneering expeditions inevitably spawned a wave of followers: to date numerous adventurers have carried out more than two dozen pre-Columbian-style raft voyages, crossing and recrossing the Atlantic and parts of the Pacific Ocean. About half of these ships sank, for one reason or another, while the other half fared reasonably well. The longest journey of a reed ship was roughly 4,000 miles. The longest of a balsa-wood raft was that piloted singlehandedly by William Willis, who sailed 11,000 miles from Peru to Australia in 1964.

Did any of these voyages prove that contact had existed between the Old and New Worlds or between Polynesia and South America?

The answer is no. They simply tested the *possibility* that such contact *could* have occurred, using the technology available at the time. To date, the only definitive proof of pre-Columbian contact between the Old World and the New is the Norse (Viking) colony at L'Anse aux Meadows, in the appropriately named Newfoundland, which has been dated to around AD 1,000.

On the Pacific side of South America, however, recent archaeological, linguistic, and genetic evidence *has* seemingly corroborated contact between Polynesia and South America, but not in the direction that Thor Heyerdahl believed it had occurred. Heyerdahl had always discounted the traditional view that the remote islands of Polynesia had been populated from west to east across the Pacific, beginning in Asia and moving gradually in the direction of South America. Instead, Heyerdahl felt that because trade winds generally blow from east to west over the Pacific, it would have been impossible for Polynesians to have sailed against them. In *Kon-Tiki*, he wrote,

> My migration theory, as such, was not necessarily proved by the successful outcome of the Kon-Tiki expedition. What we *did* prove was that the South American balsa raft possesses qualities not previously known to scientists of our time, and that the Pacific islands are located well inside the range of prehistoric craft from Peru. Primitive people are capable of undertaking immense voyages over the open ocean. The distance is not the determining factor in the case of oceanic migrations but whether the wind and the current have the same general course day and night, all the year round. The trade winds and the Equatorial Currents are turned westward by the rotation of the earth, and this rotation has never changed in all the history of mankind.

The Earth's rotation may not have changed during all of mankind's two-hundred-thousand-year history,* yet the trade winds that normally

---

*Actually, per NASA, during El Niño years the rotation of the Earth may slow ever so slightly because of the stronger winds, thus increasing the length of a day by a fraction of a millisecond (that is, a thousandth of a second).

blow from South America across the Pacific from east to west *do* routinely reverse their direction. This occurs during the weather phenomenon known as El Niño, when water in the Pacific Ocean warms, and the trade winds often reverse their direction. El Niños emerge on average every three to seven years and last anywhere from nine months to two years. Thus, Heyerdahl's contention that trade winds are constant and thus would have prevented any kind of migration across the Pacific from west to east is not correct.

Heyerdahl also seems to have underestimated, as did many other Europeans, the traditional Polynesian double, or outrigger, canoe. Instead, he remained focused on rafts constructed from either South American balsa wood or *totora* reeds. As he later wrote in his book *Early Man and the Ocean*,

> The crash landing of the balsa raft *Kon-Tiki* on the windward side of the Tuamotu islands clearly showed the greater security of a [raft] vessel of this kind, and the writer has also enough experience of ocean travel by Polynesian canoe . . . to be able to confirm that, in case of either a mid-ocean storm or coastal peril, he would unhesitatingly prefer to be on board a [raft].

The traditional Polynesian double canoe, however, which uses two canoes that have been lashed together in parallel to form a catamaran with a raised platform between them, is actually remarkably light, fast, and stable, capable of traveling long distances across the ocean. In fact, nearly two hundred years before the voyage of the *Kon-Tiki*, the renowned explorer, cartographer, and navigator Captain James Cook was one of the first to admire the Polynesians' large "sea canoes," capable of carrying fifty to one hundred people. Cook was also the first European to visit Hawaii and the first to explore and map many areas of the Pacific Ocean. While on Tonga Island in 1777, Cook wrote,

> I have mentioned that Feejee [Fiji Island] lies three days sail from [Tonga] . . . because these people have no other method of measuring

distance from island to island, but by expressing the time required to make the voyage, in one of their canoes. In order to ascertain . . . how far these canoes can sail, in a moderate gale, in any given time, I went on board one of them, when under sail, and, by several trials with the log, found that she went seven knots, or miles, in an hour, close hauled, in a gentle gale. From this I judge that they will sail, on a medium, with such breezes as general blow in their sea, about seven or eight miles in an hour.

Cook not only discovered that the Polynesian canoes could travel faster than his own ship (and, by extension, two or three times faster than the *Kon-Tiki* or the various other papyrus and *totora*-reed rafts, thus cutting down on voyage times), but that these same canoes could sail both before and *against* the wind, like a European ship. The Polynesians didn't need to wait therefore for an El Niño reversal to be able to sail from west to east toward South America. They could sail in any direction they wanted.

Cook made an additional observation that was even more startling than the speed of the Polynesians' canoes. It had to do with the Polynesian navigators who manned them:

In these navigations, the sun is their guide by day, and the stars by night. When these are obscured, they have recourse to the points from whence the winds and the waves come upon the vessel.

In other words, without knowledge of the Europeans' sextant, compass, and other navigational tools, the Polynesians were somehow able to navigate long distance accurately by using the sun, stars, and other cues. On his very first voyage, in fact, Cook took a Polynesian navigator he had met in Tahiti with him through the South Seas. The navigator's name was Tupaia and, using small shells on the beach, Tupaia created for Cook a map of the Polynesian islands that extended through a radius of some two thousand miles. Many of the islands Tupaia revealed to Cook were unknown to Europeans at the time.

After Cook's death in Hawaii in 1779, however, his discovery that Polynesian sailors were able to use a completely unknown navigational system was pretty much forgotten. For the next century and a half, European ships with single hulls and traditional navigation instruments dominated the oceans. Yet the Polynesians' traditional seafaring knowledge didn't disappear. Like the scattered master *totora*-reed boatbuilders of Lake Titicaca, traditional Polynesian navigation techniques persisted into the twentieth century, among individuals on tiny Pacific Islands strewn across thousands of miles of ocean. Before European contact, Polynesian navigators had been highly esteemed. Their specialized knowledge, in fact, was closely guarded in secret guilds and was passed down through the generations, often in the form of songs that were memorized. Little by little, however, these guilds had disappeared.

Yet in 1969—just as Thor Heyerdahl was attempting to cross the Atlantic on his reed boat *Ra I*, and as Americans were preparing to make their first landing on the Moon—an American Peace Corps worker named Mike McCoy arrived on the remote Micronesian island of Satawal. McCoy soon befriended a Polynesian named Pius "Mau" Piailug, nearly forty years old, who belonged to a long line of Micronesian navigators. Gradually, McCoy discovered that his new friend not only was an ancient-style navigator, but that he was the only one surviving in Micronesia. In short, Piailug was the last possessor of the ancient system of navigational knowledge that Captain Cook had once come into contact with and that was probably thousands of years old.

A handful of years later and across the Pacific, meanwhile, in Santa Barbara, California, a middle-aged university professor in anthropology named Ben Finney was just finishing a forty-foot replica of an ancient Polynesian sailing canoe, which he had created according to ancient designs. Finney, a specialist in Polynesia, had recently been contacted by Mike McCoy. The latter had heard of Finney's project and had told him about his unusual Micronesian friend. In 1973 Finney founded the Polynesian Voyaging Society, shipped his catamaran to Hawaii, then flew Pius Piailug to the Hawaiian Islands. Two years later and with a crew of volunteers, Piailug and Finney set sail on March 8, 1975, on Finney's catamaran, which they christened the *Hokule'a* (HOW kuw LEH ah).

The ship's name was Hawaiian for Arcturus, an important navigational star. The purpose of the voyage was to attempt to sail 2,700 miles from Honolulu to Tahiti, using only Piailug's ancient navigational skills. Thirty-three days later, the *Hokule'a* arrived safely in Papeete, Tahiti's capital. Half of the island's population turned out to witness the arrival of this ancient replica of their past and also to meet Pius Piailug, a direct link to their ancient Polynesian navigators. The "smoking gun"—the missing vessel and body of knowledge that could explain how people might have discovered and settled tiny islands strewn across thousands of miles of Pacific Ocean—had finally been found.

Not surprisingly, perhaps, and given his extensive experience in the area, Captain Cook was the first to theorize that Polynesians originally came from Asia. Today, the combined evidence of anthropology, linguistics, genetics, and archaeology has tended to corroborate what Cook suspected and what Heyerdahl spent a lifetime trying to disprove: that Polynesia had been peopled from the west, not from the east. Current linguistic evidence, in fact, points to the island of Taiwan as the ancestral homeland of the Polynesian language. Genetic evidence, meanwhile, points to Polynesians having left southeast Asia some ten thousand years ago, moving on to the area of Papua New Guinea, then crossing eastward across the Pacific Ocean. Polynesian explorers first populated the islands of Fiji, Tonga, and Samoa around 1000 BC. Other Polynesian explorers reached Hawaii—nearly three thousand miles distant—roughly 1,300 years later, in AD 300. Polynesian sailors eventually reached Easter Island—located 2,500 miles from South America's coast—sometime between AD 700 and 1200. The building of megalithic monuments on Easter Island—a tradition that was actually widespread throughout Micronesia, Melanesia, and parts of Polynesia—began soon afterward.

Polynesian explorers did not end their westward explorations at Easter Island, however. If increasing pieces of archaeological and linguistic evidence are correct, Polynesian explorers eventually beached their sail-powered catamarans on the shores of what is now Southern California, Ecuador, the Peruvian coast, and central Chile. Grooved and barbed shell fishhooks from the Chumash and Gabrielino cultures along the islands and coast of the Santa Barbara Channel in Southern California, for example, are nearly identical to those found in certain parts of Polynesia and also on the coast of Chile. Those in California have been dated between AD 900 and 1500, during the height of Polynesian expansion. Complex canoes made from planks of wood sewn together were used not only by Polynesians, but also by Southern California's Chumash and Gabrielino cultures and by the Mapuche culture along the central coast of Chile. It is unlikely that this technology was discovered independently.

Meanwhile, DNA studies of coconut palms (*Cocos nucifera*) in Ecuador have shown that this particular coconut species must have been transported by humans from the Philippine Islands, where they are native, to South America. Survival of the palms by any other method—such as coconuts carried by ocean currents—seems exceptionally unlikely. Finally, the South and Central American sweet potato (*Ipomoea batatas*), which evolved in the Americas, became widespread throughout Polynesia after arriving there by at least AD 700. The Polynesian word for sweet potato, *kumara*, is similar to the word *cumar*, used by the Canari people on Ecuador's Guayaquil coast. Current thinking is that it was Polynesians who arrived in South America, returning with the valuable root in their catamarans to the South Seas.

The combined evidence from a multiplicity of disciplines thus strongly suggests that double canoes with sails manned by Polynesians, not rafts from the New World, crossed the Pacific repeatedly and methodically, purposely seeking out new lands to inhabit and explore. While it's possible that some South Americans sailed out into the Pacific on reed or balsa-wood rafts, there seems little if any genetic, linguistic, or archaeological evidence to corroborate such an occurrence.

In perhaps a fitting irony, while Thor Heyerdahl often chided professional historians and archaeologists for their disparaging view of ancient people's seafaring abilities, when he crashed on an inhabited Pacific atoll with the *Kon-Tiki*, he himself failed to recognize the obvious vehicle of trans-Pacific migration, even when that very vehicle literally bumped into his own. As he recounted in his book of the voyage,

> At half-past five we stood in toward the reef again. We had sailed along the whole south coast and were getting near the west end of the island . . . on the beach . . . we detected a cluster of motionless black spots. Suddenly one of them moved slowly down toward the water, while several of the others made off at full speed up to the edge of the woods. They were people! . . . Now we saw a canoe being launched, and two individuals jumped on board and paddled off on the other side of the reef. Farther down they turned the boat's head out, and we saw the canoe lifted high in the air by the seas as it shot through a passage in the reef and came straight out toward us. The opening in the reef, then, was down there; there was our only hope. . . . The two men in the canoe waved. We waved back eagerly, and they increased their speed. It was a Polynesian outrigger canoe.

The solution to the age-old mystery of how Polynesia had been inhabited actually reached and docked against Thor Heyerdahl's balsa-wood raft on August 3, 1947, but the thirty-three-year-old explorer, trained in diffusionism and blinded by his own Eurocentric beliefs, was unable to recognize the very craft that had been pivotal in populating the South Seas. Heyerdahl—named after Thor, the ancient, seafaring Norse god of thunder—had been searching myopically for evidence of white, bearded gods on rafts, not brown-skinned, beardless people on canoes. And although the white gods were more than likely figments of people's imaginations, Heyerdahl nevertheless spent the remainder of his life trying to cobble together evidence to support his diffusionist belief that South America had somehow had contact with Egypt. He took his theory with him to the grave.

Thor Heyerdahl passed away on April 18, 2002, aged eighty-seven, and was honored with a state funeral in Oslo's cathedral. He was then buried where he had lived for years in Colla Micheri, an Italian seaside village that overlooks the Mediterranean Sea once crossed by Greek, Roman, and Phoenician sailors. The replica of the great Polynesian sailing craft, the *Hokule'a*, meanwhile, continues roaming the Pacific Ocean, manned by the descendants of Polynesian seafarers who are now busy training new, younger "wayfinders" in the ancient art of Polynesian navigation.

"Thor was a very good person," Paulino tells me, as we shake hands and I prepare to return to La Paz. Indeed, my own memory of Heyerdahl is one of his friendliness and of how little he was affected by his international fame. I watch as Paulino busies himself with some touch-up work on the giant *totora*-reed ship, which will soon be bound for Norway. As I walk back up the path to the highway, carrying one of Paulino's model boats in my hand, I have no doubt that it was Paulino's ancestors who built the giant reed rafts that once carried enormous stones across Lake Titicaca to the ancient city of Tiahuanaco, and that it was those same ancestors who had created the magnificent civilization that lasted for nearly a thousand years here. I also have no doubt that Paulino's ancestors needed no help other than their own ingenuity to cut, transport, and erect the enormous stones that now lie littered about that ancient city. No bearded white gods or Egyptians were necessary to create the miracle of civilization that occurred here long ago in the Andes, more than two miles above the sea. All of the evidence, in fact, points to Paulino's ancestors having arrived here long ago from Asia by land, eventually creating a series of civilizations in what are now Mexico, Central America, Colombia, Peru, and Bolivia. And that it was these same ancestors' distantly related relatives—the Polynesians—who occasionally stepped onto beaches from their double canoes. There they must have gazed in wonder at an inhabited coastline and at a distant and vast mountain chain before eventually, guided by the sun, stars, and swells, they returned to their ancient homelands, far across the seas.

7

THE END OF CHE GUEVARA (BOLIVIA)

This experience of ours is really worth taking a couple of bullets for. [If you do come] don't think of returning, the revolution won't wait. A strong hug from the one who is called and whom history will call . . . CHE.

—Che Guevara, writing from Cuba to a friend in Argentina, 1959

We learned perfectly that the life of a single human being is worth millions of times more than all the property of the richest man on earth . . . that the pride of serving our fellow man is much more important than a good income; that the people's gratitude is much more permanent, much more lasting than all the gold one can accumulate.

—Dr. Che Guevara, speaking to Cuban medical students, 1960

I've come to stay, and the only way that I will leave here is dead, or crossing a border, shooting bullets as I go.

—Che Guevara, on the eve of starting guerrilla operations in Bolivia, November 1966

Che and sixteen other guerrillas—ten Cuban, five Bolivian, and one Peruvian—walked and stumbled down the night-black trail, at the bottom of a deep canyon, and beneath the light of a small sliver of moon. The trail followed a creek hemmed in by short trees. Small potato patches emerged here and there, which the guerrillas could see only when the moonlight fell on them. Otherwise, the men in ragged, dirty clothes did their best to find their way through the black canyons created by the shadows of the trees. Che, the leader, was thirty-nine years old, wore green pants, a camouflage shirt, and a brown beret. Bound around his feet were rough pieces of cloth and leather—all that remained of boots that had fallen apart months earlier. Last March, when they had launched guerrilla operations, there had been fifty-two of them; now, seven months later, there were only seventeen—the rest having been killed or imprisoned, or having deserted. As the emaciated guerrillas followed the twisting path, they had no idea that they were nearly surrounded by an ever-tightening circle of some two hundred and fifty Bolivian soldiers, recently trained by US Green Berets.

Julia Cortez sits in her small living room, clasping her hands over and over, wringing them, full of worry. She thinks she is losing her mind. The room has a couch, a sofa, and a chair, floral wallpaper, and chintz-style pottery. At sixty-three, she wears a black skirt and a freshly starched white blouse. Her hair is gathered neatly in a bun, and her dark eyes are widely set. Her manner is open, somewhat wistful; she speaks in a very quiet voice. Forty-four years ago, Julia Cortez was one of the last people to speak with and see Che Guevara alive.

"I have serious problems with my short-term memory," she says, handing me a plate with a fresh peach and a sharp knife on it. "They're

going to do an MRI on me in Sucre, to find out what's wrong. I've already been to a doctor in Santa Cruz. It's incredible! Incredible! I forget
where I've put things! I go out and forget what I was going to do! I
have some kind of neurological problem," she says, clasping her hands
again, "and it's getting worse. My mother died a month ago, and that
has only accentuated everything. For having cried so much. I watched
her suffer for four years. I don't know what's going to happen to me
now."

Julia is a retired schoolteacher. She has a small plot of land outside
the town of Vallegrande, where she has some peach trees and raises
corn, "just for sustenance," she says. After thirty-one years of teaching,
she receives a pension that amounts to just a little more than one hundred and fifty dollars a month.

"My mother was both mother and father to me, because my father
abandoned us. We were very poor. There were eleven of us and we had
practically nothing. But my mother encouraged me to study. She was
very supportive, very diligent, very reliable." For a while, Julia says,
she was encouraged by other family members to become a nun, as that
would be a sure way of support. But Julia insisted on being a teacher.
"That's what I wanted to do."

Julia's first job was a posting to the tiny village of La Higuera (the
Fig Tree), a small cluster of adobe homes with about eight hundred
people and a two-hour walk from her own village of Pucará. It's a rugged region, with layer after layer of forested mountains in the distance
that make the view look like a Japanese woodcut. Julia taught in a small
adobe schoolroom with a dirt floor, wooden benches, a blackboard, and
about twenty primary-school kids, the children of farmers who tilled
the fields. The nineteen-year-old schoolteacher taught during the week,
then walked home on a dirt path on the weekends. A few months after
she was posted, the villagers lent her a horse to help make the journey
easier.

"There were no locked doors," Julia remembers. "The people were
very hospitable. Anyone who visited was invited into their homes to
share whatever food they had. On weekends, if I stayed over, we'd cook

something in the big [adobe] óven outside. The neighbors would come, they'd play music, and we'd share everything. It was very pretty."

Beneath the camaraderie, however, there was also plenty of poverty. The area of La Higuera, in the department of Santa Cruz, was and still is one of the poorest regions of Bolivia, a country that remains one of the poorest in the hemisphere. In 1967, when Julia was assigned as a teacher there, infant mortality, illiteracy, and poverty rivaled that of the poorest nations in Africa.

It was for some of those very reasons that the Argentine revolutionary Che Guevara launched guerrilla operations in Bolivia in 1967, the same year that Julia began work. Che, who had helped Fidel Castro come to power in Cuba, had developed a theory that a small band of guerrillas, or *foco*, could serve as a "spark" that would ignite a revolution in impoverished countries such as Bolivia. Che's guerrillas first clashed with Bolivian troops about sixty miles south of La Higuera. Their aim was to ignite a popular uprising against the Bolivian government, then to ignite similar socialist revolutions in neighboring countries, such as Peru, Brazil, and eventually Che's home country of Argentina.

Unlike Julia, Ernesto "Che" Guevara was a product of the middle class, born the eldest of five children in Rosario, Argentina, in 1928. A gifted athlete, Che excelled at sports in school, yet chronic asthma often kept him homebound. There he found refuge in books—his parents maintained a three-thousand-book library—and for the rest of his life Che was a voracious reader. One of his favorites was the epic Argentine poem *Martín Fierro*, which told the story of an Argentine *gaucho*, or cowboy, pursued by the police, one of whom changes sides due to the hero's extraordinary display of bravery. Together, the two of them go to live among the indigenous people, hoping to find a better life.

In 1951, as a twenty-three-year-old medical student, Che and a friend rode a motorcycle through South America, intent on expanding their horizons. It was the first time Che encountered some of South America's chronic poverty.

"I have visited . . . all the countries of Latin America," Che later wrote,

In the way I traveled, first as a student, then as a doctor, I began to come into close contact with poverty, with hunger, with disease, with the inability to cure a child because of a lack of resources . . . and I began to see there was something that . . . seemed to me almost as important as being a famous researcher or making some substantial contribution to medical science, and this was helping those people.

Even while a medical student, Che gradually grew to realize that bringing medicine to some isolated, impoverished hamlet was not going to cure a level of privation that had sometimes endured for centuries. To Che, working as a doctor amid the destitute was of no more use than putting a Band-Aid on a gangrenous leg instead of amputating it. It was the poverty itself that had to be rooted out. By the time he was twenty-five, Che had come to the conclusion that the only way the lives of millions of Latin Americans could ever be improved was by transforming their countries' political structures. Under most current systems, Che believed, Latin America's governments strove to preserve the wealth of a small group of privileged elites while ignoring the poor. Medicine was not going to change any of that. Only a revolution from the bottom up could.

While traveling in Mexico at the age of twenty-five, Che met a twenty-six-year-old, self-exiled Cuban lawyer and revolutionary named Fidel Castro. Castro proved to be the very catalyst Che had been searching for. On their first meeting, Castro explained that he intended to lead a small group of guerrillas to the shores of Cuba and with them topple the Cuban dictator, Fulgencio Batista. Sizing up the young Argentine doctor, Castro asked Che if he'd join them as the revolutionaries' physician. Che immediately agreed. Later he wrote that,

The truth is that after the experiences of my wanderings across all of Latin America . . . it didn't take much to incite me to join any revolution against a tyrant, but Fidel impressed me as an extraordinary man. He faced and overcame the most impossible things. He had an exceptional faith in that once he left for Cuba, he would arrive. And that once he arrived, he would fight. And that fighting, he would win. I shared his optimism . . . [It was a time to] stop crying [over social injustices] and fight.

Three years later, in 1959, Che rode with a triumphant Castro into a liberated Havana, the final prize in their protracted guerrilla war. Proven on the battlefield as a guerrilla commander and fearless to the point of recklessness under fire, Che had risen to become a *comandante* in the revolutionary army. He later became minister of industry and president of the national bank. It was during the war that Ernesto Guevara also acquired his nickname of "Che"—a uniquely Argentine expression that basically means "hey, buddy" or "friend." Che used the word so frequently when addressing his Cuban companions that they in turn used it to address him.

Six years later, with the Cuban Revolution secure yet with the island quarantined by a US economic blockade, Castro suggested that Che try to ignite the spark of continent-wide revolution. He suggested launching a war in Bolivia, where Che could help topple a president the CIA had initially helped to put in power but who had since won an election. Once war broke out in Bolivia, Castro said, revolution in neighboring countries would soon follow. Cuba would then have broken the US blockade. Guevara, now thirty-seven years old, quickly agreed. He then began to prepare himself for the enormous task of "liberating" all of South America.

In a letter written to his mother, a staunch supporter of her by-now famous revolutionary son, Che admitted that, like the fictional Don Quixote, he too was something of a dreamer: "Once again I feel below my heels the ribs of Rocinante," he said, referring to Don Quixote's faithful horse. "I return to the road with my shield on my arm . . . I believe in the armed struggle as the only solution for those peoples who fight to free themselves . . . Many will call me an adventurer, and that I am; only one of a different kind—one of those who risks his skin to prove his beliefs."

Che may have seen himself as an idealist, but the Cuban Revolution had revealed an uncompromising side of him. By 1959—in a world starkly divided between capitalism and communism—Che was a devout Marxist-Leninist who believed that capitalism was doomed and that inevitably socialism, then communism, would take its place. He also possessed an unshakable faith that the entire process could be hurried along at the point of a gun. According to Alberto Granado, who as a young medical student had accompanied Che on his motorcycle journey through South America, when Che looked through a sniper scope at a soldier and pulled the trigger, he fully believed that he was helping reduce repression by "saving 30,000 future children from lives of hunger." When Granado looked through a sniper scope, by contrast, he saw only a man with a wife and children. The difference between them, Granado said, was that Che felt certain he was ushering in a new world order.

In his book *Guerrilla Warfare*, Che summed up his new plan, "the cordilleras of the Andes will be the [Cuban] Sierra Maestra [Mountains] of Latin America; and the immense territories which this continent encompasses will become the scene of a life or death struggle against imperialism . . . This means that it will be a protracted war; it will have many fronts; and it will cost much blood and countless lives for a long period of time . . . This is a prediction. We make it with the conviction that history will prove us right."

Guevara, raised as a Catholic and later an atheist, had nevertheless become a true believer: he was now utterly convinced that Marx's prescription for how to achieve a social utopia was not just a theory—but fact.

"At which point I left the path of reason and took on something akin to faith [in communism] I can't tell you," Che wrote his parents ". . . [however] I feel not just a powerful internal strength, which I always felt, but also . . . an absolutely fatalistic sense of my mission, which strips me of all fear.

"It could be that this will be the definitive one," he warned them. "I don't go looking for it [death], but it is within the logical calculations of probabilities. If it is to be, then this is my final embrace."

Che also left behind a letter, to be read only if he did not return, for his wife and five children:

> If one day you must read this letter, it will be because I am no longer among you. You will almost not remember me and the littlest ones will remember nothing at all. Your father has been a man who acted according to his beliefs and certainly has been faithful to his convictions. Grow up to be good revolutionaries. . . . Above all try always to be able to feel deeply any injustice committed against any person in any part of the world. It is the most beautiful quality of a revolutionary. Until always, little children, I still hope to see you again. A really big kiss and a hug from Papa.

At 2:00 a.m. the guerrillas stopped and made camp, next to a large boulder near a stream. Chino Chang, the Peruvian guerrilla, could not see well at night through his glasses, so further progress was difficult. Months earlier, Che had run out of his asthma medicine and thus was wheezing heavily, his lungs constricting as if they were being crushed in a vise. The guerrillas had with them a single broken two-way radio that they could listen to but which would no longer transmit. That night, beside the stream on one of the last days of his life, Che listened through the static as a Bolivian news station broadcast an army communiqué. Then, removing a small notebook in which he'd been keeping a diary since the guerrilla war began, he wrote his final entry:

"Oct 7 [1967]. We completed the 11th month of our guerrilla operation . . . without complications until 12:30 [p.m.], when an old woman grazing her goats came into the canyon where we were camped, and we had to seize her. The woman has not given us any trustworthy information about the soldiers, saying that she knows nothing . . . from what the woman told us we figure we are about one league from [La] Higuera, one from Jagüey and two from Pucará. At 5:30, [the guerrillas] Inti, Aniceto, and Pablito went to the old woman's house where she has two daughters, one a dwarf and the

other crippled. They gave her 50 pesos telling her not to say a word to any-
one, but with little hope that she will keep her word . . . The Army issued
an unusual report [by radio this evening] concerning the presence of 250
[army] men in Serrano to keep the encircled group [of guerrillas] . . . from
getting out. They report we are hiding between the Acero and Oro Rivers.
The news seems to be a diversionary tactic."

Placing the notebook in the small leather pack he carried, Che then lay
down alongside his men and went to sleep, unaware that the communiqué
was not a diversionary tactic but rather a straightforward statement of
fact. Now, no matter what direction the guerrillas chose to head toward,
they would inevitably run into army troops, as they had been unwittingly
caught in a noose. Che was also unaware that a local farmer, the one who
tended the potato patches they were sleeping in, had detected their presence
and had gone off to alert a company of Army Rangers. Not long afterward,
while the guerrillas continued to slumber, several hundred Bolivian soldiers
began moving in.

Samaipata is a small, colorful town of whitewashed adobe buildings and
tile roofs surrounded by jungle-covered hills. Inca and Guarani sites litter the area, the Incas having arrived here in the fifteenth century during their push to conquer more territory. On July 6, 1967, three months
before their final firefight, six of Che's guerrillas commandeered a truck
and drove it boldly into town, desperate to find food and supplies as
well as medicine for Che's asthma. The guerrillas shot and killed a soldier and briefly captured ten more. They then fled, unable to find the
medicine their leader so badly needed. Che, meanwhile, had waited behind. Lately he had been riding on muleback, unable to walk.

"Now I am doomed to suffer asthma for an indefinite time," Che
wrote gloomily in his notebook that night. The guerrillas by now had
already eaten most of their horses and recently had been hungrily
eyeing Che's mule, but he would have none of it. On August 24 he

wrote, "We remained in ambush all day. At dusk the *macheteros* [trail cutters] returned with the [animal] traps, they caught a condor and a rotten cat. Everything was eaten together with the last piece of ant-eater meat. The only things remaining are the beans and whatever is hunted."

If the object of a guerrilla insurgency is to continually take the fight to one's opponent, inflicting damage on the enemy when he least expects it, then Che's weary band had long since abandoned that strategy. For the most part, chased by increasingly numerous army patrols and unable to win over the support of the local inhabitants, Che's guerrilla column was now constantly on the run. As they fled northward, they often moved at night, hiding in patches of forest cover during the day.

The guerrillas were filthy, reported a Bolivian soldier Che's men had briefly captured and released. They walked slowly, gradually cutting their way through thick brush with machetes. Che, the soldier reported, "travels by horse . . . [and] the others serve him like a God, they made his bed and brought him *yerba mate* [tea]. He smokes a pipe, of silver . . . and travels in the center [of the column]." Although he was obviously very badly off because of his untreated asthma, another prisoner reported that Che "never complained."

In Samaipata, I walk down a dirt street toward the highway that runs outside of town, hoping to find a bus going south toward La Higuera, near where Che was captured. An army Jeep passes by, then stops. The driver, a sergeant, motions me to get in. He's short, squat, brown skinned, wears an olive-green uniform, and has highly polished, jungle-style black combat boots. The sergeant is friendly but serious, has been posted to the Samaipata area for the past three years and is originally from Santa Cruz. He likes the area, he says, gesturing toward the hills. A bit later, as he drops me off on the dirt highway at an isolated tollbooth, I tell him that I'm tracing the final steps of Che Guevara, the guerrilla revolutionary. The sergeant lifts an eyebrow and turns to me. "We sure took care of him, didn't we?" he says, before driving off.

At the tollbooth a woman squats alongside the roadway, wearing long skirts and a straw hat. She brushes flies off a basket of home-made cheese-filled pastries covered with a piece of cloth. Jungle foliage cloaks the surrounding hills, and the sound of cicadas is intense, mixed with occasional bird calls. The toll man eyes me, then steps out of his booth and strikes up a conversation. He's about sixty, from Santa Cruz. He works twenty days at the booth, he says, then returns for ten days to Santa Cruz. He's then rotated to another toll both in some other isolated area. The man gestures to a small building across the road. I can see bunk beds through the open door. "That's my home," he says.

"I worked for seven years on seismic lines for petroleum companies," he says, "in the jungle. I saw a spectacled bear once, ate caiman, almost drowned in the Madidi River." He buys a cheese pastry from the woman for a boliviano and continues, munching, while she tucks the cloth back around her wares. "I worked in the Chaco, too, among the Guaranis. They still speak their own language, have hair down their backs," he says, gesturing. "They still use bows and arrows. Flat land, all of that," he says, pointing at the hills around us by contrast. "Nothing like this." He swallows the rest of his pastry, wipes the crumbs off his shirt, then peers intently at me. In the distance, I can hear the sound of a bus. The sound of the bus gets louder, and we both turn to look down the road.

"Have you seen the Nazca Lines in Peru?"

I say I have.

"Extraterrestrials landed there," he says emphatically. "It was all one big space port."

The bus pulls into sight, then grinds to a stop in a cloud of squeaks and billowing dust. Arms stick akimbo out of open windows as the woman hoists her basket and begins selling pastries in a hurry, soiled Bolivian notes and pastries quickly changing hands. The toll man talks to the driver as I climb on, and with a whoosh and a jerk, we pull out. I walk down the swaying aisle all the way to the back seat, then peer out the rear window. The toll man is standing in his booth again, looking down the deserted highway while the pastry woman sits on the side of the road, brushing her skirts as a long tube of dust spreads out behind us like a slowly expanding snake.

At daybreak on October 8, 1967, Che and his guerrillas awoke alongside a stream at the bottom of a deep canyon, called the Quebrada del Churo. Looking up, a guerrilla spotted movement on one of the ridges hedging them in. Che soon realized that somehow during the night, the Bolivian Army had taken up positions. Trapped at the bottom of a ravine about one hundred and fifty feet wide and nine hundred feet long, the guerrillas discovered that they were surrounded. It was a perfect ambush.

At 1:10 p.m. the bombardment began. Hundreds of Bolivian army troops opened up with automatic weapons and mortar fire. Soon, two guerrillas were dead and the guerrilla force scattered. Taking cover behind a large boulder near the stream, Che kept firing bursts with his rifle until a bullet struck it, rendering it useless. Soon afterward, another bullet ripped a hole in Che's beret while a third tore into his left calf. One of the Bolivian guerrillas, a man nicknamed Willy, ran to help, pulling Che up through the thick undergrowth that clung to the steep hillside, searching for a way out. As the two guerrillas stumbled forward, a Bolivian ranger suddenly stepped out from cover, trained his rifle on the two unarmed men, then ordered them to halt. Che Guevara, veteran of the Cuban Revolution, former minister of industry, medical doctor, guerrilla theorist, and potential liberator of all of South America, slowly raised his hands.

"Don't shoot!" his captor later claimed he said. "I am Che Guevara. I am worth more to you alive than dead!"

"Are you going to La Higuera?" a young woman asks me, waiting for a car that is already an hour late.

"Yes, and you?"

"I'm getting off sooner."

"Where's that?"

"Quebrada del Churo."

"The ambush site?"

"Yes! You, too?" she asks.

I tell her that I am, and ten minutes later, a car arrives and we climb in. Her name is Lucia, she's twenty-three, and is an Argentine from Buenos Aires. Lucia is pretty, has long dark hair, wears blue jean shorts, tennis shoes, and a white T-shirt, and carries a small day pack. It's been her dream for years to visit the area that Che Guevara fought in. Lucia had two weeks off from her job as a product designer and decided—*por qué no?* Why not?—to come. Like many Argentines, she is of Spanish-Italian extraction. Her parents, she says, were leftists, and as a girl, she traveled to Cuba many times. She's also white and middle class, like Che.

"In Argentina, among the young, Che's a hero," she says matter-of-factly. "We admire him—and the cause he believed in. Helping the poor."

She thinks about it a bit, then adds, "Che emanated something—a force." She looks at me and takes a long drag from her cigarette. "He was also *gorgeous*."

Lucia is not alone in her opinion. An iconic 1960 photo of Che portrays him wearing a smart-looking tunic, fashionably long hair, a scraggly (guerrilla) beard, mustache, and a black beret with a single star on it, which symbolized his rank as a guerrilla commander. Che was attending a funeral in Havana at the time for Cubans who had died from a supposed foreign attack. A Cuban photographer snapped the photo, and it was this image—Che with a determined, heroic, almost otherworldly expression—that eventually circulated around the world.

"The idea of revolution, not only the Cuban revolution, now had its symbol," a journalist wrote in Spain's *El Dominical.* "And not just any symbol, but one that was *sexy*, masculine, adventurous, noble, and— very importantly—in concert with the spirit of the times." "Would

Che have had the same impact," asked another Spanish journalist, "if Che had not had the photogenic face that he'd had—and looked more like, say, Raúl Castro [Fidel's fiercely revolutionary yet unattractive brother]?"

It's a valid point. Che had found himself not only at the right place at the right time with the right set of skills, but he also just so happened to look like a movie star.

"He was the first man I ever met who I thought not just handsome but beautiful," wrote the American journalist I. F. Stone. "He looked like a cross between a faun and a Sunday-school print of Jesus . . . [yet] he spoke with that utter sobriety which sometimes masks immense apocalyptic visions."

In addition to his looks, Che possessed a certain ineffable *je ne sais quoi* quality—one that, as with all charismatic leaders, engendered fierce loyalty among his followers. When Che appeared, wrote the Uruguayan journalist Julia Constenla de Giussani, "He had an incalculable enchantment that came completely naturally. If he entered a room, everything began revolving around him . . . He was blessed with a unique appeal."

While Lucia and I chat about Che's Bolivian strategy, we drive through semitropical woodland, occasionally passing solitary men on horseback wearing flat-brimmed black hats. Some of the riders carry a rifle slung across their backs and a lariat looped on their saddles. The car we're riding in, a black Toyota Corolla, has seen better days. For some reason, the steering wheel used to be on the right side, but has been ripped out and reinstalled on the left. All of the gauges, none of which work, have remained on the right, clinging mournfully around the hole where the steering wheel used to be, loose wires dangling from them. It's the driver's car, though, and he babies it, navigating his way carefully over deep ruts and through pools of water. The road we follow often loops past sheer edges and cliffs.

Later, as we motor through mist and past trees that have rough, lime-green lichen on their trunks that look like fur carpets, we arrive in Pucará, a village that unfolds down the side of a hill like a medieval

Italian village. Stone and adobe houses stand beside knots of men with black hats who are clustered on street corners. The men pause and stare at us as our car passes by.

Of the many setbacks Che suffered in Bolivia, perhaps none was bigger than his failure to incorporate local Bolivians like these into his guerrilla force. The farmers in the area, Che soon discovered, viewed the mostly light-skinned, bearded Cubans not as liberators but as foreigners. Foreigners who, for some indecipherable reason, had began to ambush and kill Bolivian soldiers and police.

In his 1960 manual *Guerrilla Warfare*, completed soon after the Cuban Revolution, Che wrote that "It is important to emphasize that guerrilla warfare is a war of the masses, a war of the people. The guerrilla band is an armed nucleus, the fighting vanguard of the people. It draws its great force from the mass of the people themselves." Three years later, he summed up his thinking with a stark warning: "[any] attempt to carry out this type of war without the population's support is a prelude to inevitable disaster." However, the Bolivian forces that Che was up against—some of which had recently been trained by US Green Berets in counterinsurgency warfare—knew precisely how important the local population was. They had no doubt studied Che's very own manual. Without popular support, the army knew, Che's guerrilla band would die, starved and dehydrated like a plant without water. It was thus of critical importance that Che's guerrillas not be allowed, as Mao Tse-tung had suggested, to "move amongst the people as a fish swims in the sea." It was imperative that the army, not the guerrillas, capture the "hearts and minds" of Bolivia's rural farmers and thus deny the guerrillas local support.

"Groups of Castro-Communist tendency, mostly foreigners, have infiltrated our country," the army warned the Bolivian public in April 1967, a month after fighting began, "with the sole objective of sowing chaos and halting the Progress of the Nation, carrying out acts of banditry, pillage and assault against private property. . . . The Armed Forces, conscious of its specific obligations, has been mobilized to detain and destroy the foreign invasion, as malicious as it is vandalous."

For good measure—in a country where the average income was less than $1,000 a year—Bolivia's president René Barrientos placed a $4,200 bounty on Che Guevara's head.

A few months later, in June of 1967, Che confessed in his diary his increasing frustration over the guerrilla's encounters with the local inhabitants. "The lack of peasant recruits," he wrote, ". . . is a vicious circle: to get this enlistment [of volunteers] we need to settle in a populated area, and for this we need [more] men . . . Militarily the Army's actions have been nil, but they are working on the peasants in a way that we must be very careful of as they can change a whole community into informers, either through fear of our aims or through trickery."

Che's characterization of the local farmers as "peasants," however, was an error in judging local conditions that ultimately had devastating consequences. When Che and Fidel Castro had invaded Cuba and taken refuge in the Sierra Maestra Mountains, the locals they encountered there *were* peasants; that is, they were men and women who worked for large landowners and possessed no land titles themselves. Castro quickly promised the peasants land, a promise that led many to join the revolutionary movement. In 1952 in Bolivia, by contrast, fifteen years before Che began combat operations, a reformist government had come to power that soon enacted wide-ranging land reform. Suddenly, a large percentage of Bolivia's peasants had become landowners. Unlike in Cuba, then, Che was unable to offer local Bolivian farmers the promise of land, as they already had their titles. Although the farmers' largely negative reaction to the guerrillas greatly frustrated Che, the reality was that they were being both shrewd and practical: they were simply terrified of losing the land titles they had so recently gained.

Little by little, as Che and his guerrillas marched through the remote Bolivian countryside, the army continued to work on the farmers' "hearts and minds," increasing the guerrillas' isolation and leaving them with fewer and fewer places to hide. Only in one village, Alto Seco, after Che and his guerrillas had gathered the bewildered townspeople together for a political talk, did one young man finally hold up his hand and offer to join the guerrillas. As he readied his things, one of Che's men took the volunteer aside. "Don't be silly," the guerrilla warned him, "we're done for." The comment more than likely saved the man's life.

In August, Che's forces accidently became split into two columns. The army soon wiped out the first group, which was betrayed by a local farmer. Now only seventeen guerrillas remained, and with each new confrontation, attrition was taking its toll. "The essential task of the guerrilla fighter is to keep himself from being destroyed," Che had written in 1960. Yet in Bolivia, in late 1967, Che seemed unable to prevent his group from destruction.

Che biographer Jon Lee Anderson wrote that "one can't help but conclude that [by this point] Che had become strangely detached from his own plight, an interested witness to his own inexorable march toward death. For he was [now] breaking every rule sacred to guerrilla warfare: moving in the open without precise intelligence about what lay ahead, without the support of the peasants, and knowing that the army was aware of his approach."

If there was one aspect of Che's character that remained unshakable, however, it was the fact that he was as stubborn as he was determined. Che was here to prove that a handful of well-trained guerrillas could unleash a powerful social revolution. That they could reshape the political structure of an entire country, if not the world. Defeat, therefore, was *not* an option. Che Guevara was going to either ignite a successful revolution in Bolivia, or else, as Guevara himself had said, "I've come to stay, and the only way that I will leave here is dead."

After about a twenty-minute drive from Pucará, we arrive at the spot where a trail leads down to Quebrada del Churo, the scene of Che's last firefight. Our driver, Lucia, and I begin the half-hour hike down through vegetation that would have to be cut with a machete if no path existed. It's bright, sunny, around six thousand feet in elevation, and the trail is punctuated occasionally with cornfields. Ridge after ridge extends to the horizon for as far as one can see. In the 1960s, a visiting journalist described the area as "an infernal, desolate countryside of high peaks and deep valleys," strewn with occasional villages. It seems to be perfect guerrilla habitat. Our driver says that pumas live in the forests, sometimes emerging to feed on feral goats.

On either side of the trail, orange mistletoe wraps itself around hapless plants, feeding off the plants' juices, while the path underfoot is alive with ants. We watch a trail of leaf-cutter ants stacking bits of finely veined leaves beside a hole in the ground. Later, a giant rhinoceros beetle crosses our path, black and shiny as a Bolivian soldier's combat boot. A bit further on, a smaller black beetle stands midpath, its head facing down and abdomen pointing up—warning us that, if disturbed, it might launch a direct chemical attack. The whole area we are passing through, it seems, is alive with its own miniaturized jungle warfare.

"It was a farmer who ratted the guerrillas out," says our driver, as we reach the bottom of the canyon, then start following a path through thick vegetation alongside the stream called the Churo.

"He went and told the military, and that's how the army learned where the guerrillas were."

"Shouldn't people have *ostracized* that man?" Lucia asks incredulously, picking her way over rocks. She pauses, smoking a cigarette, indignant.

The driver shrugs his shoulders.

"They were *guerrilleros*," he says.

We walk through a forested tunnel alongside the stream. Here and there in the shadows fist-sized images of Che's face emerge, ghostly white, as if from a resurrection. Someone has carefully stenciled his iconic image on the occasional tree trunk or protruding stone with spray paint. We continue walking, Che's face gazing sternly at us as we pass.

Not far ahead we arrive at a clearing with a large boulder beside a gnarled fig tree. On the boulder a visitor has scrawled *"Patria o Muerte"* ("Homeland or Death") in large letters and alongside it a white star. It was here that Che was captured. The clearing is now quiet and peaceful. The sound of water and that of a dove calling drift through the canyon. One can clearly see how the soldiers could have fired down on the guerrillas from the thickly forested hills above and how the soldiers had the

advantage of height. In the fierce firefight, two guerrillas and five soldiers were immediately killed, then Che was captured. In the ensuing
days, six more guerrillas were shot to death. Of the seventeen guerrillas
who spent the night in this area, only five eventually escaped—three of
them by hiking under cover of darkness out of Bolivia and into Chile.

The climb back up out of the *quebrada* is hot and takes an hour. We
sweat, and the steep ascent makes me breathe hard. Che, suffering from
an asthma attack and unable to put weight on his injured leg, limped up
this same slope with two soldiers supporting him. Down below, more
soldiers followed, carrying the bodies of the two dead Cuban guerrillas. Once they reached the road, the soldiers took Che to La Higuera, a
tiny village three miles further on. There, with his hands bound and his
leg wound untended, Che was thrown onto the floor of a schoolroom,
alongside the bodies of his dead companions. It was the same tiny
school where nineteen-year-old Julia Cortez taught. It was Sunday. Julia
was in the village, and she was scheduled to teach class the next day.

"That night the army celebrated Che's capture," Julia, now sixty-
three, remembers. "The army had warned us that Che was a very cruel
man, cruel and ugly. But there were rumors in the countryside that Che
was enchanted—that no bullet could touch him or penetrate his body.
That he was a sorcerer. So I was curious. At dawn the next morning,
I went to see."

Soldiers at the doorway let the young schoolteacher pass. Inside,
Julia found Che seated on a rustic wooden bench that her students
used, the room lit by candlelight. The guerrilla's hands were bound
before him with rope, and his back was against the wall. Che was filthy
and hadn't bathed in months. A CIA agent who visited him later that
day summed up Che's appearance by saying that the guerrilla leader
looked "like a piece of trash." For the young schoolteacher, however,
Che still retained his charismatic charm.

"When I went to see him, I immediately saw that he wasn't like
they had said he was. That surprised me," she says. Che asked Julia who
she was. She replied that she was a schoolteacher. From that moment
on, Che referred to her as *"la profesora,"* or "teacher."

"He was friendly, sophisticated, intelligent—and very handsome. He said I had nice eyes and legs. I asked him why, being so handsome and intelligent, he went about like that, looking like a beggar. He answered that he did it for his ideals."

After a chat, Julia left the schoolroom. Soon, other officials came in. What was his attitude? I ask.

"He replied to everyone as they were," Julia said. "If they were aggressive, then he was hard. If they treated him well, then he treated *them* well."

According to Julia, Che called for her later in the morning. She was told that he had asked to see *la profesora*.

"I went back around ten o'clock," Julia said. "They had taken him to the doorway [of the schoolroom] to take that famous photo of him with the CIA agent. Che wanted me to be in the photo, but they didn't let me. It was the last photo of him alive."

"I went inside, and we talked some more. I asked him if he had a wife, and he said he did. He said he had children in Cuba."

Che said that it was unlikely that he would see them again. When Julia asked why, he told her that three soldiers had recently entered the room and had asked him for his last wish. According to Julia, Che had made them an offer.

"They were going to shoot him," she says, "so he told them that if they did not kill him, then Cuba would make sure that the roads, health, and education would be improved in the entire area. He promised them tractors, roadways, fully equipped schools. All the basic services people needed."

"What did they say?"

She looks at me and shakes her head sadly back and forth.

"No," she says.

"Che asked me if I would bring him some food. He wanted to eat, and he wanted me to know about the offer he'd made. So that people would know about it. Because he said he'd seen so much poverty in the area. So much malnutrition. So many people with bad teeth and thyroid problems. He said he felt badly about these forgotten people."

Julia went to the house she was staying in, filled a bowl with peanut soup, then quickly returned. Che ate the soup by grabbing the bowl with his bound hands and drinking it.

"He thanked me and said that if he ever got out of this he would remember me for it. He then asked me if I would find out what was happening outside. What they were going to do with him."

Julia said she would and returned to the house where her mother had prepared lunch.

"When I told her that Che was not as they had painted him, she told me to sit down and that I shouldn't have anything more to do with him, that it was very dangerous, and that at any moment there could be another firefight. Then, while we were eating, we suddenly heard gunfire. We thought the guerrillas were attacking."

Che Guevera was standing in the schoolroom when twenty-six-year-old Felix Rodriguez, a Cuban exile and CIA agent, walked inside. Rodriguez, who had spent the last four months working with the Bolivian military and was dressed in one of its uniforms, had just made a copy of Che's two diaries with a special camera. Earlier, he'd been speaking with Che when a burst of gunfire sounded in the room next to theirs, which was a second classroom. The soldiers had just executed the Bolivian guerrilla who had helped Che in the Quebrada del Churo, a man nicknamed "Willy." "Che stopped talking," Rodriguez remembered. "He did not say anything about the shooting, but his face reflected sadness, and he shook his head slowly from left to right several times. Perhaps it was at that instant that he realized that he, too, was doomed."

Rodriguez told Che that orders had come from the high Bolivian command that he was to be executed. Che's face momentarily turned white, Rodriguez said, and then Che said quietly, "It is better like this . . . I never should have been captured alive." Rodriguez asked Che if he had any last messages.

"Tell Fidel that he will soon see a triumphant revolution in America," Che said, *"and tell my wife to remarry and try to be happy."*

Che's bravery in the face of his own death affected the CIA agent, who had been trying to reverse the Cuban Revolution for years. He stepped forward and embraced the prisoner.

"It was a tremendously emotional moment for me," Rodriguez wrote. *"I no longer hated him. His moment of truth had come, and he was conducting himself like a man. He was facing his death with courage and grace."*

Rodriguez left the room. A short while later, a short sergeant named Mario Terán entered, having volunteered to shoot Che after losing three of his comrades in the recent firefight. When the sergeant told Che to sit, Che refused. *"No, I will stand for this,"* he said, fixing him with his stare. The sergeant had been drinking and hesitated. Che, who himself had signed numerous execution orders in Havana and had once executed a man himself, reportedly told Terán, *"Calm yourself and shoot—you are only going to kill a man."*

The soldier pulled the trigger of the automatic weapon, but his aim was poor. The burst of bullets hit Che in the legs and arm. Che fell, writhing on the ground, then bit his arm to stop from yelling. The soldier pulled the trigger again. This time one of the bullets entered Che's chest, bursting his heart.

After Julia heard the rifle fire, she waited for a bit, wondering if there was a guerrilla attack. But there were no more sounds. "I waited until I couldn't stand it," she said, "with all of the tension and fear I had. Finally I made the decision to go see." Julia ran across the dirt road to the schoolhouse. There was no solider in sight, the executioner having already departed. Inside, she found that Che was no longer sitting on the bench as she had left him, but was now stretched out on his back on the ground, his arms extended, unbound, his eyes staring at the ceiling.

"It didn't seem like he was dead," she said. "His eyes were open and he was staring. I approached him and watched his eyes carefully, to see if there was any movement. But there wasn't any. He didn't move.

"I didn't know what to do. I was afraid to leave and afraid to stay. My legs felt like they had a sack of corn, *un quintal*, on each one. I couldn't walk. My legs wouldn't obey me."

Within a short while, a helicopter appeared, prearranged to carry Che's body to Vallegrande, where the army had set up operations. Soldiers laid the guerrilla's body on a stretcher and roped it to the helicopter's skids. A priest arrived. Together, he and Julia prayed for Che's soul as the helicopter lifted off and bore the guerrilla leader away.

In Vallegrande, on Malta Street, there's a chapel called the Capilla del Señor de Malta. The façade is white, and its tower the color of burnt umber. Next to the chapel is a hospital and, next to that—apparently in case things don't work out in either the church or the hospital—are two funeral parlors. It's late in the afternoon, the sun hangs like an orange, and I'm searching for the laundry room where Che's body was taken and displayed in the days following his execution. I watch as a man helps an old woman up the stairs to the chapel. Inside, a woman is singing "Ave Maria," accompanied by a piano, her voice floating out sweetly into the street. Farther down the road, an elderly woman stands in a doorway. I stop, ask directions, and then suddenly I ask her if she happened to be here when *el guerrillero* Che Guevara arrived, years ago. She says she was and motions me inside, looking both ways as if someone might see us.

The woman's name is Eva Vargas Llosa del Monte. She's eighty-five, tall and lanky. She says that her husband died seven years ago. Che was laid out on a stretcher on the cement washbasin, she says. Just behind the hospital. The whole town turned out and filed past him with soldiers standing by.

"They moved him around like he was a stone," she says. "He had no shoes, his eyes were open, his hair down to here," she says, motioning to her shoulders. "His face looked sad. Poor thing, such a cruel death he had. I cried, because I'm sensitive," she tells me. "I couldn't sleep afterwards, so I said a prayer for him."

Behind the hospital and on a sloping hill overlooking the valley, near a grove of eucalyptus and pines, I find the whitewashed adobe building that used to be a laundry room. The building has faded red tiles with gray lichen on them and is open on one side. Within it are the two waist-high cement washbasins where Che's stretcher was laid out and where women used to gossip while hand washing hospital linens. Photos from that day show Che as a lean, Christlike figure, shirtless, his head propped up, his eyes wide open with a vacant stare. Various soldiers and officials pose behind their valuable quarry; a bullet hole is clearly evident in Che's alabaster-colored chest.

The cement basin is now cold and smooth to the touch; on it, a visitor has left a vase of yellow chrysanthemums. The flowers have dried, and some of the petals have fallen lifelessly into the drain. Carved or written on the walls are hundreds of inscriptions by visitors from around the world. Countries such as Denmark, Mexico, Cuba, Argentina, Germany, France, Brazil, and Poland are all represented, bearing messages such as *"Presente!"* or "Che Lives!" or "You did not die in vain!"

Outside, the sun sinks and the wind blows softly through the trees. Forested hills rise in the distance, and church bells can be heard. At least for the pilgrims who come here, Che's story—his hopes, his struggles, and his dreams—live on. The once unremarkable laundry room has somehow been transformed into a kind of shrine, a shrine that, at least for these visitors, was once graced by a revolutionary hero or saint. Throughout the area, I'm told, people now pray to "Santo Che": "In the name of the Father, the Son, the Holy Spirit—and Che Guevara—help me in my time of need."

That evening, after dinner, I walk past the local party headquarters of the MAS, an acronym that stands for *Movimiento al Socialismo* (Movement for Socialism). Bolivia's current president, fifty-two-year-old Juan Evo Morales Ayma, is presently in his second term and, if he finishes, will be the first president in Bolivian history to complete two terms. Morales was born in an adobe home in a tiny Andean village. He became a coca-leaf–growing farmer and is the first indigenous, Aymara-speaking president in Bolivia since the country declared its independence from Spain in 1825. A critic of United States foreign policy and of the involvement of transnational corporations in Latin America, Morales is a socialist and an ally of the socialist governments of Venezuela and Cuba. Inside his presidential office in La Paz, Morales has installed a portrait of Che Guevara fashioned out of coca leaves. "Guevara is invincible in his ideals," Morales has said, president now of the very nation that once hunted down the Argentine revolutionary and had him killed. "After so many years, he inspires us to continue fighting, changing not only Bolivia, but all of Latin America and the world."

Inside the MAS office, burning the night oil, I find thirty-eight-year-old Walberto Rivas Brito, president of Morales's MAS party in Vallegrande province. He is short and strongly built, has an easy smile, and tells me an unusual story.

In October 1967, just a few miles from where Che was captured, Walberto's parents were living in a small adobe home. There, his father raised sheep, goats, and a few cows. A few days before the final ambush, the army captured one of Che's guerrillas, a man nicknamed Camba; the guerrilla was taken temporarily to Walberto's parents' home.

"The military took a photo of him in my parents' house," Walberto says. "It's in black and white, and you can see Camba tied up, alongside Colonel Gary Prado, who later became a [Bolivian] general."

Walberto, who was born six years after Che's death, says that his parents were very conservative at the time. The guerrillas, they'd been told, "were devils."

"The illiterate farmers in the area believed this," he says. "So despite their poverty, they were reactionaries."

The soldiers stationed in this particular region, however, ignored a key component of winning over his parents' "hearts and minds." Seizing their sheep and goats, the soldiers slaughtered and ate them without payment. Later they told Walberto's father that, when the time came, they would reimburse him. They never did. When he later went to town to receive payment, they laughed at and humiliated him.

"My father returned," Walberto said, "and swore that all of his kids would become revolutionaries like Che Guevara. The first book I ever read was Che's *Bolivian Diary*. My father had it. Along with other books about Cuba. All of my brothers and sisters read them. Later, we all joined [the socialist party] MAS."

Walberto's parents had fourteen children. Every one of them went to college. "Because of the sacrifices my father and mother made," Walberto says. "One by one we became doctors, lawyers, businessmen, accountants."

When he was eighteen, Walberto received a scholarship to study at a university in Cuba. He spent fourteen years on the tropical island, studying veterinary medicine and then computers.

"It was inspiring," he says of his stay. "There was a real feeling of solidarity. Cuba's education system is first class."

After Che's execution, Walberto tells me, he was buried three days later by several Bolivian soldiers and a CIA officer, secretly, in the dead of night. Che's hands had been amputated for identification, and his handless corpse was then thrown into a makeshift grave in an open field near Vallegrande's airport. Thirty years later, in 1997, a Cuban forensic team traveled to Vallegrande and located his remains. Che's body was repatriated to Cuba, and the revolutionary hero was given a large state funeral, his wife and children in attendance.

"I waited in line from six a.m.," remembers Walberto, who was living in Cuba at the time. "It took ten hours to visit his casket. It was very moving. Che was finally back home again, among people who appreciated him. I think the whole island was there." In Cuba, Walberto also met the son of the Bolivian guerrilla Willy, who'd tried to help Che to safety the day of the ambush and had been executed just before Che in the adjacent schoolroom. His son had also received a scholarship and was studying at the university, Walberto said. The two of them became good friends.

In 2004, when Walberto learned that the socialist Evo Morales was running for president, he returned to Bolivia. A year later Morales won and Walberto ran for and was elected president of the MAS party in

Vallegrande. Forty years after Che died, a socialist government had arrived in Bolivia—not with guns but through the ballot box.

"For revolutionaries like ourselves," Walberto says, "Che is [nevertheless] an example to follow. An example of the 'New Man' he was trying to build. That was his dream, no? Che didn't just talk—he showed by example. That's why we have such admiration for him. And that's why all of us who support Evo Morales are inspired by the ideals of Che. He affected us all."

On the other side of town, Julia Cortez sits in her living room, clasping her hands. Che's arrival four decades ago in her La Higuera schoolroom affected Julia deeply, too. But not in the same way it had Walberto.

Shortly after Che was executed, Julia says, people in the area began whispering:

"The teacher in La Higuera is dangerous. She's a communist. She should not be teaching our children!"

"All because I gave food to Che," Julia says. "Because I spoke with him. Because I treated him as a human being and not as an animal. Because I respected him."

That same year, an article came out in a newspaper in Vallegrande repeating the rumors and suggesting that Julia was teaching communism to La Higuera's students. None of it was true, but the rumors took on a life of their own. School authorities soon transferred Julia to a remoter town—Alto Seco. It was the same village Che and his guerrillas had occupied briefly a year before, haranguing the population. Soon signs began to appear on the town's walls, painted in red. *"La profesora es comunista"* ("The teacher is a communist"), they proclaimed. Julia was transferred again.

"It made me mad," Julia says. "I was ready to fight anyone who said something like that. Before that, I was timid."

Finally, six years after Che died, Julia was able to meet with General Joaquín Zenteno Anaya, who had commanded the 8th Division, which captured Guevara. Zenteno had visited the famous prisoner on his final day, but Che had refused to speak to him. After listening to Julia's predicament, however, the general spoke publicly about the matter.

"He said that no one was to bother me anymore. That he had been to La Higuera when Che was captured and knew the truth. That he and other military men had eaten in my home. He stood by me and said 'hands off.' After that, things calmed down."

Three years later, Julia says, Zentano was assassinated while he was an ambassador in Paris. "It was part of Che's curse," she says, clasping her hands. "Those who captured Che died in terrible ways."

President René Barrientos, for example, who ordered Che's execution, died in a mysterious helicopter crash two years later. One day his chopper, Julia says, dropped from the sky like a stone. Lt. Col. Andrés Selich, who helped capture Che and kept one of his wristwatches afterward, died in 1973. He was beaten to death by thugs working for the Bolivian dictator Hugo Banzer, whom Selich had helped seize power.

In 1981 Colonel Gary Prado, head of the Bolivian rangers who captured Che, shot himself accidentally while cleaning his gun. He's been paralyzed and in a wheelchair ever since.

Only Mario Terán, the sergeant who actually executed Che, has thus far escaped the curse, although only partially. For years he lived under an assumed name, fearful that he might be assassinated. Some say the CIA helped to protect him. Then, in 2006, Terán showed up in the Bolivian city of Santa Cruz at a free eye clinic called Operation Miracle, funded by Venezuela and staffed by Cuban doctors. Ironically, the man who had killed Che Guevara decades earlier had his cataracts removed and his sight restored by doctors from the very socialist nation that Che Guevara had helped create.

"Four decades after Mario Terán attempted to destroy a dream and an idea, Che returns to win yet another battle," the Cuban newspaper *Granma* proclaimed. "Now an old man, he [Terán] can once again appreciate the colors of the sky and the forest, [and] enjoy the smiles of his grandchildren."

A free Cuban health clinic now operates in La Higuera, Julia tells me, and helps the needy in the still-impoverished zone. Thirty-six more Cuban doctors are spread throughout the region—all volunteers.

On the last day of his life, when asked by one of his captors why he'd come to Bolivia to fight, Che replied:

"Can't you see the state in which the peasants live? They are almost like savages, living in a state of poverty that depresses the heart, having only one room in which to sleep and cook and no clothing to wear, abandoned like animals . . . the Bolivian lives without hope. Just as he is born, he dies, without ever seeing improvements in his human condition."

Some forty years later, I can't help but reflect that 60 percent of Bolivians continue to live in poverty, nearly 40 percent in extreme poverty, 80 percent have no electricity, 50 percent have no sewage system, and another 86 percent have no running water. Despite an endless stream of governments, little seems to have changed.

Meanwhile, in her living room, Julia clasps and reclasps her hands some more, thinking of the events of forty years ago and how they affected so many people. On my way out I leave her a small gift of money, for which she says she is grateful.

"It's not from me," I tell her.

She stares at me, uncomprehending.

"It's from Che."

8

THE FINAL DAYS OF
BUTCH CASSIDY AND THE
SUNDANCE KID (BOLIVIA)

A man who has had an outlaw past is never safe, no matter how straight he goes afterwards. That's the price he pays. Something out of his past life may raise up against him and wreck his life anytime.

—Matt Warner, former outlaw friend of Butch Cassidy

I came down to South America with the idea of settling down . . . In the States there was nothing but jail, the noose, or being shot by a posse. I thought maybe I could change things but I guess things at this late date can't be changed . . . I know how it's going to end . . . I guess that's the way it's got to be.

—Butch Cassidy to a friend, circa 1907, in Bolivia

I never met a soul more affable than you, Butch, or faster than the Kid, but you're still nothing but two-bit outlaws on the dodge. It's over, don't you get that? Your time is over, and you're gonna die bloody, and all you can do is choose where.

—William Goldman, screenplay, *Butch Cassidy and the Sundance Kid*

It was roughly six o'clock on a Friday afternoon, the sun sinking low, as the two gringos, both outlaws, rode over the lip of the valley and began heading down the trail toward town. San Vicente, Bolivia, was an old mining town, a cluster of sagging adobe houses with thatched roofs and a single church. A cemetery with crumbling wooden crosses surrounded by an adobe wall rose just behind town, and mine shafts with gray tailings scarred the nearby hills full of silver and zinc. At over 14,000 feet, the cold was already descending; by nightfall it would be freezing. The two outlaws had ridden all day, the day before, and the day and night before that, and were tired. In their saddlebags they carried a pair of binoculars, an English dictionary, a well-marked map of Bolivia, and hundreds of rounds of ammunition. Colt revolvers of blue-gray steel protruded from their holsters, and each had a rifle strapped to his saddle. In one of their saddlebags they also carried money—15,000 bolivianos—worth about $90,000 US. Only two days earlier they had "liberated" the money at gunpoint from a Bolivian mining company. One of the gringos, the quiet tall one, was forty-one years old, nearly six feet tall, wore a dark mustache, and rode a black mule. The other, who went by the name of "Butch," was forty-two and shorter, about five foot nine, with a thick, square jaw, sand-colored hair, and deeply set blue eyes that some said could burn a hole right through you. Butch rode a coffee-colored mule that the two had seized in the holdup. Neither knew it, but as the men and their mules plodded slowly into the outskirts of town, a few townspeople looking up at them curiously, this was the last place where either would ever seek shelter. For Butch Cassidy and the Sundance Kid—names that had made them infamous throughout North America—neither would ever leave this small, windblown Bolivian town alive.

"Tupiza, Tupiza, Tupeeezzaaa!" shouts the bus driver, opening with a whoosh the pneumatic door.

The tall, blue double-decker bus I've arrived on is covered in dust as most roads in Bolivia alternate between paving and dirt, with a heavy emphasis on dirt. Tupiza, I discover, is a small, sunny, pleasant rural city set at seven thousand feet at the base of a fold of the Andes in southwest Bolivia. After retrieving my baggage from the bus's hold, I flag down a cab and in no time at all am dropped off at the Hotel Mitru. *Mitru* means "crown" in Greek, and the hotel was founded by a Greek immigrant, Nicolás Mitru, just after the turn of the century. At first, Señor Mitru tried his hand at mining and then, after coming up empty handed, went into the hotel business. Back in his day, Tupiza boasted two hotels, both on the main plaza, the Términus and the Internacional. The hotels, small by today's standards, routinely filled with traveling businessmen, mining superintendents, merchants, laborers, and even occasional bandits traveling under aliases. On November 3, 1908, Butch Cassidy was one of them. It's to follow the trail of Butch's last robbery and of his and Sundance's final days that I've arrived in Tupiza.

Two days before Butch and Sundance rode their mules into San Vicente, the two outlaws had pulled their final holdup. In a rugged and remote area studded with tall cacti, they'd surprised two Bolivian men and a boy who were accompanying three mules, one of which carried the payroll from a mining firm, Aramayo, Franke & Co. According to Carlos Peró, the man in charge of the payroll, while they were on their way down a mule trail on a rocky hillside, near where the trail met a shallow canyon, they were stopped by two men on foot who suddenly stepped out with cocked rifles. Peró later wrote to his employers that

> On the descent of Huaca Huañusca [Dead Cow Hill], on the rugged, bottom part, we were surprised by two Yankees, whose faces were covered with bandannas and whose rifles were cocked and ready to fire at our slightest suspicious movement. In a very threatening manner, they ordered my servant . . . and my son . . . to dismount, having found me following them on foot, and immediately ordered us to hand over the

money we were carrying, to which I answered that they could search us and take whatever they wanted, as we were hardly in a position to offer any resistance. One of them [most likely Butch Cassidy] quickly began to search our saddlebags and, not finding what he was looking for, demanded that we unload our baggage, specifying that they were not interested in our personal money nor in any articles that belonged to us, but only in the money that we were carrying for the [mining] company.

The two Yankees wore new, dark red, thin wale corduroy suits with narrow, soft-brimmed hats, the brims turned down in such a way that, with the bandannas tied behind their ears, only their eyes could be seen. One of the bandits [most likely Butch], the one who came closest to and talked with me, is thin and of normal stature, and the other [most likely Sundance], who always maintained a certain distance, is heavyset and taller. Both of them carried new carbines, which appeared to be of the Mauser type, small caliber and [with a] thick barrel . . . The bandits also carried Colt revolvers, and I believe they also had very small Browning revolvers outside their cartridge belts, which were filled with rifle ammunition.

They knew that I spoke English, in which language they asked me if we were not carrying eighty thousand bolivianos [around $500,000 US], to which I replied that the sum was not quite as large as they believed. And, when I saw that there was no point in hiding anything, a search of the baggage having begun, I informed them that it was only fifteen thousand [bolivianos, or around $90,000 US]. What I said caused great anguish, momentarily silencing the bandit nearest us. As soon as they saw the package containing the cash, which was beside another very similar package, the bandit conducting the search took it and passed it to his companion without bothering with the other package, nor searching any more of the baggage, which shows that they had clear knowledge of the package with the cash. They then demanded that I give them our servant's mule—the dark brown named "Aramayo," with the [town of] Quechisla brand—which is known by all our stable hands in [the nearby city of] Tupiza . . . Keeping their eyes on us and their rifles ready, they departed with the mule.

Certainly these bandits had been in [the city of] Tupiza for some time, studying our company's habits and preparing their strike with total coolness and knowledge . . . Moreover, they undoubtedly planned their retreat carefully; otherwise they would not have left us with our animals or they would have killed us in order to avoid accusations or to gain time.

Butch and Sundance's holdup of the Aramayo, Franke & Co. payroll was the last in a long, mostly successful string of bank and payroll robberies that stretched back nearly twenty years, dating from the first bank Butch robbed in Telluride, Colorado, in 1889. At the time of his first holdup, Butch was twenty-three. Sundance, who may also have been a participant, was twenty-two. Although Sundance had already served eighteen months in prison for horse theft, and Butch would later serve eighteen months for the same, neither was ever captured for a bank robbery, despite eventually stealing hundreds of thousands of dollars and being pursued by numerous posses, thanks to rewards adding up to more than $30,000 that had been placed on their heads. The two were excellent cowboys, skilled bronco busters, seasoned and cool bank robbers—and highly accurate shots.

Butch, by most accounts, was friendly and gregarious. A biographer who interviewed many of Butch's contemporaries at the time wrote, "He never drank to excess, was always courteous to women, was free with money when he had it, and extremely loyal to his friends. All [the] old-timers . . . including officers who hunted him, were unanimous in saying, 'Butch Cassidy was one of the finest men I ever knew.' " Sundance, by contrast, was quieter, more distant, some even said shy. Their friendship nevertheless lasted for more than a decade and, despite what was often a violent and dangerous profession, neither Butch nor Sundance had ever killed a man. That is, until their final moments in Bolivia.

The two outlaws rode their mules into San Vicente, a town named after an early Christian Spanish martyr; neither knew if word of their robbery had reached town yet. Bolivia was crisscrossed by telegraph wires now, as the modern world continued to creep in, fueled by mining profits. But none connected to San Vicente yet. In a dusty street, the two inquired at the mayor's house if there were lodging. There was none, he said. The mayor suggested they might find a spare room at Bonifacio Casasola's house, in the center of town. Butch and Sundance headed that way, led by the mayor. No doubt they were outwardly relaxed yet ready to pull a gun, kick their spurs into their mules' flanks, and begin shooting at the proverbial drop of a hat. Casasola's house sat inside a patio surrounded by adobe walls with a single entrance to the dirt street outside. Butch and Sundance dismounted, led their mules through the entrance into the patio, and took their saddles off. They then entered their quarters: a single room with thick adobe brick walls, a wooden bench, a large earthenware jug, and no windows. Tired and dirty and with no change of clothes, they asked Casasola to buy some tins of sardines and a couple of beers and gave him some money to do so. Unbeknownst to either of them, only three hours earlier an armed patrol consisting of an army captain, two soldiers, and a police officer had arrived in town. The patrol was part of a region-wide mobilization hunting for the pair of outlaws who had recently stolen a mining payroll. The mayor lingered, asking them some questions. Where were they coming from? he asked. From the Argentine border, they replied. Where were they headed? South, to Santa Catalina, a town in Argentina. Butch and Sundance nevertheless asked about the trail north, in the opposite direction, the trail that led to Uyuni. The latter was the nearest town with a railway station. From there they could take the train and disappear. The mayor told them how to find the trail, bid them good evening—then hurried off to alert the soldiers.

"Butch and Sundance had no plans to rob the mining payroll," Felix Charlar Miranda, a sixty-one-year-old judge and Butch Cassidy aficionado, explains to me. "They wanted to rob the Tupiza bank, on the main square. Then a cavalry regiment arrived and decided to bivouac in one of the hotels on the plaza. For a lengthy stay. So Butch and Sundance were forced to make new plans—rash ones—and that's what got them into trouble."

I'd called Felix by phone the night of my arrival in Tupiza, thinking that we might meet for the first time the following day. "Where are you staying?" he asked. When I told him at the Hotel Mitru, he quickly replied, "I'll stop by right away, so that we don't lose any time." Sure enough, Felix soon arrived, wearing slacks and a suit jacket; he had salt-and-pepper hair, a mustache, bushy eyebrows, and intense dark eyes. Felix had lived in Tupiza all his life, had owned a television station (Channel 5, now defunct), had worked as an attorney, and presently worked as a judge. In his office lay stacks of divorce papers and a smaller stack of murder cases. Felix is the local expert on Butch and Sundance, and has converted part of his house into a sort of historical museum. Soon after meeting, he suggests we take a walk.

Outside, the adobe buildings are joined to one another, with smooth stuccoed façades and peeling layers of old posters and paint. As we walk the dark streets, lit by dim lamps, everyone seems to know him. We stop repeatedly as the judge shakes hands with passersby. *Buenas noches*, he says repeatedly. *Como están?* People stop, bow, shake hands, then continue.

"Everyone pays me their respects," Felix says, then turns toward me, lifting an eyebrow for emphasis, "except those I put in jail." Felix's father, it turns out, used to be a prison guard, and as a boy, Felix used to go into the Tupiza prison. In those days the prisoners worked outside of their cells. Felix soon struck up a friendship with a Peruvian prisoner serving a murder sentence, who taught Felix to play chess. "My father told me about why these men were inside and how the justice system worked," Felix says. "That's what got me interested in the law." Felix tells me that had Butch and Sundance been captured instead of killed, they could very well have ended up in the same prison where his father had worked.

The outlaw known as Butch Cassidy was born Robert Leroy Parker, the son of Mormon parents who emigrated from England in 1856. Born in 1866 in Beaver, in the Utah Territory, Butch was the first of thirteen children and was just a young teenager when his father decided to move the family to outside of Circleville, a tiny community about twelve miles away. The family took over a small, pine-planked cabin that had been abandoned during the Mormon–Ute Indian War and soon launched into homesteading on one hundred and sixty acres of semiarid scrubland.

It was a tough, hardscrabble existence but also a time during which Butch learned to hunt, ride, break broncos, and rope cattle. By the time he was thirteen, the friendly, sandy-haired boy had hired himself out as a cowboy on a nearby ranch. Butch's father, meanwhile, having trouble keeping his family fed, began farming additional land. When another farmer later complained, a Mormon bishop forbade Butch's father from farming the extra land, despite all the work already invested in it. Embittered, both Butch and his father took the church's decision hard. From then on, his sister Lulu later wrote, Butch did everything he could to avoid attending church.

In his midteens, Butch had a brief yet fateful encounter with a young ranch hand and part-time cattle rustler named Mike Cassidy. Cassidy soon befriended the young teenager, teaching him a number of skills. One of those was how to "appropriate" cattle from stock owners—that is, how to put one's own brand on unbranded strays, then hide them in isolated canyons before selling them as one's own. This was an era of hard winters and cattle and sheep wars, when large cattle syndicates began squeezing out the smaller ranchers and itinerant cowboys had trouble scraping together a living. Butch so looked up to Cassidy that, when he, too, began to cross over to the other side of the law occasionally, he began giving his name not as Parker but as Cassidy. For a while, Butch went by the name of Robert Cassidy. After a short stint working as butcher in Wyoming, however, he eventually picked up the final piece of the sobriquet that would stick with him for the rest of his life: Butch Cassidy.

Old-timers in the area of Circleville later remembered that by the time he was a teenager, Butch was already a crack shot. Stories circulated of the young Mormon cowboy spending hours practicing his marksmanship by drawing his gun and firing at a playing card, hitting it dead center each time. At other times, they said, Butch would ride his horse as fast as he could around a slender tree, firing at the tree and hitting it over and over again, no matter how fast he rode.

In June 1889, after knocking around the West as a cowboy and occasional cattle rustler, and breaking broncos for a dollar a day, Butch, now twenty-three, took the fateful step that would forever alter his future. At noon on Monday, June 24, Butch and three other men walked into the San Miguel Valley Bank in Telluride, Colorado, wearing boots, chaps, spurs, and gun belts, pulled out their revolvers, then announced that this was a holdup. Butch's job was to leap over the counter and remove the cash from the vault. The others made sure that no one made a move. Even split four ways, their haul of $21,000 was more money than any of them could make as hired cowboys working steadily for the next five years. In an otherwise flawless getaway, however, the quartet of newly minted desperados had a piece of bad luck. Riding hard outside of town, they galloped unmasked past an acquaintance who recognized them and who later gave their names to the posse.

"Just that little accident made all of the difference in the world to us for the rest of our lives" wrote Matt Warner, one of the three riding with Butch. "It give them a clue so they could trace us for thousands of miles and for years. Right at that point is where we broke our half-outlaw past, became real outlaws, burned our bridges behind us, and had no way to live except by robbing and stealing."

It was also during that bank robbery that Butch may have hooked up with twenty-two-year-old Harry Longabough, a young man who read about cowboys and the Wild West in dime novels while growing up in Pennsylvania and headed out west on a wagon train at fifteen. A good rider and bronco buster, Harry had already served two years in jail in Sundance, Wyoming, for horse theft, picking up the nickname the "Sundance Kid" afterward. Eventually, he and Butch would form a loose confederation of outlaws known as the Wild Bunch, which robbed trains, banks, and mining payrolls throughout the West. Butch, the former Mormon cowboy, was its charismatic leader.

Despite a string of mostly successful robberies, however, during the next decade "civilization" gradually began creeping into the western frontier, making the life expectancy of the typical outlaw shorter and shorter. "It was hard for us to understand this change that had come over the Old West," Matt Warner later wrote. "For a time, we couldn't see that what was behind it was that more railroads, telegraph lines, wagon roads, bridges, farms, cities, and settlements was blocking all the old long trails, filling up the old hiding places, and making it easier for the law to spread a dragnet over the whole country. That made it tougher each year for the horseman outlaw."

In 1900 the Union Pacific Railroad, robbed one too many times by Butch's Wild Bunch, hired a permanent posse of some of the best trackers and marksmen in the West. The railway outfitted a special train to carry the posse and their horses rapidly to the site of any robbery. Their mission was a simple one: to hunt down and capture or kill any member of the Wild Bunch they could.

For Butch and Sundance, the writing was on the wall. With the law closing in, rewards on their heads, and posses waiting to spring on them like bear traps, it was perhaps time to rethink their chosen profession. Somehow the two came up with the idea that Argentina—and the vast, wild, cowboy pampas in the south—might be the perfect place for them to start over. "Stories about ranching and homesteading opportunities in Argentina were not uncommon in American newspapers of the 1890s," Western historian Dan Buck told me. "Maybe Butch read one of them while in a barbershop."

However it came about, a decision was made. After pulling one last train robbery in Tipton, Utah, in August 1900, Butch, Sundance, and Sundance's girlfriend, Ethel Place,* boarded a steamship in New York

---

*The actual identity of Ethel Place is unknown. Because Sundance was traveling under the alias of "Harry Place" at the time, Ethel used the same last name. Later, a North

City headed for Buenos Aires. Butch was thirty-five, Sundance thirty-four, and Ethel was twenty-four.

Between 1901 and 1905, Butch and Sundance did their best to become law-abiding ranchers, homesteading "four square leagues" (roughly twelve square miles, or 7,500 acres) of government land in the Chubut Province in southern Argentina. Ethel posed as Sundance's wife, and for four years the three lived at the base of the Andes. There they bred cattle and horses, made friends with their neighbors, and lived together in a plank-wood cabin that Ethel had decorated with articles cut out of North American magazines. Butch went by the name of Santiago Ryan. Sundance and Ethel posed as Mr. and Mrs. Harry Place. An Italian immigrant who spent a night at their house later wrote that Ethel was well dressed and liked to read. He added that Ryan and Place were "tall, slender, laconic, and nervous, with intense gazes . . . Those who knew them well said they were expert shooters capable of hitting a coin in the air."

Everything went reasonably well until sometime in 1905, when Butch and Sundance received a message that would set them on the run again; a tip-off from an acquaintance that the Pinkerton Detective Agency had located them and that Argentine authorities were about to make their arrests. Almost overnight, the three abandoned their ranch and disappeared into the Andes. A few months later they emerged long enough to rob a bank in northern Argentina, their first robbery in South America, then fled across the border to Chile. Butch, Sundance, and now Ethel were bank robbers on the run again.

"You'll never know what it means to be hunted," said Matt Warner, Butch's former partner in crime. "You can never sleep. You've always got to listen with one ear and keep one eye open. After a while you almost go crazy. No sleep! Even when you know you're perfectly safe you can't sleep. Every . . . [little noise] sounds like a posse of sheriffs coming to get you!"

American journalist's typographic error transformed the name she had left in a hotel register, "Ethel," into "Etta." The latter name then gradually began appearing in news and later police accounts. Whether "Ethel" was actually her first name, however, is unknown, as that, too, may have simply been an alias she used.

At some point, probably in 1906, Ethel returned to the United States, with Sundance accompanying her. Perhaps she was tired of running from the law. Perhaps she was sad over having lost the ranch that they had devoted four years of their lives to. Butch, meanwhile, moved on to Bolivia, and Sundance soon returned and joined him. The two outlaws—now wanted in the United States *and* Argentina—decided to keep a low profile, taking jobs at the Concordia Tin Mines, southeast of Bolivia's capital, La Paz. They worked as mule tenders, used assumed names, and Butch, ever the gregarious one, soon made friends with the many expatriates working there. Recalled Percy Seibert, an American who worked with them at the time,

> The tightly knit group of Americans working the mines were bound together by the loneliness of that godforsaken place, high up in the mountains where the air was so thin we could use only a special tough breed of mule, and the only other humans were Indians. We had to rely on one another; it didn't make any difference if your neighbor was an outlaw, former western gunfighter, or fugitive from an army stockade in the States. He was all you had to share memories of the States, as a partner in chess, dominoes, or checkers, to share a drink, and to help you celebrate Christmas, New Year's and July 4th.

By November 1908, Butch and Sundance were in their early forties, had been in South America for seven years, had almost run out of money, and were visiting Tupiza, in southern Bolivia. The city had much in common with Telluride, Colorado, where Butch had robbed his first bank. Both cities lay in the middle of rich mining regions, and both possessed banks often overflowing with profits from the extraction of raw ore. Not long after they arrived, Butch and Sundance decided to rob Tupiza's main bank, which sat on the central plaza. It would be their first robbery since northern Argentina, three years earlier. As usual, the duo carefully cased the target, plotting their escape route and readying themselves for what by now was a routine job for them. Then, just as they prepared to make their move, a military detachment arrived in town, choosing the International Hotel as its headquarters. Unfortunately for the two outlaws, the hotel stood directly across from the bank.

"Butch and Sundance didn't know what to do," explains Felix Charlar, the judge. "Now they were stuck in town and had no money. And had no bank to rob. They were never going to outrun a regiment. So what were they going to do?"

I'd stopped by the judge's residence, a two-story row house that has a metal sign engraved on the door, "Felix Charlar Miranda: Abogado" (Lawyer). It's where Felix has lived for forty-five years. The house is old and made of whitewashed adobe. The foyer inside has a cement floor and cracked walls; it's crammed with so many weathered objects that it looks like an antiques store. Posters of the 1969 film *Butch Cassidy and the Sundance Kid* hang from the walls, along with a collection of turn-of-the century bric-a-brac from Tupiza's cowboy past: rusted and used Winchester rifles, revolvers, telegraph boxes, pitted spurs, and enormous iron padlocks with five-inch keys—safeguards against potential bandits who died long ago.

Felix searches through several stacks of documents, tilts his glasses down to read better, then pulls out a copy of an old local newspaper, the *Chorolque*. It's an issue dated November 4, 1908.

"I wanted you to see this," he says, using a thick forefinger to underline his point. "This shows Butch Cassidy staying at the Términus Hotel on the square," he says. "On Monday, the night before the robbery."

I peer over his shoulder and see a notice apparently routinely published in the newspapers in those days: a list of names of the various travelers staying at the town's two hotels. On the night of November 3, twelve guests had registered at the Terminus Hotel. One of them was "Santiago Lowe," an alias Butch Cassidy used in Bolivia.* Just below the

---

*Butch, at times, used "James Lowe" or "Jim Lowe" in the United States. He often used "Santiago Lowe" in Bolivia; "Santiago" is the Spanish equivalent of "James."

notice is a list of the guests who were staying at the Hotel Internacional, just across the square: "The chiefs and officers of the Albaroa Regiment." With their planned operation now spoiled, Butch and Sundance had to find another target to rob. They soon found a suitable replacement: Felix Aramayo, one of the wealthiest men in Bolivia, and his firm, Aramayo, Franke & Co.

"Butch's philosophy about banks and express companies was common in the early West," wrote James Horan, an early Butch biographer. "In the popular mind of that time they represented big business which foreclosed on farms and homes and were hated by small ranchers and farmers."

"I'm not as bad as I'm painted," Butch once told a Utah lawyer he had contacted in 1900, asking what the chances were of getting a pardon if he promised to stop robbing. "I never killed a man in my life . . . and that's gospel. I never robbed an individual—only banks and railroads that have been robbing the people for years."

After the lawyer informed him that his chances of a pardon were slim, Butch no doubt fixed his intense gaze on him and said, "You know the law and I guess you're right, but I'm sorry it can't be fixed some way. You'll never know what it means to be forever on the dodge."

Butch Cassidy may have hated big business, but in both the US and South America he got along well with common folk. In Bolivia, said Percy Seibert, who worked with Butch and Sundance off and on at the Concordia Mines from 1906 to 1908, Butch "was quite popular in the countryside, particularly with the Indian children. Whenever he went to La Paz he would always come back with sticks of candy, which he gave to the children. I can still see him coming up the trail to our place, followed by a pack of yelling, laughing kids."

On one occasion, after becoming friends and learning that his two mule tenders were actually famous outlaws, Seibert asked if they might not show him how fast they were with their guns. Butch and Sundance agreed, then rummaged around until they found some targets. As Seibert later recounted,

We walked outside, Butch and the Kid each with two beer bottles. They strapped on their six-shooters and when Butch nodded they suddenly threw the bottles high in the air. As they started to curve down, first the Kid's gun leaped into his hand and the bottles vanished into splinters, then Cassidy's followed. They repeated the same trick a few times and never missed.

The gunfire echoed in the valley like a cannonade and brought out Mrs. Seibert.

"My God, boys," she said, "what on earth are you doing?"

Butch apologized. "I'm sorry, ma'am, we were just showing Perce and Mr. Glass a little western shootin.'"

According to Seibert, by 1908 Butch, now forty-two years old and having worked since he was thirteen, was beginning to show both his age and the effects of always being on the run.

I . . . began to see a change in Cassidy. He looked older and worn; the strain was now showing. The Sundance Kid became more morose, and although we were old friends, he barely said more than the usual amenities. Their welcome [as mine employees] was also wearing thin because the army was visiting the mines unexpectedly and hinting to the owners that it might not be wise to hire these train and bank robbers.

A year earlier, in fact, the Pinkerton Detective Agency had sent a circular to as many banks in South America as possible, advising them to be on the lookout for Butch Cassidy and the Sundance Kid. The last paragraph issued a stark warning to any law enforcement agency that might attempt to apprehend them:

When attempting to arrest either [of these fugitives] officers are warned to have sufficient assistance, be fully armed, taking no risks as they will make a determined resistance before submitting to arrest, not hesitating to kill if necessary.

The two soldiers and the police inspector were sitting inside their quarters in San Vicente when the mayor arrived with some unexpected news. Two well-armed Yankees had just ridden into town, the mayor told them. One was riding a mule from the Aramayo Mining Camp, where the stolen payroll had been headed. The Yankees had asked questions about the road north to Uyuni, where the train left from, and were bunked in a room in Casasola's house. Each had a revolver and a rifle and plenty of ammunition. The police inspector wasted no time, telling the soldiers to load their rifles and to come with him to investigate. The mayor tagged along behind.

Inside their room, Butch and Sundance were eating. It was dusk and the room was already lit by candlelight. A noise or commotion must have tipped them off. Butch stood and drew his gun. Outside, two soldiers carrying rifles had entered the patio and were approaching the doorway to their room. The police inspector and the mayor stood well behind them, out in the street, trying to peer inside. Butch waited until the first soldier came near, then stepped suddenly into the doorway, aimed his pistol, and fired.

After my visit with the judge, the next morning I get up early, have breakfast, and then walk outside the hotel, where I find a Toyota Land Cruiser waiting, a blue, auxiliary gas barrel strapped on top of its rack. The hotel runs a tour agency, Mitru Tours, and for the next few days I've booked the Toyota and a driver who's also a guide. The only way to retrace the trail Butch and Sundance took to their holdup site and to San Vicente, I've learned, is with a four-wheel drive.

My driver, Enrique, is in his late twenties, was born in the tiny pueblo of San Miguel, and asks if we can take his mother there, which is along the way. I nod and soon an energetic woman with long black skirts and very few teeth climbs in. *Gracias, Señor*, she says, shaking my hand. We are soon outside the city, heading to where Butch and Sundance held up the mining payroll, a place called Huaca Huañusca.

Six months before their final robbery, Butch and Sundance had visited Santa Cruz, a frontier town in Bolivia's southeastern jungle. After exploring the area, Butch felt that he had finally found a place to start over. Some believe that the payroll heist Butch and Sundance carried out later that year was to fund another try at "going straight," this time as cattle ranchers in the Bolivian jungle. Butch soon fired off an enthusiastic letter to his expatriate friends at the Concordia Tin Mines:

> We arrived here about 3 weeks ago after a very pleasant journey, and found just the place I have been looking for 20 years. . . . This is a town of 18,000 and 14,000 are females and some of them are birds. This is the only place for old fellows like myself. One never gets too old if he has blue eyes and a red face and looks capable of making a blue eyed Baby boy. . . . Land is cheap here and everything grows good that is planted. . . . Land is worth 10 cents per hectare 10 leagues [35 miles] from here and there is some good *Estancias* [ranches] for sale, one 12 leagues [45 miles] from . . . with plenty of water and good grass and some sugar cane for 5,000 Bolivianos [around $30,000], and others just as cheap, and if I don't fall down I will be living here before long. . . . We expect to be back at Concordia in about 1 month. Good luck to all you fellows.

We travel through dry, desolate country, through forests of tall, silver cacti called *cabello pelado*, with yellow stubby fruits on top, and past ruined adobe villages, their mud and cane roofs caved in. Some of the villages, softened by time and occasional rain, look more like sand castles slowly melting back into the ground. After about an hour, we stop in the tiny town of San Miguel, where my driver was born. Corn stands in fields that stretch down to the river Salado, the tasseled ears shivering at times in the breeze. Mountains rise in the distance on the other side. Enrique's mother owns several small homes here, one with a cracked-glass window set into the straw and mud bricks. A mud oven, looking like a giant, chest-high beehive, squats nearby; his mother uses it for baking bread.

The villagers have built irrigation ditches, and under the stones in the clear, rippled water scuttle small, gray freshwater crabs. The crabs are tasty, Enrique says, when fried in oil. His mother gets out, walks into a nearby field, pulls a shaggy cornstalk from the ground, then deftly cuts up the interior of the stalk into small white pieces with a machete. She hands me one with her gnarled brown fingers, suggesting I suck on it. I do—and am surprised to find it nearly as sweet as sugarcane. His mother then shakes my hand, smiles a toothless smile, and disappears behind the village. Enrique says his mother has come to get some goat cheese to sell at the Tupiza market. Most of the village is deserted, he says, as residents have died and their children have left to find work in the cities. Many of the houses' roofs have collapsed, the buildings sinking slowly into the ground like tired elephants. Only the old people, it seems, have remained behind, living quietly among the sun-baked bricks.

A little further on, we arrive at Salo, a similar village of small thatched-roofed homes. It was here that Carlos Peró, his son, his servant, and their four mules stayed, their first night out from Tupiza, in an adobe hacienda that the mining magnate Felix Aramayo owned. The building is still there, now converted into a school with large archways in its façade.

In the distance we see an old man walking, slightly bent over with a cane, moving as if in slow motion. The old man wears gray slacks, a frayed jacket, a battered hat, and tire sandals.

"I don't seem to know you," he says, peering at us when we approach and offer our hands. The man speaks Quechua and only a little Spanish, was born in 1930, and has lived here all his life. He quickly adds that he will die here, too. His skin is leathery, like that of a tortoise. Enrique asks him in Quechua if he has ever heard a story of two gringos being killed in the area. Yes, he says, frowning. Two bandits were killed. Long ago. At Huaca Huañusca. Where did he hear about this? Enrique asks. From his parents, the man replies. The story is partially garbled. Butch and Sundance held up the payroll in Huaca Huañusca. But they *died* in San Vicente. Still, one hundred and three years after they were killed, Butch and Sundance's story still remains, as a faint echo in the memory of an eighty-one-year-old Quechua-speaking farmer.

In front of the hacienda sits a small adobe house with broken windows and a locked door. It's for the priest, the old man says. The priest comes here only once or twice a year. The old man then asks us for a few coins to buy a drink; I give him a coin worth five bolivianos. The old man thanks me, bowing formally, then heads slowly away.

From Salo, which lies along a fertile valley, we continue on, through forests of cacti of different kinds. We climb from the valley on the dirt road, then turn off onto a smaller one, heading first past a group of burros wandering among the cacti and scrub, then past a group of llamas—black, white, and multicolored. Finally, Enrique stops the car and shuts off the engine. "To reach the ambush site we must go on foot," he says.

Clouds touch the mountaintops in the distance as Enrique and I begin following a faint trail along a tiny stream flowing down a kind of *quebrada*, or shallow canyon. The creek is smooth and clear, and the water slides over black sand that has the cloven tracks of llamas pressed into it. Giant blocks of greenish-gray stone, streaked with thin lines of milky quartz, lie marooned alongside the stream bank, having fallen down from nearby cliffs. We walk past native Queñua trees, about twenty feet high with cinnamon-colored, scaly dry bark and tiny green leaves. Butch and Sundance probably tied their horses to trees like these, Enrique says. Ulála cacti sprout from the ground, higher than a man, with long white spines. Bright green circles of moss, called *yareta*, a foot round, grow low to the ground, looking like stranded brain corals. As we walk, the only sounds are those of water trickling, birds calling, and our feet occasionally stumbling over stones.

Further ahead, we turn away from the stream and follow the old mule trail up from the *quebrada*, up onto the flank of Huaca Huañusca. The trail rises, then crests a ridge, and we stop. Ahead, we can clearly see the mule trail extending up around the side of the hill for a good mile before it disappears around a curve. Behind us we can look down to the streambed we just hiked up. It's an obvious lookout spot, an excellent place for Butch and Sundance to have crouched, waiting for the mining payroll to show up in the distance, ready to spring their ambush. I sit on a ledge of rock just behind the ridge, scanning the trail on the other side, where Carlos Peró would have appeared. For the first time, I feel the presence of Cassidy and Sundance. No doubt they, too, had sat right here. Nothing in the area has really changed since then, I realize. Butch and Sundance would recognize everything.

Butch's bullet caught the first soldier in the neck, from about four paces away. The soldier fired instantaneously in return before he knew what had hit him. He then dropped his rifle, fell to the ground, and began to crawl away. The second soldier fired twice, saw there was no cover, then ran out of the patio into the street. He and the policeman then began firing through the patio door, in a crackling exchange. The bullets from the soldier's Mauser rifle easily penetrated the adobe wall of the bandits' room, making a "thump!" sound. As Butch and Sundance returned fire through the doorway, the first soldier crawled outside and died. It was the first man Butch had ever killed; now they would be accused not only of robbery but also of murder. With each passing moment, in fact, the situation for the two outlaws was getting worse and worse. Both were wounded—Butch with a bullet wound in the arm, while Sundance had been hit multiple times. Medical help, of course, was impossible. As the gunfight continued, the

mayor began rounding up townspeople to help. The army captain, meanwhile, directed those who had arrived with guns to surround the building in order to prevent the Yankee bandits from digging a hole through the wall and escaping. Wounded, pinned in by gunfire, with their only exit covered, and with armed townspeople now filling the streets, Butch and Sundance must have looked at each other. Without having to say a word, they both knew they were trapped.

From Butch and Sundance's ambush site of Huaca Huañusca, we head northwest toward San Vicente. The dirt road winds over rolling hills of yellow clumps of *ichu* grass. The whole region, with the snowcapped mountains in the distance, looks for all the world like the foothills of the Rocky Mountains in Colorado or Wyoming. Butch and Sundance must have felt quite at home here. The only difference is that the *altiplano*, at an average of fourteen thousand feet, is too high for cattle; instead, occasional groups of llamas with red tassels in their ears wander about, lifting their heads to look at us while slowly chewing. Later on, we pass sandstone buttes that look like enormous, tan-colored human skulls as clouds like giant UFOs drift over the plains and hills, discharging great masses of blue-gray water.

We cover what would normally be a day's mule ride from Salo in only a few dusty hours, rising over the crest of a hill and finding the mining town of San Vicente in a bowl-like valley below—a natural depression that Butch and Sundance rode into and from which they never returned. From above, the community looks like a typical mining town with rows of houses with corrugated tin roofs, gray tailings on the hills nearby, and entry to the town monitored by guards at gates. The silver and zinc mine is now run by a Canadian firm, Pan American Silver, based in British Columbia. Outside of town, on a slope, squats an old, adobe-walled cemetery.

We park next to a small stream that runs through town and get out, then begin walking along a row of miners' houses. The houses have small walled patios behind them, lining the dirt street. Within the patios laundry hangs in bright colors alongside small strips of llama meat, hung out to dry. Inscriptions are splayed in faded letters across the walls: *Movimiento Revolucionario Nacional!* The inscriptions refer to the National Revolutionary Movement, which came to power in the 1950s and began land redistribution for the first time in Bolivia since the arrival of the conquistadors. After the revolution and the nationalization of the mines, the national mining company, COMIBOL, tore down the old village of San Vicente, or most of it, in order to build more efficient workers' quarters with tin roofs. They then built a new adobe village for those they had displaced a short distance away. I ask a teenage boy wearing tire sandals if any old people still live in the area who might know something about the two *bandoleros* who died here a hundred years ago.

"Ask for Froilán Risso," he says. "He knows everything."

Froilán, it turns out, lives in the new village, a knot of adobe homes on dirt streets, separated from the mining town by two soccer fields. It's Sunday, and two games are in progress, the miners having formed teams and wearing uniforms. Around the pitches mostly women and children sit on the ground, eating, swapping stories, and watching the match. Their low voices fill the air, punctuated by the sounds of tennis shoes and sandals hitting the soccer balls with thuds.

In *San Vicente el Nuevo* we knock on some wooden doors, but no one answers. Everyone seems to be either at the soccer matches or else to have gone to Tupiza for the weekend. I knock on another door, and a thirtyish miner opens it, a lean man with high cheekbones and a thin white T-shirt. He's lived here only a year, he says, and doesn't know of a Mr. Risso. Finally, we find Mr. Risso's grandson, Vicente, who is thirty years old. Or actually, he finds us as he'd heard that we were searching for his grandfather. Vicente has short black hair, a stern face, and a twitch beneath his right eye. He says his grandfather is in Tupiza but might return later today. Does he know where the *balacera*, or shootout, occurred? "Yes, my grandfather showed me," he says. He stares at us solemnly while his right eye twitches some more. He wants to be paid to show us the location, he finally says. We agree on a figure and fall in behind him.

Back in the mining town, we cross a small bridge over the stream and, next to a small Evangelical church, we arrive at an adobe-lined corridor. The passageway runs between the church on the left and a newer building on the right. Midway down the corridor, on the left-hand side, rises a tall, thick wall made from old adobe bricks and with bits of pebbles and straw visible in the baked mud. The grandson stops and puts his hand on it.

"Butch Cassidy and the Sundance died just inside," he says emphatically, calling the Sundance Kid "the Sundance."

"On the other side of the wall?"

"Yes. On the other side. That's where they killed themselves."

I climb up onto the wall and look down into the courtyard of an old adobe home. A chicken is walking with halting steps, its head jerking. Laundry hangs from a line. A dog trots out, then lies down, placing its head on its paws, staring at me. The wall, the grandson says, used to be the outer wall of the room in which Butch and Sundance had their final shootout. The house once belonged to the father of his uncle, a man named Casasola, he says. I recognize the name as that of the man who had rented Butch and Sundance a room. A few years ago, Vicente says, his uncle, a very religious man, ripped down the remaining walls and built the Evangelical church. I look back down into the patio and can't help but think of Butch and Sundance's final meal: bullets, beer, and sardines.

The next morning, at dawn, after a cold night during which no shots were fired, the army captain ordered the owner of the house, Bonifacio Casasola, to go see whether the two bandits were alive or dead. The captain, who had somehow managed to miss all of the frontline action himself, reasoned that

as Bonifacio was the owner of the house, the bandits wouldn't shoot him. With the town still in shadows, Bonifacio walked slowly into the courtyard, no doubt pondering the captain's logic, then approached the doorway of the bandits' room and peeked inside. As an eyewitness later testified, "all of us [then] entered and found the smaller gringo [likely Butch] stretched out on the floor, dead, with one bullet wound in the temple and another in the arm. The taller one [probably Sundance] was hugging a large ceramic jug that was in the room. He was dead, also, with a bullet wound in the forehead."

According to some reports, the smaller man had shot his *compañero* in the forehead, then held the gun against his temple and pulled the trigger. Four days after the shootout, however, the local newspaper in Tupiza reported that the second man had been shot "in the chest" and had seven other gunshot wounds "in different parts of the body." Had Sundance died from his wounds and had Butch then killed himself? Or had Butch put Sundance out of his misery before putting the gun against his own temple and pulling the trigger? Or—as judge Felix Charlar later suggested to me—had the police and soldiers first captured and then killed them . . . and lied about it afterward?

Suicide among outlaws was not unheard of. Kid Curry, for example, who had ridden with Butch and Sundance during their glory days, had done just that four years earlier. Chased by a posse, wounded, and surrounded in a cornfield in Colorado, Curry had shot himself in the head rather than be caught, sent to prison, or hanged. Had Butch and Sundance done the same?

We have lunch, then walk up to the cemetery. The gate is open. Inside, we find the burial ground to be a crowded hodgepodge of cement tombs lying alongside graves marked with simple wood or metal crosses. Some of the crosses have small, hand-sized metal sheets fastened to their centers with details about who is buried below. Metal is a bad choice for posterity, however; even on newer graves the metal is already rusted and difficult to read.

In the middle of the cemetery rises a thick adobe archway, with an adobe wall on either side, almost cutting the cemetery in two. Passing through the archway, we come to a sign over one cement tomb that boldly states that *"Esto fue la tumba de Butch Cassidy"* ("This was the grave of Butch Cassidy"), placed there by the Pan American Silver Company. The sign, however, is incorrect. In 1994, Vicente's grandfather, Froilán, had directed a *NOVA* documentary crew to dig up this very grave. Froilán had told the crew that his father, who had been a boy of ten when the shootout occurred, had instructed him that this was where the *yanqui* bandits had been buried. The problem, however, is that the San Vicente graveyard has always been a *cementerio popular*, or public graveyard; over the years, people have dug graves beside and even on top of old ones. By the time the documentary crew arrived, the graves at San Vicente were a tangled mess, sometimes three layers thick, one grave lying on top of the other. After exhuming a skeleton three levels down that was obviously that of a gringo, the crew eventually discovered that it belonged to an unfortunate German miner who had inadvertently blown himself up with a stick of dynamite. There were no traces of Butch or Sundance.

My guide Enrique, meanwhile, tells me a theory that I've heard from others, about Butch and Sundance *not* being buried in the cemetery, which everyone has assumed. After all, only one eyewitness at the time mentioned a burial, and he said at the inquest that after searching through the bandits' belongings and having recovered the unspent mining payroll, "in the afternoon we interred them." He didn't say *where*.

"In the old days people didn't normally bury suicides in cemeteries," Enrique says. "Because everyone knew that *suicidios* went to Hell." Butch and Sundance, Enrique says, not only apparently killed themselves, but they were also *bandits*, that is, evil men. "No one in town would have wanted *bandoleros* buried in the same cemetery as their relatives." The two outlaws, Enrique believes, would have at best been tossed into a shallow grave somewhere outside of town. *"Como basura,"* he says—like trash. With a cemetery two and three levels deep and with Butch and Sundance probably having been buried in a hastily dug grave elsewhere, Enrique says, it's unlikely that anyone will ever find them.

Wandering through the graveyard, I look up at the rim of the valley that the two outlaws crested before heading down into town. After nearly twenty years on the run, Butch and Sundance made a series of compounding errors that ultimately cost them their lives. If they'd been more *ruthless* criminals, then they would have killed the three people they had robbed. No description of two *yanqui* bandits would then ever have gotten out. Nor would word of the robbery have traveled so quickly. Had they planned things better, they could have at least taken the payroll team's mules, so that Carlos Peró, his son, and his servant would have had to *walk* out, again slowing news of the robbery.

Similarly, if Butch and Sundance had decided to *avoid* San Vicente and to camp out in the hills instead, then most likely no one would ever have seen them. Finally, taking a clearly branded, stolen mule into San Vicente was another risk that backfired on them. With word out, a good description of the robbers being two well-armed *yanquis*, with new telegraph lines linking many of the towns, with a stolen mule, and with the two of them still being in the general area of the robbery two days afterward—all of those slipups ultimately cost them their lives. Butch and Sundance met their ends only a day's ride from Uyuni, where they could have taken the train to Chile or north to Oruro or La Paz and then could have vanished into a faceless crowd. Instead, they more than likely disappeared into a shallow grave in San Vicente—two anonymous bandits whose bodies no one ever claimed and have never been found.*

---

*There is one school of thought that Butch and/or Sundance survived the shootout and returned to the United States, dying as old men from natural causes. However, although Butch and Sundance had always kept up a stream of letters to family and friends in the US throughout the years, the letters from both ceased after 1908, the year of the shootout in San Vicente during which two gringos died.

In the early evening, Froilán Risso arrives in town from Tupiza. He is seventy-four years old, has creased brown skin, and wears slacks, tire sandals, and a blue baseball cap. Froilán invites me into his home and seats me on a wooden bench next to an adobe wall. He then pulls up a chair and looks at me with direct brown eyes. "What do you want to know?" he asks, in kind of a singsong voice that takes every sentence and tilts it up at the end. Froilán then asks bluntly, "How much will you *pay*?" I suggest fifty bolivianos. He suggests two hundred. After some negotiating, we agree on two hundred. Clearly, he and his grandson know how to mine Butch and Sundance's story as others would mine a rich vein of gold.

"My father was around ten when the shootout occurred," Froilán says. "He showed me where it happened and told me about it many times." His father died around 1957 or 1958, he says, and was sixty-three when he died. He then tells me the familiar story of the shootout and the suicides.

"What happened afterward?" I ask.

"They went inside and found the money and a lot of guns, modern ones, with, oof, a lot of bullets! They only found half the money, less than half! Then they took [the bodies] out into the patio, after going through their things, and buried them in the cemetery."

"What about the grave in the cemetery—the one they dug up? It turned out not to be Butch or Sundance, but a German miner."

"They didn't want to pay me," he says, referring to the documentary crew.

"So you showed them the *wrong* grave?"

"Yes."

"Do you know where Butch and Sundance are buried?"

"Yes!"

"Are they buried *inside* the cemetery—or outside?"

"Inside! But you will have to pay a *lot* for me to show you where!"

A few days later, on my final evening in Tupiza, I have dinner with the judge at a restaurant fittingly called the Alamo. I tell the judge how

Froilán had said that his father witnessed the shootout when he was a boy and insisted that the two outlaws were buried in the cemetery.

Over a plate of stir-fried *lomo saltado*, the judge leans forward, winks at me, and says, "Who knows if what Froilán Risso says is true?"

The judge then takes a swig of cold beer, sits back, and lifts up an eyebrow.

"After all, it happened a long time ago."

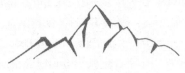

9

DARWIN, THE LAST YÁMANA, AND THE UTTERMOST PART OF THE EARTH (CHILE AND ARGENTINA)

But . . . ye shall be witnesses unto me both in Jerusalem, and in all Judaea, and in Samaria, and unto the uttermost part of the earth.

—Acts 1:18 (King James Version)

Whilst beholding these savages, one asks, Whence have they come? What could have tempted, or what change compelled, a tribe of men, to leave the fine regions of the north, to travel down the Cordillera or backbone of America, to invent and build canoes . . . and then to enter on one of the most inhospitable countries within the limits of the globe?

—Charles Darwin, *The Voyage of the* Beagle, 1839

The true barbarian is he who thinks everything barbarous but his own tastes and prejudices.

—William Hazlitt, *Characteristics*, 1837

The old woman lives in a yellow corrugated iron house outside of the naval town, down a rutted dirt road next to a stream. Smoke rises from the fitted chimney pipes and from the cluster of dwellings nearby. This is all that is left of the Yámana Indian community, a small gathering of iron houses outside of Puerto Williams on Navarino Island in Chile. It is the uttermost part of the Earth and the southernmost city in the world.

The frigid seas of the Beagle Channel suck and pull restlessly nearby, punctuated occasionally by a right, or humpback, whale that blows a greeting of stale air and frost. The old woman's sister, the second-to-last speaker of a nearly extinct language, died four years earlier, so the old woman now has no one with whom to speak her native language. Over her doorway is a sign that says *"Hai Šapakuta Sean Skáe Sean Haoa Morako,"* which means basically "You are welcome, friend." On a windswept island with thick beech forests and snowy peaks, Cristina Calderón, eighty-three years old, is the last Yámana-speaking Indian alive.

I knock on the door and hear a shuffling inside. A minute later the door opens. An old woman stands there, short yet thickly built, with shoulder-length black-and-gray hair and dark eyes. I introduce myself.

She looks at me, pauses a moment, then says in Spanish, "Come in."

In the summer of 1831, a black coach pulled by horses rode through the crowded streets of London, the capital of an English maritime empire that literally stretched round the world. Inside the carriage rode a most peculiar quartet: three natives from Patagonia and a twenty-five-year-old English sea captain named Robert FitzRoy. A year and a half earlier, while employed to map and survey the distant coast of Patagonia, FitzRoy had captured the natives and had brought them to England. A fourth had died of smallpox soon after arriving. The remaining three—a man of about twenty-five, a

boy of about fourteen, and a ten-year-old girl—had survived and, for the last year, had been receiving lessons in English language, etiquette, and gardening. Although in Patagonia the natives had gone naked and traveled by foot or in bark canoes, they were now accustomed to wearing nineteenth-century English clothing—the girl in dresses and the men in double-breasted suits, burnished leather shoes, and "proper" English hats. When introduced, they automatically exclaimed, "Hello—how do you do?" All three now spoke rudimentary English and of course their own native language, which no European knew. On this particular day, as the carriage horses clopped their way near the Thames River, the four travelers continued toward St. James's Palace. There, they had an appointment with the king and queen of England for tea.

A bit later, inside the sixteenth-century palace, the four were led past ornate drawing rooms of silk and damask, rare woods and marble and all the representative wealth of the most powerful empire in the world. In a state drawing room sat sixty-five-year-old King William IV and next to him thirty-eight-year-old Queen Adelaide. The queen had large, sympathetic eyes and a German accent. The king was wigless, had tousled white hair, and wore stockings. Soon after their arrival, attendants presented the three natives, and each said "How do you do?" before sitting down. Although the normal diet of the Patagonians was roasted mussels, sea lion meat, and occasional whale blubber, they were now treated to British crumpets, cakes, and miniature sandwiches. According to Captain FitzRoy, who planned to depart for Patagonia with his captives by the end of the year, the two monarchs were extremely curious about their visitors and about the distant land from which they hailed. Wrote FitzRoy,

> His Majesty asked a great deal about their country, as well as themselves; and I hope I may be permitted to remark that, during an equal space of time, no person ever asked me so many sensible and thoroughly pertinent questions respecting the Fuegians [of Tierra del Fuego Island] and their country.

The Queen had lost two of her own children and was especially taken with the ten-year-old native girl, whom English sailors had *nicknamed "Fuegia Basket." The girl charmed everyone she met with her impish personality and smiles. During their tea, the Queen rose from her chair, left the room briefly, then returned with one of her own laced bonnets. This she placed upon the young girl's head. The Queen then "put one of her rings upon the girl's finger, and gave her a sum of money to buy an outfit of clothes when she should leave England to return to her own country."*

Their visit over, the four bid the king and queen farewell. Two hundred miles away, the ship that would carry them back to Patagonia lay quietly at anchor in Plymouth Harbor. Her name was Her Majesty's Ship the Beagle. *She was ninety feet long and among her crew was a twenty-two-year-old pug-nosed English naturalist of whom few outside of his hometown of Shrewsbury had ever heard. Recently graduated from the university, the young man, Charles Robert Darwin, would soon join Captain FitzRoy and the three natives and set sail for Patagonia—the southernmost tip of South America.*

Robert FitzRoy, the aristocratic son of a British general and an illegitimate great-grandson of Charles II, had gone to sea at thirteen. He was only twenty-three when he received his first commission as captain, yet he'd gained his appointment through a suicide. Four months earlier, during its second year of mapping the rugged Patagonian coast, the HMS *Beagle* had been commanded by Captain Pringle Stokes. The constant cold and dangerous weather, a natural predisposition toward depression, and the enormous difficulties involved in the task, however, had weighed heavily on him. Cooped up in his cabin, the despondent Stokes withdrew a pistol, placed it against his head, and pulled the trigger. The *Beagle* was now suddenly without a captain, buffeted by howling winds amid one of the most dangerous seas in the world.

Four months later, after successfully making it to Uruguay for supplies, the *Beagle* returned to Patagonia, this time with FitzRoy at the helm. Aquiline nosed, delicate looking, deeply religious, indefatigable, an excellent officer and cartographer, FitzRoy took over the mapping of a coast where in the last three centuries hundreds of ships had gone down, often with all hands on board. As the Age of Exploration had gradually morphed into an age of commerce and imperialism, Britain had emerged as the foremost world power. In order to protect its trade routes, Britain needed to control the world's shipping lanes. To do so meant possessing not only a large fleet of ships but also accurate charts and maps with which to guide them. FitzRoy's mission was thus the same as his ill-fated predecessor's: to continue mapping the labyrinthine islands and fjords of Patagonia's coast, one of the most complex and nautically treacherous archipelagoes in the world. Only then would British shipping through the area become more secure.

Patagonia's seeming inhospitality, however, had not deterred it from having been populated by various tribes of natives who, although stark naked, were somehow able to navigate the frigid waters with only small bark canoes. First contacted in the 1500s, various tribes by now routinely approached ships or landing parties in order to gain access to the Europeans' abundant trade goods and tools. They did so, however, either by trade or theft. Thus it was that, three months into his mission, early one morning on February 5, 1831, Captain FitzRoy received a rude knock on his cabin door. As he later wrote,

> At three this morning . . . I was called up to hear that the whaleboat [used by a shore party] was . . . stolen by . . . natives; and that her coxswain and two men had just reached the ship in a clumsy canoe, made like a large basket; of wicker-work covered with pieces of canvas, and lined with clay, very leaky, and difficult to paddle . . . my boat was immediately prepared, and I hastened away with a fortnight's provisions for eleven men, intending to . . . go in search of the stolen boat.

Seven days later, FitzRoy and his sailors finally cornered some of the natives they believed had been involved in the theft. After creeping through bushes to encircle the natives' camp, the sailors had rushed forward, attempting to seize as many natives as they could. It was no easy task. "The oldest woman of the tribe was so powerful," FitzRoy wrote, "that two of the strongest men of our party could scarcely pull her out from under the bank of the stream."

While children ran screaming into the forest, two men and a woman tried to conceal themselves alongside a stream. Cornered by one of FitzRoy's men, they attacked him with stones, trying to "beat out his brains."

> Seeing the . . . [sailor's] danger, [a crew member] fired at one of the Fuegians, who staggered back and let . . . [him] escape; but immediately recovering himself, picked up stones from the bed of the stream, or was supplied with them by those who stood close to him, and threw them from each hand with astonishing force and precision. His first stone struck the master with much force, broke a powder-horn hung round his neck, and nearly knocked him backwards; and two others were thrown so truly at the heads of those nearest him, that they barely saved themselves by dropping down. All this passed in a few seconds, so quick was he with each hand: but, poor fellow, it was his last struggle; unfortunately he was mortally wounded, and, throwing one more stone, he fell against the bank and expired.

Although most of the natives subsequently escaped, a ten-year-old girl remained behind. FitzRoy's sailors named her "Fuegia Basket" after the basket-like boat his men had fashioned during the loss of their whaleboat. In subsequent days, FitzRoy captured three more natives: a roughly twenty-five-year-old man he named York Minster; a twenty-year-old man he named Boat Memory (in memory of the stolen boat, which FitzRoy never recovered); and a teenager, about fourteen years old, whom he named Jemmy Button. The boy was so named because, after encouraging him to step out of a canoe full of natives into their longboat, the English sailors had thrown the natives a shiny button "in payment."

Unable to locate his missing boat, FitzRoy now had to decide what to do with his captives. Slowly, an idea began to form in his mind:

> I became convinced that so long as we were ignorant of the Fuegian language, and the natives were equally ignorant of ours, we should never know much about them, or the interior of their country; nor would there be the slightest chance of their being raised one step above the low place which they then held in our estimation. Their words seemed to be short, but to have many meanings, and their pronunciation was harsh and guttural.
>
> I . . . [eventually] made up my mind to carry the Fuegians . . . to England; trusting that the ultimate benefits arising from their acquaintance with our habits and language, would make up for the temporary separation from their own country . . . I began to think of the various advantages which might result to them and their countrymen, as well as to us . . . educating them there as far as might be practicable, and then bringing them back to Tierra del Fuego.

The four natives were thus now made the subjects of an impromptu social experiment: could these naked inhabitants—whom FitzRoy and his sailors considered "savages"—be "civilized" by removing them to European society for a year or more, then returning them "to their country at a future time, with iron, tools, clothes, and knowledge which they might spread among their countrymen"? In other words, could native Patagonians make the leap from a hunting and gathering lifestyle with a supposed pagan belief system to agriculture and Christianity—all within a few years' time?

Three years later, the first part of the experiment had been completed. After Boat Memory had died of smallpox in England, the remaining three natives had spent nearly a year studying English and "Manners." They'd then spent another eight months returning with FitzRoy to Patagonia on the second voyage of the HMS *Beagle*. Superficially, they were radically transformed. All now routinely wore clothes, spoke basic English, and Jemmy Button, especially, loved dressing up in fine suits, waistcoats, and gloves.

As the three now peered over the bow in the stormy weather, revisiting their homeland for the first time in three years, the young Charles Darwin stood peering over the bow with them. Twenty-eight years later, in 1859, he would publish *On the Origin of Species*, a book that would revolutionize man's perception of his place in the natural world. For now, however, as an inexperienced and often seasick naturalist at the beginning of a long journey around the world, Darwin was content to observe and record his observations in his journal, including descriptions of the three Patagonians with whom he'd been living aboard ship:

> During the former voyage of the . . . Beagle . . . Captain Fitz Roy seized on a party of natives, as hostages for the loss of a boat . . . Two men, one of whom died in England of the smallpox, a boy and a little girl, were originally taken; and we had now on board, York Minster, Jemmy Button (whose name expresses his purchase-money), and Fuegia Basket.
>
> Jemmy Button was a universal favourite, but likewise passionate; the expression of his face at once showed his nice disposition. He was merry and often laughed, and was remarkably sympathetic with any one in pain: when the water was rough, I was often a little sea-sick, and he used to come to me and say in a plaintive voice, "Poor, poor fellow!" but the notion, after his aquatic life [on canoes], of a man being sea-sick, was too ludicrous, and he was generally obliged to turn on one side to hide a smile or laugh, and then he would repeat his "Poor, poor fellow!" He was of a patriotic disposition; and he liked to praise his own tribe and country . . .
>
> Jemmy was short, thick, and fat, but vain of his personal appearance; he used always to wear gloves, his hair was neatly cut, and he was distressed if his well-polished shoes were dirtied. He was fond of admiring himself in a looking glass . . .
>
> Fuegia Basket was a nice, modest, reserved young girl . . . and very quick in learning anything, especially languages. This she showed in picking up some Portuguese and Spanish, when left on shore for only a short time at Rio de Janeiro and Monte Video, and

in her knowledge of English. York Minster was very jealous of any attention paid to her; for it was clear he determined to marry her as soon as they were settled on shore.

Finally, in January 1833, three years after her last visit, the HMS *Beagle* anchored along the southwest coast of Patagonia. Captain FitzRoy soon set off in four small boats up the Beagle Channel, intent on returning York Minster, Jemmy Button, and Fuegia Basket to their native land. Darwin accompanied them and, as he later wrote,

> This channel, which was discovered by Captain Fitz Roy during the last voyage, is a most remarkable feature in the geography of this, or indeed of any other country: it may be compared to the valley of Loch Ness in Scotland, with its chain of lakes and firths. It is about one hundred and twenty miles long, with an average breadth, not subject to any very great variation, of about two miles; and is throughout the greater part so perfectly straight, that the view, bounded on each side by a line of mountains, gradually becomes indistinct in the long distance . . . This is the residence of Jemmy Button's tribe and family.

Believing at first that all four natives belonged to the same tribe, FitzRoy had gradually come to realize that they were in fact from two different ethnic groups. Upon further questioning of his captives, in fact, FitzRoy had learned that numerous tribes inhabited the southern tip of Patagonia and the Island of Tierra del Fuego, each with its own language and customs. York Minster and Fuegia Basket, it turned out, spoke the same language and were from the Akalufe tribe. Jemmy Button, by contrast, spoke a different language and was from a tribe that called themselves the Yámana. Because foul weather had made it impossible to return York Minster and Fuegia Basket to their native islands further to the east, FitzRoy had decided to return all three of them to Jemmy Button's land; York Minster and Fuegia Basket had assured the captain that they could make their way home by canoe. As

FitzRoy and Darwin sailed alongside Navarino Island, in what is now the southernmost part of Chile, they soon began seeing natives along the coast. Wrote Darwin,

> During the night the news [of our arrival] had spread, and early in the morning . . . a . . . party [of natives] arrived, belonging to the . . . [Yámana], or Jemmy's tribe. Several of them had run so fast that their noses were bleeding, and their mouths frothed from the rapidity with which they talked; and with their naked bodies all bedaubed with black, white, and red, they looked like so many demoniacs who had been fighting. We then proceeded (accompanied by twelve [native] canoes, each holding four or five people) down Ponsonby Sound to the spot [Wulaia Bay] where poor Jemmy expected to find his mother and relatives. He had already heard that his father was dead; but as he had had a "dream in his head" to that effect, he did not seem to care much about it, and repeatedly comforted himself with the very natural reflection—"Me no help it." He was not able to learn any particulars regarding his father's death, as his relations would not speak about it.

During the return voyage from England, Jemmy had indeed confided one day that he'd had a dream, a dream in which a visitor had told him that his father had died. From that moment on, Jemmy had been convinced that his father had passed away in his absence, a fact that he confirmed upon his arrival. What Darwin didn't realize was that, among the Yámanas, relatives did not speak about their dead, which was taboo. They did, however, carry out elaborate burial rituals in which they expressed their grief and sadness over their loss. Understanding neither their culture nor their language, Darwin also misread the stylized, low-key greetings between the Yámanas as evidence of a lack of empathy among them. He later wrote,

> The next morning after our arrival . . . the Fuegians began to pour in, and Jemmy's mother and brothers arrived . . . The meeting was less interesting than that between a horse, turned out into a field,

when he joins an old companion. There was no demonstration of affection; they simply stared for a short time at each other; and the mother immediately went to look after her canoe.

The family's seeming lack of affection shocked both Darwin and Fitz-Roy, both of whom assumed that this was more evidence of "savagery." Strangely, it never seemed to have occurred to the captain that seizing an adolescent boy and taking him aboard a ship for years to a distant land would not have bothered the boy's family—and of course the family had never been asked for their permission. Darwin soon learned from York Minster, however, that Jemmy's "mother had been inconsolable for the loss . . . and had searched everywhere for him, thinking that he might have been left [somewhere] after having been taken in the [Englishmen's] boat." In other words, Jemmy's mother had been as frantic about the disappearance of her son as any other mother would have been. But she had been powerless to do anything about it.

Fuegia Basket, meanwhile, had literally been seized as a hostage after at least one of the adults she'd been with was shot to death. And while FitzRoy and his crew considered the Yámanas to be thieves, what they didn't understand was that the Yámanas shared their goods among themselves. It was inconceivable that a person would ever hoard wealth and leave his companions poor. To the Yámanas, finding an abandoned boat full of equipment was akin to finding a beached whale. Within a short time, the boat's contents had no doubt been divvied up and distributed.

A week after their arrival, after helping to build two "wigwams," dig gardens, and deposit a large store of European goods for trade, Fitz-Roy and his men bade farewell to their three native captives, leaving with them a young Anglican missionary named Richard Matthews. The latter had volunteered to accompany the three Patagonians in order to "Christianize" their countrymen. Although Darwin had his doubts about abandoning a twenty-one-year-old missionary in such a wild region, FitzRoy was determined to establish a beachhead of "civilization" on Navarino Island. It was his hope that a new community would be established, one consisting of the missionary, the three "partially civilized" natives, perhaps some of Jemmy Button's family, along with several gardens now planted with turnips, potatoes, onions, and beets. The young missionary was a "lay catechist," charged by the Anglican Church to "sow" new congregations around the world. Thus, as Matthews helped to plant the gardens, he was just as determined to plant Christianity, hopefully disseminating English in the process as the new lingua franca of the region.

After another week of surveying, however, FitzRoy decided to pay a final visit to the new settlement before the *Beagle* departed for at least a year. He was shocked to learn that his mission project had quickly fallen into serious anarchy. As Darwin later wrote,

> From the time of our leaving, a regular system of plunder commenced. Fresh parties of the natives kept arriving: York and Jemmy lost many things, and [the missionary] Matthews almost everything which had not been concealed underground. Every article seemed to have been torn up and divided by the natives. Matthews described the watch he was obliged always to keep as most harassing; night and day he was surrounded by the natives, who tried to tire him out by making an incessant noise close to his head. One day an old man, whom Matthews asked to leave his wigwam, immediately returned with a large stone in his hand: another day a whole party came armed with stones and stakes, and some of the younger men and Jemmy's brother were crying.

At one point, a group of natives made it clear that they wanted to strip the young missionary of his clothes and pluck all the hairs from his body. They proposed to do so with tweezers made from mussel shells— as if the missionary were some kind of duck or sea bird. Most likely, however, this was an attempt to make Matthews appear more like themselves, to make him fit in. Yet Matthews by now had had enough. The natives had trampled the gardens. They'd seized and redistributed most of his supplies. Fearing for his life and no doubt in complete culture shock, Matthews asked FitzRoy to be taken back on board. After more than a year of preparation and seven days of proselytizing, his career as a missionary in Patagonia was over.

Also over, or so it seemed, was FitzRoy's three-year experiment in "civilizing" the region. Although disappointed, FitzRoy nevertheless still hoped that his "motives in taking . . . [Jemmy, York Minster, and Fuegia Basket] to England would become understood and appreciated among [the natives]" and that the soil on Navarino Island had indeed been seeded not only with European garden plants but also with the first roots of "civilization."

Darwin, however, with nothing invested in the social experiment and therefore a more circumspect observer, wrote that

> It was quite melancholy leaving our Fuegians amongst their barbarous countrymen . . . Poor Jemmy looked rather disconsolate, & certainly would have liked to have returned with us. I am afraid whatever other ends their excursions to England produces, it will not be conducive to their happiness. They have far too much sense not to see the vast superiority of civilized over uncivilized habits; & yet I am afraid to the latter they must return . . . I fear it is more than doubtful, whether their visit [to England] will have been of any use to them.

Roughly a year later, on March 5, 1834, Darwin's premonitions were confirmed at the same time as FitzRoy's hopes were dashed. The two had returned to Wulaia Bay to search one last time for their three native friends. On shore, FitzRoy later wrote,

> The wigwams in which I had left York, Jemmy, and Fuegia, were found empty, though uninjured: the garden had been trampled over, but some turnips and potatoes of moderate size were pulled up by us, and eaten at my table, a proof that they may be grown in that region. Not a living soul was visible anywhere . . . and an anxious hour or two passed, after the ship was moored, before three canoes were seen . . . paddling hastily towards us, from the place now called

Button Island. Looking through a glass I saw . . . a face which I knew yet could not name. "It must be someone I have seen before," said I . . . [and then] his sharp eye detected me, and a sudden movement of the hand to his head (as a sailor touches his hat) at once told me it was indeed Jemmy Button.

FitzRoy had last seen Jemmy thirteen months earlier, wearing pants, a shirt, and shoes and industriously working in his garden. Now the captain was shocked to see that, among the two canoe-loads of naked "savages"—all of whom had matted hair and bodies smeared with seal oil and grease—was his favorite protégé, Jemmy Button. As FitzRoy later wrote,

But how altered! I could hardly restrain my feelings, and I was not, by any means, the only one so touched by his squalid miserable appearance. He was naked, like his companions, except a bit of skin about his loins; his hair was long and matted, just like theirs; he was wretchedly thin, and his eyes were affected by smoke. We hurried him below, clothed him immediately, and in half an hour he was sitting with me at dinner in my cabin, using his knife and fork properly, and in every way behaving as correctly as if he had never left us. He spoke as much English as ever, and, to our astonishment, his companions, his wife, his brothers and their wives, mixed broken English words in their talking with him . . . I thought he was ill, but he surprised me by saying that he was "hearty, sir, never better," that he had not been ill, even for a day, was happy and contented, and had no wish whatever to change his way of life. He said that he got "plenty fruits," "plenty birdies," "ten guanacos in snow [winter] time," and "too much fish."

Darwin noted as well that, despite his seemingly "disheveled" appearance, Jemmy

told us he had "too much" (meaning enough) to eat, that he was not cold, that his relations were very good people, and that he did

not wish to go back to England . . . I do not now doubt that he will
be as happy as, perhaps happier than, if he had never left his own
country.

Jemmy soon explained that, not long after FitzRoy and Darwin had
left the previous year, York Minster had stolen most of Jemmy's
things one night, including his clothes, and York and Fuegia Basket
had secretly departed in a large canoe for their own islands. Jemmy
had watched, day after day, he said, for the peas, beans, and other
vegetables to sprout in the garden, but his countrymen had trampled
them. The wigwams the Europeans had built, meanwhile, were too
tall and thus too cold in winter. So they had abandoned them and
made traditional ones. As FitzRoy watched Jemmy finish his meal—
smiling and contented—he no doubt couldn't help but think of the
enormous effort he'd invested in this experiment and perhaps also of
Boat Memory's death in England of smallpox. Looking no doubt to
salvage something, he wrote,

> I cannot help still hoping that some benefit, however slight, may
> result from the intercourse of these people, Jemmy, York, and
> Fuegia, with other natives of Tierra del Fuego. Perhaps a ship-
> wrecked seaman may hereafter receive help and kind treatment
> from Jemmy Button's children; prompted, as they can hardly fail
> to be, by the traditions they will have heard of men of other lands;
> and by an idea, however faint, of their duty to God as well as their
> neighbor.

The next day, as the *Beagle* prepared to depart from the area, Jemmy
returned to shore, but only after leaving behind presents for his English friends. As sailors unfurled the ship's sails, Darwin watched as
Jemmy "lighted a signal fire, and the smoke curled up, bidding us a
last and long farewell, as the ship stood on her course into the open
sea."

Darwin and FitzRoy thus departed, never to return, embarking
on personal destinies that would include an immortal legacy, on the

one hand, and ultimate tragedy on the other. While both FitzRoy and Darwin were Anglicans, FitzRoy had gradually become more and more devout during the *Beagle's* voyage. Darwin, by contrast—unable to reconcile the fossil record he was observing during his travels with the story of creation told in the Bible—little by little began to doubt the book of Genesis, then finally began to doubt the Bible all together. As he later wrote,

> Whilst on board the Beagle I was quite orthodox, and I remember being heartily laughed at by several of the officers (though themselves orthodox) for quoting the Bible as an unanswerable authority on some point. . . . But I had gradually come . . . to see that the Old Testament from its manifestly false history of the world . . . from its attributing to God the feelings of a revengeful tyrant, was no more to be trusted than the sacred books of the Hindoos, or the beliefs of any barbarian . . .
>
> By further reflecting that the clearest evidence would be requisite to make any sane man believe in the miracles by which Christianity is supported—that the more we know of the fixed laws of nature the more incredible do miracles become . . . I gradually came to disbelieve in Christianity as a divine revelation.
>
> I was very unwilling to give up my belief . . . but I found it more and more difficult, with free scope given to my imagination, to invent evidence which would suffice to convince me. Thus disbelief crept over me at a very slow rate, but was at last complete.

Darwin's dining companion, Captain FitzRoy, meanwhile, remained steadfast in his belief that the Bible could be read not only as a religious text but also as literal history. Patagonians such as Jemmy and the Yámanas, FitzRoy believed, must have thus originally migrated from the Middle East, as they were undoubtedly the children of Adam and Eve. The reason their skins were darker than those of Englishmen, FitzRoy reasoned, was because like black Africans, Patagonians must be the sons of Cain, who killed his brother Abel. The two groups' darker skins

were the result of the "stain" left by the sins of their infamous ances-
tor. Little by little, as the Patagonians' ancestors had migrated away
from the Holy Land, certain groups must have lost their knowledge of
whence they came—of writing and agriculture and coins and clothing—
until, by the time they arrived at the bottom of South America, they
had become, FitzRoy said, "savages in the fullest sense of the word;
from which degraded condition they would not rise a step by their own
exertions."

FitzRoy published his theory of the origin of Patagonians in 1839
as a chapter in the book *Narrative of the Surveying Voyages of His Majesty's
Ships Adventure and Beagle*. Darwin, by contrast, published the results of
his own thinking twenty years later in *On the Origin of Species*. Darwin's
book, of course, was a completely radical reworking of Genesis: that
man had not been created by God in God's image but rather had *evolved*
from other animals. After receiving a copy of the book Darwin had sent
him, FitzRoy penned a reply: "My dear old friend, I, at least, *cannot* find
anything 'ennobling' in the thought of being a descendent of even the
most ancient *Ape*." Reading Darwin's book had clearly shaken the now-
retired sea captain to his very core.

*Oxford University. Saturday, June 30, 1860. Nearly one thousand
people—students, professors, scientists, and journalists—have filed into
the Museum of Natural History, ostensibly to listen to a paper about
the sexuality of plants. The real lure, however, is the promise of a debate afterward about Charles Darwin's recently published theory of
evolution—and its obvious contradiction of certain passages in the Bible.
It is also well known that, amid the audience of well-dressed Victorians
in hats, boots, and cravats, Bishop Samuel Wilberforce—famed orator,
Lord Bishop of Oxford, and member of the House of Lords—is in attendance and is going to speak afterward. Wilberforce had been involved
in the recent construction of Oxford's natural history museum—for the*

study of, as he dubbed it, the "wonders of God's creations." None doubted that he would vehemently denounce Darwin's radical new theory. Darwin had already sent word that he was ill and therefore would not be in attendance. Instead some of his most ardent supporters assembled, such as the famed zoologist Thomas Henry Huxley, who had already written several positive reviews of Darwin's book, and Joseph Dalton Hooker, the well-known botanist and Darwin's best friend. Also in attendance, seated in the center of the audience and clutching a large Bible, is fifty-four-year-old Robert FitzRoy. The former sea captain has made it known that he is now mortified that he, of all people, had selected the young naturalist to accompany him on the voyage of the Beagle. It is doubly mortifying that he had thus inadvertently helped give rise to Darwin's blasphemous theory. This, it is obvious to those who know him, causes him the "acutest pain."

After an hour and a half of a desultory lecture on plants that one observer later summed up as "flatulent," the audience finally senses that the showdown it has been waiting for is about to begin. Bishop Wilberforce, wearing the flowing robes of his office and with a cross hanging round his neck, takes the stage. Slowly and dramatically, breathing life into the vast, stuffy room, the bishop predictably begins to denounce Darwin's "crackpot" theory, a theory, as the Oxford Journal will later record, that was founded

> not on philosophical principles, but upon fancy, and he [Wilberforce] denied that one instance had been produced by Mr. Darwin on the alleged change from one species to another had ever taken place . . . and concluded, amid much cheering, by denouncing it as degrading to man, and as a theory founded upon fancy, instead of upon facts.

Turning toward the zoologist Thomas Huxley, Bishop Wilberforce—whose very profession is to serve as an intermediary between God and man—caps his speech off with both a taunt and an insult: "he begged to know," wrote the reporter from the Journal, "was it through his [Huxley's] grandfather or his grandmother that he claimed his descent from a monkey?"

Thirty-five-year-old Huxley is said to have leaned over to a friend at this moment and to have whispered "the Lord hath delivered him into my hands." Dark haired, with long sideburns, brilliant, and largely self-taught, Huxley now takes the stage. As he later wrote,

> When I got up I spoke pretty much to the effect that I had listened with great attention to the Lord Bishop's speech, but had been unable to discover either a new fact or a new argument in it—except indeed the question raised as to my personal predilections in the matter of ancestry—That it would not have occurred to me to bring forward such a topic as that for discussion myself, but that I was quite ready to meet the Right Revd . . . [Wilberforce] even on that ground—If then, said I, the question is put to me would I rather have a miserable ape for a grandfather or a man highly endowed by nature and possessed of great means of influence and yet who employs those faculties and that influence for the mere purpose of introducing ridicule into a grave scientific discussion—I unhesitatingly affirm my preference for the ape.

In the crowded room, one lady faints upon hearing Huxley's rebuttal and has to be carried outside. The crowd now erupts in shouts, laughter, and a general uproar. In the midst of the melee, a gray-haired man in a rear admiral's uniform stands up, holding a large Bible high over his head, and tries to make himself heard. It's Robert FitzRoy, now head of a meteorological department in London and aged well beyond his years. Darwin's book is an abomination, the former sea captain shouts; Darwin's ideas contradict Genesis. Wrote one observer, "Lifting an immense Bible first with both and afterwards with one hand over his head, [he] solemnly implored the audience to believe God rather than man."

Few hear the former captain, however, amid the great tumult. A despondent FitzRoy leaves quietly afterward. Five years later, at the age of fifty-nine, FitzRoy becomes increasingly more susceptible to depression. One morning, the former sea captain walks into his bathroom and slits his throat open from ear to ear. The second captain of the HMS Beagle to commit suicide.

I arrive in Ushuaia (oo SHWHY yah) in April, the beginning of fall in Patagonia. Ushuaia sits on the Argentine side of the Beagle Channel, on the southernmost rim of Tierra del Fuego Island. It's a port town, nestled on a U-shaped bay at the base of snow-covered mountains. The mountains themselves are the southernmost extension of the Andes— a tapering spine of broken gray granite, looking as stark and ragged as shark's teeth projecting from a lower jawbone.

Ushuaia is a Yámana word that means "inner harbor to the westward." It's an assortment of A-framed houses and buildings with roofs of iron and zinc and resembles a ski resort. I walk down its main street, Avenida San Martín, crowded with glass-fronted restaurants. Many display racks of lamb roasting over a fire. Pedestrians trundle past, bundled up in jackets, some headed down to the port where ships leave for Antarctica. I stop by a bakery and buy a warm *churro* stuffed with sweet *manjar blanco*, then pass by a fish market, the *Pesquera del Beagle* (Beagle Fish Market). On its front window is painted a large, southern red king crab—a five-foot-long monstrosity that looks as close to an alien life-form as anything on the planet. King crabs scuttle about in the dark at depths of up to two thousand feet. Above the town rises a thick forest of beech and evergreen trees that stretches up the flanks of the mountains. Now that it's fall, the trees are a tangle of rust, mustard, and pastel-yellow colors; some are so permanently bent over by the northerly winds that sailors once fashioned the trunks into curved braces for their boats. Beyond the treeline rises an expanse of naked black rock, then white ice and snow. Because Ushuaia is so far south, snowline here begins at a mere fifteen hundred feet.

The streets of the city climb steeply from the waterline to the hills, like a Patagonian San Francisco; here and there the corners are adorned with street signs that bear names such as Roberto Fitz Roy, Carlos

Darwin, and even Fuegia Basket. In mid-January 1833, Darwin, Fitz-Roy, Jemmy Button, York Minster, and Fuegia Basket sailed past this uninhabited bay in a flotilla of four small boats, on their way to Navarino Island, on the other side of the Beagle Channel; it was the last leg of their journey from England to return Jemmy and his companions to their native land. Wrote Darwin:

> As we proceeded along the Beagle Channel, the scenery assumed a peculiar and very magnificent character . . . The mountains were here [along Ushuaia Bay] about three thousand feet high, and terminated in sharp and jagged points. They rose in one unbroken sweep from the water's edge, and were covered to the height of fourteen or fifteen hundred feet by the dusky-coloured forest.

Jemmy's tribe, the Yámana, inhabited both sides of the Beagle Channel, crossing the open expanse with their families in bark canoes and living in numerous temporary encampments along its shores. Not surprisingly, after FitzRoy and Darwin's final departure in 1834, news about the three natives who had once visited England became scarce. For roughly the next five decades, however, Jemmy or Fuegia Basket would occasionally be spotted by foreign sailors, who were no doubt surprised to see a bark canoe approach their ship from some inhospitable shore and a naked "savage" with long matted hair shout out a greeting in English. Wrote one English sailor, who visited Wulaia Bay in 1855 and encountered Jemmy Button more than twenty years after FitzRoy had departed,

> Well, I'm blowed! What a queer thing! This beats me out and out! There's that blear-eyed, dirty-looking, naked savage, speaking as clearly to the skipper as one of us; and I be hanged, too, if he isn't as perlite as if he'd been brought up in a parlour, instead of born in this outlandish place!—Well, it is queer, and so is all the whole affair . . . lots of wild barbarians civil to us—and now one of 'em talking as plain as ourselves! It knocks me down quite!

Fourteen years later, in 1869, London's South American Missionary Society established an Anglican mission on Ushuaia Bay, consisting of a single metal house, twenty by ten feet, surrounded by a number of native Yámana huts. Two years later, a young English missionary, Thomas Bridges, arrived to take over as its head. Bridges was twenty-nine years old, stood five foot eight, had black curly hair, dark eyes, and a high forehead. Arriving with him was his English wife of two years, Mary. The Bridgeses soon had a son, Lucas, the first nonnative to be born in Ushuaia. Many years later, Lucas wrote about what it must have been like when his parents first arrived:

> As they were rowed ashore . . . this Ushuaia, of which she [Bridges's wife, Mary] had heard so much, was new, strange and rather frightening. Behind the . . . [pebble] beach the grassland stretched away to meet a sudden steep [hill] less than a quarter of a mile from the shore. Between shore and hill were scattered wigwams, half-buried hovels made of branches roofed with turf and grass, smelling strongly . . . of smoke and decomposed whale-blubber or refuse flung close outside. Round the wigwams dark figures, some partially draped in otter-skins, others almost naked, stood or squatted, gazing curiously at the little boat as it approached the beach.
>
> Some canoes lay hauled up on the . . . [shore], and in others women were fishing or paddling alongside the schooner, trying to barter fish or limpets for knives or those great delicacies introduced by the foreigners, biscuits and sugar. These . . . [people] were wanderers, attracted by the wish to see what the white men were doing in Ushuaia.

Thomas Bridges, who had been abandoned as a baby and left in a basket on a bridge in Bristol, England (hence his last name), was adopted by missionaries. His adoptive parents later moved to the Falklands, a cluster of islands that lies about three hundred miles off the coast of southern Argentina. By the late 1850s, missionaries from the Falklands had begun to transport small numbers of Yámana Indians from

Patagonia to the Falkland mission on Keppel Island, in an effort to learn their language and to Christianize them. Growing up amid the visiting Yámanas and their children, Bridges eventually became the first non-native to become fluent in their language. It was also on Keppel Island that Bridges began to write down Yámana words and expressions, a lifelong interest that eventually resulted in the only Yámana dictionary ever created. Gradually, as he learned their language, Bridges began to realize that many famous explorers—including Darwin, who believed the short, powerful natives had previously been cannibals—had gotten the Yámanas completely wrong. As his son Lucas later wrote in his classic book *The Uttermost Part of the Earth,*

> The belief that the Fuegians were cannibals was not the only mistake Charles Darwin made about them. Listening to their speech . . . [Darwin] got the impression that they were repeating the same phrases over and over again, and therefore came to the conclusion that something like one hundred words would cover the whole language. We who learned as children to speak . . . [Yámana] know that, within its own limitations, it is infinitely richer and more expressive than English or Spanish. My father's . . . *Dictionary* . . . contains no fewer than 32,000 [Yámana] words and inflections, the number of which might have been greatly increased without departing from correct speech.

The Yámana language, for example, has five different words for snow while English has only one. English also has about seventeen different words for family relationships while Yámana has about fifty, and so on.

The more he got to know them, the more Bridges also grew to respect the Yámanas' ability to flourish in an area where Europeans—convinced of their own superiority—had previously been unable to survive. Just twenty years earlier, for example, a group of Anglican missionaries had attempted to found a mission on Picton Island in the Beagle Channel. The seven men—unable to speak the local language and with no experience whatsoever hunting or fishing in Patagonia—slowly starved to death. Next to the body of the reverend leading the group, fragments of a letter were found that he'd written, while delirious, about the death of one of their members:

> The Lord has seen fit to call home another of our little company. Our dear departed brother left the [beached] boat on Tuesday afternoon, and has not since returned. Doubtless he is in the presence of his Redeemer, whom he served faithfully . . . days without food . . . heaven.

Elsewhere, the same drama had been repeated throughout the centuries—beginning with a Spanish attempt to colonize the area in 1583. In that year twenty-four ships had set out for Patagonia from Spain. Eight subsequently sank in fierce storms, and all but four of the remainder soon abandoned the expedition. The surviving ships entered the Magellan Strait and unloaded three hundred Spanish colonists in a bay on the strait's northern shore. All eventually died from starvation and, fittingly, the area was later christened Port Famine. By the time Thomas Bridges arrived in Ushuaia, European explorers had studded the rugged topography of Patagonia with names that described their frequent life-and-death struggles with the elements: Port Famine, Desolation Island, Fury Harbor, Useless Bay, Mount Misery, and so on.

The Yámanas and their ancestors, by contrast, had lived successfully amid the islands and channels of Patagonia for at least the last six thousand years. As did many other indigenous groups, they used names that described the ecology of the land, which mirrored their understanding of it. There was, for example, *Tushcapalan*, or the Kelp Island of the Flying Loggerhead Duck; *Lapa-yusha*, the Coast of Conch Shells; *Alacushwaia*, the Bay of the Flapping Loggerhead Duck; *Tuwu-jlumbiwaia*, Black Heron Harbor; and so on. The food they subsisted upon—seals, cormorants, penguins, fish, birds, eggs, mussels, and other shellfish—were abundant, if you knew where and when to look for them. Wulaia Bay—the heart of Yámana territory on Navarino Island, where Darwin and FitzRoy had returned Jemmy Button—is by most accounts a biological wonderland. The sheltered bay's shallow waters possess innumerable ecological niches that are filled with a vast smorgasbord of food for anyone skilled at harvesting it. As Jemmy Button explained to a shocked FitzRoy on their last meeting, he was "hearty, sir, never better," and had "plenty fruits, plenty birdies," "ten [roughly two-hundred-pound] guanacos in snow [winter] time," and "too much fish."

Indeed, Bridges gradually learned that the Yámanas knew not only how to fish, but also how to harpoon seals and sea lions, dive for mussels and shellfish, build canoes, construct shelters, skillfully navigate Patagonia's unpredictable seas, conduct important rituals, recount myths, marry, raise children—and have fun. Charles Darwin—who knew nothing about anthropology and regarded the Yámanas as "savages"—nevertheless recognized that Jemmy "did not wish to go back to England." Yet, despite his repugnance to matted hair and seal oil, Darwin was nevertheless able to understand the essential core of the issue: that is, whether or not a "savage" in his natural environment was content. "I do not now doubt," Darwin later wrote, "that . . . [Jemmy] will be as happy as, perhaps happier than if he had never left his own country."

The Achilles' heel of the Yámanas, it turned out, was not the "inhospitable" nature of Patagonia, but rather two riches they "possessed" that were soon coveted by foreigners. The first was the newly discovered shipping lane connecting Europe with Asia, which the Yámana unfortunately lived alongside. The second was the abundant marine life—the penguins, whales, sea lions, and other marine animals that thrived in their waters. Europeans and Americans, for example, both coveted whales—especially sperm whales—for their oil and blubber, in addition to seals for their pelts. In fact, Captain FitzRoy himself had marveled at the sheer abundance of its wildlife during his first voyage to Patagonia in 1828–1830:

> In the tideway, at the narrow passage, the sea teemed with fish; over which hovered . . . [cormorants] and other sea-fowl, preying upon

the small fry that were trying to elude their voracious enemies, the porpoises and seals, thousands of which were seen sporting about as we proceeded on our way. Whales were also numerous in the vicinity, probably because of an abundance of the small red shrimp [krill], which constitutes their principal food.

FitzRoy, to his credit, clearly understood a food chain when he saw one. The coastal areas of southern Patagonia actually contain some of the richest upwellings of nutrient-rich waters in the world. Entire food chains as intricate as rain forests flourish here, beginning with microscopic plankton and ending with squid, toothfish, seals, albatross, whales, and—in the area of the Beagle Channel for thousands of years—harpoon-wielding Yámana natives. The ocean might be cold, frigid even, but it was filled with wildlife that could be hunted.

Eleven years after the *Beagle*'s final visit, a twenty-two-year-old sailor and future novelist named Herman Melville rounded Cape Horn and sailed through Yámana territory in 1844. Melville's ship was part of a veritable armada of American and European whaling and sealing ships. In Melville's most famous novel, *Moby Dick*, his character Ishmael explains why he sought whales in such distant parts of the world:

> Chief among these motives was the overwhelming idea of the great whale himself. Such a portentous and mysterious monster roused all my curiosity . . . these, with all the attending marvels of a thousand Patagonian sights and sounds, helped to sway me to my wish. With other men, perhaps, such things would not have been inducements; but as for me, I am tormented with an everlasting itch for things remote. I love to sail forbidden seas, and land on barbarous coasts . . . [although] it is but well to be on friendly terms with all the inmates of the place one lodges in.

Just a few years before Melville's visit, the crew of another American whaling ship—perhaps wishing to be "on friendly terms" with the local "inmates"—was surprised when a naked woman in a bark canoe approached them, hailing them in English. It was Fuegia Basket, a dozen years after her return from England—the only woman in Patagonia who spoke English. According to members of the crew, Fuegia called out, "How do? I have been to Plymouth and London!" Later, she conversed in English with the captain and "stayed a few days." Then, just as abruptly, she climbed back into her canoe and soon disappeared amid rugged headlands that were bordered by the sea.

In Ushuaia I walk along a peninsula that stretches out into the bay, forming one shore of the harbor. The windswept peninsula is covered in tall yellow grass and affords wonderful views of the Beagle Channel. In the distance Navarino Island looms up, a smudge of green with white mountains; to the east lies the city, spread out along the harbor's north-ern shore. I wander about the peninsula, my jacket zipped tight due to a biting cold wind, searching for the site of the original Anglican mis-sion and Thomas Bridges's home. Ushuaia no longer has an Anglican church but has a Catholic one, *Nuestra Señora de La Merced* (Our Lady of Mercy). The Anglican mission shut its doors in 1910. I walk by a cluster of old naval buildings with peeling white paint and several large rusted anchors lying abandoned in front, then climb over a metal fence. Along the top of the bluff I finally find a white triangular monument, about five feet high, marking the site of Bridges's home. The monument is studded with a variety of small bronze plaques and one of them, fas-tened here in 1998, says

En Memoria de los misioneros Anglicanos que murieron hace 100 años:
Thomas Bridges, July 15, 1898.

("In Memory of the Anglican Missionaries who died one hundred years ago"). The tiny plaque is the only reminder of the original English settlement in Ushuaia. The English, after all, are not popular here— a much larger monument stands beside the quay that reads *Las Malvi-nas son Nuestras*, meaning "The Falklands Are Ours," placed there after the Falklands War, and using the Spanish name for the islands, *Las Malvinas*.

The Bridgeses lived on this peninsula for a dozen years, gradually teaching an increasingly sedentary group of Yámanas the arts of European agriculture and how to raise sheep and cows. In a sense, they were reproducing European subsistence patterns along a narrow stretch of wild Patagonian coast. In 1882, ten years after the Bridgeses arrived, a French physician, Paul Hyades, visited the mission. The doctor was part of a French scientific expedition staying on nearby Hoste Island and was curious about the mission's inhabitants. He later wrote that

> An impression of melancholy imposes itself when one first sees the few English houses, all of the material brought from Europe, installed in this somber surrounding, as if lost at the end of the world . . . This impression lingers when one disembarks and becomes aware of the natives . . . dressed as they are, possessing relatively comfortable huts and some even owners of well-kept gardens. But none seems any happier than the Fuegians we just left [on Hoste Island], naked in their canoes, going as they well please, in search of their daily sustenance.

Eventually, anthropologists discovered that going naked was a useful strategy for the Yámanas. Since rain and water spray were constant, the Yámanas wore no clothes because clothes quickly became wet and were practically impossible to dry. Instead, the Yámanas covered themselves with seal or whale oil, which served as a protective barrier, and never went anywhere without taking fire with them. While it was the woman's job to dive for mussels and shellfish in the frigid waters, Yámana men tended the fire, made the canoes, and hunted seals and other animals. When the Yámanas got wet, they dried themselves next to the nearest fire. Europeans who got caught in wet clothing in Patagonia, by contrast, often died of pneumonia or hypothermia. When missionaries began to insist that the natives wear clothes, scores of Yámanas soon died as a result. The missionaries learned too late that even the Yámanas' long matted hair, which the missionaries encouraged them to cut off, was useful: it served as insulation against the frigid weather. To make matters worse, the Yámanas who frequented the mission and hence tried to adapt to soggy clothing, short hair, and a more sedentary lifestyle, also caught European-introduced diseases. As the French doctor Hyades later wrote,

> More than one of those . . . [Yámanas] who passed one or two years in . . . [Ushuaia], and through work and good behavior acquired a little house, and a cultivated plot of land, suddenly, without regret, left all their possessions to resume their life in the canoe. These savages are aware that those who settle in . . . [Ushuaia] rapidly lose their habit of supplying their own needs by means of the traditional industries. Their sons no longer know how to make canoes, nor harpoons to hunt . . . [sea otters] or seals, and they find themselves dependent on the good graces of the English for their food. They also flee from [Ushuaia] . . . because the sickness there is more fatal than elsewhere, be it consumption or other imported diseases.

Adding to the gradual loss of their culture and their exposure to imported diseases loomed something equally dangerous: the loss of their native foods.

"The destruction of the seal and sea lion rookeries was the beginning of the end for the Yámanas and other coastal sea nomads" says Ernesto Piana, a wiry, gray-haired archaeologist who has worked in the Ushuaia area for the last thirty years. Piana, a chain-smoking Argentine, is passionate about the Patagonian archipelago and its wild, windswept seas. He works for CADIC (*Centro Austral de Investigaciones Científicas*), a scientific investigation center housed in a group of buildings that resembles an ochre-colored naval ship run aground. The center lies just to the west of where the Bridges once had their mission.

The Yámanas' ancestors, Piana tells me, arrived some six thousand years ago, after the retreat of the last glaciers. Before that, the Beagle Channel and the Strait of Magellan had been filled with ice; only when the Earth warmed did the channels fill with water and Tierra del Fuego become an island. For the next six thousand years, Piana says, the Yámanas and their ancestors had a pretty smooth time of it, until the arrival of the first Europeans.

"The Europeans sailed down in their ships and began slaughtering animals in their rookeries," Piana says. "The Yámanas never did that. The Europeans not only wiped out the local population of whales, but they also wiped out penguins, seals, and sea lions.

"The Yámanas inhabited these islands and coasts for thousands of years," he continues, tipping some cigarette ash into a small glass container. "There are thousands of middens along the coast, *thousands.*"

Middens, Piana explains, are the mounds of discarded mussel and other shells that pile up after years of harvesting and eating shellfish. Heated in a fire, bivalves relax their muscles, the shells open, and their hot contents can be quickly devoured. The Yámana then threw the shells onto a pile outside their huts. *Ondagumakona* is a Yámana word that means "to pick mussels off clusters, one by one, from a canoe."

Piana takes a pull on his cigarette and fixes me with intense dark eyes. His ancestors were Italian. "The Yámanas' food supplies collapsed," he says. "They began to starve to death. By the time the missionaries began to gather them together in the late nineteenth century, they were already weakened. Then the epidemics arrived."

Jemmy Button, it so happened, was one of the first to go. Inoculated against smallpox in England in 1833, Jemmy was last seen in Wulaia Bay in 1863 by a group of visiting Anglican missionaries. A few months after they left, an epidemic hit Navarino Island. Scores of Yámanas died, including Jemmy, who was in his mid-fifties at the time. A missionary who met Jemmy's wife soon afterward wrote that "Her face was visibly impressed with sorrow; and, pointing with her finger towards the sky, she gave me to understand by looks more than words, the cause of her grief, and how great it was." Jemmy's family cremated his body, as was customary, on a funeral pyre.

So ended the life of the man who as a fourteen-year-old boy had been whisked away from his canoe by foreigners, taken to England, and presented to the king and queen—only to be felled later in life by one of the foreigners' many diseases. The epidemics—brought to the area no doubt by the fur sealers and whalers—soon became common. Tuberculosis hit the Ushuaia mission in 1882, killing dozens of natives, none of whom had resistance to the bacterial disease. Two years later, a measles epidemic struck Ushuaia and the surrounding area with devastating effect. Lucas Bridges, Thomas Bridges's son, remembered that "the natives were dying at such a rate that it was impossible to dig graves fast enough. In outlying districts the dead were merely put outside the wigwams or . . . carried or dragged to the nearest bushes." Sickness then struck Navarino Island again, the natives' impermanent huts quickly filling with the dead. A look at the census records for the Yámanas in the area shows a traditional population pyramid turned completely upside down:

1833: @ 3,000 Yámanas

1908: 170 Yámanas

1947: 43 Yámanas

2014: 1 Yámana

The inverse was true for Ushuaia's nonnative population:

1871 3 English inhabitants (Thomas Bridges, his wife, and their daughter)

1914 1,558 inhabitants

1947 2,182 inhabitants

2014 65,000 inhabitants

The Bridgeses did what they could to try to stave off the rapid decline of the Yámanas but, having no control over the epidemics, there was little they could do. Bridges, however, did begin to wonder whether he should remove his family—and some of the Yámanas—to a more isolated area, beyond the reach of the sealers, whalers, and Argentine settlers. Eventually, he began to fixate on an untouched area beside a small bay, about sixty miles east of Ushuaia. He would later call it Harberton.

It's a two-hour drive to the *estancia*, or ranch, of Harberton, which lies along the rich blue waters of the Beagle Channel, on the southern edge of Tierra del Fuego. The dirt road wends its way around low snow-covered mountains, through groves of birch and coigüe trees, around small streams that have been dammed by imported Canadian beavers, and over small wooden bridges. A-framed houses appear now and then, tucked away amid the trees, isolated and alone. Gradually, the homes become fewer and fewer until they disappear altogether. During winter, the road is clotted with snow; only if you have snow shoes or a four-wheel drive can you get through.

It's midmorning when I reach the edge of the ranch, a cluster of old red-roofed white buildings set amid rolling hills of knee-high grass and scattered forest, alongside a bay on the Beagle Channel. The ranch is called Harberton after the town in England where Mary Bridges was born. In 1884, as epidemics raked Ushuaia and the Argentine Navy arrived to formally install a subprefecture there—thus finally taking possession of the area—Bridges clearly saw the writing on the wall. Lowering the British flag over the mission and running up the Argentine flag, Bridges soon petitioned the Argentine government for land on which to establish a sheep farm. Argentina had just spent the previous five decades successfully clearing the *pampas* of the Tehuelche Indians, who lived further north amid the vast *pampas* and who hunted guanacos. Evidently, the government was feeling magnanimous as it eventually ceded Bridges fifty thousand acres. A few years later, the now forty-four-year-old reverend resigned from the mission, then left with his family and a large group of Yámanas, launching himself into the sheep-raising business.

Although Bridges was the first to do so, other settlers soon began carving up the island of Tierra del Fuego, about the size of Ireland, into sheep ranches. This despite the fact that much of the island was already inhabited by the Selknam (also known as the Ona) Indians, who lived by hunting guanacos. While Bridges made a point of finding work for the natives, most of his fellow ranchers did everything they could to rid the island of its original inhabitants, some of whom had turned to hunting sheep as the guanacos disappeared. A few settlers had even begun hiring hunting parties to massacre native families en masse in their camps.

Those few who survived were forcibly taken to a Salesian mission

on Dawson Island in the Magellan Strait. There, the formerly independent natives were soon relegated to a sedentary lifestyle of gardening,
sewing, woodworking, and prayer. Here too, however, in this last artificially concentrated population, epidemics soon arrived. An Italian priest
named Father Fagnano, who gradually witnessed the natives' dwindling
numbers, actually wept during his last visit to the Dawson mission in
1902; he had been unable to ignore the fact that the number of crosses
in the mission's cemetery was now larger than the remaining population. Another Salesian wrote, in a way summing up the entire missionary effort in Patagonia, that "[Sometimes] an action that requires [so
much missionary] sacrifice does not guarantee success." Of the one
thousand Indians who entered the Dawson Mission between 1889 and
1898, only twenty-five were left by the time the mission closed in 1911.
All the rest had died.

Lucas Bridges, who spoke both Yámana and Ona, later described a
visit to the Dawson mission at its height in the late 1890s:

> I was on a little steamer which touched at . . . Dawson Island, where,
> it was said, about seven hundred Ona were confined. The women
> were employed making blankets and knitting garments under the
> training of the [Salesian] Sisters, and a number of men were working
> in a saw-mill cutting timber, largely for shipment to Punta Arenas.
> When I went into the saw-mill and made a remark to these fellows
> in their own language, they crowded around me.
>
> . . . These Indian workers were "decently clad" in discarded
> or shop-soiled garments, generally some sizes too small for them.
> Looking at them, I could not help picturing them standing in their
> old haunts, proud and painted, armed with bows and arrows and
> dressed, as of yore, in *goöchilh, oil* and *jamni* (head-dress, robe and
> moccasins).
>
> Some of them knew me by sight and many others by report. I am
> afraid that the work came to a standstill and the lay brothers showed
> some annoyance at the interruption, so I retired. Later, however,
> when they broke off work, I was able to have a talk with Hektliohlh
> [a native Bridges knew]. He seemed to have nothing whatever to

complain of with regard to his treatment, but was terribly sad at his captivity. Looking with yearning towards the distant mountains of his native land, he said:

"*Shouwe t-maten ya.*" ("Longing is killing me.")

Which was actually the case, for he did not survive very long. Liberty is dear to white men; to untamed wanderers of the wilds it is an absolute necessity.

Lucas's father, Thomas Bridges, died in 1898, of stomach cancer, at the age of fifty-six. His mother, Mary, remained a few years at Harberton and then returned to England, where she passed away some two decades later. The couple's three sons, Despard, Lucas, and Will, eventually married and continued to run the Harberton sheep farm, which gradually grew and prospered. Today the ranch is still there, run now by Thomas Bridges's great-great nephew, Thomas Goodall, and his American-born wife, Natalie. The *estancia* no longer operates as a sheep farm but as a tourist attraction: it now caters to tourists who want to visit the oldest ranch in Tierra del Fuego.

The main house—built in Devon, England, then disassembled, shipped, and reassembled here more than a century ago—has a tea room with large glass windows that look out onto the bay. Visitors here can order scones, coffee, tea, and jam. On the hillsides sprout beech trees dripping with pale green lichen. Some of their branches are marbled with an edible orange fungus that Charles Darwin discovered and is now named *Cyttaria darwinii*. Ancient middens of crumbling mussel shells also abound. I stroll about the grounds and find a midden near the Bridges family cemetery. The mound is knee-high, about six feet across, and composed of ink-colored mussel shells. I lift some up; they are soft with age and crumble between my fingers. Years ago—a hundred, a thousand?—a native woman once dove into the sea, wrestled these mussels off the ocean floor, then swam back to her canoe, depositing them inside. Some of the middens have native skeletons buried within: a few small children in one; an adult woman in another. The mounds are now the only visible signs that indigenous people once lived here.

Inside the main house Thomas Goodall stands behind a counter in the wooden tea room. He's in his midseventies, wears blue overalls, has yellow, peg-like teeth, speaks Spanish with an unusual accent that includes English-pronounced *r*'s, and tells me bluntly that he does not "do" interviews. His wife, Natalie, on the other hand, is seventy-five and amiable. She's a scientist and admits that her husband can be abrupt.

"He was like that when I first visited here, on a lark, in 1962," she tells me. Natalie is from Ohio, went to Kent State University, has a master's degree in biology, and taught school. She has blue eyes and curly gray hair and is presently laid up in bed after a knee operation. Her bedroom is stocked with wood furniture, photos of families and friends, and piles of papers that she's working on—mainly a variety of science reports.

When she was young and landlocked, Natalie dreamed of escaping the Midwest and finding adventure. By chance she read Lucas Bridges's account of life at the southern extreme of Tierra del Fuego. It was while reading those pages that she *knew* she had to visit Ushuaia and the Bridgeses' *estancia* at Harberton.

"There was no road out here [to Harberton] then," she says, "no visitors. I arrived in Ushuaia on a DC-3 plane. Shortly after I got there I requested to visit Harberton by radio. Tom was managing the ranch and refused," she says, laughing. "He didn't want to have anything to do with me!" Natalie was persistent, however, and eventually found her way out to the ranch—staying for three weeks. "Tom wasn't very friendly" she says, "but his mother was." That was in December of 1962. Somehow, during those three weeks, something clicked and Tom thawed out a bit. He later visited Natalie in Ohio. A month later, the two were married. Natalie has been living in Tierra del Fuego, the tip of Patagonia, ever since.

"I first began studying the flora," she says. "At the same time, I started noticing bones and skulls washed up on the coast, so I began collecting them. Dolphin skulls, whale skulls, things like that."

In 1973 scientists from a US expedition to the Antarctic whose mission was to study whales and dolphins paid a visit to Harberton.

"Would you like to see some skulls?" Natalie asked them. They nodded, she said, "but you could tell they were bored." Fifteen minutes later, the scientists were slapping each other on the back. Among Natalie's collection, it turned out, they discovered extremely rare skulls of the spectacled porpoise, a dolphin that looks like a tiny version of a killer whale. Until then, only eight specimens existed in the world. Natalie had found thirty-five. "If you want more, I'll go find some," she nonchalantly said—and she did.

Soon, Natalie was receiving funds from the National Science Foundation and later from the National Geographic Society, whose magazine profiled her in 1971. Natalie now runs the "Southernmost Marine Bird and Mammal Museum, Acatushún," based at Harberton. The museum and research center is full of the reassembled skeletons of spectacled and Commerson's dolphins, beaked whales, Southern fur and leopard seals, and other creatures found in the southern seas. By now, Natalie and her assistants have collected about three hundred spectacled porpoise skulls and more than 2,700 marine mammal skeletons. In 1998 Kent State University awarded her an honorary doctorate.

As I prepare to leave, Natalie tells me that last year, some forty-five seals washed up on the coast, when usually there are only one or two. "It may be that the ocean is getting warmer," she says, "due to global warming." Higher temperatures can kill off the krill, she says, and without the krill, the seals and other marine life can starve. "It's all about ecology."

I ask her about the name of her museum, Acatushún. "It's a Yámana word," she says. "But I don't know what it means. It's what they called this part of the coast."

"Are there any natives who still speak Yámana?"

"Just one," she says. "On Navarino Island. In Puerto Williams."

She runs a hand down her leg cast and readjusts herself in bed.

"Her name is Cristina Calderón."

Three days later, I'm on a Zodiac crossing the Beagle Channel, from the Argentine port of Ushuaia to Chile's Navarino Island. The inflatable boat has a low plastic roof for protection against the waves. The sky is gray, the sea the color of slate and with strong swells. The skipper stands in the open behind, dressed in foul-weather gear that includes a ski mask, goggles, and a baseball hat. *Es feo* ("It's ugly"), he tells me bluntly before we take off. Sea birds dip and rise as we skim along the backs of cresting swells, sometimes slamming into the troughs. The Zodiac shudders, then scoots up another swell again. About midway, we see the fluke of a whale.

"Humpback!" the skipper shouts.

Looking back across the Beagle Channel, I can see the crescent harbor of Ushuaia and the final, dragon-like tail of the Andes Mountains, stretched out behind it in a rather majestic and jagged chain that eventually slinks into the sea further south at Cape Horn. To the north rise two snowcapped peaks, obscured by clouds. One is Mount Darwin; two hundred miles further north is Mount FitzRoy—both Andean peaks now pay homage to a naturalist and a captain, once genial dining companions—whose voyage through this area ultimately changed the world.

On Navarino Island we disembark at a tiny port that consists of a small bay and a single wooden wharf. We then transfer to a mud-spattered SUV and begin heading south, following a dirt road that skirts through the forest and along the coast, the car jouncing and hot inside, the sea looking blue and cool and inviting. About an hour south, a woman flags us down, and we stop and let her in. She wears a long checkered coat, is about sixty, and has lived on Navarino Island for fifteen years. She has a face as lined and weathered by the elements as granite that has been scoured by glaciers. The trees here, too, are contorted, bent permanently southward from the constant winds. The woman tells me she's been out cutting firewood and will return to pick it up in a few days.

"For the winter," she says.

Another hour south we arrive in Puerto Williams, a town of twenty-two hundred inhabitants. Those who live here boast of living in the southernmost city in the world. It is, if your criteria for a "city" is a few thousand inhabitants. If not, then the sixty thousand people who live in Ushuaia, thirty miles across the Beagle Channel in Argentina, can claim the title.

The afternoon is sunny and the air freshly scrubbed from rain. I walk down a street, the gabled houses in town all brilliantly lit, their corrugated iron roofs so many rectangles and squares of pale green, blue, black, or red. Piles of firewood lie stacked alongside or in front of each house—the remains of coigüe or lenga beech trees. All heating in Puerto Williams comes from the small hatcheted pieces of wood that are thrown into metal furnaces. Outside, small round metal chimneys poke through the roofs, exhaling constant plumes of black and milk-colored smoke over town.

It's late in the afternoon by the time I find a fisherman's house that doubles as a bed and breakfast. The owner's name is Nelson. He's brown skinned with dark eyes and shows me to a room that is heated with hot water pipes. The bedroom's only window is already frosted. Nelson's originally from Concepción, on Chile's northern coast. He is forty-two years old and has been a fisherman all his life. Ten years ago, he risked setting crab pots down in an area where no fisherman had dared to go crabbing before, due to its treacherous nature. Nelson soon hit the jackpot, finding so many Southern king crabs and making so much money that he was able to buy his present house with cash. Nelson christened his new place the Hostal Paso McKinlay, named after the channel where he'd made his fortune.

"The crabs were this size," he says, holding his thick, lined hands out for a four-foot spread. I ask him where, after a lifetime spent on the sea, the roughest seas are. He thinks a minute, then says "Las Malvinas" (the Falklands). He shakes his head slowly from side to side. *Es lo peor*, (It's the worst), he says.

Sixty miles northwest of Puerto Williams, on the back side of Navarino island, lies Wulaia Bay, which I reach a few days later. Wulaia is still accessible only by boat as there are scarcely any roads on the island. It's the same bay where Darwin and FitzRoy left Jemmy Button, York Minster, and Fuegia Basket in 1833. The bay is surrounded on three sides by tall, forest-covered hills that slope down to the water, while the bay itself is dotted with tiny forested islets, low to the water and looking like the overturned hulls of boats. I follow a path up into the hills, the trail covered in small, fall-colored beech leaves, then emerge onto a bluff with magnificent views over the bay. It has recently rained, so the ground is cold and damp. Water drips from the trees.

Wulaia was once the heart of Yámana territory, and the area is still strewn with abundant shell middens. One hundred and seventy-eight years ago, the HMS *Beagle* anchored here and was soon surrounded by dozens of canoes filled with excited Yámana Indians. Other canoes remained out on the bay, the women fishing or diving as children cried and the smoke from small fires in the canoes, set upon wet clay, curled up into the sky. Now the bay is quiet and eerie. There are no signs of life other than birds calling in the forest or trees moving in the wind. The area where Jemmy and the *Beagle*'s crew once created gardens is now knee-high in yellow grass. In the distance, clouds shift their shapes, slowly scudding along the sea. To the north, I can just see Button Island, green and forested, where Jemmy lived and where his body was later cremated. Now, not a soul lives there.

In 1873, nine years after Jemmy died, a canoe showed up at Ushuaia, across the Beagle Channel. Inside was Fuegia Basket, who had not been seen in years. Thomas Bridges had taken up residence in Ushuaia only a year earlier, but he of course had heard of her. As Lucas Bridges recounted,

> It was my father's first meeting with her. He found her strong and well; short, thickset and with many teeth missing from a mouth that was large even for a Fuegian. When he tried sounding her memory, she recollected London and Miss Jenkins, whose special charge she had been. She also retained memories of Captain FitzRoy and the good ship Beagle, and recalled such words as "knife," "fork," and "beads." When my mother showed her two children . . . she seemed greatly pleased, and said "Little boy, little gal." All else she appeared

to have forgotten, including the art of sitting on a chair, for when offered one she squatted beside it on the floor.

Fuegia's husband, York Minster, it turned out, had been killed years earlier, she said, in retaliation for the murder of another man. Fuegia had remarried and was now in her early fifties. Although Bridges did his utmost to get her to recall her religious training, "all recollection of it had faded entirely from her mind."

A decade later, in 1883, two years after Darwin died, Thomas Bridges came across Fuegia one last time, on what is now called Cook Island, at the northern end of the Beagle Channel. "She was about sixty-two years of age," Lucas Bridges wrote, "and nearing her end. He found her in a very weak condition and an unhappy state of mind and did his best to cheer her with the beautiful Biblical promises in which he himself so firmly believed." It was the final time, he said, that Fuegia Basket—the last of the natives who had once visited England—was ever seen.

A few days after visiting Wulaia Bay, I walk south out of Puerto Williams, along the road leading to Ukika, the Yámana settlement. In the early part of the nineteenth century, the only remaining Anglican missionary in the area, Reverend Williams, petitioned the Chilean government for land for the Yámanas. The government granted it at Mejillones, which is Spanish for "mussels." Mejillones is a small bay on the northwestern shores of Navarino Island; it was the only land the Yámanas ever received. For years, many Yámana families lived along the bay's edge, in wooden houses with zinc roofs, fishing, diving for mussels, tending small herds of sheep, and occasionally hiring themselves out as workers on various ranches. In 1958 the Chilean Navy relocated the remaining Yámanas to a tiny settlement on the Ukika River, just east of Puerto Williams. The navy built a small cluster of wooden houses with corrugated metal siding and sloping metal roofs, set amid a grove of beech trees. I walk up to one of them, a small yellow house whose roof is a mix of rust and green paint. Smoke streams from a chimney stovepipe. I knock on the door and hear footsteps inside. The door opens, and Cristina Calderón, the last Yámana speaker on Earth, stands before me. "Come in," she says in Spanish.

Cristina is about five feet two with gray-black, shoulder-length hair parted down the middle, wide-set brown eyes, and a firm, no-nonsense face. She is eighty-three years old and was born in 1928 on a sheep ranch on Navarino Island.

"My mother, my brothers and sisters, we all spoke Yámana growing up around the house," she tells me, balancing her great-niece, four-year-old Tamara, on her knee.

"There used to be more of us speakers, but they died. The last person I could speak my language with was my sister, Úrsula. She died four years ago."

Úrsula, she says, loved Mejillones, or Mussels, Bay. When she grew ill, she kept saying that she wanted to return there.

"Her daughter took her there finally," Cristina says, "just before she died."

Now no one lives on the bay. Only the Yámana cemetery remains, rising from a grassy field alongside the road. The cemetery is an assortment of wooden crosses, surrounded by a wicker fence and backed by trees that look out over the Beagle Channel.

Cristina's father disappeared soon after she was born, she says, and her mother died when she was five. Her mother's sister and her uncle then raised her and her six brothers and sisters. She never went to school, she said, because there was no school where they lived.

When Cristina was sixteen, she found work on a sheep ranch, helping out in the kitchen and taking care of the owner's children. Eventually, she married a Spanish-speaking Chilean. She and her husband found work in the 1950s on Harberton Ranch, with the Goodall family, the descendants of Thomas Bridges. "That was before Thomas Goodall was married," she says. She lived in a small cottage for ten years on the Harberton property and has fond memories of living there. Cristina eventually had six children; all work as fishermen except for one who works on a cruise ship. None of them speak Yámana.

"I never married a Yámana," she tells me, "so I couldn't teach my children. They grew up speaking Spanish."

A hundred years ago sixteen indigenous languages were spoken in Chile; now seven of those have already gone extinct. In the wider world, of the seven thousand or so languages that are spoken today, roughly half are spoken by fewer than three thousand people. Linguists estimate that between 50 percent and 90 percent of all of the languages presently spoken on Earth will disappear within the next fifty years.

"Languages are not simply vocabulary lists or sets of grammatical rules," says the anthropologist Wade Davis, but "old-growth forests of the mind." Languages are products of unique cultures, he says, cultures that reflect "different ways of being, thinking, and knowing." When a language goes extinct, it "reduces the entire range of the human imagination."

"What will happen to the Yámana language now," I ask Cristina, "since you're the last speaker? Is anyone else learning it?"

"My niece is," Cristina tells me. Her niece is a teacher, married to a German, and both she and her husband know some Yámana words. "My niece helped me write my book," she says.

Cristina fetches a slim red paperback and shows me its title: *Hai Kur Mamašu Shis*. It means in Yámana, "I want to tell you a story." The book is a collection of myths that she and her sister Úrsula learned from the older Yámanas when growing up. Despite the title, it's written in Spanish by her granddaughter, Cristina Zórraga, who transcribed the myths.

When she was a young girl, Cristina tells me, she witnessed the last Yámana initiation rite, what the Yámanas called the *Chexaus*. The elders built a large, oval-shaped shelter, she said. Some of the elders wore headbands of white albatross feathers, which symbolized the foam of the sea. Others dressed up as spirits, such as the fierce *winefkar* or the *yetaite*. There was nonstop singing and dancing. A fire was lit within the shelter, and two or three young teenagers, called *ushwaala*, were led inside to learn the Yámana myths, the sacred rites and songs. They were there to learn what it meant to be Yámana. The *Chexaus* was a sort of "school," Cristina says, and usually would last for weeks, even months. In the old days, if a beached whale were found, the Yámanas would gather and use the whale as an excuse to throw a *Chexaus*, as the constant supply of food allowed them to take a sort of holiday. The last *Chexaus* took place when Cristina was too young to be initiated herself. "That was the last one we ever held," she said. "It was beautiful."

I buy a copy of her book and ask her to sign it, without really thinking about the request. Cristina opens it carefully, flips a few pages, and then, on the frontispiece dedicated to her sister, Úrsula, she carefully scrawls out "c r i s t i n a," in rough letters. Each letter stands alone and looks as if it has been engraved with a penknife.

As she scrawls out her name, I suddenly realize that Cristina, the last Yámana speaker, never learned how to read or write.

Two days later I'm on a cruise ship, the *Via Australis*, heading out of Ushuaia. It's night, and the ship glides down the Beagle Channel, on its way to Cape Horn, the southernmost island off South America and the southernmost island that the Yámanas once inhabited. Nowadays on Cape Horn there's only a lighthouse run by the Chilean government and a single Chilean family, which changes every year. On the island's shore—long feared by sailors—protrude the quiet remains of shell middens. To the Yámanas, this craggy, forlorn outpost—the last outburst of the Andes—was home.

Earlier in the day, at dusk, I'd strolled along the top deck, witnessing a humpback whale lift its black fluke and then dive, slowly wending its way to winter feeding grounds off Antarctica, perhaps singing to other whales deep beneath the sea.

Cristina had told me that her son worked here, in the ship's galley, making the repeated run from Ushuaia to Cape Horn and then to Punta Arenas and back, stopping at various ports along the way. During our voyage, the ship had passed blue-green glaciers that routinely "cracked" in the sun, shifting their contents abruptly into the sea.

I ask a steward to arrange a meeting and, one night outside the galley, the door opens. A man steps out. Cristina's son is about five foot three, wears black slacks, a dark shirt, and a white apron. He has thick salt-and-pepper eyebrows, brown skin, and a puzzled look on his face. Nearly two centuries earlier, the HMS *Beagle* had cruised these same waters, taking on board a young Yámana boy known as Orundellico in his own language and Jemmy Button to others. Now, nearly two centuries later, I chat with the son of the last Yámana speaker, a man who works on a ship that caters to wealthy travelers from around the world. His name is David, he is fifty-five years old, and he tells me that he's an assistant cook.

"I never learned my mother's language," he says, looking a bit wistful. "Because my father only spoke Spanish.

"And now," he says, wiping his hands on his apron, "I'm afraid it's too late."

NOTES

PREFACE

PAGE

vii *All men dream*: Thomas Edward Lawrence, *Seven Pillars of Wisdom* (Anchor Books: New York, 1991), 24.

xix *O most serene and gracious Lord*: Pedro de Cieza de León, *The Travels of Pedro de Cieza de León* (London: Hakluyt Society, 1864), 2.

CHAPTER 1: THE HUNT FOR PABLO ESCOBAR AND THE SEARCH FOR EL DORADO (COLOMBIA)

1 *"He stated that [Colombia]"*: John Hemming, *"The Search for El Dorado"* (New York: Dutton, 1979), 101.

1 *"Sometimes I am God"*: Elizabeth Mora-Mass, *"De Medallo a 'Metrallo' "* (Bogotá: 1986), 16.

1 *"Someday, and that day may never come"*: Mario Puzo and Francis Ford Coppola, in Jenny M. Jones, *The Annotated* Godfather: *The Complete Screenplay* (New York: Black Dog & Leventhal Publishers, 2009), 26.

7 *"They came to our town"*: Roberto Escobar, *The Accountant's Story: Inside the Violent World of the Medellín Cartel* (New York: Grand Central Publishing, 2009), 7.

8 *"My mother was crying"*: Ibid., 7–8.

8 *"Our road was illuminated"*: Ibid., 8.

9 *"The immeasurable violence and pain"*: Sture Allén, *Nobel Lectures, Literature 1981–1990* (Singapore: World Scientific Publishing Company, 1993), 23.

10   *"When the Spaniards set their eyes"*: Carmen Millán de Benavides, in J. Michael
      Francis, *Invading Colombia: Spanish Accounts of the Gonzalo Jiménez de Quesada Expe-
      dition of Conquest* (Pennsylvania: Pennsylvania State University Press, 2007), 68.

10   *"Marching along on the campaign"*: Juan de San Martín and Antonio de Lebrija, in
      J. Michael Francis, *Invading Colombia*, 59–61.

10   *"The men who went on these ventures"*: John Hemming, *El Dorado*, 50.

11   *"The next day they continued"*: Anonymous, in J. Michael Francis, *Invading Colom-
      bia*, 64–65.

11   *"[The captured chief] Sagipa responded"*: Ibid., 110.

12   *As the guests lounged in their chairs*: Mark Bowden, *Killing Pablo* (New York: At-
      lantic Monthly Press, 2001), 30.

15   *"Then I stood before the mirror"*: Hugo Martínez, interview with the author,
      March 2013.

15   *"I liked to read stories"*: Ibid.

15   *"When you first become a cadet"*: Ibid.

16   *"If you love this girl"*: Ibid.

17   *"In all parts of the Indies"*: Pedro Cieza de León, *The Travels of Pedro Cieza de León,
      AD 1532–50, Contained in the First Part of His Chronicles in Peru* (London: Haklyut
      Society, 1864), 352–53.

23   *"El Dorado," the Englishman said quietly*: anonymous, *New York Times*, Oct. 27,
      1912, 58.

23   *"The lake is drained as dry"*: Ibid.

26   *"Escobar was a criminal"*: Hugo Martínez, interview.

26   *"Pablo promised"*: Roberto Escobar, *The Accountant's Story*, 38.

27   *"Cocaine's popularity has spread"*: Richard Steele, "The Cocaine Scene," *News-
      week*, May 30, 1977, 20–21.

29   *"Escobar wanted it both ways"*: Hugo Martínez, interview.

33   *"I was constantly attending funerals"*: Ibid.

34   *"One of the radios"*: Roberto Escobar, *The Accountant's Story*, 146–47.

34   *"Colonel, I'm going to kill you"*: Mark Bowden, *Killing Pablo*, 205.

35   *"I'm here, but I don't see it"*: Hugo Martínez, interview.

36   *"The question," Pablo Escobar*: Ibid.

37   *"If I fail"*: Ibid.

40   *"It's just too dangerous"*: Ibid.

41   *"Pablo made phone calls"*: Roberto Escobar, *The Accountant's Story*, 245.

43   *"I've got him located!"*: Hugo Martínez, interview.

44   "Momento, momento": Ibid.

45   *Between 2006 and 2015*: Claire Schaeffer-Duffy, "Counting Mexico's Drug Vic-
      tims Is a Murky Business," *National Catholic Reporter*, March 1, 2014.

CHAPTER 2: EVOLUTION AND DENIAL IN THE GALÁPAGOS (ECUADOR)

51   *"And God made the beasts of the earth"*: The Bible: *Authorized King James Ver-
      sion* (London: Oxford University Press, 2008), 2. Note: most contemporary

scholars believe that what is now known as the book of Genesis was written during the time of King Solomon in Israel (970–931 BC).

51   *"The main conclusion arrived"*: Charles Darwin, *The Descent of Man* (New York: Penguin, 2004), 676.

51   *"I was fascinated"*: Phillip Johnson, "How the Evolution Debate Can Be Won," *Revival Times*, 6, issue 11 (London: Kensington Temple London City Church, Nov. 2004), 1.

52   *"What you see depends"*: Eugene Taurman, personal conversation, April 2015.

53   *"It is the fate of every voyager"*: Edward J. Larson, *Evolution's Workshop: God and Science on the Galapagos Islands* (New York: Basic Books, 2001), 75.

55   *"Take five and twenty heaps"*: Herman Melville, *The Encantadas and Other Stories* (Mineola, NY: Dover Publications, 2005), 21.

58   *"On land they were not able"*: Fray Tomás de Berlanga, *Letter to His Majesty . . . describing his Voyage from Panamá to Puerto Viejo*, In *Colección de Documentos Inéditos relativos al Descubrimiento, Conquista y Organización de las Antiguas Posesiones Españolas de América y Oceania*, tomo XLI, cuaderno II (Madrid: Imprenta de Manuel G. Hernandez, 1884), 540.

59   *"On Passion Sunday"*: Ibid., 541.

60   *"Little but reptile life"*: Herman Melville, *The Encantadas*, 22.

60   *"Early in my school-days"*: Charles Darwin, *The Life and Letters of Charles Darwin* (London: John Murray, 1887), 33.

61   *"You care for nothing but shooting"*: Ibid., 32.

65   *"a burning zeal"*: Ibid., 68.

69   *"If an organized body"*: James Hutton, *An Investigation of the Principles of Knowledge and of the Progress of Reason, from Sense to Science and Philosophy*, Vol. 2 (Edinburgh: Strahan & Cadell, 1794), 500.

72   *"I trust I shall make my"*: Terry Mortenson, *The Great Turning Point: The Church's Catastrophic Mistake on Geology* (Green Forest, AZ: Master Books, 2004), 225–26.

73   *"In crossing the Cordillera"*: Robert FitzRoy, *Narrative of the Surveying Voyages of His Majesty's Ships* Adventure *and* Beagle, *Between the Years 1826 and 1836, Describing Their Examination of the Southern Shores of South America, and the* Beagle's *Circumnavigation of the Globe*, Vol. II (London: Henry Colburn, 1839), 667–68.

74   *"My own mind is convinced"*: Ibid., 666.

75   *"From my ignorance in botany"*: Charles Darwin, *Narrative of the Surveying Voyages of His Majesty's Ships* Adventure *and* Beagle, *Between the Years 1826 and 1836*, Vol. III, 629.

75   *"I probably collected second"*: Ibid.

76   *"All the small birds"*: Robert FitzRoy, *Narrative*, Vol. II, 503.

76   *"After dinner a party"*: Ibid., 353.

77   *"I industriously collected"*: Charles Darwin, *Charles Darwin's* Beagle *Diary* (New York: Cambridge University Press, 1988), 356.

82   *"Monday the fourteenth"*: Benjamin Morrell, *A Narrative of Four Voyages to the South Sea* (New York: J & J Harper, 1832), 192–93.

83   *"On passing the currents"*: Ibid., 194–95.

83   *"The next day, a light breeze"*: Charles Darwin, Beagle *Diary*, 405.

83   *"the fragments of Lava"*: Ibid., 399.

84   *"I have [mockingbird] specimens"*: Richard Keynes, *Fossils, Finches and Fuegians: Charles Darwin's Adventures and Discoveries on the Beagle* (London: HarperCollins, 2002), 371–72 (italics mine).

87   *"These islands appear paradises"*: Charles Darwin, Beagle *Diary*, 353.

87   *"The houses are very simple"*: Ibid., 356.

92   *"ZOOLOGICAL SOCIETY"*: Edward J. Larson, *Evolution's Workshop: God and Science on the Galápagos Islands* (New York: Basic Books, 2001), 76.

94   *"I never dreamed that islands"*: Charles Darwin, *The Voyage of the* Beagle (New York: Signet Classic, 1988), 341.

96   *"The most striking and important"*: Charles Darwin, *On the Origin of Species by Means of Natural Selection, or the Preservation of Favored Races in the Struggle for Life* (London: John Murray, 1902), 357–58.

97   *"It is interesting to contemplate"*: Ibid., 440–41.

99   *"I just skimmed"*: Charles Darwin, *The Life and Letters of Charles Darwin*, Vol. II (New York: D. Appleton and Co, 1898), 411–12.

100 *"The mystery of the beginning"*: Charles Darwin, *Life and Letters*, Vol. I, 282.

CHAPTER 3: DEATH IN THE ANDES: THE CAPTURE OF SHINING PATH LEADER ABIMAEL GUZMÁN (PERU)

102 *"Their burning conviction"*: Eric Hoffer, *The True Believer: Thoughts on the Nature of Mass Movements* (New York: Harper, 2010), 74.

102 *"The philosophers"*: Karl Marx, "Theses on Feuerbach," in Karl Marx and Lawrence H. Simon, *Selected Writings* (New York: Hackett, 1994), 101.

102 *"Revolution is not a dinner party"*: Mao Tse-tung, quoted in Lee Feignon, *Mao: A Reinterpretation* (Chicago: Ivan R. Dee, 2002), 41.

103 *"From the moment"*: Abimael Guzmán, *Presidente Gonzalo Rompe el Silencio* (Lima: El Diario, July 24, 1988), 26 (author's translation).

110 *"unfurling the dawn"*: Gustavo Gorriti, *The Shining Path: A History of the Millenarian War in Peru* (Chapel Hill: University of North Carolina Press, 1999), 28.

119 *"My son, take care"*: Elena Iparraguirre, quoted in Santiago Roncagliolo, *La Cuarta Espada* (Barcelona: Debate, 2007), 243 (author's translation).

119 *"When I met him"*: Susana Guzmán, *En Mi Noche Sin Fortuna* (Barcelona: Montesinos, 1999), 201 (author's translation). Note: although Ms. Guzmán's book is a novel, the Peruvian writer Santiago Roncagliolo, in his book *La Cuarta Espada: La Historia de Abimael Guzmán y Sendero Luminoso* (Barcelona: Debate, 2007), reproduces a letter from Ms. Guzmán, who told him that the account of a particular character (Manuel) in her novel was actually nonfiction, or true, and was based on her half brother, Abimael (Santiago Roncagliolo, *La Cuarta Espada*, 28).

120 *"A lot of blood was shed"*: Abimael Guzmán, *Presidente Gonzalo Rompe el Silencio*, 46 (author's translation).

121 *"I don't know exactly what happened"*: Santiago Roncagliolo, *La Cuarta Espada*, 39 (author's translation).

121 *"This girl . . . actually decided"*: Susana Guzmán, *En Mi Noche Sin Fortuna*, 151–52 (author's translation).

122 *"He was one of the best students"*: Miguel Ángel Rodrígez Rivas, quoted in Abimael Guzmán, *De Puno y Letra* (Lima: Manoalzada, 2009), 23 (author's translation).

122 *"Their reality opened my eyes"*: Abimael Guzmán, quoted in "Exclusive Comments by Abimael Guzmán," *World Affairs* (Summer 1993), 156, issue 1, Heldref Publications, p. 54. Note: these are "Transcribed excerpts" of an "exclusive" tape recording of Shining Path leader Abimael Guzmán from a Dincote, Counterterrorism Directorate, cell in Lima, September 1993.

124 *"Let's remember, that"*: Abimael Guzmán, *Presidente Gonzalo Rompe el Silencio*, 40 (author's translation).

125 *"The intellectuals"*: Abimael Guzmán, quoted in "Exclusive Comments by Abimael Guzmán," p. 53.

126 *"Comrades, we are entering"*: Abimael Guzmán, quoted in "We Are the Initiators," in Orin Starn, et al., *The Peru Reader: History, Culture, Politics* (Durham, NC: Duke University Press, 1995), 314.

130 *"Amid the smoke and pestilence"*: Mario Vargas Llosa, *The Real Life of Alejandro Mayta* (New York: Farrar, Straus and Giroux, 1986), 200–201.

137 *"Chief, what are you watching?"*: Víctor Tipe Sánchez, *El Olor de la Retama: La Historia Escondida Sobre la Captura de Abimael Guzmán* (Lima: Grupo Siete, 2007), 133–34 (author's translation).

139 *"I can't believe what my eyes are seeing"*: Ibid., 289 (author's translation).

140 *"Halt! We're police!"*: Ibid., 308 (author's translation).

141 *"Shut up, God dammit!"*: Ibid., 309 (author's translation).

143 "Tenemos el cachetón!": Ibid., 310 (author's translation).

143 *"You had to know quite a bit"*: Francesca Ralea, *Así Cayó Abimael Guzmán* (Buenos Aires: *Página 12*, June 24, 2001), 23.

143 *"Doctor," the minister asked*: Benedicto Jiménez Baca, interview with the author, January 2011.

150 *"The armed insurrection"*: Nelson Manrique, "Notas Sobre Las Condiciones Sociales De La Violencia Politica En El Peru," *Revista de Neuro-Psiquiatria*, 56: 235–240, 1993; 239.

151 *"Doctor, it's time to go"*: Víctor Tipe Sánchez, *El Olor de la Retama*, 323.

CHAPTER 4: THE RISE AND FALL OF HIRAM BINGHAM, "DISCOVERER" OF MACHU PICCHU (PERU)

153 *"Yesterday I had a glorious flight"*: Alfred M. Bingham, *Explorer of Machu Picchu: Portrait of Hiram Bingham* (Greenwich, CT: Triune Books, 2000), 317.

153 *"I warn you"*: Ovid, Mary Innes, translator, *The Metamorphoses of Ovid* (London, Penguin Books, 1955), 96.

161 *Lizarraga, 1902*: Alfred M. Bingham, *Explorer*, 13.

161 *"Something hidden!"*: Rudyard Kipling, "The Explorer," in *Rudyard Kipling's Verse, Inclusive Edition* (Garden City: Doubleday, 1920), 120.

162 *"Agustín Lizarraga is the discoverer"*: Alfred M. Bingham, *Explorer of Machu Picchu*, 19.

162 *"From a crude scrawl"*: Hiram Bingham, *Inca Land* (Boston: Houghton Mifflin, 1922), 324.

162 *"I found it."*: Hiram Bingham, *Lost City of the Incas* (London: Weidenfeld & Nicolson, 2002), 23.

165 *"The Incas were, undeniably"*: Hiram Bingham, "In the Wonderland of Peru," *National Geographic* 24, no. 4 (1913), 473, 477.
    The Criminal Excavation: Alfred M. Bingham, *Explorer*, 307 (author's translation).

167 *"considerable amount of mental depression."*: Christopher Heaney, *Cradle of Gold: The Story of Hiram Bingham, A Real-life Indiana Jones, and the Search for Machu Picchu* (New York: Palgrave Macmillan, 2010), 237.

168 *"It seems to me a strange thing"*: Ibid., 243.

169 *"The most thrilling moment"*: Hiram Bingham, *Further Explorations in the Land of the Incas, National Geographic* 29, no. 5 (May 1916), 445.

170 *"Not far from Patallacta"*: Ibid., 446.

173 *"I suppose that in the same sense"*: Alfred M. Bingham, *Explorer*, 26.

174 *"All the ruins were cleaned"*: Christopher Heaney, *Cradle of Gold*, 219.

176 *"to the sharp iron edge I came"*: Mark Eisner, *The Essential Neruda: Selected Poems* (San Francisco: City Lights Books, 2004), 71.

CHAPTER 5: ICE MAIDENS, VOLCANOES, AND INCAS (PERU)

177 *"These children [to be sacrificed"*: Johan Reinhard, *The Ice Maiden: Inca Mummies, Mountain Gods, and Sacred Sites in the Andes* (Washington, DC: National Geographic Society, 2005), 77.

177 *"Some females included in the sacrifices"*: Father Bernabé Cobo, *Inca Religion and Customs* (Austin: University of Texas Press, 1990), 112.

177 *"Human nature would not allow"*: Ibid., 8.

181 *"We settled in Chinchero"*: Ed and Chris Franquemont, "Learning to Weave in Chinchero," *The Textile Museum Journal* 26 (1988), 55.

182 *"I'd been really really sick"*: Abby Franquemont, interview with the author, November 27, 2012.

184 *"As a child I'd seen pictures"*: Ibid.

189 *"Her spinning was so fine"*: Nilda Callañaupa Alvarez, *Weaving in the Peruvian Highlands* (Cusco: Centro de Textiles Tradicionales del Cusco, 2007), 15.

189 *"When I was growing up"*: Ibid., 14.

191 *"the art and wisdom of a people"*: Jose Maria Arguedas, *The Fox from Up Above and the Fox from Down Below* (Pittsburgh: University of Pittsburgh Press, 2000), 268.

192 *"the route followed"*: Ibid., 269.

192 *"There were vast numbers"*: Pedro Pizarro, in John Hemming, *The Conquest of the Incas* (New York: Harcourt, Brace, Jovanovich, 1970), 135–36.

193 *The [Inca] king*: Father Bernabé Cobo, *Inca Religion and Customs*, 244–45.

195 *"My father was insistent"*: Nilda Callañaupa Alvarez, *Weaving in the Peruvian Highlands*, 16.

195 *"I continued learning to weave"*: Nilda Callañaupa Alvarez, interview with the author, November 2010.

195 *"You would think the grandmothers"*: Ibid.

196 *"A week later"*: Ibid.

197 *"O Sun . . . [our] father"*: Father Bernabé Cobo, *Inca Religion and Customs*, 120.

201 *"Young people were not learning"*: Nilda Callañaupa Alvarez, interview with the author, November 2010.

201 *"Creating a cooperative"*: Ibid.

213 *"So for the three days"*: Tim Wells, interview with the author, November 2010.

214 *"I had been going out"*: Nilda Callañaupa Alvarez, *Weaving in the Peruvian Highlands* (Cusco: Center for Traditional Textiles; 2007), 101.

215 *"It's not an 'apprenticeship' "*: Tim Wells, interview with the author, November 2010.

216 *"[An Inca] mummy bundle"*: Johan Reinhard, *The Ice Maiden*, 24.

217 *"Some of the women"*: Cieza de León, *The Travels of Pedro de Cieza de León, A.D. 1532–50* (New York: Haklyut Society, 1964), 146.

226 *"My mind raced"*: Johan Reinhard, *The Ice Maiden*, 30.

227 *"I couldn't hoist"*: Ibid., 32–33.

227 *"According to the chroniclers"*: Ibid., 28–29.

229 *"She was the age of Shakespeare's Juliet"*: Ibid., 208.

230 *"On behalf of the people of Peru"*: Ibid., 152–53.

CHAPTER 6: THE *KON-TIKI* VOYAGE, WHITE GODS, AND THE FLOATING ISLANDS OF LAKE TITICACA (PERU AND BOLIVIA)

233 *"I asked the Indians"*: Juan de Betanzos, in Roland Hamilton, *Narrative of the Incas* (Austin: University of Texas, 1996), 10.

233 *"I was no longer in doubt"*: Thor Heyerdahl, *Kon-Tiki: Across the Pacific by Raft* (New York: Rand McNally, 1967), 25–26.

235 *"Once in a while"*: Ibid., 13.

240 *"These Uros are barbarous"*: Antonio de Calancha, *Crónica Moralizada de Antonio de la Calancha*, Vol. 1 (Barcelona: Pedro Lacavalleria, 1639), 650.

240 *"They raise a large amount of reeds"*: Jose de Acosta, *Natural and Moral History of the Indies* (Durham, NC: Duke University Press, 2002), 83.

247 *has a mere twenty-six native species*: Ben Orlove, *Lines in the Water: Nature and Culture at Lake Titicaca* (Berkeley: University of California Press, 2002), 118.

248 *"Ages ago"*: Hiram Bingham, *Inca Land* (Boston: Houghton Mifflin, 1922), 68.

250 *"The [Andean] Indians, [worshipped]"*: Father Bernabé Cobo, *Inca Religion and Customs* (Austin: University of Texas Press, 1990), 6.

250 *"These Indians used two names"*: Ibid., 10.

256 *"Tihuanaco . . . is famous"*: Pedro Cieza de León, in Alan Kolata, *Valley of the Spirits: A Journey into the Lost Realm of the Aymara* (New York: Wiley, 1996), 64.

257 *"[When] . . . I asked the natives"*: Ibid.

257 *"he tried to find out"*: Father Bernabé Cobo, *Inca Religion and Customs*, 145.

258 "received news that": Pedro Sarmiento de Gamboa, *Narrative of the Voyages of Pedro Sarmiento de Gamboa* (London: Haklyut Society, 1907), 159.

258 "In ancient times": Roland Hamilton, *Narrative of the Incas*, 8.

259 "Viracocha . . . [then] ordered": Pedro Sarmiento de Gamboa, *Narrative*, 33.

259 "In [the city of] Tiaguanaco": Father Bernabé Cobo, *Inca Religion and Customs*, 13.

259 "working his miracles": Pedro Sarmiento de Gamboa, *Narrative*, 36.

259 "He told them that people": Ibid.

269 "They knew how to build reed boats": Thor Heyerdahl, *The Ra Expeditions* (Garden City, NY: Doubleday, 1971), 297.

272 "[Reed] boats of this distinctive type": Ibid., 29–30.

274 "Who were right, the isolationists": Ibid., 31.

275 "Here was a large pyramid": Ibid., 115.

277 "My migration theory": Thor Heyerdahl, *Kon-Tiki*, 297.

278 "The crash landing": Thor Heyerdahl, *Early Man and the Ocean* (Garden City, NY: Doubleday, 1979), 32.

278 "I have mentioned that Feejee": Captain James Cook, *A Voyage to the Pacific Ocean*, Vol. 1 (London: G. Nicol, 1785), 376.

279 "In these navigations": Ibid.

283 "At half-past five": Thor Heyerdahl, *Kon-Tiki*, 167.

CHAPTER 7: THE END OF CHE GUEVARA (BOLIVIA)

286 "This experience of ours": Jon Lee Anderson, *Che: A Revolutionary Life* (New York: Grove Press, 1997), 424.

286 "We learned perfectly": Che Guevara, *The Motorcycle Diaries* (Melbourne: Centro de Estudios Che Guevara, 2003), 173.

286 "I've come to stay": Jon Lee Anderson, *Che*, 702.

289 "I have visited": Che Guevara, *The Motorcycle Diaries*, 84 (photo caption).

290 "The truth is": Jon Lee Anderson, *Che*, 309.

291 "Once again I feel below my heels": Richard L. Harris, *Death of a Revolutionary: Che Guevara's Last Mission* (New York: Norton, 1970), 49.

292 "saving 30,000 future children": Jon Lee Anderson, *Che*, 571.

292 "the cordilleras of the Andes": Che Guevara, *Guerilla Warfare*, Brian Loveman, ed. (Lincoln: University of Nebraska Press, 1985), 193.

292 "At which point I left the path": Ibid., 165–66.

292 "I feel not just a powerful internal strength": Ibid., 434.

292 "It could be that this will be the definitive one": Ibid., 633.

293 "If one day you must read": Ibid., 634.

293 "Oct 7 [1967]": Che Guevara, *The Bolivian Diary: Authorized Edition* (New York: Ocean Press, 2006), 223.

294 "Now I am doomed": Jon Lee Anderson, *Che*, 725.

295 "We remained in ambush": Che Guevara, *The Bolivian Diary*, 216.

295 "travels by horse": Jon Lee Anderson, *Che*, 729.

297 "Don't shoot!": Ibid., 733.

298 *"The idea of revolution"*: Albert Garrido, "Los Últimos Lugares de Che: Tras la Huella de un Mito," *El Periódico Dominical* (Madrid, June 14–15, 2003), 55 (author's translation).

299 *"Would Che have had the same impact,"*: Guillermo Cabrera Infante, "Entre el Fracaso y El Error," *El Periódico Dominical* (Madrid, June 14–15, 2003), 52 (author's translation).

299 *"He was the first man I ever met"*: Christopher Hitchens, "Goodbye to All That," *New York Review of Books,* July 17, 1997.

299 *"He had an incalculable enchantment"*: Jon Lee Anderson, *Che,* 516.

300 *"It is important to emphasize"*: Che Guevara, *Guerrilla Warfare,* 49–50.

300 *"[any] attempt to carry out this type of war"*: Ibid., 183.

300 *"Groups of Castro-Communist tendency"*: Jon Lee Anderson, *Che,* 729.

301 *"The lack of peasant recruits"*: Che Guevara, *The Bolivian Diary,* 182.

302 *"Don't be silly"*: Henry Butterfield Ryan, *The Fall of Che Guevara* (New York: Oxford University Press, 1997), 122.

302 *"The essential task of the guerrilla fighter"*: Che Guevara, *Guerrilla Warfare,* 55.

302 *"one can't help but conclude"*: Jon Lee Anderson, *Che,* 730.

302 *"an infernal, desolate countryside"*: Henry Butterfield Ryan, *The Fall of Che Guevara,* 128.

304 *"like a piece of trash"*: Jon Lee Anderson, *Che,* 736.

306 *"Che stopped talking"*: Felix Rodriguez, *Shadow Warrior* (New York: Simon and Schuster, 1989), 168.

306 *"It is better like this"*: Ibid., 169.

307 *"Tell Fidel"*: Ibid.

307 *"It was a tremendously emotional moment"*: Ibid.

307 *"No, I will stand for this"*: Henry Butterfield Ryan, *The Fall of Che Guevara,* 154.

307 *"Calm yourself and shoot"*: Jon Lee Anderson, *Che,* 738.

310 *"Guevara is invincible in his ideals"*: "Bolivian Leader Joins in Tribute to Che Guevara," *Seattle Times,* Oct. 8, 2009.

311 *After Che's execution*: Note: Walberto's story appears confirmed by Richard Gott's account, "On the Ribs of Rocinante," *London Review of Books* 19, no. 16, Aug. 29, 1997, 5.

313 *"Four decades after Mario Terán"*: Rory Carroll, "Cuban Doctors Restore Eyesight of Che's Killer," *Guardian,* Oct. 1, 2007.

314 *"Can't you see the state"*: Jon Lee Anderson, *Che,* 735.

CHAPTER 8: THE FINAL DAYS OF BUTCH CASSIDY AND THE SUNDANCE KID (BOLIVIA)

315 *"A man who has had an outlaw past"*: Matt Warner, *Last of the Bandit Riders: Revisited* (Salt Lake City, UT: Big Moon Traders, 2000), 114.

315 *"I came down to South America"*: James David Horan, *The Authentic Wild West: The Outlaws* (New York: Crown Publishers, 1977), 281–82.

315 *"I never met a soul more affable"*: William Goldman, *Four Screenplays with Essays* (New York: Applause Books, 1995), 68.

317 *"On the descent of Huaca Huañusca"*: Anne Meadows, *Digging Up Butch and Sun-
     dance* (New York: St. Martin's Press, 1995), 230–32.

319 *"He never drank to excess"*: Charles Kelly, Anne Meadows, and Dan Buck, *The
     Outlaw Trail: A History of Butch Cassidy and His Wild Bunch* (Lincoln: University
     of Nebraska, 1996), 4.

323 *"Just that little accident"*: Matt Warner, *Last of the Bandit Riders*, 46.

324 *"It was hard for us"*: Ibid., 88.

324 *"Stories about ranching and homesteading"*: Dan Buck, personal communication,
     December 2013.

325 *"tall, slender, laconic, and nervous"*: Anne Meadows, *Digging Up Butch and Sun-
     dance*, 5.

325 *"You'll never know what it means to be hunted"*: Charles Kelly, Anne Meadows, and
     Dan Buck, *The Outlaw Trail*, 311.

326 *"The tightly knit group of Americans"*: James David Horan, *The Authentic Wild
     West*, 286.

328 *"Butch's philosophy about banks"*: Ibid., 235.

328 *"I'm not as bad as I'm painted"*: Charles Kelly, Anne Meadows, and Dan Buck, *The
     Outlaw Trail*, 167–68.

328 *"You know the law"*: Ibid., 169.

328 *"was quite popular in the countryside"*: James David Horan, *The Authentic Wild
     West*, 281.

329 *"We walked outside"*: Ibid., 283.

329 *"I . . . began to see a change in Cassidy"*: Ibid., 286.

329 *"When attempting to arrest"*: Ibid., 273.

331 *"We arrived here about 3 weeks ago"*: Anne Meadows, *Digging Up Butch and Sun-
     dance*, 98–99.

338 *"all of us [then] entered"*: Ibid., 264–65.

338 *"in the chest"*: "El Chorolque" Año III, no. 99 (Tupiza, Bolivia, November 11,
     1908), page 1, reprinted in Max Reynaga Farfán, *Turismo Adventure* (Tupiza:
     Tupac Katari Printers, Oct. 2006), 13 (author's translation).

339 *"NOVA documentary crew"*: *NOVA*, "Wanted—Butch and Sundance," PBS docu-
     mentary, Oct. 12, 1993.

CHAPTER 9: DARWIN, THE LAST YÁMANA, AND THE UTTERMOST PART OF THE EARTH (CHILE AND ARGENTINA)

343 *"But . . . ye shall be witnesses"*: The Bible: *Authorized King James Version* (London:
     Oxford University Press, 2008), 147.

343 *"Whilst beholding these savages"*: Charles Darwin, *Narrative of the Surveying Voy-
     ages of His Majesty's Ships* Adventure *and* Beagle, *Between the Years 1826 and
     1836, Describing Their Examination of the Southern Shores of South America, and the
     Beagle's Circumnavigation of the Globe*, Vol. III (London: Henry Colburn, 1839),
     236.

343 *"The true barbarian"*: William Hazlitt, *Characteristics: In the Manner of Rochefou-
     cault's Maxims* (London: J. Templeman, 1837), 119.

345 *"His Majesty asked a great deal"*: Nick Hazelwood, *Savage: The Life and Times of Jemmy Button* (New York: St. Martin's Press, 2001), 94.

347 *"At three this morning"*: Captain Robert FitzRoy, *Narrative of the Surveying Voyages*, Vol. I, 391–92.

348 *"The oldest woman of the tribe"*: Ibid., 399.

348 *"beat out his brains"*: Ibid., 398.

348 *"Seeing the . . . [sailor's] danger"*: Ibid.

349 *"I became convinced"*: Ibid., 405.

349 *"I . . . [eventually] made up my mind"*: Ibid., 458–59.

349 *"to their country at a future time"*: Ibid., 459.

350 *"During the former voyage of the . . . Beagle"*: Charles Darwin, *The Voyage of the Beagle* (New York: P. F. Collier & Son, 1909), 211–12.

350 *"Fuegia Basket was a nice, modest, reserved young girl"*: Ibid., 213.

351 *"This channel"*: Ibid., 222.

352 *"During the night the news"*: Ibid., 226.

352 *"The next morning after our arrival"*: Ibid., 226–27.

353 *"mother had been inconsolable"*: Ibid., 227.

354 *"From the time of our leaving"*: Ibid., 230.

355 *"It was quite melancholy"*: Ibid., 231.

355 *"The wigwams in which I had left York"*: Captain Robert FitzRoy, *Narrative*, Vol. II, 323–24.

356 *"But how altered!"*: Ibid., 324.

356 *"told us he had 'too much' "*: Charles Darwin, *Voyage*, 234.

357 *"I cannot help still hoping"*: Captain Robert FitzRoy, *Narrative*, Vol. II, 327.

357 *"lighted a signal fire"*: Charles Darwin, *Voyage*, 234.

358 *"Whilst on board the Beagle"*: Peter Nicols, *Evolution's Captain: The Dark Fate of the Man Who Sailed Darwin Around the World* (New York: Harper Collins, 2003), 293–94.

359 *"savages in the fullest sense of the word"*: Captain Robert FitzRoy, *Narrative*, Vol. II, 649.

359 *FitzRoy published his theory of the origin of Patagonians*: Ibid.

359 *"My dear old friend"*: Peter Nicols, *Evolution's Captain*, 311.

360 *"acutest pain"*: Adrian Desmond, *Darwin: The Life of a Tormented Evolutionist* (New York: Warner Books, 1991), 495.

360 *"not on philosophical principles"*: Edward Caudill, *Darwinian Myths: The Legends and Misuses of a Theory* (Knoxville: University of Tennessee Press, 1997), 44.

360 *"he begged to know"*: Leonard Huxley, *Life and Letters of Thomas Henry Huxley*, Vol. 1 (New York: D. Appleton & Company, 1901), 197.

361 *"the Lord hath delivered him"*: Ibid.

361 *"When I got up"*: Adrian Desmond, *Darwin*, 497.

361 *"Lifting an immense Bible"*: Ibid., 495.

363 *"As we proceeded along"*: Charles Darwin, *Voyage*, 225.

363 *"Well, I'm blowed!"*: Nick Hazelwood, *Savage: The Life and Times of Jemmy Button*, 174.

364   *"As they were rowed ashore"*: Lucas Bridges, *The Uttermost Part of the Earth* (New York: Dover, 1988), 59.

365   *"The belief that the Fuegians were cannibals"*: Ibid., 34.

366   *"The Lord has seen fit"*: Charles Dickens, *The Household Register of Current Events, for the Year 1852* (London: Bradbury and Evans, 1852), 110.

367   *"I do not now doubt"*: Charles Darwin, *Voyage*, 234.

367   *"In the tideway"*: Captain Robert FitzRoy, *Narrative*, Vol. I, 139.

368   *"Chief among these motives"*: Herman Melville, *Moby Dick* (Boston: St. Botolph Society, 1922), 11.

369   *"How do?"*: Nick Hazelwood, *Savage*, 326.

370   *"An impression of melancholy"*: Ann Chapman, *European Encounters with the Yamana People of Cape Horn* (New York: Cambridge University Press, 2010), 519.

371   *"More than one of those . . . [Yámanas]"*: Ibid., 522.

372   *"Her face was visibly impressed with sorrow"*: Ibid., 407.

373   *"the natives were dying"*: Ibid., 538.

375   *"[Sometimes] an action that requires"*: Placard in the Museo Regional Salesiano in Punta Arenas, Chile, April 2011.

375   *"I was on a little steamer"*: Lucas Bridges, *The Uttermost Part of the Earth*, 266–67.

381   *"It was my father's first meeting"*: Ibid., 83–84.

382   *"all recollection of it had faded"*: Ibid., 84.

382   *"She was about sixty-two years of age"*: Ibid.

384   *"Languages are not simply vocabulary lists"*: Wade Davis, *The Wayfinders: Why Ancient Wisdom Matters in the Modern World* (Toronto: House of Anansi Press, 2009), 3.

ACKNOWLEDGMENTS

During the years it took to research and write this book, I inevitably owe many people a great deal of thanks. Literally hundreds of people helped me, in one way or another, and so I'd like to acknowledge my gratitude to some of them here.

First, I owe many thanks to my editor at Simon & Schuster, Bob Bender, who was enthusiastic from the moment I pitched this book idea and who remained enthusiastic throughout. Bob was and is as solid an editor as one could hope for. Many thanks also to Johanna Li, a fine editorial assistant, and to my agent, Sarah Lazin.

A number of specialists and readers were kind enough to take the time from their busy schedules to read portions of this book and to offer their insightful comments. Many thanks to Dr. Johan Reinhard, Dan Buck, Bart Lewis, Joanne MacQuarrie, and Henry Butterfield Ryan, for their comments. If any errors have remained in the manuscript, I am solely to blame.

While traveling the length of the Andes, many people contributed contacts, references, advice, or other help along the way. Others generously agreed to interviews and willingly shared some of their amazing stories. I am grateful to all of them.

In Colombia, I would like to thank General Hugo Martínez Poveda, Maria Ines Carrizosa, Dominic Streatfield, Tim Pratt, Herman and María van Diepen, Jose Vicente Arizmendi, and Roberto Escobar.

In Peru, I would like to thank the late Thor Heyerdahl, who was kind enough to invite me to visit him while he was excavating the Moche ruins of Túcume, Alfredo Ferreyros, Stefan Zumsteg, Luz Maria Lores Garrido Lecca, Max Hernández, Andre Baertschi, José Koechlin von Stein, Paul Cripps of Amazonas Explorers (who organized my hike on the Inca Trail), Nick Asheshov, Eleanor Griffis de Zúniga, the late Enrique Zileri Gibson, Francisco Diez Canseco Távara, Keefe Borden (with whom I first visited the Shining Path guerrillas in Canto Grande Prison), Gustavo Gorriti, Victor Tipe Sánchez, Benedicto Jiménez Bacca, Maritza Garrido-Lecca, Nilda Callañaupa Alvarez, Tim Wells, the late Chris Franquemont, Abby Franquemont, Olga Huamán, Jenevieve Doerr, Judith Crosbie, Johan Reinhard, François Patthey, the Center for Traditional Textiles, and Walter Bustamante Cano.

In Bolivia, I would like to thank Juan and Elsa Lujano of the Uros Islands, Judge Felix Charlar Miranda, Dan Buck, Fabiola Mitru and Tupiza Tours, Froilán Risso, Mario Giorgetta, Waldo Barahona Ruiz, Paulino and Porfírio Esteban, Julia Cortés, Walberto Rivas Brito, and Lucía Presta.

In Chile, I would like to thank Cristina Calderón, David Calderón, Denis Chevallay, Simon Gardner, and the very helpful staff of the Martin Gusinde Anthropological Museum in Puerto Williams, on Navarino Island.

In Argentina, I would like to thank Ernesto Luis Piana, Natalie Goodall, and the staffs of the Museo Regional Salesiano in Punta Arenas and of the Museo Mundo Yámana in Ushuaia.

Finally, I would like to express my love and gratitude to Ciara Byrne, who joined me once I reached Patagonia and who, once again and more than anyone else, helped to make this book a reality.

INDEX

Page numbers in *italics* refer to maps.

Banzer, Hugo, 313
Barbados, 237, 269
Bardem, Javier, 142
barley, 199
Barrientos, René, 301, 313
barter system, 184
Bartolomé Island, Galápagos, 78, 80
Batista, Fulgencio, 290
Beagle, HMS, 52, 53, 60, 62, 64, 72,
    76n, 78, 79, 83–85, 87, 90–92, 97,
    346–47, 349, 351, 354, 360, 361,
    368, 381, 386
Beagle Channel, 344, 351, 362, 363, 365,
    368, 369, 371, 373, 374, 379, 380,
    381, 382, 383, 385
Beaver, Utah, 322
Becerra (Peruvian GEIN agent), 140–42
beetles, 64
Belgium, 88
Belief systems, altering perceptions of
    reality, 52, 67–68, 73–74, 94, 99,
    102, 124, 225, 227–28, 274, 284,
    292, 358, 361
Bennett Monolith, Bolivia, 271
Berlanga, Tomás de, 57–59, 86
Beth (Inca Trail hiker), 156, 158, 170–71
Bible, 343, 382
    creation theory of, 56, 61, 71–72, 85,
        100–101, 358
    literal interpretation of, 58–59, 68, 71,
        73, 95, 98, 358–60
bicycle racing (Colombia), 18, 46, 47
Bingham, Alfreda Mitchell, 157, 159,172
Bingham, Hiram, xviii, 153, 154–63,
    165–76
    accomplishments of, 159, 171–72
    ambition of, 155, 160, 171
    background and youth of, 156–57, 173
    death and burial of, 174, 175, 176
    debated heroism of, 154–57, 171
    downfall of, 158–59, 167–68, 171–72
    in illegal antiquities trade, 154, 155,
        156–58, 166, 174
    on Lake Titicaca, 248
    Machu Picchu "discovered" by, 150–63,
        173, 248
    marriages of, 157, 172
    mistress of, 172
    political career of, 159, 172
birds:
    Darwin's collection of, xviii, 52–53,
        75–77, 92, 94

Darwin's misjudgements and
    oversights about, 52–54, 56, 75–77,
    91–95
of Galápagos, 88, 95–97
on Lake Titicaca, 248
tameness of, 58, 76–77
see also specific species
Bloque de Búsqueda (Colombia), *see* Search
    Bloc
blue-footed boobies (Galápagos Islands),
    57, 58, 78
boatbuilders, 237, 254, 266–70
    competition for, 268
Boat Memory (Alakaluf/Kawésqar native),
    348, 349, 357
boats:
    papyrus reed, 269
    Polynesian outrigger/catamaran,
        278–83
    totora reed, 247, 248, 253, 263, 265,
        266n, 270, 270n, 272, 276, 280,
        284
bobo (clown; fool) (boobie birds), 57
bocachico (fish), 8
bocachiquiar, murder by, 7–8
Bogotá, Colombia, xvi, 5, 11, 16, 18–19,
    30, 31, 39, 41, 42, 50
    Castellana neighborhood of, 2
    Chico Norte neighborhood of, 13
Bogotá, Muisca chief, 9–11
Bolivia, 201, 241, 274
    altiplano of, 254–55, 262, 335
    author's journey to, xvii–xviii, 254–70,
        295–300, 302–6, 317, 321, 327,
        328–34, 335–37, 338–42
    Butch and Sundance in, 315–22,
        326–42
    in cocaine trade, 25
    dying villages of, 332–33
    Guevara's failed insurrection in,
        125–26, 286–314
    Guevara's misjudgment of local
        populace of, 300
    Lake Titicaca in, 237, 238, 241, 254,
        256–59, 263, 265–66
    land distribution in, 301, 336
    poverty in, 288–89, 301, 305, 310,
        313–14
    socialist government of, 312
    terrain of, 299, 302–3, 331–33
    volcanic zone of, 224
Bolivian Diary (Guevara), 311